ELECTRIC SOUND

THE PAST AND PROMISE
OF ELECTRONIC MUSIC

JOEL CHADABE

State University of New York at Albany

Prenticc Hall, Upper Saddle River, New Jersey 07458

Library of Congress Cataloging-in-Publication Data

CHADABE, JOEL.
 Electric sound: the past and promise of electronic music / by Joel
Chadabe.
  p. cm.
 Includes index.
 ISBN 0-13-303231-0
 1. Electronic music—History and criticism. I. Title.
ML1380.C43   1997
786.7—dc20   96-29349

Editorial director: *Charlyce Jones Owen*
Acquisitions editor: *Norwell Therien*
Editorial/production supervision
  and interior design: *Edie Riker*
Cover design: *Bruce Kenselaar*
Cover photo illustration: *Carl Howard*
Buyer: *Bob Anderson*
Editorial assistant: *Lee Mamunes*

This book was set in 10/12 Sabon by East End Publishing Services
and was printed and bound by Courier Companies, Inc. The cover
was printed by Phoenix Color Corp.

 © 1997 by Prentice-Hall, Inc.
Simon & Schuster / A Viacom Company
Upper Saddle River, New Jersey 07458

Printed in the United States of America

10   9   8   7   6   5   4   3   2

ISBN   0-13-303231-0

PRENTICE-HALL INTERNATIONAL (UK) LIMITED, *London*
PRENTICE-HALL OF AUSTRALIA PTY. LIMITEd, *Sydney*
PRENTICE-HALL CANADA INC., *Toronto*
PRENTICE-HALL HISPANOAMERICANA, S.A., *Mexico*
PRENTICE-HALL OF INDIA PRIVATE LIMITED, *New Delhi*
PRENTICE-HALL of JAPAN, INC., *Tokyo*
SIMON & SCHUSTER ASIA PTE. LTD., *Singapore*
EDITORA PRENTICE-HALL DO BRASIL, LTDA., *Rio de Janeiro*

FOR
FRANÇOISE & BENJAMIN

CONTENTS

PREFACE

If electronic music had been a political platform, John Philip Sousa, famed composer of *Stars and Stripes Forever* and many other marches, would probably have voted for the opposition. He writes:

> And now, in this the twentieth century, come these talking and playing machines, and offer again to reduce the expression of music to a mathematical system of megaphones, wheels, cogs, disks, cylinders, and all manner of revolving things, which are as like real art as the marble statue of Eve is like her beautiful, living, breathing daughters. . .

> When a mother can turn on the phonograph with the same ease that she applies to the electric light, will she croon her baby to slumber with sweet lullabys, or will the infant be put to sleep by machinery?

Sousa may not be alone in equating electronic technology with something mathematical, mechanical, and downright unmusical, but as we learn from a 1950s popular song, phonographs and love *do* mix:

> Put another nickel in,
> In the nickelodeon.
> All I want is lovin' you
> And music, music, music!

And in any case, Sousa's point is a little confused. Is he against recordings? Or more broadly, all manner of revolving things? Or technology in general? My sense is that it's a general anti-technology diatribe. Yet even Sousa might have agreed that the technologies of musical instruments—whether the wood and glue of a violin case, the mechanical hammers and levers of a piano action, or the electronic microprocessors used in synthesizers—have reflected the times and places of their inventions. The violin, for example, made with hand tools and containing no moving parts, is a product of seventeenth-century European pre-industrial-age technology. The piano, a wooden machine with many moving parts, is a product of nineteenth-century European industrial-age technology. Indeed, throughout history and throughout the world, people have used available technology to make music. It should come as no surprise that electronic circuits are used to make musical instruments in the twentieth-century electronic age.

My point, however, goes deeper than the normality of building a musical instrument with electronics. My point is that the electronic musical instrument, in its myriad forms, has particular promise. It may well turn out to be the *most* beneficial to humans and the *most* enjoyable, rewarding, and expressive instrument that has ever existed.

•

The development of the electronic musical instrument through the twentieth century has involved a multitude of composers, engineers, scientists, and entrepreneurs. With different personalities, backgrounds, skills, and goals, they composed music, built instruments, conducted research, formed companies and, in general, contributed to the cumulative body of concepts, artistry, and techniques that defines the electronic musical instrument in its current forms.

Some composers contributed by using existing technology in such creative ways that their compositions led to the invention of new instruments. Some composers directly stated their need for new technology. As early as 1916, for example, Edgard Varèse wrote, "We also need new instruments very badly . . . In my own works I have always felt the need for new mediums of expression." Some composers actually developed new technologies. And some composers contributed by developing new technologies even when they had the wrong idea. Herbert Eimert, for example, cofounder of the Cologne tape studio in 1951, wrote: "Electronic music exists only on tape . . ." In fact, Eimert was twice wrong. There *were* electronic instruments before 1951; *and* tape music, at least as Eimert knew it, was short-lived. Luciano Berio, definitely on the right track in the mid-1970s, put it clearly and made a positive suggestion: "I think that the electronic tape piece is dead . . . it should be kept either at home or, if it is soft enough, in a restaurant."

Engineers contributed, of course, by designing and building instruments, albeit sometimes they disagreed on basic issues. Harry Olson, for example, designer of the RCA synthesizers, saw benefit in avoiding the noise elements of traditional instruments: "Conventional instruments produce various noises . . . These undesirable noises do not exist in the electronic music synthesizer." Hugh Le Caine, on the other hand, designer of many innovative instruments in Canada, saw benefit in *including* the noise elements of traditional instruments: "These effects . . . add to the expressive power of the instrument . . ."

Scientists contributed through research in psychoacoustics and other related fields. Some scientists contributed by publishing theories, even nonmusical theories, that shed light on the issues raised by new musical technologies. Shannon and Weaver's formulation of Information Theory in *The Mathematical Theory of Communication* (1949), for example, led Harry Olson and Herbert Belar to begin work on a probabilities-based composing machine at RCA's Sarnoff Laboratories in Princeton; it led to Lejaren Hiller's seminal work in algorithmic composition at the University of Illinois; it interested John Pierce at Bell Telephone Laboratories in his work with computer-generated sound; and it made a strong impression on Werner Meyer-Eppler at the University of Bonn, Germany, giving impetus to his experiments in electronically generated sound that brought him a step closer to the Cologne studio.

Entrepreneurs contributed by forming companies, turning ideas into products, and making those products available to the public.

●

The history of the electronic musical instrument, in short, is a complexity of many stories. Each of the stories, in itself, describes a coherent step-by-step progression of work along a certain path. And the paths often run along parallel lines. At any given moment, one group of people in a particular context was working out a certain set of ideas, which led to the next ideas, while at the same time, elsewhere, another group in another context was working out different ideas, which led to other ideas, and so on. And along the parallel paths of all of those stories, there are milestones. Those milestones mark an overall chronology which is the basis for the organization of this book.

The first milestone marks the development of the early electronic instruments, built by pioneering individuals during the first half of the twentieth century—from Thaddeus Cahill's Telharmonium in 1906 to the RCA Mark II Electronic Music Synthesizer in 1957.

The second milestone marks the opening up of music to all sounds, beginning with John Cage's early work in the mid-1930s and continuing into the first round of tape studios in the 1950s. By 1967, Hugh Davies' *International Electronic Music Catalog* could state that approximately 7,500 tape compositions had been written or were in progress since 1951. Tape music was an idea whose time had come, and it spilled out of the studios into performance spaces, festivals, and a broad-based technology-and-art culture.

The third milestone was the growth of synthesizers from their roots in mainframe computers and analog systems in the 1960s to become commercially successful electronic musical instruments in the 1970s and 1980s. As electronic technology evolved from vacuum tubes to transistors in the 1960s, from transistors to integrated circuits in the 1970s, and from integrated circuits to microprocessors in the 1980s, so evolved the technology of electronic musical instruments from large, expensive, institutional systems to small, relatively inexpensive, personal systems.

The fourth milestone, on a path that paralleled the development of the hardware instruments, was the formulation of new ideas for making music and playing instruments. Those ideas, which dealt ultimately with concepts of interaction, challenge the very nature of the way we've traditionally thought about music and musical instruments.

•

My goal in this book is to make the history of electronic music clear for any interested person, whether professional, student, nonelectronic musician, or observer. Given that goal, I thought about the extent to which technical explanation might be appropriate. Reasoning that professionals don't need it, that nonelectronic musicians and observers don't want it, and that students can very easily find it elsewhere, I concluded that technical explanation would serve little purpose and that it might just bog things down. There is little of it in these pages.

At the same time, I did not take pains to avoid using the normal terms of the field, such as *synthesizer, oscillator, frequency modulation*, and so on, because those terms are part of the electronic music landscape. My advice to nontechnical readers, consequently, is simply to derive some meaning from the context in which unfamiliar terms are used and read on. In a sea novel of the early nineteenth century, Patrick O'Brian describes the harbor of Port Mahon as containing "hundreds of feluccas, tartans, xebecs, pinks, polacres . . ." Well, who knows exactly what they were? And what does it matter if we don't know? They were just part of the scenery.

I would, however, like to define the term *electronic music*. Electronic music includes all music made with electronics, whether specifically with computer, synthesizer, or any other special equipment. I view the use of the term in much the same way that we'd use the term *orchestral music*, for example, to designate music played by an orchestra. Among other terms in current use, *computer music* too specifically connotes music made with general-purpose computers, *synthesizer music* is too specifically related to synthesizers, and *electroacoustic music* suggests, at least to me, systems that combine electronic and acoustic sound generators. Electronic music, to my way of thinking, is the generic term, even if in Germany it may cause confusion with *elektronische Musik*, which refers specifically to the philosophy of the Cologne studio in the early 1950s.

Yet understood even in a generic sense, the term *electronic music* has meant different things to different people at different times. In the tape-music and technology-in-art world of the 1950s and 1960s, electronic music was considered by many composers to be something special, exploratory, not based on conventional pitches or harmonies. Most composers created sounds purposefully different from the familiar and friendly sounds normally played by acoustic instruments. "If you want a clarinet sound," a composer might have said at the time, "go out and hire a clarinetist." And the term *electronic music* was therefore often linked to an aesthetic that, well, to put it softly, did not seem to certain critics to embody time-honored values of beauty in music. One 1960s review, for example, began:

> Composers who rival Cage in fetching weird, electronic and dreamworld sounds and patterns of sounds out of their busily inventive New Age brains and out of the turmoil of modern life . . .

Some critics went so far as to express fear of machine takeover, as in this review excerpt from the 1950s:

> We ask ourselves whether truly this is the beginning of a new world or whether perhaps the world . . . is about to perish. There are people who earnestly and seriously fear this, where music becomes the slave of the machine . . .

But by the 1980s, the meaning of the term had changed. Any sound, including the sounds of clarinets and other acoustic instruments, could be produced electronically. Electronic music had become more of a medium than a style, and the music was differentiated from the particular electronic system or instrument with which it was played, as indicated, for example, in this review excerpt from 1986:

> The actual musical input seemed unimaginative, compared with the ingenuity that had presumably gone into the devising of the electronic system.

That was a good review. It was good because it differentiated between the electronic musical instrument and the music it played. It was an early step toward the fifth milestone, yet to be reached. The fifth milestone will mark the resolution of still-unresolved design issues and the crystallization of still-forming concepts into the many potential forms of the electronic musical instrument. The electronic musical instrument, after all, can take any form. It can play any music. And it can be played in any way. In one form or another, and played in one way or another, it just may meet everyone's musical needs.

● ● ●

ACKNOWLEDGMENTS

In the course of writing this book, I talked with more than 150 composers, researchers, and entrepreneurs who discussed their work with me, told me their stories, and explained their ideas. Many of them are friends and colleagues.

I acknowledge with gratitude the invaluable information provided by Sydney Alonso, Marco Alpert, Jon Appleton, Robert Ashley, Larry Austin, Milton Babbitt, Frank Balde, Jean-Baptiste Barrière, Marc Battier, François Bayle, David Behrman, Gerald Bennett, Luciano Berio, Peter Beyls, John Bischoff, Georges Bloch, Lars-Gunnar Bodin, Richard Boulanger, Chris Brown, Earle Brown, Herbert Brun, Donald Buchla, Warren Burt, William Buxton, Tristram Cary, Xavier Chabot, Chris Chafe, John Chowning, Gustav Ciamaga, Christian Clozier, David Cockerell, Nicolas Collins, Perry Cook, Roger Dannenberg, James Dashow, Mario Davidovsky, Hugh Davies, Paul DeMarinis, Giuseppe Di Giugno, Christopher Dobrian, Charles Dodge, Jacob Druckman, David Dunn, John Eaton, Jean-Claude Eloy, Simon Emmerson, Giuseppe G. Englert, Terry Fryer, Emmanuel Ghent, Johannes Goebel, Peter Gotcher, Chris Halaby, Sten Hanson, Jonathan Harvey, Kurt Hebel, Pierre Henry, Felix Hess, Brian Hodgson, Jim Horton, Al Hospers, Martin Hurni, Toshi Ichiyanagi, David Jaffe, Ikutaro Kakehashi, Gottfried Michael Koenig, Gregory Kramer, Francisco Kröpfl, Ronald Kuivila, Joan La Barbara, Paul Lansky, Alcides Lanza, Otto Laske, Pierre Lavoie, Vincent Lesbros, George Lewis, Roger Linn, Cort Lippe, Annea Lockwood, Alvin Lucier, Tod Machover, Bill Maginnis, Chris Mann, Philippe Manoury, Tony Martin, Dorothy Martirano, Salvatore Martirano, Max Mathews, Barton McLean, Priscilla McLean, Stephen Montague, Robert Moog, F. Richard Moore, Dexter Morrill, Gordon Mumma, Gary Lee Nelson, Phill Niblock, Tom Oberheim, Pauline Oliveros, Dave Oppenheim, Yann Orlarey, Stephen Paine, Gerard Pape, Maggi Payne, Bruce Pennycook, Tim Perkis, John Pierce, Larry Polansky, Miller Puckette, Eliane Radigue, Michel Redolfi, Tom Rhea, Jean-Claude Risset, Curtis Roads, Rene Rochat, Xavier Rodet, Neil Rolnick, David Rosenboom, Robert Rowe, Manfred Rürup, André Ruschkowski, Joel Ryan, Frederic Rzewski, Kaija Saariaho, Sylviane Sapir, Carla Scaletti, Andrew Schloss, Ramon Sender, Denis Smalley, Dave Smith, Julius Smith,

Laetitia Sonami, Laurie Spiegel, Bruno Spoerri, Carl Stone, Morton Subotnick, Ivan Tcherepnin, Richard Teitelbaum, Stan Tempelaars, Daniel Teruggi, Barry Truax, David Tudor, Tamas Ungvary, Woody and Steina Vasulka, Barry Vercoe, Alvise Vidolin, Felix Visser, Michel Waisvisz, David Wessel, Lachlan Westfall, Jane Wheeler, Antony Widoff, Jan Williams, Trevor Wishart, Iannis Xenakis, Joji Yuasa, David Zicarelli, Peter Zinovieff, and Richard Zvonar.

I also acknowledge with gratitude the many people who provided me with materials, information, and insights on a wide range of related subjects. Warren Burt sent materials on developments in Australia, Marc Battier and Jean-Baptiste Barrière provided information on and reports from IRCAM, François Bayle lucidly explained the history of the GRM, Emmanuel Favreau and Daniel Teruggi provided information on technical developments at the GRM, Folkmar Hein gave me materials on electronic music in Germany, Billy Klüver and Lowell Cross provided materials on EAT and the 9 Evenings festival in 1966, Curtis Roads shared certain sections of a computer-music manuscript in progress, Patte Wood and Marcia Bauman provided historical information on CCRMA, Alvise Vidolin gave me a wealth of information on developments in Italy, Joji Yuasa was my first guide in understanding the early days in Japan, Takehiko Shimazu was able to answer some detailed questions about the NHK studio, Eliane Radigue introduced me to Pierre Henry, Landa Ketoff provided materials regarding the SynKet, and Garrett Bowles made available materials from Pauline Oliveros' archives at the University of California at San Diego. Joseph Schepis assisted in certain background research. Conversations with Laurie Spiegel were helpful in clarifying issues of interaction. Reynold Weidenaar gave me a prepublication copy of his magnificent book on the Telharmonium. Andre Smirnov shared his knowledge of Theremin's life and work. Hugh Davies and Tom Rhea offered historical insights, a wide range of leads, and valuable information.

My thanks also to the several people who, at various times, read copies of my manuscript and made comments. Don Byrd, Neil Rolnick, and Randy Neal read the book in outline form in May 1993 and offered both encouragement and ideas. Antonino Carnevali, physicist, verified the science passages. Rita Putnam read a manuscript in progress in the summer of 1994 and offered editorial suggestions that were extremely helpful in making the book readable and coherent. Tom Rhea and Christopher Dobrian read and corrected parts of the manuscript at different times during 1995 and 1996. Nathaniel Reichman read parts of the manuscript in its final stages and made some useful observations. Françoise Chadabe, my wife, helped with translations from French and general editing. Benjamin Chadabe, my son, helped at first by transcribing taped material, then by helping me organize and format the photographs, and finally by reviewing the manuscript and making a large number of extremely perceptive corrections and suggestions.

—*Joel Chadabe*
Albany, June 1996

CHAPTER ONE

THE EARLY
INSTRUMENTS

The history of music technology—including innovations in tuning systems, musical instrument designs, studies in acoustics, and in general, an exploratory attitude toward music and sound—goes far back in time. Ling Lun, for example, in twenty-seventh-century B.C. China, devised the tuning of the pentatonic and chromatic scales. Pythagoras, in sixth-century B.C. Greece, related numerical frequency ratios to pitch intervals, such as 2:1 for the octave. Vitruvius, in first-century B.C. Rome, analyzed theater acoustics to conclude that sound projected best from a stage with a curved back-shell. Ptolemy, in second-century Egypt, devised the Ptolemaic Sequence, in effect a diatonic scale. Francisco de Salinas, in sixteenth-century Italy, developed a meantone temperament. Marin Mersenne, in seventeenth-century France, investigated the speed of sound and other acoustical matters. Arp Schnitger, in seventeenth-century Germany, tuned an organ to equal temperament, thereby, in Harry Partch's words, "setting the clavier stool" for three-year-old Johann Sebastian Bach and setting the stage for the next 300 years of Western music.

There were, of course, the conservatives, among them Plato: "Any musical innovation is full of danger to the whole State, and ought to be prohibited . . ."

There were also the poets and visionaries, among them E.T.A. Hoffmann who, in the nineteenth century, wrote:

"Exactly," said Lewis. "Now, in the case of instruments of the keyboard class a great deal might be done. There is a wide field open in that direction to clever mechanical people, much as has been accomplished already; particularly in instruments of the pianoforte genus. But it would be the task of a really advanced system of the 'mechanics of music' to observe closely, study minutely, and discover carefully that class of sounds which belong, most purely and strictly, to Nature herself, to obtain a knowledge of the tones which dwell in substances of every description, and then to take this mysterious music and enclose it in some sort of instrument, where it should be subject to man's will, and give itself forth at his touch . . ."

"The object at which it aims," said Lewis, "is the discovery of the most absolutely perfect kind of musical sound; and according to my theory, musical sound would be the nearer to perfection the more closely it approximated such of the mysterious tones of nature . . ."

And there were the designers and builders of original instruments, in fact sometimes *very* original instruments. Don Nicola Vicentino, for example, in sixteenth-century Italy, built the *Archicembalo*, a "harpsichord" with thirty-one tones to the octave and six banks of keys. Jean-Baptiste de La Borde, in 1759, in Paris, constructed the *Clavecin Electrique*, a sort of keyboard-controlled carillon in which suspended bells were struck by clappers charged with static electricity. Nikolay Obukhov, a Russian composer, in 1918, devised an inaudible instrument which he called *Ether*, theoretically capable of producing sounds from five octaves below to five octaves above the audible range of frequencies. And special honors go to Luigi Russolo: first, for his dedication to Futurist music and, second, for his courage in facing the airborne vegetable.

Russolo's manifesto of March 11, 1913, entitled *L'Arte dei Rumori* (The Art of Noises) and dedicated to Francesco Balilla Pratella, a friend and Futurist musician, set forth his ideas. He wrote:

Dear Balilla Pratella, great Futurist composer,

In Rome, in the Costanzi Theatre, packed to capacity, while I was listening to the orchestral performance of your overwhelming Futurist music, with my Futurist friends, Marinetti, Boccioni, Carrà, Balla, Soffici, Papini and Cavacchioli, a new art came into my mind which only you can create: the Art of Noises, the logical consequence of your splendid innovations . . .

We cannot see that enormous display of power represented by the modern orchestra without feeling profound disappointment at the feeble acoustic results. Is anything more ridiculous than the sight of twenty men furiously bent on redoubling the mewing of a violin? All this will naturally make music-lovers scream, and will perhaps stir the sleepy atmosphere of concert halls. Let us now, as Futurists, enter one of these hospitals for anaemic sounds . . .

Here are the six families of noises of the Futurist orchestra which we will soon create mechanically:

1. Rumbles, Roars, Explosions, Crashes, Thuds, Booms.
2. Whistles, Hisses, Snorts.
3. Whispers, Murmurs, Mutters, Rumbles, Gurgles.
4. Creaks, Rustles, Buzzes, Crackles, Scrapes.
5. Noises obtained by percussion on metal, wood, skin, stone, terracotta, etc.
6. Voices of animals and men: Shouts, Screams, Groans, Shrieks, Howls, Laughs, Wheezes, Sobs.

In this inventory we have included the most characteristic basic noises . . .

Later that year, with percussionist Ugo Piatti, Russolo began to build the *intonarumori*, instruments which were boxes of various sizes, each with a crank in the back, a sound-generating mechanism inside, and an amplification horn in front. A lever, mounted on top of each box, was used to adjust pitch. On April 21, 1914, at the Teatro Dal Cerme in Milan, Russolo conducted the first *Gran concerto futuristica* with an orchestra of eighteen formally dressed musicians playing gurglers, cracklers, howlers, thunderers, exploders, hissers, buzzers, and crumplers. Following the performances of three of Russolo's compositions, and not to be outdone, the audience threw vegetables, accompanying itself with vocal sounds such as whistling, booing, and hooting; and the concert eventually degenerated into fist fights between Futurists and non-Futurists, with the last musical sound of the evening, one imagines, the sirens of the arriving police.

•

Although there were odds and ends of experiments during the nineteenth century, such as Elisha Gray's *Musical Telegraph* in 1874 and William Duddell's *Singing Arc* in 1899, the first major electronic instrument was Thaddeus Cahill's *Telharmonium*. The Telharmonium represented not only exceptional technological achievement, it also represented exceptional entrepreneurial drive. It was visionary and radical. Looking back, in fact, it seems as if the visions came in series. In 1627, in his essay "New Atlantis," Francis Bacon foresaw Cahill's idea:

We have also sound-houses, where we practice and demonstrate all sounds, and their generation . . . We have also means to convey sounds in trunks and pipes, in strange lines and distances.

And Thaddeus Cahill foresaw Musak. In 1897, at a time when automobiles were rarely seen and when few homes had electricity or telephones, his first patent for an electronic musical instrument, entitled *Art of and Apparatus for Generating and Distributing Music Electronically*, was granted. His idea was to build an electronic music synthesizer, generate music with it, and broadcast that music via telephone lines to restaurants, hotels, and private homes. In 1898, in Washington, D.C., he began work on his instrument.

By 1901, the Telharmonium, as it came to be known, was sufficiently finished to attract initial financing from Oscar T. Crosby, retired army engineer, businessman, and world traveler. Crosby brought in Frederick C. Todd, businessman and sportsman, as a partner, and together they organized a fund-raising dinner at the Maryland Club in Baltimore. While the Telharmonium was played in Washington, the assembled group of bankers and businessmen in Baltimore listened to Handel's *Largo* emanate from a special horn attached to a telephone receiver. It was a success. Following a few months of financial discussions and contracts signed, Crosby formed New England Electric Music Company as a New Jersey corporation.

In 1902, New England Electric Music Company leased a large space in the Cabot Street Mill, a factory-type building in Holyoke, Massachusetts. Cahill moved the prototype instrument from Washington and proceeded to build a new and improved Telharmonium. In 1904, he made a successful transmission from Holyoke to New Haven, Connecticut. When it became clear that more capital was needed, Crosby established New York Electric Music Company, also as a New Jersey corporation, to raise funds more effectively in New York. New Jersey, incidentally, for many reasons of corporate law, was considered at the time to be a preferred state in which to incorporate.

In 1905, investments were coming in, the Telharmonium was moving toward completion, and Crosby successfully negotiated an agreement with New York Telephone Company wherein New York Telephone Company would lay special telephone lines for the purpose of transmitting the Telharmonium's music throughout New York City. By 1906, Cahill had approximately fifty people working for him in what was, in effect, a factory for electrical machinery. The Telharmonium's sounds were produced by combining sine waves generated by dynamos whose outputs were linked through a complex switching system. The sounds were heard through horns attached to telephone receivers fitted with especially thin diaphragms for better bass response.

In March 1906, the new instrument began to attract attention in the press. A glowing article appeared in *Electrical World*. Parts of the article were reprinted in *The New York Times*. In July 1906, in an article in *McClure's Magazine*, Ray Stannard Baker wrote that the best music, because it could now be transmitted into homes, would be available to the poor. Cahill stated, also in Baker's article, that he preferred to call his instrument the *Dynamophone*.

During the summer of 1906, the Telharmonium was disassembled—reports at the time estimated its weight at 200 tons—and moved via railway boxcars to a building at Broadway and 39th Street, in the middle of New York City's glittering theater district. The dynamos and switching system, which gen-

The Telharmonium performance console in Telharmonic Hall, December 1906.
Photo courtesy Reynold Weidenaar.

erated mechanical noise as well as electricity, were installed in the basement. The performance console was placed in the Music Hall, a comfortable room on street level with a circular divan in the middle and potted plants and ferns placed around and about to conceal loudspeakers. At the New York opening, on September 26, 1906, Crosby gave an exuberant welcoming speech and a concert was performed.

Meanwhile, telephone cables were being laid up and down Broadway to convey the Telharmonium's sounds to nearby restaurants. Café Martin, magnificent and large, on 26th Street between Fifth Avenue and Broadway, became the first subscriber; and on November 9, 1906, at a banquet hosted by Crosby in one of Café Martin's private dining rooms, the sounds of the Telharmonium were heard by a group of happy guests and compared to a softer, sweeter organ, to flutes and horns, and to other instruments.

Those softer, sweeter sounds, however, were apparently causing confusion on the telephone lines. Although the Telharmonium and telephones had their separate cables, the cables were running side by side through the same conduits and there was crosstalk. Telephone conversations were interrupted by Rossini overtures. Irate telephone users complained. In late November 1906, New York Telephone Company informed Crosby that it intended to terminate its 1905 agreement to supply telephone lines to New York Electric Music Company; and Crosby, facing the inevitable, expressed hope that New York Telephone Company would assist him in obtaining a New York City franchise to lay his own transmission lines.

The winter season was eventful. Louis Sherry's, a well-known restaurant at 44th Street and Fifth Avenue, subscribed. In December 1906, the Telharmonium's music was piped through normal telephone lines to the Museum of Natural History on 81st Street. In January 1907, a concert series open to the public was announced. The building at 39th Street and Broadway was, for the first time, called Telharmonic Hall. There was a transmission to the Casino Theatre across the street. There were numerous receptions and overtures made to the financial and cultural elite. The Normandie Hotel, the Waldorf-Astoria Hotel, and other hotels became subscribers. Some wealthy individuals began to subscribe for their private homes. And the public concert series got off to a successful start. The number of concerts quickly increased from two to four each day and there were demonstrations of "tone building." Music was piped to external loudspeakers for the auditory pleasure of passers-by. Celebrities came to listen, among them Walter Damrosch and Giacomo Puccini.

Meanwhile, in 1906, Lee De Forest had patented the audion, a definitive breakthrough in vacuum tube technology. On February 27, 1907, particularly interested in the audion's application in wireless transmission, De Forest made a wireless transmission of the Telharmonium's sounds from Telharmonic Hall to the Yale Club, several blocks away. A few days later, he established a receiving station at the Normandie Hotel, a block away. On March 5, the chief electrician at the Brooklyn Navy Yard, five miles away, complained that naval wireless signals were being interrupted by Rossini overtures. On March 7, De Forest put a receiver on top of The New York Times building, which led to publicity, speculation, and a business proposal from De Forest to New York Electric Music Company to disseminate Telharmonium music by wireless. New York Electric Music Company, perhaps unfortunately, declined to do business with De Forest until wireless transmission became commercially dependable. And as the concerts, demonstrations, luminary visits, and general activities continued through the spring, some technical problems became more apparent. Reynold Weidenaar writes:

> It did run perfectly in tune with itself, but frequently the whole machine ran too slow, drifting down in pitch . . . The instrument's other limitations—"robbing," where adding voices depleted the volume, so that a many-toned chord could be softer than a single note; "diaphragm crack," where each staccato note sounded like the rap of a metal mallet; the impossibility of producing more than two, and later three, timbres simultaneously; the exaggerated "growling" of bass notes close together . . .

Crosby, meanwhile, was dealing with a peculiar business problem. Although the application for a New York City franchise to lay cables had to come from a New York State corporation, there was no legislation permitting a New York State corporation to be formed for transmitting music. The solution, clearly, was to have the necessary legislation passed by the state government. Consequently, Crosby went to Albany, the state capital, and drafted a bill. On May 6, the bill was signed into law. On May 7, he formed New York Cahill Telharmonic Company. Shortly afterward, he applied for a New York City franchise to lay cables. To encourage a speedy approval of his application, he submitted rosy financial projections with high franchise royalties due New York City. *The Brooklyn Times*, on June 15, 1907, predicted that he would have the franchise within a year.

In the absence of a sufficient number of subscribers, however, New York Electric Music Company was losing money. Crosby had approached AT&T for support and collaboration, but AT&T had declined. To make matters worse, the general financial climate was declining through the spring and summer. As the situation continued to deteriorate, Crosby quit the company, built a house in Virginia, and business control passed to Frederick C. Todd. By October, the so-called Panic of 1907 was causing financial grief everywhere. A new concert season opened in Telharmonic Hall in November, but as the general woe worsened, the concerts became fewer and finally stopped in February 1908. There were no telephone lines, no subscribers, and no income. In May, New York Electric Music Company collapsed. Telharmonic Hall was locked up.

Cahill, however, determined to keep the project alive, went to New York, dismantled the abandoned Telharmonium, shipped it back to Holyoke, and began work on a third, improved Telharmonium. In early 1910, the New York City Board of Estimate asked New York Cahill Telharmonic Company if it was still interested in a franchise and was informed that the company was reorganizing and that a new proposal would be made. In April 1910, Cahill demonstrated the new Telharmonium in Holyoke to a group of 200 people from New York, Boston, and other places. In December 1910, Cahill and his brothers completed their purchase of the stock of New York Cahill Telharmonic Company; and Thaddeus Cahill, now president, renegotiated the franchise contract that had been proposed by Crosby as part of the original application in 1907. Finally, in March 1911, Cahill had a franchise. In April 1911, a building on West 56th Street was leased. In August 1911, the new Telharmonium was installed.

But it was the beginning of the end. In February 1912, the new Telharmonium was demonstrated at Carnegie Hall, but with little press coverage. Demonstrations continued into the spring, but there were no investments. And competition materialized in the form of a new Wurlitzer organ. Wireless transmission was increasingly commanding public attention. The company's debts accumulated. In December 1914, New York Cahill Telharmonic Company declared bankruptcy.

A few months later, in April 1915, Lee De Forest filed a patent entitled *Electrical Means for Producing Musical Notes*. He had found that the audion could be used as an oscillator. The audion, in other words, could produce sounds at a tiny fraction of the cost of Cahill's dynamos.

•

In August 1920, in Moscow, Leon Theremin demonstrated and performed what he then called the *aetherphone*, later known as the *theremin*, for fellow students and staff at the Physico Technical Institute. The theremin was a cabinet about one foot deep, eighteen inches wide, and about two feet high, placed on a table or stand. Emerging from the top right of the cabinet was a thin vertical rod, which was the pitch antenna. A loop, the volume antenna, was mounted horizontally on the left side of the cabinet. Theremin played it by moving his hands in the air. When his right hand moved closer to the pitch antenna, it caused the pitch to go higher. When his left hand moved closer to the volume antenna, it caused the sound to get softer. The sound was somewhere between a viola and a clarinet, smooth and lyrical, sometimes reminding listeners of the human voice. Theremin later said, "I conceived of an instrument that would create sound without using any mechanical energy, like the conductor of an orchestra."

Seeming, as Nicolas Slonimsky commented, "to carry out Lenin's dictum that 'socialism is proletarian dictatorship plus electrification,'" Theremin demonstrated his instrument for the delegates at the 8th All-Russia Electro-Technical Congress in October 1921. The performance led to a private concert for Lenin, which in turn led to a free railway pass to facilitate another 150 or so performances in Russia. And then, in 1927, Theremin took his instrument on tour to Frankfurt, Berlin, London, and Paris, where listeners were amazed that electronics could be used to such magical and musical ends as to allow a musician to perform by making movements in the air. Theremin became a celebrity.

On December 21, 1927, he arrived in New York. His first appearance, in the Plaza Hotel's Grand Ballroom on January 24, 1928, was a private demonstration-concert arranged under the auspices of Walter Damrosch, Vincent Astor, Edsel Ford, Fritz Kreisler, and others, with guests including Sergei Rachmaninoff, Arturo Toscanini, and Joseph Szigeti. That first appearance was followed by a public concert at the Metropolitan Opera House on January 31, 1928. And that concert was followed by many more demonstrations and concerts and by the continuing attention of many of New York's artistic elite. Theremin and three students performed four theremins with the New York Philharmonic on August 27, 1928, playing Rachmaninoff's *Vocalise*, Liszt's *Hungarian Rhapsody #1*, and other music.

RCA acquired a license for the commercial manufacture of the theremin. Joseph Schillinger, also a recent arrival from Russia, and subsequently known for his statistics-based compositional method, worked with Theremin to design the RCA version of the instrument and, as part of its promotion, wrote his *Airphonic Suite for RCA Theremin and Orchestra* (1929). RCA, in promoting

*Leon Theremin playing the theremin in 1927.
Photo courtesy Robert Moog.*

their new product, gave assurance that *anyone* could play the theremin, or at least anyone who could hum or whistle. It was a lot to assure considering that the theremin was a relatively unfamiliar instrument, that it offered no tactile feedback, and that however easy it may have been to play badly, it required great physical discipline to play well. RCA built 200 theremins, found it not immediately profitable and, consequently, as Robert Moog put it, "dropped it like a hot potato . . ."

The theremin's first virtuoso was Clara Rockmore, a violinist who also arrived in New York from Russia in 1927. She had met Theremin shortly after her arrival and worked intensively with his instruments during the next several years. In fact, Theremin had built several novel instruments in the early 1930s, among them the *Terpsitone*, a musical floor that allowed a dancer to control pitch and volume by body position. Rockmore later recalled that, at one of Theremin's concerts in 1932 which included the Terpsitone, Theremin asked her to perform because "none of the dancers who tried it could carry a tune." Her first solo theremin recital, playing an instrument built especially for her by Theremin and accompanied at the piano by her sister Nadia Reisenberg, was at Town Hall in New York on October 30, 1934. Moog describes her technique:

Ms. Rockmore actually uses fingering patterns to play the most rapid passages. For instance, if she were to play an upward arpeggio, she would start on the lowest note with right hand tilted back and fingers withdrawn. To play the next note she would abruptly move her hand forward from the wrist, while keeping her right arm motionless. The third note would be played by rapidly extending the little finger, and the fourth note by extending one or two more fingers while simultaneously turning the wrist sideways to bring the newly-extended fingers nearer to the pitch antenna. She would then continue the arpeggio by moving her whole arm closer to the pitch antenna while drawing her hand and fingers back, then repeating the above-described succession of movements. At the same time, she may articulate each individual pitch by rapidly shooting the fingers of her left hand into the volume antenna loop, then withdrawing them, to silence the tone during the very short periods of time that her right hand moves from one pitch to another . . .

In 1938, Theremin was abducted by Soviet agents and returned forcibly to the Soviet Union. In fact, according to Andre Smirnov, director of the Theremin Center in Moscow, it was well known that Theremin had been working as an agent for the KGB since the early 1920s and that he had not done a particularly good job for them; and consequently, it would make sense to speculate that with war pending, the KGB would have found him more valuable in Moscow than in New York. After a few months back in Moscow, Theremin was imprisoned, and following a few months of physical labor, he was put to work at developing aircraft radar. In 1947, he invented a bugging device for the KGB, for which he was awarded the 1947 Stalin Prize of 100,000 rubles. By the 1960s, he had become a professor of acoustics at Moscow University, working mainly on naval acoustics and noise suppression.

Leon Theremin playing the theremin (left) and talking with Robert Moog (right) at Stanford University in 1991. Photos by Renee Moog.

In 1991, at the age of 95, he came back to the United States for a visit. He performed at a concert at Stanford University. His daughter Natasha also played Rachmaninoff's *Vocalise* on one of her father's theremins, accompanied by Max Mathews playing his Radio Baton. He had reunions with old friends in New York, among them Clara Rockmore. And in the course of an interview with Robert Moog, Theremin recalled his 1921 performance in Moscow and his encounter with Lenin:

> In the Soviet Union at that time everyone was interested in new things, in particular all the new uses of electricity . . . And so Vladimir Ilyich Lenin, the leader of our state, learned that I had shown an interesting thing at this conference, and he wanted to get acquainted with it himself. They asked me to come with my apparatus, with my musical instrument, to his office, to show him. And I did so. I played Glinka's *The Lark*, which he loved very much . . . He stood up, moved to the instrument, stretched his hands out, right hand to the pitch antenna and left to the volume antenna. I took his hands from behind and helped him. He started to play *The Lark*. He had a very good ear, and he felt where to move his hands to get the sound—to lower or raise the pitch. In the middle of this piece I thought that he could, independently, move his hands. So I took my hands off his and he completed the whole thing independently, by himself, with great success and with great applause following . . .

It is not so often that a head of state tries out the latest electronic musical instrument and, yet more exceptionally, plays it well.

●

Many electronic instruments were developed through the 1920s and 1930s, and most of them—such as the Gnome, the Syntronic organ, the Photona, the Hardy-Goldthwaite organ, the Rangertone organ, the Wave organ, the Polytone organ—were ephemeral.

Some of them were interesting. Jörg Mager's *Sphärophon*, for example, demonstrated in 1926 at Donaueschingen, Germany, was similar to a theremin but capable of timbral gradations and discrete pitches. Mager went on to develop other instruments, among them a keyboard version of the Sphärophon. René Bertrand's *Dynaphone*, demonstrated in 1928 in Paris, somewhat resembled the top half of an old clock. It was played by turning a pointer, something like a clock's hand, to select pitches while operating various knobs and buttons for volume and timbre. There was the *Givelet/Coupleux Organ*, a five-octave electronic organ with a full pedal keyboard, introduced in 1932 in Paris by Armand Givelet, engineer, and Eloy Coupleux, organ builder, after a decade of collaborative experimentation on various electronic instrument designs. A bit further out from the mainstream, there was Nikolay Obukhov's *Croix Sonore*, completed in 1934 in Paris, basically a theremin in the form of a cross about six feet high which, according to Obukhov, a mystic, "attracts us like a message from another world." A bit closer to the mainstream, there was Georges Jenny's *Ondioline*, a three-octave monophonic keyboard with variable timbre and vibrato, developed in 1938 in Paris and manufactured in various forms into the 1960s.

The *Trautonium* and the *Ondes Martenot* were particularly distinctive. In 1928, Friedrich Trautwein, acoustician, and Paul Hindemith, composer, established a studio for musical experiments at the Hochschule für Musik in Berlin. Hindemith experimented with sound by, among other things, changing the speeds of phonograph turntables. Trautwein developed the Trautonium. In playing the Trautonium, a performer controlled pitch by pressing a finger against a wire at some point along its length, thereby putting the wire in contact with a metal bar, closing a circuit, and producing a note. The performer pressed another bar to control articulation. With expert use of the independent pitch and articulation controls, a performer could achieve considerable nuance and expression. Timbres were chosen by means of simple switches. Altogether, the Trautonium was an instrument sophisticated enough to inspire Paul Hindemith to write his *Concerto for Solo Trautonium and Orchestra* (1930). And it was a good enough idea that Oskar Sala, who had been a student of Trautwein's, developed the *Mixturtrautonium*, an improved two-manual version of the original instrument, and used it to compose music and sound effects for films, including sound effects for Hitchock's *The Birds*. In 1962, Lejaren Hiller visited Sala at his studio at MARS Film in Berlin and reported: "Sala is convinced of the necessity of *performing* music to achieve the results he wants. He improvises much of his music for films directly on the instruments while watching film proofs . . ."

Also in 1928, Maurice Martenot presented his Ondes Martenot at the Paris Opera. He performed by inserting a finger in a ring and pulling a ribbon left or right, causing pitches to change correspondingly lower or higher. While his right hand was occupied playing the ribbon, his left hand was employed at a small panel to the left of the keyboard, varying loudness and activating different timbres by manipulating various controls. A few years later, although the ribbon was and remained a distinguishing feature of the Ondes Martenot, Martenot added a keyboard that could be used independently or in conjunction with the ribbon. He also placed a lever under the keyboard, to be pushed upward by the right knee to control continuous timbral changes.

Martenot actively promoted his instrument. After his successful premiere in Paris, he performed a European tour, following which he brought the instrument to New York. In December 1930, he played with the Philadelphia Orchestra. A world tour followed. At the Exposition Internationale de Paris of 1937, there were demonstrations and concerts by Ondes Martenot ensembles of up to twelve musicians. Many composers—among them Olivier Messiaen, Darius Milhaud, Arthur Honegger, Jacques Ibert, André Jolivet, Edgard Varèse, Maurice Jarre, and Pierre Boulez—played the Ondes Martenot and incorporated it into some of their compositions. In 1960, the Paris conservatory offered classes in Ondes Martenot performance, taught by Martenot at his Ecole d'Art Martenot in Neuilly, on the outskirts of Paris. But the Ondes Martenot, although interesting and novel for a certain circle of musicians, never really achieved mainstream status. Martenot apparently was not commercially minded. As Jean-Claude Eloy, one of the students at Neuilly, recalls:

> He was making the instruments one by one in his atelier, maybe three per year. We said to him, "You ought to industrialize it," but he was not that type of person, not a technician, not a businessman. He was a musician and a philosopher who was following an idea . . .

Laurens Hammond, on the other hand, developer of the first commercially successful electronic instrument, certainly was commercially minded. The Hammond electronic organ, introduced in 1935, quickly achieved mainstream status. For many years, people said "Hammond" when they meant "electronic organ."

●

Hugh Le Caine, a scientist at the Canadian National Research Council in Ottawa, worked during World War II on microwave transmission. In 1945, after the war, he turned some of his attention to building what he called the *Electronic Sackbut*, a performance-oriented synthesizer with an unusual capability for fingertip control of expression and nuance. By 1948, he had finished a working prototype. He describes it:

> The keyboard facilitates rapid execution of scales and arpeggios. In distinction to the conventional keyboard, the Sackbut keys are constructed in such a way that by applying a lateral (side) pressure to the key such subtleties of pitch control such as a smooth slide from one note to another, the vibrato or wavering pitch which a violinist produces by rocking his finger back and forth on the string, and the occasional use for musical purposes of sounds which are not on the musical scale or are off the pitch can be produced. The extent of the pitch change in any direction produced by this lateral pressure may be made as much as an octave either way. To produce long slides and other special effects a continuous pitch control is placed behind the keyboard in such a way that when the finger is moved along the control the pitch varies gradually over the range of the keyboard.
>   To control the loudness of a note the player controls the vertical pressure on the key. Not only gradual crescendi and diminuendi but changes in attack may be produced in this way. If the player uses the gradual pressure a violin-like attack results. If he strikes the key a blow, a sharp attack is produced. Since it is all too easy for the electronic instrument to have a

tone of monotonous purity, means of introducing irregularity have been included. One device produces an effect similar to a rasp in the voice or the buzzing produced by a trumpeter. Another mechanism produces breath tone as sometimes heard in the flute. These effects of course are introduced in only small amount and only occasionally, but they add to the expressive power of the instrument and avoid the monotonous purity of the "electronic tone."

Through the late 1940s and into the 1950s, Le Caine worked extensively on musical projects in his home studio. In 1953, as his interest in music was becoming increasingly known within the Canadian National Research Council, he was invited to speak about his instruments to the Scientists' Wives' Association. In his presentation, he used a taped example of himself performing the opening clarinet solo from Gershwin's *Rhapsody in Blue* on the electronic Sackbut. In 1954, he presented additional lectures and demonstrations both for the public and for the staff at the National Research Council. As a result of these presentations, the National Research Council established a

Hugh Le Caine demonstrating the Electronic Sackbut in 1954. While his right hand is playing notes on the keyboard, controlling volume by pressure and pitch bend by moving each key left and right, his left hand is controlling timbre. Photo courtesy Gustav Ciamaga.

music laboratory for him, the purpose of which was to develop electronic musical instruments that could be manufactured by Canadian companies.

•

The Canadian National Research Council had a point. By the mid-1950s, the eventual commercial potential of electronic musical instruments was becoming clear. Many companies entered the field. Following its brief early entry with the theremin, RCA *re*-entered the field, once again briefly.

Milton Babbitt, who had joined the Princeton University faculty in 1938, had read articles about optical soundtracks: "They were ecstatic reports of any kind of sound or continuity by drawing on film, and the people at RCA, at that time Harry Olson, thought it sounded like fun, so we began to play around a little with optical sound." Tape recorders became available in the late 1940s, but as Babbitt said, "I didn't want to splice tape—tape was just not my medium." In 1957, when RCA announced the *Mark II Electronic Music Synthesizer*, an improvement on the Mark I of a few years earlier, Babbitt got seriously interested. The Mark II was a floor-to-ceiling wall-to-wall synthesizer built by Harry Olson and Herbert Belar at RCA's Sarnoff Laboratories in Princeton. The Mark II offered, in Olson's words:

> the possibility of entirely new tone complexes and combinations which cannot be achieved with conventional instruments. Furthermore, in the case of conventional instruments, the musician is limited to the use of lips, mouth, ten fingers, two hands and two feet to perform the different operations. This limitation does not exist in the electronic music synthesizer. Conventional instruments produce various noises such as the rushing of wind in wind instruments, bow scratch in the viol family, various clatters and rattles in plucked and struck-string instruments, and mechanism rattle in any instrument in which keys, valves, levers and shafts are used. These undesirable noises do not exist in the electronic music synthesizer. With the advent of the electronic method for the production of musical tones, new musical compositions can be written which take advantage of the superior characteristics of the electronic music synthesizer.

Charles Wuorinen, who used the Mark II to provide the basic sound material for his *Time's Encomium* (1969), described it as:

> a 750-vacuum-tube affair in which information was encoded by a fiendish combination of 4-bit binary switches, banks on the walls and console of this nearly room-sized machine, and two particularly clever paper drives, each of which would encompass two channels of information. Holes were punched in the paper that then passed over a metal roller to which contact was made by a set of brushes. The brushes were arranged so that they would lie over the holes that passed beneath, mak-

ing continuous contact. Time was represented on the machine as the number of holes at a certain rate of the paper drive. Pitch and other information was represented in binary numbers by a combination of preset switches and banks of holes in the paper.

And Babbitt tells the story:

> I talked to Harry Olson and he agreed that if [Vladimir] Ussachevsky and I were willing to learn how to use it, he would be grateful, and we could evaluate it and decide which universities might be interested in purchasing it. Vladimir and I went there many times each week, early in the morning, under a cloak of industrial secrecy. They checked us for cameras. Vladimir would eat a Hershey bar and we would work in an un-air-conditioned room. But he decided early on that it wasn't the way for him, so I was left on my own.

A collaboration formed nonetheless. Babbitt, Ussachevsky at Columbia University, and Otto Luening (also at Columbia), approached the Rockefeller Foundation for funding to establish the Columbia-Princeton Electronic Music Center and purchase the Mark II. As Babbitt recalls, "Vladimir and I met hundreds of times with lawyers to knock out a contract, and then came the fateful day when we got our money from the Rockefeller Foundation and we said to RCA that we'd like to have this machine—so they charged us $10,000, gave us the blueprints, and put it all in our place at 125th Street." The Mark II was installed at the newly organized Columbia-Princeton Electronic Music Center in 1959. Babbitt continues:

> Then came a great two years when I worked with Peter Mauzey and other engineers to make it practical. Peter was great. We worked morning, noon, and night, and learned the machine inside and out. Those were two years of experimentation, and the engineers changed a great deal of the machine. Varèse came to the studio—he had had no hands-on experience with any instrument—and he got excited. Stravinsky came up one Saturday morning and got so excited he had a heart attack. We had to get a cab and get him back to the hotel. He told me all the things he wanted me to do for him. He wanted to hear all kinds of rhythmic combinations that he was afraid to compose.
> The machine was extremely difficult to operate. First of all, it had a paper drive, and getting the paper through the machine and punching the holes was difficult. We were punching in binary. The machine was totally zero, nothing predetermined, and any number we punched could refer to any dimension of the machine. There was an immense number of analog oscillators but the analog sound equipment was constantly causing problems. I couldn't think of anything that you couldn't get, but other

Milton Babbitt at the RCA Mark II Electronic Music Synthesizer in the mid-1960s. Photo courtesy Milton Babbitt.

composers gave up—it was a matter of patience. Max Mathews once said to me, "You must have the mechanical aptitude of Edison to work with that synthesizer," and I said, "No, I've got the patience of Job." I became irritated with the mechanics of the machine very often. I had to troubleshoot all the time and I was completely dependent upon Peter Mauzey. But I learned a lot of tricks, how to cut down on programming time with presets and so on. There were many people who would look at this machine and say, "It's a computer." But it never computed anything. It was basically just a complex switching device to an enormous and complicated analog studio hooked into a tape machine. And yet for me it was so wonderful because I could specify something and hear it instantly.

Babbitt's principal compositions with the Mark II were *Composition for Synthesizer* (1961), for tape alone; *Vision and Prayer* (1961), for tape and soprano, with text based on a poem by Dylan Thomas; *Philomel* (1963), for tape and soprano, with text based on a poem by John Hollander; and *Ensembles* (1964), for tape alone. In all of the music that Babbitt composed with the Mark II, the subtlety of the musical texture, based on precise changes in timbre and timing, was amazing. Indeed, changes could be made to happen so fast, with timings so tight, that it led Babbitt to reconsider his notions of timing and ensemble when working with live performers. As he said, "I realized there was a tremendous discrepancy between what we could specify and hat could be done by performers." Babbitt was surprised in both ways—what bunded possible was sometimes impossible, and what seemed impossible was sometimes possible. Harvey Sollberger, superb flutist, provided one example. As Babbitt recalls, "I wrote a trill which had thirty-two alternations a second, and Harvey said, 'I can produce that,' but he couldn't—and we soon learned where the hand was never faster than the ear." On the other hand, Babbitt composed *Vision and Prayer* for soprano Bethany Beardslee. As Babbitt tells it, "In the notation, I simplified some of the rhythms ever so slightly so they would not look preposterous, and she called me two days later and said, 'Either the tape is wrong or my score is wrong—it throws me off completely.'" Babbitt sums it up:

> In a nutshell, we had to learn a whole new set of limitations of the human perceptual apparatus. And that was really what concerned us for the next decade or more. I often went to the studio and tried things and it wasn't what I predicted. And then my problem was how to get what I wanted to get. It was a long hard road. I was perfectly willing to work long and hard hours and produce relatively few pieces.

But why? Why long and hard hours? What exactly was the allure? Babbitt answers:

> The notion of having complete control over one's composition, of being complete master of all you survey (and please remember that in the mid-1950s, the possibilities for performance of exacting difficult music were rare), the prospect of having one's music performed and performed adequately, to hear one's music as it was conceived . . . Where could one turn? It seemed to be a practical solution, a musical solution, a conceptual solution, and it removed one from an inappropriate milieu of presenting it to people who were not prepared and not interested.

The end came in 1976. A group of thieves broke into the studio from the roof and "stole everything that was stealable. The wiring was destroyed," Babbitt said, "and I never used the synthesizer again."

•

The RCA Mark II Electronic Music Synthesizer marked the end of the era of the early electronic instruments. Thaddeus Cahill had characterized the era when, in November 1907, at a demonstration of the Telharmonium for the Music Teachers' National Association, he said, "The composer of the future will have . . . not merely the known and approved tones of the orchestra, but many shades and nuances heretofore unattainable." Cahill, in other words, had predicted new sounds.

New sounds, but not new music. The Telharmonium had played Rossini overtures, Theremin had played Glinka, Le Caine had played *Rhapsody in Blue*, the engineers of the Mark II programmed Irving Berlin's *Blue Skies*. And although avant-garde composers such as Hindemith, Varèse, Babbitt, and others used electronic instruments to perform their music, their musical ideas had been formed independently of the instruments. The early electronic musical instruments, in short, opened the door to future developments but embodied no new musical ideas.

There was one notable exception. Percy Grainger, an Australian composer, had long been interested in what he called "Free Music." In 1938, he wrote:

> Music is an art not yet grown up . . . Existing conventional music (whether 'classical' or popular) is tied down by set scales, a tyrannical (whether metrical or irregular) rhythmic pulse that holds the whole fabric in a vise-like grasp and a set of harmonic procedures (whether keybound or atonal) that are merely habits . . . It seems to me absurd to live in an age of flying and yet not be able to execute tonal glides and curves . . . Free Music demands a non-human performance. Like most true music, it is an emotional, not a cerebral product and should pass direct from the imagination of the composer to the ear of the listener by way of delicately controlled musical machines. Too long has music been subject to the limitations of the human hand . . . A composer wants to speak to his public direct. Machines (if properly constructed and properly written for) are capable of niceties of emotional expression impossible to a human performer. That is why I write my Free Music for theremins—the most perfect tonal instruments I know.

Grainger was at the time living in the United States. He had met Theremin in New York and was impressed that the theremin could play any pitch; thus, when Theremin disappeared from New York in 1938, Grainger decided to develop his own *Free Music Machine*. In 1944, he met Burnett Cross, a scientist, and they began a collaboration to build it. Cross describes the project:

> Grainger wanted a composer's machine, not one for the concert hall. As he said, he wanted to hear in actuality the sounds he had heard in his mind for many years . . . The Free Music Machine had to be able to play any pitch within its range. It was to be free of the limitations of speaking in half tones, or quarter tones or eighth tones for that matter . . . The machine had to be able to go from pitch to pitch by way of a controlled glide as well as by a leap . . . The machine had to be able to perform complex irregular rhythms accurately, rhythms much too difficult for human beings to execute . . . The machine had to be workable by the composer. It was not to require a staff of resident engineers . . .

After several earlier versions, including one that was labeled in a diagram as the "Kangaroo Pouch method of synchronizing and playing eight oscillators," the final version of the Free Music Machine was finished in the mid-1950s. It read separate graphs for pitch and volume, each graph painted along its appropriate band on a five-foot wide roll of plastic that was rolled through the machine. Light was passed through the graphs to photocells which controlled the frequencies of oscillators. The pitch oscillator was heard directly. The volume oscillator's output modulated a flashlight bulb which in turn modulated another photocell which controlled a preamplifier circuit. Durations, and consequently rhythms of arbitrary complexity, were specified by calculating relationships between the length of a line in the graph and its speed through the photocell apparatus.

The Free Music Machine grew out of Grainger's musical ideas. By itself, it was too personal to inspire a revolution. But Grainger's sense of musical freedom was in the air. And while so many new electronic instruments were being developed during the first half of the century, a musical revolution was indeed brewing.

• • •

CHAPTER TWO

THE GREAT OPENING UP OF MUSIC TO ALL SOUNDS

As if models of a synchronous universe, every musical composition and painting of the Newtonian period—roughly from 1600 to 1900—reflected one line of time. In every musical composition, there was but one line of chord progressions to which all notes were synchronized. In every painting, there was but one line of travel for a viewer's eyes, one perspective to which all objects were synchronized. Newton, in his *Principia* (1687), called that one line of time *Absolute Time*:

> Absolute, True, and Mathematical Time, of itself, and from its own nature flows . . . All motions may be accelerated and retarded, but the True, or equable progress, of Absolute Time is liable to no change . . .

It was and still is a matter of common sense to view the universe as synchronous. When we say "We'll see you at 7," we do so knowing full well that our watches are ticking at the same rate, that we are all synchronized to a single line of time.

But common sense is not the only reality. At the beginning of the twentieth century, it had become clear that the universe—atoms, light quanta, stars—extended to smaller and larger items than could be seen by the naked eye. And Einstein, in the Special Theory (1905), portrayed an asynchronous universe of multiple clocks, where each clock relative to other clocks ticked faster or slower according to the speed with which it traveled through space.

The idea of relative speed is easy to understand. A train that moves at 60 mph, for example, is in fact moving at 60 mph faster than the surface of the earth; and when we pour coffee in that train, the coffee pours straight down because it too is moving at 60 mph and is, consequently, at rest relative to the train. What is neither easy to understand nor verifiable in common sense is that, because it is moving faster than the surface of the earth, the train's "clock" is ticking more slowly than a clock on the surface of the earth. As proposed in the Special Theory, the faster something moves, the more slowly its time passes. Einstein's universe, in short, was a multiplicity of parallel and asynchronous timelines.

•

The idea of an asynchronous universe was in the air. It's not that early twentieth-century poets, musicians, and artists read Einstein. It's just that some of them sniffed the new idea and saw things in a new way. As they looked around, they saw simultaneous and asynchronous activities, or processes, or "stories," each developing at its own rate. In *Lundi Rue Christine* (1913), for example, Guillaume Appollinaire juxtaposed unrelated phrases and fragments as if they were "plucked" from independent and parallel storylines:

> *Three lit gas jets*
> *The proprietress has bad lungs*
> *When you've finished we'll play a hand of backgammon*
> *An orchestra conductor who has a sore throat*
> *When you come to Tunis I'll give you some kef to smoke*
>
> *This seems to rhyme*

It was liberating. Indeed, *anything* could seem to rhyme. Anything could go together with anything else. It was as if the world had opened up. "We must throw wide the window to the open sky," Claude Debussy wrote through Monsieur Croche. "Music was born free; and to win freedom is its destiny," Ferruccio Busoni wrote in his *Sketch of a New Aesthetic of Music*. In the new music of the early twentieth century, chords and melodies were "plucked" from different keys and juxtaposed in a multiplicity of new combinations; as in, for example, Igor Stravinsky's *Le Sacre du Printemps* (1913), so large in scale, so complex in its combinations and superimpositions of rhythms, chords and melodies, so rich in the originality of its musical invention, that the riot at its premiere seems a reasonable public reaction; or as in Charles Ives' *Putnam's Camp*, finished in 1914 as part of his orchestral suite *Three Places in New England*, where campfire songs and marches are superimposed as asynchronous and simultaneous processes in a free-for-all celebration of the Fourth of July.

Everything thinkable was possible, including the plucking of *found objects* from their normal environments and contexts and juxtaposing them with other found objects in artworks. Pablo Picasso's *Still Life with Chair Caning* (1912), for example, contains a piece of oilcloth and hemp rope. *Man with a Hat*, one of several *papiers collés* finished by Picasso also in 1912, is a cubist drawing in charcoal and black ink of a man's face and upper torso, with blue paper and newspaper cutouts glued to the surface. Nor was Picasso alone in using found objects. His first assemblages were the beginning of a twentieth-century mainstream that included works by Georges Braque, Juan Gris, Marcel Duchamp, Kurt Schwitters, Hannah Höch, Man Ray, Jean Tinguely, Robert Rauschenberg, and many other artists. Although Duchamp, in particular, did raise a few eyebrows from time to time, particularly with his so-called *ready-mades*, the use of found objects in the visual arts was normal.

In music, on the other hand, the use of found sounds was abnormal, controversial, and sometimes technically problematic. *Parade*, for example, produced at the Châtelet Theatre in Paris on May 18, 1917, conceived by Jean Cocteau, designed by Pablo Picasso, choreographed by Léonid Massine, with music by Eric Satie, was received with scant applause and an abundance of critical hostility. Satie, doubtless speaking for generations of composers before and after, responded to one of the more negative critics with the postcard: "Sir and Dear Friend, You are only an arse, but an arse without music." And the critic, demonstrating thereby how right Satie was, sued Satie. At the conclusion of an excited trial, during which Cocteau was in momentary physical conflict with the courtroom police, Satie was given an eight-day suspended sentence. Yes, *Parade* was controversial. And there were technical problems. The found-sound devices planned by Cocteau hadn't worked well. Cocteau later wrote:

> The score of *Parade* was intended to serve as a background to suggestive noises . . . in effect, noises played an important role in *Parade*. Practical problems (lack of compressed air, among others) deprived us of these "trompe l'oreille" sounds—dynamo, Morse code machine, sirens, steam engine, airplane motor—which I used just like "trompe l'oeil"—newspaper, cornice, artificial wood—is used by painters. We could hardly make the typewriters heard.

The sweetest example of found sounds in those early days was the use of recorded nightingales during a performance of Ottorino Respighi's orchestral piece *Pines of Rome* in 1924. The loudest example was George Antheil's use of an airplane engine on stage for his *Ballet Mécanique* in 1926. The *Ballet Mécanique* was noted by, among others, Ezra Pound, who wrote:

> Antheil has made a beginning; that is in writing music that couldn't have been written before. His musical world is a world of steel bars, not of old

stone and ivy. With the performance of the *Ballet Mécanique* one can conceive the possibility of organizing the sounds of a factory, let us say, of boiler plate or any other clangorous noisiness, the actual sounds of the labor, the various tones of the grindings . . .

•

John Cage was the first composer to focus on the use of found sounds, and one route to Cage is through Marcel Duchamp. At first as an amusement, Duchamp mounted a bicycle wheel upside down on a stool in his studio. Later, in 1913, he saw it in a more serious context, as a prototype *readymade*, as he called it. Other readymades followed, among them *In Advance of a Broken Arm* (1915), a snow shovel with the title written on the back of the blade, and *Fountain* (1917), a porcelain urinal with the inscription "R. Mutt, 1917" painted on the front. Of *Fountain*, Duchamp wrote:

> Now Mr. Mutt's fountain is not immoral, that is absurd, no more than a bathtub is immoral. It is a fixture that you see every day in plumbers' show windows.
>
> Whether Mr. Mutt with his own hands made the fountain or not has no importance. He CHOSE it. He took an ordinary article of life, placed it so that its useful significance disappeared under the title and point of view—created a new thought for that object.

L.H.O.O.Q. from 1919, a so-called "rectified" readymade, was a reproduction of the *Mona Lisa* with a mustache and goatee drawn on it. It was described by its creator as:

> a combination readymade and iconoclastic dadaism. The original, I mean the original readymade is a cheap chromo 8 x 5 on which I inscribed at the bottom four letters which pronounced like initials in French, made a very risqué joke on the *Gioconda*.

La Gioconda is the Italian name for the *Mona Lisa*. L.H.O.O.Q. is in fact five letters (but who's counting?). The risqué joke is in the French pronunciation of the five letters as *elle a chaud au cul*, which means, in roughly equivalent jargon, "she's got a hot ass"—which, as Duchamp remarked, explained her smile. Duchamp had a talent for scandal, as did John Cage. And Cage, from his point of view, felt a particular affinity for Duchamp's work, as well as a friendship for the man and, one might guess, empathy with the mischievousness of his personality. Several of Cage's compositions involve Duchamp in the title or in some other way. There is a series of graphics from 1969 called *Not Wanting to Say Anything About Marcel* and a wonderful mesostic, one of the *36 Mesostics Re and Not Re Duchamp*, which is:

> since other Men
> mAke
> aRt,
> he Cannot.
> timE
> is vaLuable.

But whereas Duchamp started by discovering a readymade in his own studio, Cage started by defining concepts of musical structure that were independent of any particular sound. As he said, "Structure in music is its divisibility into successive parts . . ." Of his *Construction in Metal* (1939), Cage wrote:

> I felt the need of finding some structural means adequate to composing for percussion. This led me eventually to a basic reexamination of the physical nature of sound. Sounds, including noises, it seemed to me, had four characteristics (pitch, loudness, timbre and duration), while silence had only one (duration). I therefore devised a rhythmic structure based on the duration, not of notes, but of spaces of time . . .

Cage defined the parts before putting in the sounds. Of his *Sonatas and Interludes* (1948), he wrote, "the structure . . . was one hundred measures of two-two time, divided into ten units of ten measures each . . . combined in the proportion three, three, two, two . . ." In other words, Cage conceptualized musical structure as an array of empty glasses of predetermined sizes to be filled with sounds or silences. His silent piano piece, originally titled *4'33"*, makes the idea crystal clear. It is, in effect, three empty glasses. The score specifies only a structure of three silent parts, and the note to the score explains, partly by example, the concept:

> The title of this work is the total length in minutes and seconds of its performance. At Woodstock, NY, August 29, 1952, the title was 4'33" and the three parts were 33", 2'40", and 1'20". It was performed by David Tudor, pianist, who indicated the beginnings of parts by closing, the endings by opening, the keyboard lid. However, the work may be performed by any instrumentalist or combination of instrumentalists and last any length of time.

Cage's idea of structure had its most important consequence in his corollary idea that any sound or silence might fill the glasses. In *Construction in Metal*, Cage filled them with percussion sounds. In *Sonatas and Interludes*, he filled them with prepared piano sounds produced by various rubber wedges, screws, and other items placed between the strings of a piano, the goal of which was to turn a piano into a keyboard-controlled percussion ensemble. He also filled the glasses with found sounds. In *Imaginary Landscape #1* (1939), he called for variable-speed phonograph turntables. In *Imaginary Landscape #3* (1942), it was tin cans and electronic oscillators. *Imaginary Landscape #4* (1951) was for twelve radios, and *Imaginary Landscape #5*, finished in January 1952, used material from forty-two phonograph records. Cage had expressed his interest in found sounds as early as 1937 when he said:

> I believe that the use of noise to make music will continue and increase until we reach a music produced through the aid of electrical instruments which will make available for musical purposes any and all sounds that can be heard . . . whereas, in the past, the point of disagreement has been between dissonance and consonance, it will be, in the immediate future, between noise and so-called musical sounds.

By "noise," Cage meant found sounds. By "musical sounds," he meant, well . . . As he put it:

> Wherever we are, what we hear is mostly noise. When we ignore it, it disturbs us. When we listen to it, we find it fascinating. The sound of a truck at fifty miles per hour. Static between the stations. Rain. We want to capture and control these sounds, to use them not as sound effects but as musical instruments . . . If this word "music" is sacred and reserved for eighteenth- and nineteenth-century instruments, we can substitute a more meaningful term: organization of sound.

•

In his approach to using found sounds, Pierre Schaeffer, in Paris, followed Cage's lead. By training a radio engineer and by profession an announcer for Radiodiffusion Française (RF), Schaeffer had been able to establish an embryonic research facility at RF in Paris as early as 1942, during the German occupation. At first called Studio d'Essai, it was renamed Club d'Essai in 1946 and served as a base for experiments in radio-theater and music.

In 1948, Schaeffer got another idea. As he wrote at Easter: "Certainly the idea of a concert of locomotives is exciting. Sensational." On May 3, he wrote, "Here I am en route to the station at Batignolles, with a sound truck and naively treasuring my false good idea." The composition, which contains juxtaposed sections of locomotive steam and wheel sounds, their periodic rhythms punctuated with whistles, was called *Etude aux Chemins de Fer* (Railroad Study). It was significant because it was the first recorded assemblage of sounds and, as such, it launched a new technique and gave rise to a new way of thinking about music. In an entry dated May 15, Schaeffer introduced his term *musique concrète*:

> This determination to compose with materials taken from an existing collection of experimental sounds, I name *musique concrète* to mark well the

place in which we find ourselves, no longer dependent upon preconceived sound abstractions, but now using fragments of sound existing concretely and considered as sound objects defined and whole . . .

Schaeffer completed a series of five short musique concrète studies in 1948: *Etude aux Chemins de Fer* was the first, to be followed by *Etude aux Tourniquets*, with sounds from toy tops and percussion instruments; *Etude Violette*, using piano sounds recorded for Schaeffer by Pierre Boulez; *Etude Noire*, also using piano sounds recorded for Schaeffer by Boulez; and *Etude Pathétique*, using sounds from saucepans, canal boats, words sung and spoken, a harmonica, and a piano. There was one more piece in 1948, the *Diapason Concertino*, based on piano sounds recorded for Schaeffer by Jean-Jacques Grunenwald.

Following a spirited reception of the *Etudes* as heard in a radio concert called *Concert de Bruits* (Concert of Noises), broadcast on October 5, 1948, Schaeffer asked the RF administration for a team of assistants. In 1949, he was joined by Pierre Henry as co-researcher and Jacques Poullin as technician and the first culmination of their joint efforts was a live concert of musique concrète on March 18, 1950, at the Ecole Normale de Musique in Paris. The concert included the first performance of *Symphonie pour un Homme Seul* (Symphony for One Man Alone), a Schaeffer-Henry collaboration. The original version, as played in that concert, contained twenty-two movements—some of them called by classical names such as *Partita*, *Valse*, and *Scherzo*, and some using spoken words and rhythmic patterns produced by percussion instruments. A later version by Henry reduced the number of movements to twelve.

Pierre Henry was important in the collaboration. As a free-lance musician, he had made the music for a film called *Voir l'Invisible* (To See the Invisible), and as he recalls, "At that point I wanted to meet Pierre Schaeffer— I had heard the *Etudes de Bruit* and I wanted to show him what I'd done because I thought he was very close to what I wanted to do." Henry had gone to see Schaeffer just as Schaeffer was looking for a composer to work with him on research in sound. Henry started to work on *Symphonie pour un Homme Seul* and, as he puts it, "I found my voice." Henry continues:

A lot of the *Symphonie*. . . was taken from pieces that I'd composed before. We transformed them. We worked with very primitive equipment and, even more, the loudspeakers weren't very good so we couldn't hear very well what we should do. It needed a lot of imagination. And I was very surprised at the success of the first experiments. People wanted to hear them. They were interested because we made new sounds that suggested an extraordinary instrument.

Working with Schaeffer was an intellectual challenge. I was very young, twenty or twenty-one years old, and it was formative for me. I was there twelve hours each day. He came from time to time and modified what I had done. He was perhaps more intellectual than I was at the time, and I was more of a musician. He was more theoretical, I was more expressive. The first years were the discovery of sound. After that it became more formal—"Pierre, do this phrase, do more of that sequence . . ." Schaeffer gave ideas, suggestions, orders . . . He was in charge of the studio and I was a salaried employee. Afterwards, I worked for myself. But there, I worked for Schaeffer.

In those days before RF acquired tape recorders, Schaeffer and Henry recorded sound by cutting directly into a disc with a lathe. Sounds were edited by playing back several discs simultaneously and switching between them with a mixer. Henry's description of composing *Symphonie pour un Homme Seul* with, as he put it, "primitive equipment" was from today's perspective certainly appropriate.

•

Other composers had also experimented with found sounds. During the 1920s and 1930s, Darius Milhaud, Percy Grainger, Paul Hindemith, and Ernest Toch, at different times and with different intents, had experimented with variable-speed phonographs as a means to transform recorded sound. Primitive perhaps, but at the time it was the only technology available. The phonograph with a hollow cylinder had been invented by Thomas Edison in 1877; the gramophone with a flat disc had been invented ten years later by Emile Berliner; and by the 1920s, the gramophone, often called a phonograph, had become a commercial item. The serious problem in phonograph technology, however, was that a phonograph recording could not be edited. For a period during the 1930s, optical recording, in particular the early work of Norman McLaren in Canada and Yevgeny Sholpo in Russia, seemed to have possibilities. But the first real solution to editing was magnetic recording on tape.

The history of magnetic recording begins in the late nineteenth century. The September 8, 1888 issue of *The Electrical World* carried an article entitled "Some Possible Forms of Phonograph," written by Oberlin Smith, an American engineer. Smith began as follows:

> There being nowadays throughout the scientific world great activity of thought regarding listening and talking machines, the readers of *The Electrical World* may be interested in a description of two or three possible methods of making a phonograph which the writer contrived some years ago, but which were laid aside and never brought to completion on account of a press of other work.

Smith, in other words, published his ideas in the hope that others, less pressed for time than he was, might develop them. He went on to suggest that a thread or ribbon of magnetizable material, or possibly material coated with magnetizable dust, could provide a basis for recording and playing back sound.

In 1898 in Denmark, Valdemar Poulsen had the same idea. He proceeded to invent what he called the Telegraphone, a machine which recorded sound magnetically on a steel wire, and presented it at the Paris Exposition in 1900, winning the grand prix for scientific invention. Articles were published in scientific magazines, among them *Scientific American*, *The Electrician*, *Annalen der Physik*, and *Comptes Rendus*.

In 1903, American Telegraphone Company was founded to manufacture and market Poulsen's device. Advertisements appeared featuring Phoebe Snow, a famous model of the time, happily playing stenographer with her dictating-machine Telegraphone. Phoebe Snow, however, was far more beautiful than the Telegraphone, which remained ugly, heavy, difficult to use, and expensive. There were, nonetheless, occasional sales, among them to E. I. Dupont de Nemours & Company for a central dictation facility in their Wilmington, Delaware, office. And there were more than occasional lawsuits, one of them brought by E. I. Dupont de Nemours & Company because the dictation machines did not work. Other lawsuits were brought by unhappy shareholders. By the 1920s, all manufacture had ceased and the sole activity of the American Telegraphone Company was litigation.

In 1925, Kurt Stille and partners founded Telegraphie-Patent Syndikat Company in Germany to license the manufacture of magnetic recorders. There were two important licensees: Ludwig Blattner and Karl Bauer. Blattner developed the Blattnerphone, which used a steel band instead of a wire as the recording medium (an idea, incidentally, which had also occurred to Poulsen). In 1930, the British Marconi Company bought Blattner's company and, with the cooperation of Stille Laboratories, developed an improved Marconi-Stille steel tape machine that was used by the BBC at its studios at Maida Vale in London. It was described as presenting the "risk of instantly decapitating anyone within reach of its whirling steel tape . . ." The reels weighed twenty-two pounds and turned at an impressive speed. The recording engineers were located in an adjoining room in case the steel tape broke and "thrashed ungovernably about . . ." Editing the tape was a matter of welding. Although not user friendly by later standards, its use was occasionally distinctive, as on Christmas Day, 1932, when it was used to broadcast a speech by King George V.

Karl Bauer, meanwhile, organized Echophone Company to manufacture the Dailygraph, a wire recorder that featured cartridge containment of the wire. Echophone Company was purchased in 1932 by C. Lorenz Company which manufactured and marketed an office dictation machine called the Textophone.

In 1927, a United States patent describing a recording tape of powdered magnetic material was issued to J. A. O'Neill. In 1928, a German patent describing a recording tape of powdered magnetic material was issued to Fritz Pfleumer. In 1931, Pfleumer succeeded in interesting I. G. Farben in developing plastic-backed tape. He also interested Allgemeine Electrizitäts Gesellschaft (AEG) in developing tape machines. In 1935, AEG introduced the new

Magnetophone at the German Annual Radio Exposition in Berlin with the first example of plastic tape. It was less expensive than steel tape, which was a major benefit, but it felt like sandpaper and created clouds of dust as it passed through the recorder.

By the mid-1930s, magnetic recording was established as an emerging technology. Wire and steel tape recording were of acceptable quality; plastic tape seemed promising; Lee De Forest's audion had become commercially available for use in the amplification of weak signals; and AC biasing techniques, invented in 1921 by Wendell L. Carson and Glenn W. Carpenter of the United States Naval Research Laboratory, were used to improve the signal-to-noise ratio in recording and playback. In 1936, the London Philharmonic Orchestra, Sir Thomas Beecham conducting, was recorded at I. G. Farben headquarters at Ludwigshafen, Germany.

Improvements, of course, continued during World War II. Several American companies, among them Brush Development Company, Armour Research Foundation, H. G. Fischer Company, and General Electric, developed wire recorders for military and commercial use. During the same period, AEG improved the use of plastic tape. By 1945, the AEG Magnetophone had a frequency response of up to fifteen kilohertz at a tape speed of thirty inches per second. Colonel Richard Ranger, a pioneer in the design and manufacture of tape recorders, recounts his entry into Berlin with the allies in 1945 :

> The center of the Magnetophone production was the AEG in the part of Berlin which finally came under the French. I found that there were parts for eighteen machines available which had not been assembled. The French agreed to let them be assembled and the eighteen were to be apportioned six to the French, six to the British and six to the United States. When I came back some weeks later, I found that the first had gone to the French, the second to the British and the third was to go to the French. Well, we finally got that straightened out . . .

Additional examples were shipped to the United States from Frankfurt. And interest in tape recording took a major jump forward. Magnecord, Rangertone, and Ampex were formed in 1946, spurring interest at Minnesota Mining and Manufacture (3M) to develop a better plastic tape. The problems with the AEG tape were low output, the necessity of playing it at high speed, and lack of uniformity in its response. Dr. W. W. Wetzel, then head of the physics section of the 3M research division, put together a team to develop a new oxide coating for plastic tape, while other groups at 3M developed manufacturing technologies. In 1947, the first commercial tape was produced with a black oxide coating. And Bing Crosby entered the field. Again, Richard Ranger:

> Bing Crosby started transcription broadcasting using discs in 1946. But building a finished program on disc by retranscribing from disc to disc

took time and degraded the quality with successive generations, so it was decided to test out all the available media . . . In the summer of 1947 Bing came to New York for a program and it was recorded at WJZ in New York, on disc and film. . . They then asked us how long it would take us to come up with a tape version. We quite surprised them by saying, "Would tomorrow evening be all right?" . . . In a couple of months all the Crosby shows were from tape spliced together . . .

In the fall of 1947, 3M finished the development of a new magnetic material, a red oxide, which made possible a fifteen-kilohertz frequency response at a lower tape speed (seven and one-half inches per second) and greatly improved uniformity, all of which, in short, resulted in a lower cost, longer playing, and higher fidelity tape. In 1948, the market began major expansion as Bing Crosby Enterprises became a distributor for the new Ampex 200 tape machine. In 1949, two things happened: Magnecord introduced the first stereo tape machine. And the first commercial splicing block was introduced.

•

The story of the Paris studio continues. The first performance of *Symphonie pour un Homme Seul* on March 18, 1950, had been problematic, in large part because of technical complexities in manipulating turntables and mixers. Those problems led Schaeffer to suggest, in 1951, that Jacques Poullin build the *pupitre d'espace*, a mechanism for distributing sound throughout the space of a concert hall. Schaeffer also conceived of two special tape recorders—the *Phonogène*, a variable-speed variable-pitch tape recorder, and the *Morphophone*, a tape recorder with multiple heads allowing for various delay and desynchronizing effects—which were built by Poullin. Pierre Henry composed *Aube, Microphone Bien Tempéré, Musique sans Titre, Concerto des Ambiguités*, and *Astrologie*, among other pieces, and he worked with Schaeffer on *Orphée*, a musique concrète opera first performed at the Théâtre de l'Empire in Paris on July 6, 1951.

In 1951, Schaeffer reestablished the studio, with tape recorders, as the Groupe de Recherche de Musique Concrète. It quickly got busy: André Hodeir composed *Jazz et Jazz* (1951), for piano and tape; Pierre Boulez composed *Etude I sur un Son* (1952) and *Etude II sur Sept Sons* (1952); Olivier Messiaen composed *Timbres-Durées* (1952); Karlheinz Stockhausen composed *Etude* (1952); Michel Philippot composed *Etude I* (1952); and Pierre Henry composed *Vocalises* (1952) and *Antiphonie* (1952), among other works, while working on revisions to *Orphée*. Schaeffer was mainly engaged in the formulation of a theory of sound objects.

Orphée was performed again as *Orphée 53* at the Donaueschingen Musiktage, a prestigious festival in Germany, on October 10 and 11, 1953. Its reception at Donaueschingen, however, was problematic. Henry recalls:

*Pierre Henry at the pupitre d'espace in a concert at the Salle
de L'Ancien Conservatoire in Paris in 1952. Induction coils
were used to pass the signal from channel to channel.
Photo courtesy Pierre Henry.*

There was a riot. Everyone in the room was against it. They shouted.
They made more noise than the loudspeakers. But that was normal
because there were so many new sounds. It wasn't in the tradition of the
contemporary music of the time, and it was for this reason that the
German public revolted against it. But I was happy that the public took
it so seriously. And it gave me taste for combat, to battle against the public until they understood the music.

Shortly after the performance at Donaueschingen, Schaeffer became
occupied with radio projects in the French colonies in North Africa. Henry
remained at the studio in Paris and composed *Le Voile d'Orphée* (1953),
among other works. As he explained, "*Le Voile d'Orphée* existed within the
larger *Orphée*, but because Pierre Schaeffer had nothing to do with its composition, I kept it as my own." And the studio remained generally busy. Jean
Barraqué composed *Etude* (1953); Darius Milhaud composed *La Rivière
Endormie (Etude Poétique)* (1954), for mezzo soprano, narrators, orchestra,
and tape; and Edgard Varèse came to the studio from New York, at Schaeffer's
invitation, to compose some of the tape part to *Déserts* (1954), for orchestra
and tape. Schaeffer kept in touch and came back from time to time.

In 1955, Maurice Béjart visited the studio and that same year choreographed *Symphonie pour un Homme Seul*. It was successful. As Henry said, "It was the *Symphonie* . . . that made Béjart famous." In 1956, Henry composed *Haut Voltage* specifically for Béjart's dance company. As he said, "It gave me a taste to make concerts theatrical—the effectiveness of the lights, the visual activities . . ." Henry and Béjart began a fifteen year collaboration.

In 1957, Schaeffer returned to Paris. In 1958, Henry left his position at RF and, in 1959, established the Studio Apsome and began to work again as a professional composer. Henry remembers:

I left because he wanted me to leave. All of the studio equipment that was used before 1958 was locked up because Schaeffer wanted to start from zero. He thought that I was dangerous for the formation and functioning of a new group. And, yes, I did want to work independently. I financed the Studio Apsome by my professional work. I made recordings. I made montages for my clients. I did publicity, films. It was auto-financed, with-

Pierre Schaeffer in 1952 with two different versions of the phonogène, a variable-speed tape recorder built by Jacques Poullin. On the left is the phonogène à coulisse, in which the tape speed is controlled with a handle to produce continuous change from 0 to 76 centimeters per second. On the right is the phonogène à clavier, in which the tape speed is controlled by a keyboard to produce twelve discrete pitch levels. Photo courtesy GRM.

out help. There was a lot of music for film, lots of discs, lots of events with the public, with lights . . .

Henry worked with other composers, among them Eliane Radigue. And into the 1960s, he composed several important works, including *La Noire à Soixante* (1961), *Le Voyage* (1962), *Variations pour une Porte et un Soupir* (1963), and *Apocalypse de Jean* (1968). *Variations pour une Porte et un Soupir* (Variations on a Door and a Sigh) was exceptional in the simplicity of its sound sources and the ingenuity with which the sounds were used. As Henry describes it, "It was a question of recording a door in a way that there was a form to the sound, a grain, a color, like an instrument, and the rest was the sound of a sigh, a breath—there was no transposition, no treatment, it was only a montage and little bit of mixing."

Meanwhile, in 1958, with Luc Ferrari and François-Bernard Mâche, and also with Michel Philippot and Iannis Xenakis, Schaeffer established a new studio called Groupe de Recherches Musicales (GRM). Xenakis, in particular, emerged as an original and significant voice. As he put it, "The idea of musique concrète was that you could use all sorts of sounds or noises—I discovered the noises." And what was it like to work at GRM? Xenakis describes it:

At that time, there was no teaching of the system there. We didn't have any specific training. It was really free. We had some people working with us, helping, and they did whatever you told them to do. They were paid.

He adds, pensively, "I was not paid." In his early tape pieces at GRM, he used recorded acoustic sounds modified by tape manipulations—changing speed, playing backward, splicing—and mixing, but without electronic processing such as filtering and modulation. His compositions, however, were not juxtaposed "objects," as in normal musique concrète, so much as they were complex sound-masses that transformed in time as the result of shifting distributions and densities of small, component sounds. His experiences in the Greek resistance during World War II had shaped his sense of sound as sharp, powerful, striking, never pretty, never insipid. In his words:

It's interesting for me because I've been in musical environments that were made not only with individual sounds but also with large numbers of sounds. When I was in the resistance in Athens, there were multiple sounds, many people shouting at the same time, in thousands of cries. And I was amazed by the changes in the sounds. Another thing. I used to go camping around Attica, and I heard the cicadas and the raindrops on my tent, and I was always charmed by these noises.

In composing *Diamorphoses* (1957), Xenakis used the sounds of jet engines, car crashes, earthquake shocks, textures of sliding pitches, and other noiselike sounds, and sometimes contrasted them with thin, high bell sounds. *Concret P.H.* (1958) is a minimal, short piece based on the grainy, sandy sounds of burning charcoal, with varying density and register achieved by the overlays of tapes played at different speeds. *Orient-Occident* (1960), composed for a UNESCO film by Enrico Fulchignioni comparing sculpture and art of different cultures and times, was based on the sounds of bowed boxes, bells, and metal rods, sounds from the ionosphere, and a speed-altered excerpt from Xenakis' orchestral work *Pithoprakta*. In composing *Bohor* (1962), Xenakis used the sounds of bracelets, other jewelry, and a Laotian mouth organ. He remembers:

> I did *Bohor* with all sorts of sounds with bracelets. I had some necklaces from Iran. I was interested in the tiny sounds because you could expand them and find different sounds in them. I dedicated the piece to Schaeffer. He hated the piece.

By 1960, Radiodiffusion Française had become Radio Télévision Française (RTF) and in the new context of television, Schaeffer proposed to the RTF administration a plan to create Le Service de la Recherche, an organization that would include GRM but expand its experiments to include visuals. The administration accepted Schaeffer's proposal, and the new *Service* was established in a beautiful ivy-lined brownstone in Passy, an elegant section of Paris. Also in 1960, François Bayle began to work with Schaeffer in the dual capacity of student and general administrative and public relations assistant.

In 1963, Bayle became a salaried administrator in GRM, Radio Télévision Française became Office de Radio Télévision Française (ORTF), and Schaeffer was writing *Traité des Objets Musicaux*, a book of essays on musique concrète. In 1966, Schaeffer's book was published and Bayle became Director of GRM. In 1974, ORTF was partitioned into several organizations, among them Radio France and Institut National Audiovisuel (INA). GRM was administratively incorporated into INA and relocated inside the remarkable, round Radio France building in Paris. It was the beginning of a new line of technical development. And looking back, Bayle makes an important point:

> Musique concrète wasn't at all a music of noises, not at all a music of provocation. It was the contrary. It was a music that uses all the resources that are available to us, a music that uses all the sounds of life. Musique concrète sounds have meanings for us, as photographs and films have meanings. They show life as we experience it, as we live it in the everyday world.

●

The story of the Cologne studio begins in 1948. Homer Dudley, from Bell Telephone Laboratories at Murray Hill, New Jersey, visited Werner Meyer-Eppler, director of the Institute of Phonetics at the University of Bonn,

Germany. Dudley showed Meyer-Eppler a newly developed *vocoder*, a device for electronically processing vocal sounds.

What followed was a two-year flurry of lectures, demonstrations, meetings, and collaborations. Meyer-Eppler used taped examples of the vocoder's sounds to illustrate a lecture called "Developmental Possibilities of Sound" at a Tonmeister conference in Detmold in 1949. Robert Beyer, from the Westdeutscher Rundfunk (WDR) in Cologne, at that time called the Nordwestdeutscher Rundfunk (NWDR), heard the lecture and began a cooperative relationship with Meyer-Eppler to advance the cause of electronic music. In August 1950, Meyer-Eppler and Beyer presented lectures under the general heading of "The World of Sound of Electronic Music" at the International Summer School for New Music at Darmstadt. Herbert Eimert heard the lectures and joined forces with Meyer-Eppler and Beyer. Later in 1950, Harald Bode delivered a *Melochord*, his keyboard-controlled electronic instrument, to Meyer-Eppler in Bonn. Meyer-Eppler used Bode's Melochord to create examples of electronically generated sounds, which he then presented in a lecture called "Possibilities of Electronic Sound Production" at Darmstadt in July 1951. Beyer gave a lecture entitled "Music and Technology," and Eimert delivered a lecture called "Music on the Borderline." Later, in October, at another Tonmeister conference in Detmold, Meyer-Eppler gave another lecture, this time called "Sound Experiments," to a group which included Fritz Enkel, technical director of the WDR. The culminating event took place on October 18, 1951, at the WDR in Cologne. It was a meeting involving Meyer-Eppler, Beyer, Eimert, Enkel, and others of the WDR technical staff at which it was resolved to establish a studio at the WDR "to follow the process suggested by Dr. Meyer-Eppler to compose directly onto magnetic tape." That same day, the WDR broadcast "The World of Sound of Electronic Music," a forum with Meyer-Eppler, Beyer, and Eimert as participants.

Construction of the Cologne studio started in late 1951 and went into 1952. Meanwhile, in early 1952, Bruno Maderna worked with Meyer-Eppler in Bonn to compose *Musica su Due Dimensioni*, for flute, percussion, and tape, which was performed that summer at Darmstadt to an audience that included Pierre Boulez, Karel Goeyvaerts, Gottfried Michael Koenig, and Karlheinz Stockhausen, all of whom were invited to work in the Cologne studio. The program notes read, in part: "*Musica su Due Dimensioni* is a first attempt to combine the past possibilities of mechanical instrumental music with the new possibilities of electronic tone generation . . ."

Maderna's piece, the first composition associated with the Cologne studio, was nonetheless not typical of the studio's philosophy. It was Eimert, as the studio's first director, who initially set the tone, so to speak. His idea was that electronic music, or *elektronische Musik* as the Cologne approach came to be called, was an extension of serialism.

Serialism was an approach to musical structure that was considered by many composers during the 1950s to be extremely important, indeed so important as to approach the status of historical imperative. One may retrospectively wonder how something so cold as serialism could generate such heat, but apparently it did. As Pierre Boulez most emphatically put it, "I, in turn, assert that any musician who has not experienced—I do not say understood, but, in all exactness, experienced—the necessity for serialism is *useless.*"

Historically, serialism was an outgrowth of the so-called "twelve-tone system," formulated by Arnold Schoenberg during the early 1920s as a method for basing an entire composition on a single "row" of twelve notes. The German symphonic tradition, with its fundamental aesthetic of unity and economy of material, had been based largely on techniques of motivic development; and for Schoenberg, who saw himself as taking the next step in that tradition, manipulating the row was the contemporary equivalent of developing motives. But Schoenberg had structured only notes according to the row and, further, used his rows intuitively to create traditional textures of melody and accompaniment. It was Anton Webern, Schoenberg's student and far more radical than Schoenberg, who provided the model for the European serialists. In his *Symphony, Opus 21* (1928), for example, Webern used the row to derive a timbral structure as well as a pitch structure. And the notes were undifferentiated as melody and accompaniment. In a lecture in 1932, he referred to the idea of notes as all deriving equally from the row and all forms of the row as being equally important: "Goethe's primeval plant; the root is in fact no different from the stalk, the stalk no different from the leaf, and the leaf no different from the flower; variations of the same idea."

The European serialists of the early 1950s considered themselves post-Webern. For them, serialism was a compositional technique wherein every aspect of a composition—not only notes, but also loudness, timbre, duration, type of attack, and every other imaginable parameter of a sound—could be based on and derived from the same row, or *series*, thereby producing a kind of total structure wherein every detail was organized. For Eimert, the promise of elektronische Musik was more things in sound to organize. He saw the possibility for a microscopic resolution of sound to the level of the individual partial. He wrote:

> It is certain that no means of musical control could have been established over electronic material had it not been for the revolutionary thought of Anton Webern . . . Alone among the twelve-tone composers, Anton Webern conceived the row non-subjectively . . . In his work, for the first time, we see the beginnings of a three-dimensional row technique—of what, in short, we know as *serial technique* . . . everything, to the last element of the single note, is subjected to serial permutation . . . This electronic music is not 'another' music, but is serial music . . . Talk of 'humanised' electronic sound may be left to unimaginative instrument makers.

Karlheinz Stockhausen began to work at the WDR studio in May 1953. His first pieces in Cologne were *Studie I* (1953) and *Studie II* (1954), in which he used serialist techniques to determine the frequencies of sine waves. In distinct contrast with the Paris school, which focused on sounds recorded with a microphone, *Studie I* and *Studie II* were produced from electronic sound sources only. It was, in fact, an extremely laborious process, as the WDR studio at the time had very few electronic sound sources. Its sound-generating equipment consisted of a single sine wave generator, a white noise generator, Bode's Melochord, and a Monochord, actually a modified Trautonium built expressly by Trautwein for the WDR studio.

At the beginning, the sine wave generator was the preferred source because it offered the finest resolution in controlling sound according to serialist procedures. A *partial* (or *overtone*, as it is sometimes called) is a sine wave, and the idea was that by combining several sine waves at different frequencies any sound could be constructed. Since there was only one sine wave generator, however, the technique was to record four sine waves successively on each track of a four-track tape recorder, then play them back together through a mixer onto a monophonic tape recorder, then copy the result back onto one track of the four-track tape recorder, then record three additional sine waves onto the three remaining tracks, then play them back together onto a monophonic tape recorder, and so on. Finally, echo and reverberation effects were used to shape the final sound. As Stockhausen described it:

> a sine-wave is recorded on tape, a second, third, etc., is added. Electrically controlled, each sine-wave is given its own intensity curve, and then the intensity curve of the entire complex ("envelope") is once more regulated. The duration of the sound is fixed by measuring the tape in centimetres in cutting it—the speed of the tape is 30 or 15 inches per second. Thus, one by one, the sounds are put together and catalogued. When all the sounds for a composition have been prepared on the tape, the pieces are stuck together according to the score, and if necessary, are superimposed again by means of several synchronised tape-recorders . . .

During 1953 and 1954 , many composers worked at Cologne, and the works of these first years—Stockhausen's *Studie I* and *Studie II*, Herbert Eimert's *Glockenspiel* and *Etüde über Tongemische*, Karel Goeyvaerts' *Komposition #5*, Henri Pousseur's *Seismogramme*, and Paul Gredinger's *Formanten I/II*—were presented on October 19, 1954, at a concert called "Music of Our Time," which was subsequently broadcast by the WDR on December 9. As Gottfried Michael Koenig recalls, "When I went to Cologne in 1954, the studio was full of activity—it was an atelier-like situation, very attractive, where people were busy doing things."

Stockhausen, in particular, was moving into a position of leadership. He had studied with Olivier Messiaen at the Paris Conservatory from January 1952 to May 1953, and during that time in Paris, he had worked in Pierre Schaeffer's studio. That work had led him to reflect upon the structure and distinction of different sounds:

Wherein lies the difference between instrumental sounds, between any audible events: violin, piano, the vowel "a," the consonant "sh," the wind? In the group "musique concrète" in Paris during 1952 and 1953, I made many analyses of instrumental sounds—especially percussion, recorded in the Musée de l'Homme—also of speech and noises of all kinds. The sounds and noises were recorded in various kinds of rooms (anechoic chamber, room with normal acoustic, reverberation room). Electro-acoustic apparatus: filters, oscillographs, etc., was used to determine the sound characteristics . . .

In Stockhausen's *Gesang der Jünglinge* (1956), the first major work to be composed in the Cologne studio, the sounds recorded with a microphone were of a boy soprano's voice reading from the apocrypha to the Book of Daniel. Of the nine verses used, three words—*Preiset den Herrn* (Praise the Lord)—are often repeated, and according to the context, *jubelt* (exalt) is often substituted for *preiset*. About the semantic content of the words, Stockhausen wrote:

The lines and words can also be permutated without altering the actual meaning . . . if the word "preiset" occurs at one moment and the word "Herrn" at another—or vice versa—the listener is reminded of a word connection which he has always known . . . the concentration is directed upon the sacredness; speech becomes ritual.

Concerning the sounds of the words, he continued:

In the composition, sung tones must be blended with electronically produced ones to form a mutual sound-continuum . . . in a selected scale of electronically-produced sounds, single steps are replaced by sung speech-sounds. We only have a homogenous sound-family if sung sounds sound at certain places like electronic sounds, electronic sounds like sung ones. In order to achieve the greatest possible homogeneity . . . a twelve-year old boy sang all the necessary sounds, syllables, words and at times groups of words, too, which we recorded on tape and transformed, employing various methods of orientation as to pitch, duration, intensity and articulation of timbre . . .

According to the "colour"-continuum, the composition was based on the idea of a "speech-continuum": at certain points in the composition, sung groups of words become comprehensible speech-symbols, words; at others they remain pure sound qualities, sound-symbols; between these extremes there are various degrees of comprehensibility of the word. These are brought about either by the degree of permutation of the words in the sentence, syllables in the word, phonemes in the syllable, or by blending one form of speech with speech- or sound-elements foreign to the context . . .

The intention, therefore, is, by selecting individual steps from a sound-word continuum, to let "speech" proceed from the composition . . .

The original version was in five tracks, played through five loudspeaker groups arranged around the hall. Different strains of material were made to circulate through the space in carefully calculated paths—one sound-group, for example, might move in a trajectory from loudspeaker-group 1 to loudspeaker-group 2, while another sound-group might travel a different trajectory through other loudspeakers—with the goal of making them more differentiated, more clearly heard, more comprehensible. Stockhausen wrote:

> In my *Gesang der Jünglinge*, I attempted to form the direction and movement of sound in space, and to make them accessible as a new dimension for musical experience. The work was composed for five groups of loudspeakers, which should be placed around the listeners in the hall. From which side, by how many loudspeakers at once, whether with rotation to left or right, whether motionless or moving —*how* the sounds and sound-groups should be projected into space: all this is decisive for the comprehension of this work. The first performance took place on May 30th, 1956, in the main broadcasting studio at Cologne Radio Station. Today there are already quite a number of electronic spatial compositions . . .

In its organization of a sound continuum in discrete and gradated steps, in the permutations of the elements of sounds, and in the structural significance of musical detail including the spatial distribution of sound, *Gesang der Jünglinge* projects a serialist way of thinking. But it also represents a step taken away from serialism in its warmth, in its intuitive musicality, and in its pointillistic "clouds" of sound which were composed in what Stockhausen referred to as *statistical form*.

In 1960, Stockhausen finished *Kontakte*, his next major electronic work, after two years of practical experimentation. Yet further from serialism, *Kontakte* was based on what Stockhausen called *moment form*, wherein each moment was a miniature structure that stood on its own, independent from any overall structural continuity. And although the sounds were generated electronically, the musical phrases and the nature of the sounds were in large part suggestive of performance with percussion instruments and piano. Indeed, the title *Kontakte* (Contacts) points to connections between electronics and acoustic instruments. *Kontakte* exists in two versions, one for tape alone and another for performance with metal, skin, and wooden percussion instruments and piano. The first performance, on July 11, 1960, at a WDR music festival, was of the combined version: Christoph Caskel played percussion and David Tudor played piano and percussion.

By the mid-1960s, Stockhausen's tape compositions had become increasingly like musical films conceived as international epics. As a camera records

Karlheinz Stockhausen at the rotation table in the WDR Studio in 1958. This photo shows Stockhausen's method at the time for achieving sound distribution in a concert hall. As the table is turned, the loudspeaker on it projects a sound in different directions. The sound is picked up at slightly different times by four directional microphones, placed at different positions around the table, and the signal from each microphone is recorded on one track of a four-track tape. When the tape is played back in a concert hall, the signal from each track is routed through a different loudspeaker. Photo courtesy Stockhausen-Verlag.

visual events that are then brought together and edited into their final continuity as a film, so Stockhausen increasingly used a microphone to record sounds, and sounds that were recorded apart in space and/or time were brought together and electronically processed, edited, and mixed into their final continuity on tape. His *Telemusik*, for example, composed during a visit to Japan in 1966, contained sounds "from the Imperial Japanese Court (the Gagaku Players), from the happy isle of Bali, from the southern Sahara, from a Spanish village fiesta, from Hungary, from the Shipibos of the Amazon . . ." *Hymnen* (Anthems), finished in Cologne in 1967 but global in its geography and time scale, contained the national anthems of countries around the world. Further, in both *Telemusik* and *Hymnen*, the sounds were transformed by a process that Stockhausen called *intermodulation*, which meant that certain characteristics of one sound were used to transform certain characteristics of another thereby achieving, since the sounds came from so many countries, a poetic metaphor for international interaction. Would that real countries in the real world could intermodulate so easily, or that the real world's perceptions of structure could grow so seamlessly from the juxtapositions of collage forms to interconnectedness. As Stockhausen later wrote regarding *Telemusik*:

> Today, only three years later, I can already say that *Telemusik* has come to be the beginning of a new development. The situation of the "collage" of the first half of this century has been overcome. *Telemusik* is *not* a collage anymore. Rather, through the process of intermodulation, old objets trouvés and new sounds, which I produced in the electronic studio, are combined into a higher unity: a universality of past, present and future, of distant places and spaces: *Tele-Musik*.

Regarding *Hymnen*, Stockhausen wrote:

> National anthems are the most well known music that one can imagine. Everyone knows the anthem of his own country, and perhaps those of several others, or at least their beginnings. When one integrates in a composition known music with unknown, new music, one can hear especially well *how* it was integrated: untransformed, more or less transformed, transposed, modulated . . . Naturally, national anthems are more than that: they are "loaded" with time, with history . . .
>
> Numerous compositional processes of inter-modulation were applied in *Hymnen*. For example, the rhythm of one anthem is modulated with the harmony of another; this result is modulated with the dynamic envelope of a third anthem; this result in turn is modulated with the timbral constellation and melodic contour of chosen electronic sounds . . .

Stockhausen had succeeded Eimert as Director of the WDR studio in 1962, and during his tenure to 1980, the studio's equipment list grew more diverse to include eventually analog and digital synthesizers, among them an EMS Synthi-100, an EMS vocoder, and an Emulator. And although his work was the best known work to come out of the studio, Stockhausen was by no means the only composer to work at the WDR. The first group of composers, as represented in the 1954 concert, continued to work at the studio and they were joined through the years by many others, among them Giselher Klebe, Gottfried Michael Koenig, Ernst Krenek, Bengt Hambraeus, Franco Evangelisti, György Ligeti, Herbert Brun, Bo Nilson, Mauricio Kagel, Konrad Boehmer, Petr Kotik, Michael von Biel, Johannes Fritsch, Wlodzimierz Kotonski, Eugeniusz Rudnik, Peter Eötvös, David Johnson, Mesias Maiguashca, Bernd Alois Zimmermann, York Höller, Roger Smalley, Jean-Claude Eloy, Tim Souster, Luc Ferrari, Rolf Gehlhaar, Iannis Xenakis, Thomas Kessler, and Joseph Riedl.

•

Roughly simultaneously with the establishment of the Cologne studio in 1951, in Tokyo a group of four composers—Joji Yuasa, Toru Takemitsu, Hiroyoshi

Suzuki, and Kazuo Fukushima—along with several painters, a poet, a pianist, and a technician formed what they called the Jikken Kobo (Experimental Workshop). As Yuasa remembers, "It was an experimental time in Tokyo— there was a lively atmosphere and we aimed to do things in combined arts." Nobody in the group owned a tape recorder, but in 1953, Sony (at that time called Tokyo Tsushin Kogyo) provided access to its studio so that experiments in tape music could begin.

Also in 1953, a group of radio producers, engineers, and composers began tape music experiments at NHK (Nippon Houso Kyokai / Japanese Broadcasting Corporation) in Tokyo. In late 1954, the NHK studio officially opened its doors. The principal composers involved were Toshiro Mayuzumi, who had earlier worked in Schaeffer's studio in Paris, and Minao Shibata. Mayuzumi's first work had in fact predated the NHK studio. His *XYZ* (1953), a study in musique concrète done at the studio of the Bunka Hoso, was among the first tape pieces done in Japan. His first pieces composed at the NHK studio were *Etude I* (1955), a study in different techniques, and *Aoi no Ue* (1957), an integration of technology and tradition which used electronics in a Noh-theater context. Shibata's first piece was *Musique Concrète for Stereophonic Broadcast* (1955) which was simulcast that year on two different bands to achieve its called-for stereo effect. Makoto Maroi, a younger composer, visited Cologne for several months in 1955 and subsequently influenced the development of the NHK studio along Cologne lines. And he worked with Mayuzumi in composing *Shichi no Variation* (1956, Variations on Seven), which was influenced by the tuning proportions in Stockhausen's *Studie II*.

Eventually, other composers also worked in the NHK studio, among them Toshi Ichiyanagi and Joji Yuasa. Ichiyanagi had studied in New York from 1956 to 1961, first at Juilliard (he recalls, "but there was of course no electronic studio at that time"), then at the New School with Henry Cowell and John Cage, and later privately with Cage at Stony Point. In 1961, when he returned to Tokyo, he was commissioned by NHK to work in the new studio where he finished *Parallel Music* (1962), a combination of taped sounds and live sounds processed via a microphone. As he recalls, "It was very lively, very stimulating, and we had a very good relationship with engineers so we could try things."

Yuasa had previously worked at the NHK studio doing incidental music for radio dramas and documentaries that had been commissioned by the NHK drama department. By 1963, as he put it, "I was more or less known, so the NHK music department commissioned me to make electronic music." His *Projection Esemplastic* (1964) was based on what he called the *plasticity* of time and space. In his words, "I tried to compose throughout with bent sounds including portamenti and sound forms which have the shape of glissandi . . . I was strongly attracted to the fact that intervalic and timbral conditions are metamorphosed by the plasticity of time when it is changed continuously through tape speed alteration."

Many composers were also working at the Sogetsu Art Center, an alternative space in Tokyo for artistic and technical experimentation. Zyunosuke Okuyama, technician, invented a pen with a recording head such that signals could be written by hand directly onto tape. Yuasa used the pen to create a piece called *Aoi no Ue* (1961)—he explains, "Same name as Mayuzumi's piece, different music"—and Takemitsu used the pen to make a musical score for his film *Kaidan*. Following 1961, Ichiyanagi also worked at the Sogetsu Art Center. He was, in fact, influential in arranging for John Cage and David Tudor to be invited to Japan in 1962.

•

Meanwhile, on May 9, 1952, at a Composers' Forum concert at Columbia University in New York City, Vladimir Ussachevsky presented five electronic studies that he'd done with his own and borrowed equipment. One outcome of the concert was a friendly review by Henry Cowell in *Musical Quarterly*, October 1952, which ended: "We wish him well." Another outcome was an invitation from Otto Luening to present his work in August 1952 at the Bennington Composers' Conference at Bennington College in Vermont. It marked the beginning of a collaboration. That summer, Luening and Ussachevsky received an invitation to present their works as part of a contemporary music concert series produced by Leopold Stokowski at the Museum of Modern Art in New York. They accepted the invitation, then started to compose the music using, among other things, a reverberation device built for them by Peter Mauzey, a young engineer. It's Luening's story:

> We transported our equipment in Ussachevsky's car to Henry Cowell's house in Woodstock, New York, where we spent two weeks. With a borrowed portable tape recorder, an oversized wooden speaker, and old carpeting to deaden sound, we went to work. Using a flute as the sound source, I developed two impressionistic, virtuoso pieces, "Fantasy in Space" and "Low Speed." The latter was an exotic composition that took the flute below its natural range, but with certain acoustic combinations and the help of Mauzey's reverberation box, the flute was made to sound like a strange new instrument . . . Ussachevsky began work on an eight-minute composition that used piano as the primary sound source . . .
>
> This primitive laboratory was brought to Ussachevsky's living room in New York City, where we completed the compositions. With more borrowed equipment we added the final touch to our works in the studio of the basement of Arturo Toscanini's Riverdale home, at the invitation of David Sarser, the Maestro's sound engineer . . .

The concert took place on October 28, 1952, and included Ussachevsky's *Sonic Contours* and Luening's *Low Speed*, *Invention*, and *Fantasy in Space*. It was the first concert of its kind in the United States—as Jay

Harrison wrote in the *New York Herald Tribune*, "The result is as nothing encountered before . . ."—and it was subsequently broadcast by WNYC in New York and WGBH in Boston. Luening and Ussachevsky were also invited to do a demonstration and interview on the *Today* show on NBC television. Luening describes it:

> We were met at the studio by a member of the Musicians Local 802, who asked if I had a union card. I said, "No, but if any flutist in the union can improvise the program, I will be glad to have him take over." That settled the matter. A crew of eight engineers tried to connect Mauzey's little box, but it would not work. Five minutes before the telecast, Mauzey was finally allowed to operate his machine . . .

In April 1953, Luening's and Ussachevsky's music was presented at a festival at Radiodiffusion Française in Paris. In the summer of 1953, they did a short piece for Leopold Stokowski's CBS radio program called *Twentieth Century Concert Hall*. Also in 1953, they presented their music at a concert supported in part by the Musicians Performance Trust Fund and the Musicians Union; and an announcement from the stage that the concert probably signaled the eventual end of live music, as Luening recalled, "did not seem to detract from the audience's genuine interest." There was a commission from the Louisville Symphony Orchestra to compose a piece for tape and orchestra, a small grant from the Rockefeller Foundation to purchase a tape recorder, a brief stay at the MacDowell Colony to write a ballet for the American Mime Theater, a commission from the Los Angeles Philharmonic, and in June 1955, a grant from the Rockefeller Foundation to look into studios in the United States and Europe. Luening:

> We wrote a report for the Rockefeller Foundation on the state of experimental music in Europe and the United States, including recommendations about the best program to be followed here.
> Our studio in the Ussachevsky living room was moved to my apartment. We then reported to President Kirk of Columbia University that unless we could have space on campus, our whole program would be seriously jeopardized. Soon afterwards, we were provided with suitable quarters—the charming "Charles Adams" house, located on campus at the site of the former Bloomingdale Insane Asylum . . .

The Columbia University studio was born. It was soon to be transformed, however.

In 1955, RCA demonstrated the Olson-Belar Sound Synthesizer . . . Davidson Taylor, director of the School of Arts at Columbia University, suggested that we try to obtain the synthesizer on loan. Ussachevsky wanted very much to pursue this possibility, and I wrote to several RCA executives . . . Our report to the Rockefeller Foundation included a detailed description of the equipment and personnel needed . . . Our application was approved with the recommendation that we procure the RCA synthesizer . . .

That Milton Babbitt, on the faculty of Princeton University, had also been interested in the RCA Mark II Electronic Music Synthesizer led to the involvement of Princeton University in the grant application. In January 1959, the Columbia-Princeton Electronic Music Center, containing the RCA Mark II Electronic Music Synthesizer and several tape studios, was established.

In 1960, Mario Davidovsky arrived in New York from Argentina. He began by working with Bulent Arel. As he recalls, "I assisted him and by imitation I absorbed his techniques—so in a certain way he was my teacher, and a wonderful one, a wonderful teacher." And what was it like to work in the studio? He answers:

Life at that time was being in the studio. There was nothing else. I remember staying up to thirty-six hours at a time, taking catnaps and crossing

Otto Luening (left) and Vladimir Ussachevsky (right) in one of the tape studios at Columbia Princeton Electronic Music Center in about 1960. Photo courtesy Robert Moog.

Broadway to buy sandwiches and coffee and going back to the studio. My colleagues were doing the same thing. Every little sound was like a discovery. We were starting to decode the potential of what was sitting in front of us, using each piece of equipment and then relating it to the others. In a way, we were building an instrument, a very special sort of instrument. Technically, I was totally naive. But I was also having my own ideas.

In order for me to keep some psychological continuity while going into this new territory, I found ways of translating things that were known to me, that reflected my past tradition. I found that it was possible for me to think of a phrase made of a sequence of sounds, of timbres, dynamics, registers. I shaped gestures following the sculptural shape of a melody. I found that it was almost impossible with that technology to produce long sounds that were beautiful—they would tend to become dull. But I found that sounds of short duration and percussive-like sounds were accessible. To me, the most important ability was to articulate the music by shaping the sound. If it was a simple sound, let's say a sharp attack and a decay, I could do it with a splice at the beginning and then a long decay in the mixer. Or if I was working on a percussive sound, I would take an inch of that sound and make a tape loop—so that I heard the sound every few seconds—and then I would take that sound, go to a filter, mixer, another filter, reverb unit, and so on, so the sound would reappear in slightly different dressings, and then I would use the mixer as a way of balancing all of these elements in order to shape the timbre.

On May 9 and 10, 1961, the center presented its first two concerts. The programs included Davidovsky's *Electronic Study #1*, Halim El-Dabh's *Leiyla and the Poet*, Ussachevsky's *Creation-Prologue*, Babbitt's *Composition for Synthesizer*, Arel's *Stereo Electronic Music #1*, Luening's *Gargoyles for Violin Solo and Synthesized Sound*, and Charles Wuorinen's *Symphonia Sacra*. It was a lot of music for one year's work, and it was just the beginning. As Luening later reported, "From 1960 to 1970, more than 225 compositions by more than 60 composers from 11 countries were produced . . ." When Ussachevsky retired in 1979, Davidovsky became director. As he said, "My major goal was not so much to get involved in technical research but rather in creating music."

•

Luciano Berio was in the audience at the Museum of Modern Art on October 28, 1952. As he remembers, "The sound was very new for me—I became enthusiastic and I became friends with Ussachevsky and Luening." He then established a studio in Milan. He tells it:

A few weeks later, I went back to Milano and a few months later, in 1953, I met Bruno Maderna. He had already worked on electronic music in Germany. I convinced the radio—I was occasionally writing music for the radio, in any case—to establish a studio for electronic music. I was the one that was responsible for it because I was there more than Bruno. He was travelling and conducting a lot, but he was like my older brother there. Alfredo Lietti was also very interested. He was one of the technical chiefs at the Milano station, and I asked him if he was ready to help us. And he did.

In 1955, the Studio di Fonologia Musicale was established at the RAI (Radio Audizioni Italiane / Italian Radio Broadcasting) studios in Milan with Luciano Berio and Bruno Maderna as artistic directors, Alfredo Lietti as technical director, and Marino Zuccheri as technician.

One basis for the studio was radio sound. As Alvise Vidolin points out, "radio had come to be seen as a new stage, or rather a new medium for shows, in which the principal ingredients were voice, music, sounds, and noise." In 1954, Berio and Maderna had collaborated in composing *Ritratto di Città* specifically for radio broadcast. *Ritratto di Città*, a sound portrait of Milan during the course of a day, with text by Roberto Leydi, had been an important step in exploring the value of audio art created specifically for radio broadcast. In 1956, Berio stated a need for further exploration: "the idea of a radiophonic art and aesthetic has not yet been defined . . ." Many of the pieces composed in the Studio di Fonologia Musicale were commissioned by the radio specifically for broadcast.

There were also purely musical concerns. Compared with the rigorous musique concrète approach of the Paris studio and with the strict serialist philosophy of the startup Cologne studio, the Milan studio was not tied to any particular ideology or method. As Berio said, "Bruno and I immediately agreed that our work should *not* be directed in a systematic way, either towards recording acoustic sounds or towards a systematic serialism based on discrete pitches." At the same time, Berio's musical ideas provided an initial focus, a starting point for his own work, and a kind of *personality*, one might say, for the studio in general:

> The idea of the studio was the interaction between acoustics and musical form, the coordination of timbre and harmony. It was important for me to work with Joyce's words, to extract certain sound qualities and to transform them by speeding up or superimposing them into something else. I felt a constant need of dealing with sounds as evolutionary phenomena, not static, always changing, but always for musical reasons. For me, the experience of electronic music generated a view of form, of musical structure, different from instrumental music. And so the Studio di Fonologia was always open to exploring the interaction between the acoustical dimensions of sounds and musical forms.

The Studio di Fonologia Musicale was for a brief period in the vanguard of European studios. With its complement of nine oscillators as well as other state-of-the-art equipment, it was for its time exceptionally well equipped. Alfredo Lietti, who designed the studio, echoed Berio's and Maderna's artistic openness and cooperative spirit:

> The musician may have a clear idea of the sound he desires to obtain, but it is, naturally, a musical idea. To the technician interested instead in the physical data of the sound, it's a question of whether it can be produced electronically. It's obvious that the difficulty can be overcome only by a reciprocal effort of understanding.

Berio's first important tape piece at the Milan studio was *Thema–Omaggio a Joyce* (1958). He had been studying onomatopoeia in poetry with Umberto Eco, and among the texts they examined was the beginning of the eleventh chapter of James Joyce's *Ulysses*. Here are some brief excerpts:

> *BRONZE BY GOLD, THE HOOFIRONS, STEELYRINING IMPER-*
> *thnthn thnthnthn.*
> *Chips, picking chips off rocky thumbnail, chips. Horrid!*
> *And gold flushed more.*
> *A husky fifenote blew.*
> *Blew. Blue bloom is on the*
> *Gold pinnacled hair.*
> *A jumping rose on satiny breasts of satin, rose of Castille. . .*
>
> *Boomed crashing chords. When love absorbs. War! War!*
> *The tympanum.*
> *A sail! A veil awave upon the waves . . .*
>
> *A moonlight nightcall: far: far.*
> *I feel so sad. P. S. So lonely blooming.*
> *Listen!*
> *The spiked and winding cold seahorn. Have you the? Each and for*
> *other plash and silent roar.*
> *Pearls: when she. Liszt's rhapsodies. Hissss.*

The text, which became the basis for all of the sounds in *Thema*, was first recited on the tape by the magnificent singer Cathy Berberian. Then Berio selected elements and began to work with them. He said, "What I emphasized and developed in *Thema* is the transition between a perceivable verbal message and music . . ." Certain text elements were suggestive of musical figures. For example, "IMPER-thnthn thnthnthn" suggested a trill. "Chips, picking chips" suggested staccato. "A sail! A veil awave upon the waves" suggested glissando or portamento. Sibilant and vowel sounds were derived from the text—as in "a sail, a sail . . . a veil awave . . . hissss hiss . . . I feel so . . . bl bl bloo blooming

. . . rhapsody . . . hisss soft hisss . . ."—and organized in changes from discontinuous to periodic to continuous. All of the sounds were subjected to electronic processing, primarily filtering with one-third-octave filters, and tape editing, including superimposition at different time and pitch scales and the construction of fragments into various musical articulations. For example, at one point the *bl* of "blooming" is repeated to make a stutter sound, the *ooo* is extended as a musical sound, the *sss* becomes a continuous hiss; and many of the sounds are abstracted to a point of unintelligibility only to reappear as recognizable words, reflecting the shifts in Joyce's text between onomatopoeia and semantic meaning. *Thema* is remarkable in that all of its myriad and detailed sounds are derived from the text. Indeed, the texture of *Thema*, its rhythm and its play with the sounds and meanings of words and phonemes, parallels and extends the musicality of Joyce's text. Berio said it, but Joyce might have said it as well: "I attempted to establish a new relationship between speech and music, in which a discontinuous metamorphosis of one into the other can be developed . . ." And *Thema* is all the more remarkable in light of the way it was composed. Berio describes the experience:

> At that time, techniques and procedures were quite time consuming. Everything was done by cutting and splicing tape . . . In order to create certain effects, some sounds had to be copied sixty, seventy, and eighty times, and then spliced together. Then these tapes had to be copied further at different speeds in order to achieve new sound qualities more or less related to Cathy Berberian's original delivery of the text. I was interested in constant and controlled transformation from discontinuous to continuous patterns, from periodic to nonperiodic events, from sound to noise, from perceived words to perceived musical structures, and from syllabic to a phonetic view of the text . . . I didn't surrender to the difficulties . . . It's surprising now to think that I spent several months of my life cutting tape while today I could achieve many of the same results in much less time by using a computer.

Among the pieces done by other composers in the Milan studio, Henri Pousseur's *Scambi* (1957) was distinctive. For one thing, it was based on procedures rather than a fixed structure, as Pousseur later said, "to experiment on the electronic level with the idea of open, variable form . . ." Different versions were made at different times by Pousseur, Berio, and Mark Wilkinson. For another thing, all of its sounds were made with white noise. White noise, which sounds like hiss, or steam, or waterfalls, is a wide-range smear of sound energy undifferentiated by pitches or timbre. As Michelangelo specified shape by chipping at his block of marble with a chisel, so Pousseur specified crisp, clear, and pitched sounds by chipping at his block of white noise with an electronic chisel called a *filter*. Pousseur differentiated the sounds by pitch, timbre, and reverberation and then edited the sounds into sequences on tape.

Cage did a tape realization of his graphic score *Fontana Mix* (1958). During a four-month period during the summer of 1958, with the technical assistance of Marino Zuccheri, Cage used random numbers as a guide to snipping and splicing little bits of tape from several different reels of sound material recorded and/or found in Milan and from Italian radio. And amongst the traffic sounds, dog barking, and so on, there's a fleeting moment where a radio voice says, "Qui c'é folkloristica," meaning "Here there's folklore." Considering that it showed up randomly, and considering the nature of the assemblage of sounds to which it seems to refer, that fleeting moment is certainly worth a fleeting smile. And there was the occasion for another smile. During that same period in Milan, Cage was featured on *Lascia o Raddoppia* (Nothing or Double), an Italian television quiz show. In five appearances, he presented several of his compositions. He also won the equivalent of about $6,000 for answering questions about mushrooms.

Berio's last tape work in Milan was *Visage* (1961). Within an ambience of electronically generated sounds, Cathy Berberian sang and recited mostly abstract vocal sounds suggestive of the formation of words and language. Different from *Thema*, the vocal sounds in *Visage* were used as they were recorded, without electronic manipulation and with a minimum of editing. *Visage* is, as Berio described it, "purely a radio-program work: a sound track for a 'drama' that was never written . . . based on the sound symbolism of vocal gestures and inflections with their accompanying shadow of meanings and their associative tendencies . . ."

Shortly after finishing *Visage* in 1961, Berio left Milan to live in the United States, and following his departure, the studio progressively changed. Maderna, of course, had also worked in the studio during the 1950s—his best known works of the period include *Continuo* (1958), *Invenzione su una Voce* (1960), and *Serenata III* (1961)—but because he became busier with conducting engagements in the 1960s, his work in the studio became more occasional, although it did include *Le Rire* (1962), *Tempo Libero* (1972), and a few other compositions. Other composers who worked in the studio through the 1960s and 1970s included Girolamo Arrigo, Nicoló Castiglioni, Aldo Clementi, Franco Donotoni, Pietro Grossi, Marcello Panni, and Camillo Togni.

Luigi Nono, originally introduced to electronic music by Maderna, became the studio's principal composer. Nono was there as the studio's equipment was updated in the mid-1960s, and he worked there until the studio closed at the end of the 1970s. His first composition was *Omaggio a Vedova* (1960), which was his only work to use only electronically generated sounds. He often combined live instrumental and vocal performance with electronic sounds on tape. And he often based his compositions on social and political themes. His next works were *La Fabbrica Illuminata* (1964, The Illuminated Factory), composed with factory sounds recorded at Italsider, a steel plant at Genova; *Ricordati Cosa Ti Hanno Fatto in Auschwitz* (1966, Remember What They Did to You in Auschwitz), which was derived from his incidental music for a play by Peter Weiss and which combined high, thin electronic sounds with multiple choruses and a soprano melody, projecting the effect of terrible anguish; and *Non Consumiamo Marx* (1969, We Aren't Consuming Marx), which included sounds from political demonstrations during 1968.

•

Because equipment was expensive and technical knowledge was necessary, most of the first studios were established at institutions where budgets and technicians were available. But there were, at the same time, a few composers sufficiently ingenious and stalwart to forge ahead and form personal studios. Tristram Cary's studio in London, for example, was among the first of the independents. Cary's story starts when he was demobilized from the British navy in 1946:

> We all knew about tape recorders but nobody had seen one—we had aboard the ship a very poor wire recorder—but what seemed quite clear was that tape was going to make possible editing sound in a way that was not possible before. So I spent my gratuity, the gratuity you get when you're demobilized from the service, to buy equipment. My gratuity was £50 which was equivalent I guess to $1,000 of today's money. I was able to buy a disc recorder for which I made pickups that ran behind the cutting head in the same groove, so I had echo effects. I also had a playback turntable that would do anything from 12 rpm to 200 rpm and was reversible. And in those days, Lisle Street, just behind Leicester Square in London, was full of junk electronic shops. There were war surplus supplies from Britain, Germany, America, everywhere, and a lot of this gear was brand new. So for a few shillings or a few pounds you could buy the most exquisitely made stuff, things like bomb sights, airborne cameras, all sorts of things from which you could make elaborate delay gear and that kind of thing. And I bought my first tape recorder in 1952.

Cary then wrote to several BBC producers. As he reports, "Three of them replied, two of them saw me, and one of them gave me a little job." By the end of 1955, he was working regularly for the BBC and his studio, of course, was continually growing. By 1957, he had three tape recorders, a number of turntables, and three or four oscillators, some entirely home constructed and some built with kits. He adds, "I was using recorded sound most of the time because my electronic facilities were fairly limited." But limited though his facilities may have been, through the 1950s he did the music for a lot of films, among them *The Lady Killers* (1955), *Time Without Pity* (1955), *Town on Trial* (1956), *The Flesh Is Weak* (1957), *Tread Softly Stranger* (1958), and *The Little Island* (1958), an animated film by Richard Williams. Of *The Little Island*, in particular, he remembers:

It really put my studio and my ideas into high gear. Dick had no money, of course. Nobody had any money. He said, "Look, you're obviously good at film music, and I've got this film I'm trying to make and I've got no money so I can't commission music. But I'd like you to help me choose some library tracks." Well, I saw the line tests and I was very impressed, and I said to Dick, "You've got to have properly composed music with this." So I borrowed money on my house and we went into this thing together because, whatever kind of production you're making, you can't skimp on the music.

The Little Island won the Best Experimental Film of the Year award in Venice in 1958, it was shown at the 1958 World's Fair in Brussels, and it won the 1959 British Film Academy award for Best Cartoon of the Year. Cary continues:

Meanwhile, at about this time I bought a cottage in the country, in Suffolk, in Fressingfield. There was no electricity when I moved in, but I had a great big hut in the garden and I made a spacious studio. I moved in properly in 1962, when there *was* electricity, but even then we were on the end of the line run, sharing the transformer with the local farmer. Whenever he started up his agricultural equipment, my voltage dropped. So I had considerable problems with voltage regulation. The Fressingfield studio, nonetheless, depending on the money, got quite good. All of it was built by me in between things, when I had a spare day or a spare hour. Very often what happened was that I came across a creative problem that became a technical problem. I wanted to create a certain sound, and I knew how I could do it, but it needed a special gadget. So I would stop being a composer for the moment and build something, with the result that the studio became as most studios in those days, very personal matters. It became a studio for me doing the things that I wanted to do.

Among those things, through the 1950s and 1960s, Cary completed many instrumental and electronic concert compositions. There was electronic ambient music for the Industrial Section of the British Pavilion at EXPO '67 in Montreal: "I decorated the whole place with sound." And there were many electronic scores for BBC radio and television, among them *Macbeth* (1959), of which he recalls, "It seemed perfectly obvious to me that the way to do the witches was with electronics." There were also Craig's *The Children of Lir* (1959), Macneice's *East of the Sun and West of the Moon* (1959), Cocteau's *La Machine Infernale* (1960), Jennifer Dawson's *The Ha-Ha* (1963), Ionesco's *The Killer* (1964), Peake's *The Rhyme of the Flying Bomb* (1964), and Ray Bradbury's *Leviathan '99* (1968). And there was *Doctor Who*, a BBC science fiction series for which Cary composed a considerable amount of incidental music. Cary recalls a visit to the *Doctor Who* studio with one of his children who saw a Dalek, one of the show's salt-shaker-shaped villainous creatures, and said, as Cary tells it, "It's pretty primitive, Dad. I don't think it will be a great success." Cary continues:

> In those days, a million years it seems before sync devices like SMPTE code, timing was the main problem, and *The Dead Planet* (Serial B) had long tracks of atmosphere stuff (e.g. a faintly menacing alien forest with strange creatures) interspersed with sudden events that had to be in sync. A given scene could only be roughly timed at rehearsal in some hall away from the studio, and the show only moved into the studio just before the recording. Videotape was used, but the show was recorded as if it were a live transmission. So I used two or three tape machines. Red track was the main holding track with the continuous, non-sync stuff covering the general atmosphere of a scene while Green track carried short events like a menacing close-up or an exploding Dalek to be punched in at the right moment over Red.
>
> I aimed at rich sounds which were different from normal aural experience. One always had to remember that the final product would be heard on the absurd speakers used in the average TV, so things that relied for their effect on extreme bass or top, or even being loud, were out. Sometimes, in fact, I played a track through the family TV's audio to hear the effect. In long tracks, I would use loops, but such long ones that nobody would hear them as loops. At Fressingfield, I sometimes had loops going out through the window and round mike stands set among the cabbages outside. And living in four acres of space gave other opportunities to explore unusual environments, like the strange echoes produced in wells, tanks, and oil drums. They were breaking up railways at the time, and I had a blacksmith make a railway-line metallophone for me (tuning not accurate), which made a huge noise. That sound in particular was interesting both slower and faster, and also recorded at a distance. In fact, I got some fascinating results from a very long way, like 200 yards from the microphone, done in the middle of the night when the birds were asleep.

Cary did the music for several more episodes, including *Marco Polo*, *The Gunfighter*, and *The Mutants*. Of *The Mutants*, in 1972, he reflects:

> Compared to the early ones, this was hi-tech in every way. Colour gave the opportunity for special visual effects, and my studio was as good as it ever got. *Who* was often fun, but in the end it was a bit samey. *Another* space travel sound, *another* alien invasion.

•

Among the ingenious there were also Louis and Bebe Barron who founded a personal studio in New York. They had begun as early as 1948 to work with taped sounds and simple electronic circuits and they then went on to do several electronic film scores, among them *Bells of Atlantis* (1953) and *Forbidden Planet* (1956). They were there in 1951 when John Cage and David Tudor launched the Project for Music for Magnetic Tape in New York. Tudor recalls:

> It was John's idea. It was John who supplied the ideas and motivation. And the project actually began because our friend Paul Williams gave us some money. He was a godsend. The spirit was to be all inclusive, so one of the first endeavors that we made was to categorize sounds. The Barrons acted as sound engineers, as a team. They worked with us for several months. Then, because the money was running out, John took the tactic that we should record all the necessary material, so the last monies were spent with the objective that we would have all the material in our hands necessary to complete the splicing. The Barrons helped to record and prepare all the material . . .

The Barrons recorded approximately 600 sounds to provide the initial material for the project. Tudor continues:

> I worked closely with John in the first year. We established a method of working. The main work was splicing tape for *Williams Mix* . . . John and I were impoverished. There was no money to throw around. I recall that at one point the money was in danger of running out, and so John and I made an assessment of what had to be done so that the funds would last until the completion of *Williams Mix*, and subsequently Paul gave us another sum of money to help continue. Then Earle came and offered to help. And spent more and more time helping.

In mid-1952, Earle Brown arrived in New York and immediately started to work with Cage. Christian Wolff and Morton Feldman also became involved with the project and composed pieces, but Brown and Cage did most of the work. Brown continues:

> I lived in the Village on Cornelia Street. John lived on Monroe Street, underneath the Williamsburg Bridge. There's no subway because it's diagonally crosstown, so I used to walk to John's loft every morning. The cutting and splicing happened at John's loft . . . John and I worked on opposite sides of a big table . . . We usually worked from ten in the morning until four or five in the afternoon and then we usually went to meet Morty and Merce Cunningham and Carolyn Brown at the Cedar Bar or one of our apartments. Fridays, John and I used to go to Suzuki's lectures at Columbia.

The cutting and splicing was for Cage's *Williams Mix*, finished in late 1952. Cage first created a library of snippets of tape, catalogued as *A* (city sounds), *B* (country sounds), *C* (electronic sounds), *D* (manually produced sounds, including normal music), *E* (wind-produced sounds, including voice), and *F* (small sounds requiring amplification to be heard). The sounds were further classified: the letter *c* indicated control and predictability, the letter *v* designated lack of control or unpredictability; and both *c* and *v* were applied to pitch, timbre, and loudness in that order. The designation *Bvcv*, for example, would indicate a country sound of uncontrolled pitch, known timbre, and uncontrolled loudness. Cage then created a score for the piece, in effect a graphic plan, using a procedure derived from the *I Ching*, the ancient Chinese *Book of Changes*. The procedure was to toss three coins six times to generate a random number between 1 and 64 and to use the resulting random numbers to select, from corresponding listings in several charts, what type of sound from the library was to be used, where among any of eight tracks it was to be placed, the durations of the sounds and silences, and the shapes (attacks and decays) of the sounds as they were physically cut into the tape. Brown continues:

> We simultaneously cut and spliced John's *Williams Mix* and composed with his three coins by chance, using the *I Ching*. Anybody could toss the three coins and write down heads, heads, tails, do it again, tails, heads, heads, do it again, oh, three tails. . . Anybody could do it, so when anybody would come to visit, John would hand them three coins and tell them how to do it and everybody would be sitting around tossing coins. That was the composing part of it, completely by chance, and the coins referred to, first, the kind of sound, then duration, then how the attacks and decays were cut. We cut the attacks and decays into the tape with demagnetized razor blades. We put the score under a glass plate on the table, and then lay the tape on it, and cut exactly to the pattern. John used to suggest that it was like following a dressmaker's pattern . . .
>
> The pieces of tape were in regular legal size envelopes, white envelopes, bunched up. We didn't have them on reels or anything. We had them in a cardboard box in one corner of John's loft, and there were maybe 150 or 175 envelopes, each marked "A," "B," "C" . . . up to seven categories, and then we'd go over and paw through the envelopes until we came to the right one, as called for by the chance process. We'd pick up the envelope, take the piece of tape over, lay the tape on top of the glass under which was the score, and cut and splice exactly as was called for. Then we applied the pieces of recording tape onto splicing tape and then, between pieces of recording tape, we rubbed talcum powder so the splicing tape wouldn't be sticky. After we did this, and we'd gotten a minute or so finished, we used to go over to Colonel Richard Ranger's studio in New Jersey to make copies on a solid piece of tape. We didn't even have a tape machine. We couldn't hear anything. All we had were razor blades and talcum powder, no tape machine, it's true. If we'd needed to use one, we could have gone to the Barrons' studio. But John was

doing it by chance. He didn't need to hear. You only need to hear when you're doing something by taste.

It took so long, so bloody long, and it was boring to do all that cutting and splicing. John and I sat at opposite sides of the table and we talked about everything in the world. . . we would talk about Suzuki, we'd talk about profound things, banal things, we smoked cigarettes all the time. We would usually end up at three in the afternoon and neither one of us would have any cigarettes left, so we would smoke the butts. And nearly every day we would go across the street from John's loft and buy a big hero sandwich, and John would make terrible black coffee.

We both joked a lot. I could be funny, John could be funny. We would get on each other's nerves once in a while. I'd argue with him about something, and he'd get riled up a bit. I remember one thing that we argued about was that he liked to say that any sound in the world could be in the library of the Music for Magnetic Tape project, and I would say, "John, that's impossible, you can't get the sound of a whale, ten fathoms down, into the library," and he'd say, "It could be." Philosophically, he didn't eliminate any sound, but when he said that any sound could be in the library, I said, "That's impossible. You can't get every sound in the library."

After *Williams Mix*, Cage and Brown worked together on Brown's *Octet*:

Having finished *Williams Mix*, there were a lot of scraps of tape. We knew we were going to have a concert at the University of Illinois Arts Festival, March 1953, and I wanted to do a piece, so I tried to think quickly about how to make a piece . . . And I worked out a way to do the piece, based on density. I used a book of random sampling tables. I would get the length of a piece of tape, say fifteen inches, and then I would come up with how many pieces of tape would fit into that fifteen inches, and then I would take some pieces of tape and then I would chop them so that I had relatively equal lengths to fit into fifteen inches. Maybe four inches might have seven fragments, but never more than ten . . . So I made *Octet*, for eight mono tapes and eight loudspeakers surrounding the audience because *Williams Mix* is that way too, eight tapes for eight loudspeakers. I remember what John said about *Octet*. He said, "It sounds like a snowfall."

The March 1953 concert at the University of Illinois Arts Festival included *Williams Mix*, *Octet*, and pieces by Wolff, Stockhausen, Eimert, Boulez, Luening, and Ussachevsky. Brown remembers:

We had eight mono Magnacorders on stage and eight loudspeakers equidistantly spaced around the auditorium. The funny thing is that people would come into the concert hall and they would see this stack of eight Magnacorders on stage, and at that point everybody was frightened to death of electronic music, so they would look at the stage and they would sit in the back. But right behind them were loudspeakers.

The project ended in 1954 as both Cage and Brown moved on to other things. As Brown said, "I don't remember why it stopped actually. I guess I needed a job."

●

In parallel with the development of the early instruments, with Duchamp's and Cage's early work, with the invention of the tape recorder and the opening of the first studios, indeed in parallel with the entire early development of electronic music, Edgard Varèse had pursued his ideas about what has been called "the liberation of sound." Varèse had met Busoni in Berlin as early as 1907 and later commented on Busoni's famous statement ("Music was born free. . .") by saying, "It was like hearing the echo of my own thought." In Cage's words:

> More clearly and actively than anyone else of his generation, he established the present nature of music. This nature . . . arises from an acceptance of all audible phenomena as material proper to music. While others were still discriminating "musical" tones from noises, Varèse moved into the field of sound itself . . .

Why was Varèse' work so significant? Prior to the twentieth century, orchestration had been inseparably linked to melody, rhythm, and chord progressions, as color had been linked with the objects depicted in painting, such as green grass, blue sky, and so on. As Hector Berlioz said, in *A Travers Chants*, "Orchestration is, in music, the exact equivalent of color in painting." In the general artistic upheaval at the beginning of the twentieth century, sound and color became increasingly independent aspects of music and painting. Arnold Schoenberg, for example, in his *Harmonielehre* (1911), proposed the idea of a *Klangfarbenmelodie*, a "sound-color melody," which based musical structure on sound. And Wassily Kandinsky wrote in 1912 that "colors are not used because they are true to nature but because they are necessary to the particular picture." Varèse put it perfectly when he said:

> The role of color or timbre would be completely changed from being incidental, anecdotal, sensual or picturesque; it would become an agent of delineation like the different colors on a map separating different areas, and an integral part of form.

In Varèse' *Intégrales* (1926), for woodwinds, brass, and percussion, the pitches that the instruments play, their loudnesses, their spacings in orchestral chords, their crescendos, attacks, and durations, were important because of the way they contributed to a composite timbre. In all of his music, Varèse' concern with timbre as a primary musical quality led him to shape sounds so unconventionally that his orchestration approached, as Milton Babbitt put it, "nonelectronic synthesis." In *Ionisation* (1931), Varèse used percussion instruments to create a repertoire of unpitched sounds. And he used a siren. As he later said, "I have always felt the need of a kind of a continuous flowing curve that instruments could not give me. That is why I used sirens in several of my works."

In 1916, Varèse said, "Our musical alphabet must be enriched . . . We also need new instruments very badly . . . In my own works I have always felt the need for new mediums of expression." In 1927, he contacted Harvey Fletcher, director of acoustic research at Bell Telephone Laboratories, to investigate the possibility of access to a laboratory, but then and afterward, Fletcher, although sympathetic, was unable to support the request. Varèse had formed a friendship with René Bertrand in Paris in 1913, and in 1932, in another attempt to find support for researching new instruments and sounds, he applied to the Guggenheim Foundation to do collaborative work with Bertrand. In February 1933, Varèse wrote the following as a clarification of his application:

> The acoustical work which I have undertaken and which I hope to continue in collaboration with René Bertrand consists of experiments which I have suggested on his invention, the Dynaphone. The Dynaphone (invented 1927–28) is a musical instrument of electrical oscillations somewhat similar to the Theremin, Givelet and Martenot electrical instruments. But its principle and operation are entirely different, the resemblance being only superficial. The technical results I look for are as follows:
>
> 1. To obtain absolutely pure fundamentals.
> 2. By means of loading the fundamentals with certain series of harmonics to obtain timbres which will produce new sounds.
> 3. To speculate on the new sounds that the combination of two or more interfering Dynaphones would give if combined in a single instrument.
> 4. To increase the range of the instrument so as to obtain high frequencies which no other instrument can give, together with adequate intensity.
>
> The practical result of our work will be a new instrument which will be adequate to the needs of the creative musician and musicologist. I have conceived a system by which the instrument may be used not only for the tempered and natural scales, but one which also allows for the accurate production of any number of frequencies and consequently is able to produce any interval or any subdivision required by the ancient or exotic modes.

Edgard Varèse in the 1950s. Photo by Roy Hyrkin. Courtesy Ann McMillan archive at Electronic Music Foundation.

By no means the last important composer to be turned down by the Guggenheim Foundation, Varèse' luck began to change many years later. In 1954, Pierre Schaeffer invited him to Paris to complete the tape parts to *Déserts*, a work combining orchestral and taped sounds. In 1957, he gained access to the Philips Laboratories in Eindhoven, Holland, where a special studio was created for him with sophisticated equipment and the support of a group of technicians and advisors. He went to Eindhoven to compose *Poème Electronique*. And he crossed paths with Iannis Xenakis.

Xenakis had arrived in Paris from Athens in November 1947, following his activities in the Greek resistance during and after the war. As he said, "I was a civil engineer—I was on my way to the States, but I stopped in Paris and I thought, 'Well, why not?'" He soon found a position with Le Corbusier, one of the most prestigious and interesting architects in France: "I got to Le Corbusier through an acquaintance and I started calculating beams and columns and floors for the Marseilles building." (The Marseilles building was *L'Unité d'Habitation*, one of Le Corbusier's best known works.) After a while, Xenakis got interested in architecture and asked Le Corbusier if he could work on an architectural project. Le Corbusier agreed and, as Xenakis recalls, "We started doing the monastery of La Turette, which I designed completely from beginning to end." Among other Le Corbusier commissions, Xenakis also worked on the Assembly Hall for Chandigarh, India.

In January 1956, Philips Corporation in Eindhoven asked Le Corbusier to design their pavilion for the 1958 Brussels World's Fair. Le Corbusier replied: "I will make you a *poème électronique*. Everything will happen inside: sound, light, color, rhythm . . ." Xenakis continues:

> They asked Le Corbusier to design something and Le Corbusier asked me to design something. At that time, I was very much interested in shapes like hyperbolic paraboloids, things like that; and so I organized them to form a shell in which we could produce sounds and images on the walls. I did the designs and I showed them to Le Corbusier and he said, "Yes, of course."

The World's Fair opened in May 1958. The Philips Pavilion also opened, and its sound-and-image show, created by Xenakis, Varèse, and Le Corbusier, was repeated several times every day. The sound consisted of Xenakis' short and gritty *Concret P.H.* (1958) followed by Varèse' *Poème Electronique*. Le Corbusier's colored lighting formed a backdrop to his projected images—pictures of animals (monkeys, shellfish, birds), religious objects and art from different cultures (Buddha, Giotto, masks, sculptures), parts of the Eiffel Tower, Laurel and Hardy stills, nuclear explosions and other war imagery, and buildings from different countries—which were shown continuously. By the end of 1958, more than two million people had visited the Philips Pavilion, heard the music, seen the projections. Varèse later described the event as:

> a spectacle of sound and light, presented during the Brussels Exposition in the pavilion designed for the Philips Corporation of Holland by Le Corbusier, who was also the author of the visual part. It consisted of moving colored lights, images projected on the walls of the pavilion, and music. The music was distributed by 425 loudspeakers; there were twenty amplifier combinations. It was recorded on a three-track magnetic tape that could be varied in intensity and quality. The loudspeakers were mounted in groups and in what is called "sound routes" to achieve various effects such as that of the music running around the pavilion, as well as coming from different directions, reverberations, etc. For the first time, I heard my music literally projected into space.

Indeed, Varèse thought of his sounds as objects of different shapes and materials with dynamic properties and tendencies, existing in and moving through a musical space. He said:

> There is an idea, the basis of an internal structure, expanded and split into different shapes or groups of sounds constantly changing in shape, direction, and speed, attracted and repulsed by various forces. The form of the work is the consequence of this interaction.

The sounds in *Poème Electronique*, many of them the result of electronic processing, are derived from percussion and melody instruments, bells, sirens, electronic tone generators, machines, and voices. There are simple sound objects, consisting of a single sound such as a percussive stroke. There are complex patterns of different sounds. There are extended rhythmic figures, articulated in percussion; smooth hyperbolic curves, contrasted with buzzing, shaking, and fluttering sounds; and staccato, pitched sounds combined in short melodic phrases. Born in 1883, Varèse was in his mid-seventies in 1958. He was a mature musician whose ideas and style had developed through the first half of the century. *Poème Electronique* was the ultimate statement of tape music as musique concrète. It marked the end of the beginning.

● ● ●

CHAPTER THREE

EXPANSION
OF THE
TAPE MUSIC IDEA

In 1954, Pierre Boulez visited Buenos Aires. He met with Francisco Kröpfl and Mauricio Kagel, gave them a score to Stockhausen's *Studie I*, and conveyed the latest technical information from Cologne. Although Pierre Schaeffer's work had already been heard in Argentina, and although Kagel had composed a bit of musique concrète for an industrial exhibit, Boulez' visit provided a new impetus. Kröpfl began some private experimentation and searched for a place to start a studio.

In 1958, with technician Fausto Maranca and some schematics from the Studio di Fonologia in Milan, Kröpfl founded the Estudio de Fonologia Musical within the structure and physical space of the acoustics laboratory at the School of Architecture, University of Buenos Aires. He made a deal with the university: "In exchange for time and space in the acoustics laboratory, we made acoustic measurements for the School of Architecture and for industry." Kröpfl and Maranca also adapted and designed specific equipment for music. They adapted a tape recorder, for example, to record and play at varying speeds; they designed a photocell-based envelope controller which read shapes cut out in cardboard; and they built a reverberation chamber which measured, as Kröpfl remembers, "about ninety cubic meters—so we had between eight and ten seconds of reverberation time." Kröpfl used the reverberation chamber in his *Ejercicio de Impulsos* (1960, Studies on Pulses). He then finished other compositions, among them *Dialogos I* and *Dialogos II*. And he joined the music faculty at the University of Buenos Aires.

In 1963, CLAEM (Centro Latinoamericano de Altos Estudios Musicales/ Latin American Center for Advanced Musical Studies) was established at the Instituto Di Tella in Buenos Aires with funding in large part from the Rockefeller Foundation and with equipment selected initially by Mario Davidovsky. In 1966, Fernando von Reichenbach redesigned the CLAEM studio by installing a central studio-control system. He also invented what was called the *Graphic Converter*, a device that allowed a composer to specify controls by drawing them on a strip of paper which was read by a video camera. Kröpfl became musical director of CLAEM in 1967, and many composers worked there during those several years, among them Alcides Lanza, Eduardo Kusnir, Jose Maranzano, Ariel Martinez, and Pedro Caryevschi.

By 1968, the Instituto Di Tella, a large organization which supported a wide range of activity in the arts, was having financial problems. There were also political problems, primarily because the theater group of the Instituto Di Tella was, as Kröpfl put it, "quite critical of the military government." At the end of 1971, the Instituto Di Tella was closed and CLAEM was dissolved. The equipment was moved to CICMAT (Centro de Investigaziones en Communication Massiva, Artes y Technologia / Center for Studies in Mass Communication, Art, and Technology), newly formed by the municipality of Buenos Aires. Kröpfl was appointed director of the CICMAT contemporary music department. In 1973, the Estudio de Fonologia Musical was also dissolved, for reasons, in Kröpfl's words, "conceivable only by a Latin American." But the CICMAT studio was another beginning.

•

In 1959, the University of Toronto received its first *Multi-Track Tape Recorder*, built by Hugh Le Caine at the National Research Council and so-named by Le Caine to indicate its ability to play back several tapes simultaneously. Gustav Ciamaga joined the University of Toronto faculty in 1963 and became director of the electronic music studio in 1965. He recalls:

> When I came in, there were two Multi-Track Tape Recorders, the prototype and an update. In the updated version, you could play sixteen channels of pre-recorded sound through a sixteen-input mixer which was controlled by sixteen touch-sensitive keys. It was a performance instrument. The National Research Council had been interested in commercializing it if it looked better and if it could be debugged, so Hugh had done a dress up of the original prototype. But by the time we had it refined, no one was interested in it. It would have been a very expensive instrument for its time—the original projections were between $25,000 and $30,000.

•

Studios were forming not only in Buenos Aires and Toronto, but in Berlin, Munich, Freiburg, Warsaw, Rome, London, Stockholm, and many other places. Indeed, hundreds of new studios formed throughout the world during the late 1950s and early 1960s. Some were institutional studios. Many were personal studios. Specific studios were distinctive for specific reasons.

The Radiophonic Workshop, at the BBC's Maida Vale studios in London, was distinctive not only because of the sounds it produced for Third Programme radio dramas, not only for its musical backgrounds for normal radio and television shows, not only for its broadcasts to schools and science programs, but also because it produced sound effects for *Doctor Who*, the first electronic music media hit.

The Radiophonic Workshop opened on April 1, 1958, following a year's experiments by a group of musicians, producers, and writers who had taken their cues, so to speak, from the radio studios in Paris, Cologne, and Milan. Among the experiments had been sounds produced by Desmond Briscoe for the Third Programme radio production of Samuel Beckett's *All That Fall*. In Briscoe's words:

> Beckett's script was remarkable, really remarkable. He wrote "silence" and "pause," quite obviously differentiating between the two. When he demanded sounds, he didn't say they had to be made in any particular way . . . Eventually we did away with natural sounds altogether, and simulated—for instance—the sounds of people walking with a simple drum rhythm . . . when we faded up the replay knob of the recording machine while it was still recording, we produced tape feed-back . . . usually known as "flutter-echo" . . . when the "Up-Mail" train hurtles through the sleepy station, the effect was heightened by all the sounds clattering and reiterating . . .

Radiophonic sound was, as Brian Hodgson called it, "applied electronic music," similar to musique concrète except that it functioned to reinforce the emotions and moods of radio and television productions. Hodgson joined the Radiophonic Workshop in 1962 while it was still a new idea. He recalls:

> In those days, it was one room with a budget of £2000 as a one-time payment to set it up. There was an engineer called "Dickie" Bird, quite an amazing character, and he had two junior engineers working with him. They built the place and they kept it running. There was one filter, some oscillators which Dickie actually made from kit, a frequency-modulated oscillator that we called a "wobbulator." The Motosacoche tape recorders took about fifteen seconds to come up to speed, but once up to speed they'd stay locked all day. To repair them, you pushed a button on the front and they rose majestically into the air, and you repaired them from underneath like a motorcar. They would keep recording even while being repaired. If you wanted to scare a producer, you would push the button and he'd see the recorder ascend into the air before his eyes. The

mixing desk was a BBC design, a low level mixer, so if you faded out one channel you had to compensate the main level by 3 db, but it had very low noise. There was a large echo machine that was so crackly that we turned it on the day before we wanted to use it, so it would get all the crackles out of its system.

The BBC had this funny rule at the beginning. They didn't want anyone staying more than three months. A doctor friend of a senior manager thought that people would have nervous breakdowns because of exposure to strange noises and they didn't want any loonies on their staff. The great advantage was that a lot of composers went through the system and were exposed to the possibilities.

Doctor Who, a science fiction series in which the hero travels through time and space in a telephone booth, started in 1963. Although Tristram Cary and other composers provided music for later episodes, Ron Grainer, a well-known television composer, was hired to compose the theme music. But because Grainer had no knowledge of electronic music technology, Delia Derbyshire, a staff composer at the Radiophonic Workshop, was asked to realize Grainer's score. Hodgson recalls, "Delia took the manuscript and realized it, and when Grainer came back he said to Delia, 'Gracious me, did I write that?' and she said, 'Most of it.'" Hodgson did the sound effects. He modulated an actor's voice to get the sound of the Daleks, villains that looked and sounded like salt shakers. But the sound of the time-machine takeoff remained a problem. Hodgson didn't want it to be like a spaceship. As he said, "No whooshes, no motors, or things like that." And then, he got an idea: "I got this concept . . . of tearing the fabric of time . . ."

Well, one might say that *Doctor Who* itself tore the fabric of time. It was initially expected to run for a few episodes, but it turned out to be a twenty-three year success. Musique concrète had reached its largest and youngest public.

•

The Swedish Radio in Stockholm was distinctive for supporting and promoting a new approach to combining music and text. Oyvind Fahlström's *Fåglar i Sverige* (Birds in Sweden), broadcast by the Swedish Radio in 1963, served as an initial model. Then, in 1965, the Swedish Radio commissioned six music-and-text works from Lars-Gunnar Bodin and Bengt Emil Johnson under the collective name *Semicolon*. In 1966, Bodin, Johnson, Sten Hanson, and others formed a music-and-text discussion and presentation group at Fylkingen, a cutting-edge new music organization in Stockholm. In 1967, the Swedish Radio commissioned Bodin's *CYBO I*, Johnson's *Semicolon: Adventure Along the Way*, and Åke Hodell's *Structures III*, and then organized performances of the commissioned works at a concert at the Museum of Modern Art in Stockholm and broadcast the concert live.

During the evening of September 3, 1967, on a visit to Hilversum, Holland, and following a day's conversation with many other European representatives of radio art, Bodin and Johnson coined the term *text-sound composition* to describe a sound art that, in its concern for the sounds of words as well as their semantic meanings, combined music and poetry. And, along with Hanson and others, they continued to develop and define the text-sound approach into the 1970s and 1980s. Johnson's *1/1970; (bland) 1* (1970), for example, consists primarily of sounds taken from language but, in his words, "reduced to a kind of characteristic inarticulate utterance devoid of semantic significance . . ." In Bodin's *For Jon III* (1982), different words are abstracted by electronic processing and linked by a synchronizing pulse, as Bodin explained, "to 'freeze' the words by repeating dissected fragments for certain time periods . . ." In Bodin's *On Speaking Terms* (1986), the poems range from verbal meaning to completely abstract sounds such that, as Bodin said, "all the textual layers start out from the same point but gradually glide apart . . ."

Meanwhile, in 1968, Hanson became the leader of the Fylkingen text-sound group, a member of the Fylkingen board of trustees, and the person responsible for producing Fylkingen's concerts, approximately sixty per year. He recalls, with a nostalgic smile, "I did everything, all the administration . . ." And, having composed *Che* (1968), *How Are You* (1969), and the trilogy *fnarp(e)* (1970), *Oips!* (1971), and *Ouhm* (1973), he emerged as one of the principal pioneers of text-sound.

•

Since radio stations normally used tape recordings in broadcasting, it was perfectly natural that electronic or recorded sounds should be broadcast from tape. But the traditional way to present music to the public remained the concert hall, and playing tapes did pose a problem in concert situations. Who, after all, enjoys sitting in a darkened theater watching inanimate loudspeakers? And why would one go to a concert hall to hear something that could be played on a stereo at home? The problem was how to make the playing of tapes lively in a concert.

One solution was the creation of an extraordinary concert environment, an environment that one could not create at home, as in Varèse' *Poème Electronique* and Stockhausen's *Gesang der Jünglinge*. And one aspect of an extraordinary environment was the spatial distribution of sound. Indeed, ever since Pierre Schaeffer's *pupitre d'espace* in 1951, the spatial distribution of sound was thought of as an important if not essential element in the public presentation of tape music. In Joji Yuasa's *Icon* (1967), for example, composed at the NHK studio in Tokyo, sounds moved at the same time clockwise and counterclockwise at different speeds through a pentagonal array of loudspeakers surrounding the audience. John Cage subtitled *Birdcage* (1972) as "twelve tapes to be distributed by a single performer in a space in which people are free

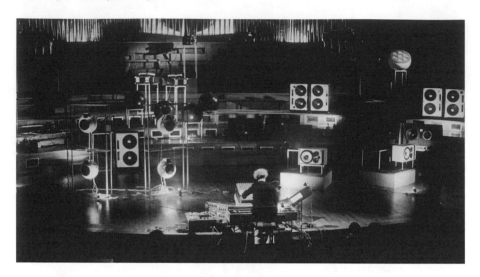

François Bayle (seen from behind) seated at the control board for the Acousmonium in the Salle Olivier Messiaen, Maison de Radio France, at a concert presented by GRM in December 1980. Photo courtesy GRM.

to move and birds to fly." And in 1974, François Bayle created the *Acousmonium*, a loudspeaker orchestra created specifically for playing tapes. The Acousmonium consisted of eighty loudspeakers of various sizes placed across a stage at different heights and distances from the proscenium. As Bayle specified it, "The placement of loudspeakers is organized according to their qualities—extreme bass, bass, midrange, high, super-high—their power, their quality, and their direction—convergent, divergent, direct, reflected, indirect . . ."

Further, the spatial distribution of sound was, in Bayle's view, a means to expose the interior structure of sound, what he called the *morpho-concept*. He explains:

> The morpho-concept has to do with the evolution of a sound—its timbre, shape, contour, elasticity, structure—as against the idea of notes. And the projection of sound into space is an integral part of that. It puts you inside the sound. It's like the interior of a sound universe.

•

Another solution was to put a performer on stage along with the loudspeakers. This idea might have found its ultimate commercial statement in Karaoke, but Karaoke embodies only one relationship between recorded music and performer, that of accompanist and soloist, whereas the literature of tape-and-performer pieces contains many different relationships. In Stockhausen's *Kontakte*, for example, the performers do a parallel and simultaneous performance, synchronized and related to the tape, which adds a live dimension to the tape and brings its performance correctly within the environment of the concert hall.

In Mario Davidovsky's *Synchronisms #6* (1970), the pitches of electronic sounds on tape are integrated so well with the notes played by a pianist that it seems as if the tape simply makes the piano larger. Davidovsky said, "The proposition of *Synchronisms* is stretching an instrument by adding electronic sounds and stretching electronic sounds by having a performer capable of the nuance of phrasing that the tape didn't have at the time—so they both add something to the combination." Further, Davidovsky saw the concert hall as having a demarginalizing effect on electronic music: "With a live instrumentalist on stage, I could introduce electronic sounds in a presentable and civilized way to a larger audience and have the audience accept the sounds as aesthetically valid."

Jacob Druckman began working at the Columbia studio in the mid-1960s. As he said, "I went in with the idea of doing more complicated rhythms than human beings could do—I began by splicing tape with a ruler." But it didn't work as expected: "I very quickly discovered that the intellectual precision that I wanted was not at all effective when I heard it played back." And so his ideas changed and he began to use tape, in his words, "to exaggerate human qualities—I was most fascinated with those sounds that included human energy." In his *Animus I* (1966), for tape and trombone, the tape contains mostly processed trombone sounds and the dramatic concept of the piece extends from that idea. As Druckman explains, "Like looking in a mirror and perhaps seeing a hostile, competitive image, I had the idea of a trombone player who's playing in a desultory fashion and the tape becomes his mirror, in effect another trombonist but with a hostile, competitive stance."

The use of tape with live performance, however, poses a question: Although the composer may have intended that the tape function as an accompanist, or as another performer, or even as an orchestra, wasn't the tape machine insensitive and unyielding to a musician's fluctuations in tempo? And the answer is yes. But in some cases that was good. Davidovsky observes, "Despite the rhythmic aspect of the tape being totally unyielding, performers can still do small rubatos, taking some freedom in the interpretation, and somehow compensate for it, because the tape is totally reliable in sustaining the rhythm." Jan Williams, percussionist, conductor, and performer of contemporary music since the 1960s, answers:

It was always possible to develop a sense of timing based on the tape. Since the tape was always moving at the same speed, it became like an aural score, and coordinating with it in the process of rehearsing became easier. The fixed nature of the tape allowed me to rely on it. I don't know how it happened exactly, but it seemed to be possible to develop a sense of the passage of time not based on seconds but based on events on the tape.

When synchronization between performer and tape was important, a composer typically supplied a graphic roadmap, or score, that showed the performer the timings of the taped sounds, and the performer typically used a stopwatch to follow the score. At least, that was Earle Brown's intention in his *Times Five* (1963), composed in Paris. He tells the story:

> As usual, I wanted instruments involved . . . and the idea of the title *Times Five* came from the fact that the five instruments would be in the center of a big "X" of crisscrossed loudspeakers . . . Luciano Berio had a group at that time. He said, "Why don't you write a piece for my group?" And that was the instrumentation: flute, trombone, harp, violin, cello. The title *Times Five* also relates to multiplying the instruments. Almost all of the material on the tapes are instrumental sounds because I wanted to multiply the instruments. I loved the idea of people in the audience seeing five people but walls of instrumental sound would be coming at them.

Brown recorded instrumental sounds and brought the tapes into the studio at Le Service de la Recherche. He continues:

> They had a machine that was variable speed, with a large lever. You could speed up or slow down the tape . . . I remember playing with the variable speed lever. I would wait until the orchestra chord hit, and I did what Bruno Maderna called the "karate chop," fingers vertical, and, *whap* . . . I would vary the speed of the tape, and before the sound ceased, I'd be back at fifteen inches per second. In other words, I wanted to start the sound with the real sound of the instruments and end the sound with the real sound of the instruments, but in between do something else. I wanted that violent attack and then squirming like a car skidding on ice . . .
>
> Luciano conducted the first performance of *Times Five*. The tape runs continuously for 17'15" and the instruments are coordinated with it. There are five sections with different kinds of material. The sections are not supposed to begin on an exact cue, but the conductor needs to have a general orientation as to where the tape is, so the structure is given in timings. You start a stopwatch at the beginning, and at 4'37" you know that the tape is into section two and you go from section one to section two, but not on the exact beat. When Luciano conducted it in that concert, he was about five minutes into the piece, and he looked at me. I was in the back with the tape machine. He looked at me and said, silently, "I forgot to start the watch," so he didn't know where the hell he was in the structure of the piece. And when the tape ended at 17'15", Luciano kept right on conducting the orchestra, and finally I signaled to him "it's over, it's over, it's over."

Salvatore Martirano's *L's G.A.* (1968), for gas-masked politico, helium bomb, a triple-projection film by Ronald Nameth, and two-channel tape recorder, was based on a text written by Martirano after Lincoln's Gettysburg Address with one-liners taken from M. C. Holloway's poetry. In a performance, Holloway, who played the gas-masked politico, stood in front of the projections, coordinating his physical movements with his filmed "shadow" on the center screen and coordinating his voice with the tape. The music was finished in early 1967, before the film. As Martirano tells it, "Suffering from the 1960s tangle of wires and cold solder joints, I thought about gas and bought an aviator's helmet at an army surplus store and combined it with a gas mask, and stuck a microphone in the gas mask, so the politico had a microphone which wouldn't have a problem with feedback—the two minutes at the end is when the politico breathes the helium and his voice rises hysterically."

L's G.A. grew out of Martirano's *Underworld* (1965), for four actors, four percussionists, two string basses, tenor sax, and two-channel tape. As he explained, "In *Underworld*, which was composed of different forms of wailing, laughing, yes and no, the burden of meaning is carried by inflection—my intention was to turn Lincoln's speech into a histrionic sequence of stereotypes representing the diverse attitudes of politicians who were using L's words to justify opinion over the spectrum." Is it true, then, that the dramatic intent of *L's G.A.* was to show that the Vietnam War was a perversion of the values expressed in Lincoln's speech? Martirano answers: "I was against the war, no doubt about that, but when I did the piece, I was thinking of it more like a soap opera—in fact, the whole idea of the organ came from soap operas." *L's G.A.* ends with Saint-Saen's *My Heart at Thine Sweet Voice*. As Martirano recalls, "It was played on a Magnavox, a really cheezy organ, by Don Smith, who played it in C-major and didn't get it quite right." He processed the tape with filtering and feedback and then played it back on two different tape recorders, which got slightly out of sync. He then recorded the result on a third. In performance, it's played loudly, with flowers opening on the screens.

•

Some composers allowed for a flexible synchronization between performers and taped sounds. In his *MAP* (1971), for example, Lukas Foss created a game for tapes and performers in which four players interact with instrumental sounds previously recorded on tapes. In a performance, the stage or playing area is divided into four zones, each the base position for one player. Bells of various shapes and sizes are hung from the ceiling in between the players' zones, as if in a wilderness area, with the audience seated around the players, as if around a boxing ring. The performance develops as a series of contests, or rounds, in which the performers play together, stop together, react quickly, imitate the taped sounds, or connect fragments. At the end of each round, a referee declares a loser. At the end of the performance, the winner plays or sings a solo in celebration of victory.

When he began to work on *MAP* in 1970, Foss' intention was to create a piece in which performers would improvise with electronic sounds on tape. As rehearsals progressed, however, he concluded that the electronic sounds were functioning too much as a score; and that realization came more or less at the same time as the idea of creating a game, the rules for which would produce, as he put it, "a music that would happen by itself." In a diary-history of the development of the piece, Foss noted for May 2, 1970:

> The answer perhaps: a game. Invent a game the rules of which will make the music happen. A game which ensures the consistent grouping and regrouping of the musicians. Solos, duets, trios happen of their own accord and in different corners of the stage, like inventions of territories (the Japanese game "Go?"). The traditional gamesmanship of musicians: to play the right note at the right time, is replaced by plain gamesmanship: how to come out ahead.

•

Jean-Claude Eloy's approach was to store sounds on tapes and, in performance, flexibly mix those sounds with a live musician's sounds. His tapes for *Yo-In* (1980, Reverberations), composed at the Institute of Sonology in Utrecht, included boat sirens recorded in the Turkish Bosporus, African birds, and he tells us, "Another friend who is a *chasseur de son* gave me some thunder sounds, I got myself some aircraft sounds, and I found a recording of an atomic explosion—made," he adds, "from very far away." He then went to Cologne to visit percussionist Michael Ranta. He describes it:

> Visiting him at his home in Cologne, I discovered that he had many wonderful instruments. He had a company that was importing instruments from all over Asia. I told him, "Here, I'm looking for a sound of this quality which matches this tape," and he listened, and we tried different instruments, and we looked for something to match, musically, dramatically, acoustically, visually, spiritually.

In a performance of *Yo-In*, subtitled *Music for an Imaginary Ritual*, a personage-percussionist leads the performance through four acts—*Aube* . . . (Dawn, the Call, the Ritual of Imploration), *Midi* . . . (Noon, Unification, Ritual of Integration), *Crépuscule* . . . (Twilight, Meditation, Ritual of Contemplation), and *Nuit* . . . (Night, Exorcism, Ritual of Liberation)—which represent different moods, poetic ideas, and families of sounds. At a performance at the Museum of Modern Art in Paris in February 1981, the space was divided into four stations around the audience, each station consisting of a group of loudspeakers and a group of percussion instruments. The quantity (more than 200) and variety of the percussion instruments—they included drums, chimes, bells, cymbals, mallet instruments; all other manner of instruments from throughout Asia, South America, the Pacific, and Europe; and carpenter's tools such as hammer and electric drill—were impressive. Ranta, the personage-percussionist, performed each act at a different station, leading the audience's attention from one station to another during the course of the evening. Eloy was seated behind a formidable control console, processing Ranta's percussion sounds with a Serge analog synthesizer and mixing them with the sounds from the tapes.

In his *Erkos* (1991), inspired by and composed for Junko Ueda, a Japanese Satsuma-Biwa player and Shômyo singer, Eloy carried the idea further. He tells it:

> I used to meet her in Japan but she was living in Europe when I wrote the piece. So I told her to come to the WDR studio, where I was working, and for two days I sampled her voice and instrument. I made a chorus with her voice, from two lines to 150 lines of polyphony and heterophony. So she sings and plays sometimes as soloist, sometimes in duets and trios, sometimes with orchestras and choruses like mirror galaxies of herself. The playback of the tapes is very interactive. I have a configuration of DAT tapes for a playback system which allows me to start the tapes at different points and follow her performance. So the DAT tapes are rarely superimposed in exactly the same way—they have several floating points of time relationships, and the details are different in each performance.
>
> I care very much about the space and the loudspeaker placement. She's in front of the stage, in the center, in a special position . . . Speakers are under the podium in front of the public. Behind her there are other speakers looking backward. Then in front, on both sides, I have two large speakers on the stage. In the rear I have two other large speakers. And high up in the far front and in the back of the hall, I have mono mixes, so I can completely play around her. Sometimes it seems that the sound is coming from her. Other times it grows all around the space, or in the far distance. The source is really the human being singing and playing, and all the work in the studio is to enlarge that, to multiply it. But it is always coming from her.
>
> The text is a Hindu prayer to the Great Goddess. The soloist acoustically becomes the Goddess who creates and absorbs all the energies, all the worlds, all the sounds.

•

John Cage's idea was simultaneous yet unsynchronized, *non*-interactive performances. His recording of the stories of *Indeterminacy* (1958), for example, is juxtaposed with David Tudor's performance of solos from the *Concert for Piano*. Cage's tape realization of *Fontana Mix* (1958) is often played simultaneously with a performance of *Aria*. In *HPSCHD* (1969), seven harpsichordists play at their own tempos along with the playback of Lejaren Hiller's fifty-one tapes. *Roaratorio* (1979) is in that tradition.

Based on James Joyce's *Finnegans Wake*, *Roaratorio* is the biggest example of simultaneous performance, a culminating event, "an Irish circus," as Cage called it. In its first performances, Cage read his *Writing for the Second Time through Finnegans Wake*, a series of mesostics derived from the book, while several Irish musicians played Irish folk music on traditional instruments and sixty-two channels of tape were played back, collectively conveying all of the sounds mentioned in *Finnegans Wake*.

Roaratorio was the result of three invitations: from Klaus Schöning at the WDR in Cologne for some music to accompany a radio reading of *Writing for the Second Time through Finnegans Wake*; from Pierre Boulez at IRCAM in Paris to compose a work there; and from the Festival d'Automne in Paris to create an evening of music for an event called *Autour de Merce Cunningham*. As Cage said, "I tried to have this one project . . . satisfy also all the other requests for work." He continues:

My first idea was to read through the book again . . . to make a list of the sounds I noticed mentioned in it. Recording those it seemed to me would bring the book to music. This resulted in a very long text called *Listing through Finnegans Wake*. Many of the sounds I found were difficult to imagine. How would they be made? I began to have doubts . . . My doubts had to do with the relation between the work to be done and the available time and personal energy, mine and that of John Fullemann who had agreed to do the sound engineering for the project . . . However, my father, the inventor, used to say, "If somebody says can't, that shows you what remains for you to do" . . .

Furthermore all along I had in the back of my mind the plan to make a circus of Irish traditional music. Ballads, at least. After all, Joyce himself had sung in the streets of Dublin . . .

In May Klaus Schöning and I met in Lyon in France. I was on tour with the Merce Cunningham Dance Company. Schöning had agreed to write to radio stations all over the world in order to ask for sounds from places mentioned in the *Wake* . . . We went through my *Listing through Finnegans Wake* several times extracting categories, for instance, various kinds of music, instrumental and vocal, various kinds of humanly produced noises, shouts, laughter, tears, various birds and animals, sounds of nature, water, wind, etc. We made a schedule: June 15 to July 15, a trip by the Fullemanns and me to Ireland to collect sounds and record music; July 15 to August 15: work in the studio at IRCAM to put everything together . . .

I hope that someday it can be heard with separate channels for each track, between sixty and seventy of them, with live musicians and myself reading and the Cunningham Dance Company performing. Merce Cunningham is half Irish and one of the characters in *Finnegans Wake* is poor Merkyn Corningwham . . .

John Cage, about 1970. Photo by James Klosty.
Courtesy The John Cage Trust.

•

Cage also differentiated between playing a tape in public and using tapes in performance: as he said, "Tapes *can* be used very effectively in performance." In his *Rozart Mix* (1965), for example, performers make, repair, change, and play tape loops on as many tape machines as are available for a performance. In Stockhausen's *Solo für Melodieinstrument mit Ruckkopplung* (1966, Solo for Melody Instrument with Feedback), a performer's sounds are played into a microphone, recorded, and played back at various times from an extensive tape delay system, superimposed and transformed, providing a counterpoint with which the performer continues to play. Alvin Lucier's *"I Am Sitting in a Room"* (1969) begins with a performer recording the following words:

> I am sitting in a room different from the one you are in now. I am recording the sound of my speaking voice and I am going to play it back into the room again and again until the resonant frequencies of the room reinforce themselves so that any semblance of my speech, with perhaps the exception of rhythm, is destroyed . . .

A performance of *"I Am Sitting in a Room"* requires two tape recorders, a microphone, and a loudspeaker. The instructions to the performer read as follows:

> Record your voice on tape through the microphone attached to tape recorder #1. Rewind the tape to its beginning, transfer it to tape recorder

#2, play it back into the room through the loudspeaker and record a second generation of the original recorded statement through the microphone attached to tape recorder #1. Rewind the second generation to its beginning and splice it onto the end of the original recorded statement on tape recorder #2. Play the second generation only back into the room through the loudspeaker and record a third generation . . . Continue this process . . .

Lucier later said:

> I didn't choose to use tape, I had to, because in order to recycle sounds into a space, I had to have them accessible in some form. Tape, then, wasn't a medium in which to compose sounds, it was a conveyor, a means to record them and play them back one after another in chronological order . . . I was interested in the process, the step-by-step, slow process of the disintegration of the speech and the reinforcement of the resonant frequencies . . . the signal goes through the air again and again . . . the space acts as a filter; it filters out all of the frequencies except for the resonant ones . . .

•

Eliane Radigue did not use tape to create a performance. She used performance to create a tape. She had begun working with tape during the 1950s as an assistant to Pierre Henry, and she had continued composing with tape into the 1960s. Then, in 1968, she discovered audio feedback as a means for controlling sound, and it pointed her in a new direction. In her words:

> I was fascinated. I found the sounds very expressive. I controlled the levels of the sounds and I moved the microphone, all with great simplicity. What fascinated me was the fragility of the sounds, that I could change just a tiny thing, like moving my finger slightly on a potentiometer, and it would change the sound enormously.

In 1969, she composed a series of continuous sound environments. One of them was *Usral*, a collaboration with sculptor Marc Halpern at the Salon des Artistes Décorateurs à Paris, where she combined three tape loops of slightly different durations to make a continual, long sound that gradually evolved. As she said, "When you make three tapes that play together in that way, the sound goes through an evolution in changing timbres, and this technique allowed me to make a music something like Paul Verlaine wrote, '. . . qui n'est jamais ni tout à fait la même ni tout à fait une autre . . .' ('. . .that is never exactly the same and never exactly something else . . .')." She began to work with synthesizers in 1970: "With a synthesizer instead of a tape machine and microphone, I had a far better way to do the things that interested me, with a far better control—and with these techniques, I could make sounds that change almost imperceptibly, and I learned to modify the sounds *tout douce-ment*, very lightly, almost like a caress."

Why, then, did Radigue use tape? For one thing, her goal in performance was to achieve a sound without directionality, a sound that permeated the space without even the suggestion of a performer. At a performance of her *847* (1973) at The Kitchen in New York, the sound was "oozing from the walls," as Tom Johnson described it at the time in *The Village Voice*. And at a performance of her *Kyema* (1988) in 1993 at the Eglise de Cimiez in Nice, France, as she describes it, "The audience was bathed in sound without knowing where the sound was coming from."

For another thing, she used tape because precision in mixing her sounds was crucial to her music: "I use tape because my pieces are made up of sounds that crossfade into other sounds, and at the moment of overlap there's an interaction between the two sounds, and it's crucial to get the timing right—there's a delicacy and great difficulty in getting it right, and if I was doing a live performance in a concert and it wasn't right, I'd have to start again."

•

Radigue's way of using tape was typical of a generally new approach that developed through the 1960s. The new tape music was not collage, not based on juxtapositions of sound objects. It was usually the result of a studio performance done with a minimum of editing, if any at all. In composing *It's Gonna Rain* (1965), for example, Steve Reich performed the relative speeds of tape loop playbacks. He describes it:

> The voice belongs to a young black Pentecostal preacher who called himself Brother Walter. I recorded him along with the pigeons and traffic one Sunday afternoon in Union Square in downtown San Francisco. Later at home I started playing with tape loops of his voice and, by accident, discovered the process of letting two identical loops go gradually out of phase with each other. In the first part of the piece the two loops are lined up in unison, gradually move completely out of phase with each other, and then slowly move back to unison . . . Finally, the process moves to eight voices and the effect is a kind of controlled chaos, which may be appropriate to the subject matter—the end of the world.

Pauline Oliveros performed *I of IV* (1966) onto tape. In the summer of 1966, en route from her previous position at the Mills College Tape Music Center to a new position at the University of California at San Diego, Oliveros attended a six-week studio course at the University of Toronto. She set up an interactive performable system involving tone generators, tape delays, and amplifiers to produce combination tones, repetitions, layering of sounds, and different kinds of reverberation. She then played a keyboard, but because so much happened automatically in the tape delay system—sounds were record-ed, then played back several times at different time intervals and continually mixed with new sounds at different pitches, producing different combination tones—she was sometimes surprised by the results. She recalls:

> I wanted to bypass editing, if I could, and work in a way that was similar to performance . . . As I was making *I of IV*, I was also listening to it. At one point in the piece there's a rather climactic scream-like melody that sweeps through most of the audible range. When that started coming out, I didn't expect it; it was incredible and very delightful. I was laughing and was amazed at that particular moment. . . .

Jean-Claude Eloy composed *Gaku-no-Michi* (1978, The Ways of Sounds) in Tokyo during several visits in 1977 and 1978 using, in his words, "about a total of seven months of studio time, full time, every day of the week." The structure of *Gaku-no-Michi* was based on transformations between sounds, as he puts it, "from abstract to concrète, from concrète to abstract, from concrète to concrète, and from abstract to abstract, giving the skeleton of the piece." Being in Japan, he decided to record Japanese sound material, but the question was, as he recalls, "What are Japanese sounds?" He recorded cultural sounds, such as traditional music and religious ceremonies, and daily life sounds as they were heard in streets, subways, department stores, and gardens. Sometimes he went far afield to find a special sound. He remembers, "I had to go very far out of Kyoto to find a *shishiyodoshi*—it's bamboo that fills with water, then moves like a seesaw to empty the water on a stone." And then, in the studio, he worked with the sounds and gradually defined a structure. He describes the process:

> I transformed the sounds. I accumulated the transformed materials. And then I paused and listened and tried to find which families of sounds mixed well with other families. I tried to be systematic. I made extensive notes in a book. I did piles of experiments to see what went well with what. And then I made groupings of materials, small moments, maybe a few or several minutes, a combination of sounds mixed together. Progressively, step by step, I arrived at longer and more complex sections, scored on paper or improvised onto tape. Finally, I reached the level of the final mixes. For some of them, it was like an actual performance, sometimes thirty minutes long, non-stop, with many tapes. I called all the assistants and rehearsed several times before recording. It was like per-forming a piano concerto. Same concentration, same rehearsals before. Same need for total silence around.

Although Maggi Payne, in San Francisco, occasionally used synthesized sounds, as in *Phase Transitions* (1989), composed with a Roland D-550, her basic materials were usually recorded acoustic sounds. As she said, "The focus is to take natural sounds and transform them using equalization, convolution, phase vocoding—whatever resources are available." Sometimes those natural sounds were made specifically with a certain effect in mind. Referring to *White Night* (1984), she explains: "I took a word, looped it in a digital delay, and overlayed it so many times that the rhythmic quality became very disguised, resulting in an undulating surface texture with a continuous sound." Sometimes she found sounds through an impressive sensitivity to the presence of lawyers, as, for example, the sounds for *Liquid Metal* (1994). In her words:

> Oh, man, did you ever hear a Harley close up going down a canyon? It's time variant—the pitch, the amplitude—and also it's so spatial. We were canoeing out on a stream. It looked like it might be pristine, but there were lawyers on Harleys roaring down the canyon road. All you heard were Harleys, cars, and bicycles going by.

Sometimes her sounds came from other ideas and feelings. In discussing her concept for *Airwaves* (1987), for example, she commented: "I have a great affinity for the desert and an incredible appreciation for the people who live in these remote places—I got tangled in the idea that their sense of reality is very different from ours." The source materials for her sounds, in short, came from many different places, and they were accumulated and combined in a studio. Why? Payne answers:

> Control. And detail. The mix in the studio is subtle, it's detailed, and so critical to the way the piece sounds that I don't think it can be re-created in a live situation. Subtle variations are critical to the life of the piece. The mix is intensely difficult, but it's the only way to bring a dynamic quality into the piece, a structural element. I'll do twenty-five mixes before I can settle on one.

Phill Niblock also used tape for precision in mixing. Filmmaker as well as composer, his films—all silent, shot in China, Brazil, Portugal, Hong Kong, Mexico, and many other countries and locales—deal with the motions of everyday labor. One sees the backs of laborers, or their tools, or their hands, plowing, picking, fishing, manufacturing, weaving, cooking. As he said, "I'm looking at the movement of people working without trying to influence the way we think about it." And one sees minimalist, changing patterns.

His approach to composing was also minimalist, also with changing patterns. First, he recorded single notes played on acoustic instruments at pitches that were separated only by microtones. For *A Trombone Piece* (1977), for example, trombonist James Fulkerson was recorded playing various tunings of a single note in three different octaves. As Niblock describes the process, "We went to a studio and recorded tones that were 'A's and sharp 'A's, approximately two minutes per tone, and then I edited that material by taking out the breathing sounds and spaces in between the tones—but I left in the trail-off of one note and the attack of the next note . . ." Then, he mixed the pitches together to make sustained, complex, slowly shifting sounds with gradually developing changes in color, shape, and feel.

•

Tape was used by composers whenever tape was essential to gather, store, and transport sounds. The amazing multilevel sounds in Maryanne Amacher's *Sound Characters* (1989), for example, could not have been done without accumulating and mixing sounds on tape. And, like Eliane Radigue, Amacher filled spaces with her sounds. Her *Music for Sound-Joined Rooms*, for example, from which *Sound Characters* is derived, provided aural environments that occurred simultaneously in adjoining rooms such that the sounds, slightly different in each of the rooms, "tuned" the spaces and one's passage through them.

Annea Lockwood's *A Sound Map of the Hudson River* (1982) was a single manifestation of her *River Archive*, a collection begun in the mid-1960s of recordings of the world's rivers. She explains the idea:

> The sound of one section of a river is distinct from that of another section. And water passes over many different surfaces at many different rates, so the resultant textures tend to be really intimate, and really complex, and quite absorbing to listen to . . . When I record, I'm aiming for a lot of presence . . . I'm eliminating all ambient sound that's extraneous to the water—the wind, the birds. The focus is on the water.

How else but with a recording medium could the sound of a river, for example, be heard in a concert hall? Or at home? How else but with recording could one convey the closeness of water? As Lockwood puts it, "I view the whole world of electronic media as a sophisticated transportation system, as a means for me to bring sounds which otherwise can't be transported into people's living rooms."

• • •

Chapter Four

Out of the Studios

Question: "How do you perform electronic music without tape?" Answer (said with a shrug of the shoulders and rising inflection): "Take away the tape." After all, most tape studios by 1960 contained filters, modulators, amplifiers, and various other sound-processing equipment, and in general, all manner of audio equipment was easily available. Why not use these devices, without tape, in performance?

Cage, true to form, had done it early on. In *Cartridge Music* (1960), his idea was, as he said it, "to make electronic music live." And, as one would expect, he took an exceptional approach. In his continual quest to find any and all sounds that could be heard, in *Cartridge Music* he looked to "small" sounds:

> The title *Cartridge Music* derives from the use in its performance of cartridges, that is, phonograph pick-ups into which needles are inserted for playing recordings. Contact microphones are also used. These latter are applied to chairs, tables, wastebaskets, etc.: various suitable objects (toothpicks, matches, slinkies, piano wires, feathers, etc.) are inserted in the cartridges. Both the microphones and cartridges are connected to amplifiers that go to loud-speakers, the majority of the sounds produced being small and requiring amplification in order to be heard . . .

Cage's score to *Cartridge Music*, like his score to *Fontana Mix*, consists of graphic materials on transparent plastic sheets which a performer can overlay in different juxtapositions to devise a specific structure for a particular performance. Most of Cage's scores from the period—for example, *Fontana Mix* (1958), *Variations I* (1958), *Variations II* (1961), *Variations III* (1963), *Variations IV* (1964)—are based on similar open-ended structural principles. The title *Cartridge Music* is a bit unusual among Cage's titles in that it specifically suggests electronic sounds, but even when a title did not indicate specific sounds, Cage often performed with electronics, and the open-ended scores gave him a way to structure different performance situations, including collaborative situations with other musicians.

The idea for *Variations V*, for example, came when, as Merce Cunningham said, "Cage decided to find out if there might not be ways that the sound could be affected by movement, and he and David Tudor proceeded to discover that there were . . ." *Variations V* was performed by the Merce Cunningham Dance Company on July 23, 1965 at Lincoln Center in New York City, with music performed and created by John Cage, Malcolm Goldstein, Frederick Lieberman, James Tenney, and David Tudor, films by Stan VanDerBeek, and video images by Nam June Paik. It also included twelve poles, actually modified theremins, built especially for the performance by Robert Moog and placed throughout the stage. The idea was that the dancers would move within the sensitivity ranges of the poles, thereby triggering sounds. Cunningham remembers, "I did wonder about our feet stepping on the wires . . ." There were also photoelectric cells at the bases of the poles, which triggered additional sounds. Cunningham continues:

> The general principle as far as I was concerned was like the doors automatically opening when you enter a supermarket. The dancers triggered some of the sound possibilities, but the kind of sound, how long it might last, the possible repetition or delaying of it, was controlled by the musicians and technicians who were at the numerous machines on a platform behind and above the dance space. They utilized tape machines, oscillators, and shortwave radios . . .

There were also objects—a plant, a pillow, a pad, a table, and two chairs—to which contact microphones were attached and which, when moved or touched by the dancers, produced yet additional sounds. *Variations V* contained a lot of ways to trigger sounds, and as if to put a period at the end of the sentence, Merce Cunningham, at the end of the dance, rode a bicycle around the stage, its wheels wired for sound.

•

Cage's general approach was to define a "territory" and use all of the sounds within that territory as the sound material for a composition. In *Williams Mix*, the territory was the world; in *Cartridge Music*, it was sounds requiring amplification; in *Birdcage*, it was birds and nature; in *Roaratorio*, it was *Finnegans Wake*. Cage's electronic music was different from that of his contemporaries, Stockhausen's for example, because Cage's structures were based on process and random juxtapositions rather than fixed relationships between sounds. His electronic music suggests a happy anarchy where all things can be and coexist as themselves. It does not convey control, technique, expertise; it does not convey personal, subjective, poetic expression. It does convey a sense of adventure, of totality, of all things being available to us in the world around us—of exuberance, discovery, surprise, and good humor. In performing *Child of Tree* (1975) with a deadpan concentration that would have put Buster Keaton to shame, Cage plucked spines from a cactus, thereby producing amplified pings and blurps. If Cage had been in the audience watching his own performance, he too would have laughed.

Stockhausen's music, on the other hand, does convey control, technique, and expertise. In the summer of 1964, he installed a tamtam in his garden and began the series of experiments that led to *Mikrophonie I* (1964). In his words:

> I undertook an experiment in which the tamtam was excited with various objects that I found around the house—objects of glass, cardboard, metal, wood, rubber, synthetics. At the same time, I held and moved with my hand a directional microphone that was connected first to an elec-

John Cage and Karlheinz Stockhausen, about 1958.
Photo courtesy The John Cage Trust.

tronic filter with a potentiometer for volume control, and then to an amplifier and loudspeaker. In so doing, I used the microphone to listen to the tamtam, the way a doctor examines a patient with a stethoscope. Meanwhile, a technician, who was sitting in the living room, freely altered the adjustment of the filter and potentiometer . . .

Rehearsal of Karlheinz Stockhausen's Mikrophonie I in November 1973 at WDR in Cologne. The photo below shows, from left to right, Aloys Kontarsky, Péter Eötvös, Harald Bojé, and Joachim Krist performing at the tamtam. The photo on the right is Stockhausen controlling the sounds. Photos courtesy Stockhausen-Verlag.

It was on the basis of this experiment that *Mikrophonie I* was composed. With various materials, two players excite the tamtam; two other players pick up the vibrations with directional microphones. Distance between the microphone and tamtam (which influences the dynamics and timbre), relative distance between the microphone and the point of excitation on the tamtam (influencing pitch, timbre, and above all determining the spatial impression of the sound, ranging between distant, echoing and extremely close), and rhythm of microphone movement are prescribed in an appropriate notation. Each of two more players activates an electronic filter and potentiometer. They again shape the timbre and pitch (through a combination of filter adjustment and volume control) and the rhythm of the structures (through the metrically notated alteration of both instrument settings) . . .

Stockhausen did many electronic performance pieces, among them *Mixtur* (1964), for instrumental ensembles and ring modulators, and *Mikrophonie II* (1965), for twelve singers, Hammond organ, and ring modulator. *Prozession* (1967), *Stimmung* (1968), *Aus den Sieben Tagen* (1968), and *Mantra* (1970) called for voices and/or acoustic instruments with some form of electronic processing. In general, his approach was to use electronics to transform acoustically produced sounds. He was also interested in issues of continual growth in skill, knowledge, and expertise. In 1967, for example, he said:

Recently I worked four days in our studio. At the end, I had to spend another four or five days analyzing what I had done in order to write it down. It is an awful thing for me. But without what I describe there will be no culture whatsoever in the new dimension. If I make a thing, I'm not only interested in the result; I'm interested in the learning; I'm interested in the initial culture. Let's say we have no score, but we do have a tape. The tape alone doesn't help enough for study. We can listen, yes; we can get a kind of idea; it may stimulate other things one can do. But one is really not able to go further in that direction. There wouldn't be any scientific or philosophical or musical progress in our culture if one couldn't learn from one's forefathers.

•

Learning from one's forefathers, however, is not the only wisdom. History can perpetuate unwanted baggage as well as verified knowledge; and for a whole new generation of composers in the 1960s, particularly in the United States, the point was to step out of history. The world was wide open for new ways of doing things.

One of the new centers of activity was San Francisco. At the San Francisco Conservatory, Pauline Oliveros and Ramon Sender pooled equipment from, as Oliveros put it, "hither and yon," and on December 18, 1961, organized a tape concert called *Sonics I*, with works by Sender, Oliveros, Terry Riley, Phil Winsor, and an improvisational piece for instruments and tape played by Sender, Oliveros, Riley, Winsor, and Laurel Johnson. Soon after the first concert, Sonics formed as a group, consisting initially of Sender, Oliveros, Johnson, and Winsor, soon to be joined by Morton Subotnick and Tony Martin. They had few resources but much ingenuity. Oliveros' *Time Perspectives*, played on that first Sonics concert, was a four-channel composition done with two roughly-synchronized stereo tapes. She had composed it with a SilverTone tape recorder purchased from Sears Roebuck, which had the feature that you could hand-wind the tape while recording. As she later described it, "I had a variable speed machine." How did she make the sounds? Oliveros explains:

> I would record acoustic sounds using cardboard tubes as filters. I'd put a microphone at one end of a cardboard tube and a sound source at the other. I used different sized tubes to get different filter characteristics. Sometimes I'd clamp a sound source to the wall so the wall would act as a resonator and then record it at 3-1/2 or 7-1/2 inches per second and use the hand winding to vary the speed. I used a bathtub as a reverberation chamber . . .

Sonics continued through the winter of 1961 and into the summer of 1962 with many concerts. On April 20, the concert included Gordon Mumma's *Vectors and Densities*, Subotnick's *Mandolin*, *Opera Three* (a group improvisation), James Tenney's *Collage #1* and *Blue Suede*, Sender's *Parade*, and *Opera Four* (a group improvisation with the same participants as *Opera Three*). On June 11, Sender's *Tropical Fish Opera*, performed by Sender, Subotnick, Oliveros, and Loren Rush, used a tank of tropical fish as a score. As Sender sensitively described it, "Certain areas on the sides of the tank were marked off and whenever a fish swam into that area he or she became a note or dynamic indication." Then came *Smell Opera with Found Tape*. Subotnick tells the story:

> One of us had found a tape in an alley. We sealed it and brought it to the auditorium. The Ann Halprin Dance Company had bought these little personality perfume kits, and they went around interviewing people in the audience—letting them choose their scents—and spraying them. Tony Martin did lights. Then we unsealed the tape and played it. It turned out to be a psychodrama about a girl who had a child out of wedlock with a minister giving her advice. The next day, the headline was "Concert Literally Stinks," and the critic couldn't get the smell out of his clothes. The Conservatory didn't want us there anymore.

Undaunted, Subotnick and Sender found a house on Jones Street, on Russian Hill in San Francisco, and carried on. Subotnick continues:

The house was going to be torn down, and so it was fine for us to have it for nothing, to keep tabs on it. It had a large dining-living room that would seat about 100 people. The studio area was the dining room. So we took whatever we had massed together at the Conservatory, and we brought it all over to Jones Street. There was a woman, Agnes Albert, who said she would give us money if we incorporated, so she could write it off. So we got a lawyer and incorporated. It cost about $100. Then we called Agnes and she sent us a check for $25.

The corporation was called the San Francisco Tape Music Center. As Subotnick explains, "At that point, there was a big battle between the Stockhausen elektronische Musik and the Schaeffer musique concrète, and we

Morton Subotnick (left) and Ramon Sender (right) drink coffee in 1964 in front of the three-track Ampex tape machine at the San Francisco Tape Music Center. As Sender tells the story, "That tape recorder had been built from the ground up by a young high school engineer in the Ampex labs. He did everything, including laminating his own heads. And one of our patrons was Eldon Corl, who worked for Ampex. Eldon called us one day and said, 'You want a deal, here it is.' So we went down and looked at it. It was a beast standing six feet tall in his bedroom. His newer version was transistorized and it fit into a briefcase, so he was happy to unload this one. But it did things that no other tape recorder could do. It had no erase head. We could set the tape tension reel so that the tape would creep past the record head. By playing tapes at fast speeds I could create complex sounds and key them into a piece." Photo courtesy Ramon Sender.

wanted to bridge these differences by calling it 'tape music,' which could be anything that was on tape." Subotnick had a tape recorder, Sender had a few things, and they went to Palo Alto to see Eldon Corl, a sales representative for Ampex. Corl had an experimental three-track recorder (one track each for left and right stereo and one for the middle) which he lent to the center. As Subotnick recalls, "It was five or six feet tall, and the power supply was as big as a chair—the power supply blew up before the first performance." Michael Calahan, a high school student, became their technician. As Subotnick remembers, gratefully, "He would borrow pieces of equipment from his high school."

Subotnick and Sender produced a concert series. On December 3, 1962, the concert included Luigi Nono's *Omaggio a Vedova*, James Tenney's *Blue Suede*, André Boucourechliev's *Texte II (1st Version)*, a composition for actors directed by Lee Breuer, André Boucourechliev's *Texte II (2nd Version)*, and Mario Davidovsky's *Study #2*. On February 4 and 5, 1963, the concert included a painting event with Robert Lavigne, Sender's *Kronos*, Pousseur's *Trois Visages de Liège*, and Subotnick's *Music from Galileo*. *City Scale*, organized by Ken Dewey, Ramon Sender, and Tony Martin in early spring 1963, was the culminating event of the season, with different activities organized at different locations in the city and the audience carried around in trucks. As Sender recalls, "It was an era of happenings and we decided we'd do one." He continues:

> We used the city environment as totally as possible and many of the events were presented as ambiguously as possible so that audience members wouldn't know whether a certain event was planned or just happening: the arrival of the audience at a park overlooking the mission district coincided with the confrontation of two gangs . . . And after we did this, I said, "Well, I don't know what we could do to top this." And somebody jokingly said, "Well, we can burn the house down."

Subotnick continues:

> Everything got reviewed, but the address was never mentioned because we couldn't meet the fire laws. It was a volatile season. The police came once. Ramon and I were paying for everything out of our own pockets, so we rented out rooms to artists and poets. But most of them were on drugs and they weren't paying their rent anyway, and we were afraid of being busted.

So Subotnick and Sender decided to do it in a more legitimate way. They found a place on Divisidero Street which had two auditoriums. They rented one auditorium to KPFA, a Bay Area radio station, to do live performances. KPFA renovated the auditorium, made a broadcast booth, and installed a piano. They rented the other auditorium to the Ann Halprin Dance Company. The attic became the tape studio which included, incidentally, the rebuilt three-track Ampex from Jones Street. With access to the auditorium that KPFA had renovated, Subotnick and Sender continued what they had started at Jones Street. Just in time, it might be added, because there was a fire in the house on Jones Street. As Sender remembers, "I was back there saying goodbye to some sub-tenants, when I noticed an odd orange glow from the attic . . ." In fact, Sender had moments earlier gone in, seen an empty fuse socket and put in a fuse, then come out again into the street. He remembers:

> It was quite a show. A windy night. The fog was coming in. The whole roof went up. The fire engines came and some of our audience people came. They had heard about it on the radio. They said things like, "Well, you sure outdid yourself." It self-fulfilled our prophesy.

The first season at Divisidero Street, however, was more spectacular than the fire. Tony Martin, multimedia artist, created films, lighting, and visuals for other people's works and composed many of his own. There was a concert of Luciano Berio's music—Berio had come to San Francisco to teach at Mills College—in which Ann Halprin danced to *Visage*. Lee Romero did liquid projections on Pyrex glass, projected as a light show with overhead projectors. Stockhausen visited. Salvatore Martirano visited. Three composers from Sweden—Folke Rabe, Jan Bark, and Arne Milnas—came to study on a grant from the Swedish government. In March and April 1964, Pauline Oliveros organized a three-concert, six-day festival called *TudorFest* which featured John Cage's work and included David Tudor, Alvin Lucier, and Toshi Ichiyanagi. Oliveros and Tudor collaborated on *Duo for Accordion, Bandoneon, and Possible Mynah Bird Obbligato, Seesaw Version*, in which the seesaw spun around slowly on a Lazy Susan with the mynah bird suspended overhead, hopefully to make a sound. There was also a performance of Cage's *Atlas Eclipticalis*, performed by Oliveros, Subotnick, Stuart Dempster, Loren Rush, John Chowning, and Stanley Shaff, with Sender conducting. Oliveros sums it up: "That was a major event for us—I pushed the boundaries of the Tape Music Center."

Events continued into the next seasons. There were numerous compositions finished and performed by Subotnick, Oliveros, Sender, Martin, and others, among them Martin's *Room* (1964), for film, slide projections, three musicians, and a tape recorded at his loft on the Embarcadero with traffic and ocean sounds. With combined projections including sequences of hand-painted and overlaid slides, sixteen-millimeter films, and improvisations involving the manipulation of liquids and various objects on the transparencies of overhead projectors, Martin created stage-sized, continually changing imagery something like paintings in motion. There were group improvisations at every concert. And there were collaborative performances. In November 1964, Terry Riley's *In C*, which had been commissioned by the San Francisco Tape Music Center, was first performed. In February 1965, Steve Reich's *It's Gonna Rain*—another commissioned work—was played. And in January 1966, there was the Trips Festival. Sender organized it. He tells the story:

I started burning out on the Tape Center and wanted to do something different, like Sunday morning new age church rituals. Peyote got me interested in moving out of concert performance and into ceremonial behavior. At that point Tony said, "Why don't you look up Stewart Brand? He's doing a multimedia show, 'America Needs Indians.'" So the Trips Festival was co-produced by myself and Stewart Brand. Ken Kesey was our star, but he was on the lam from the cops when the Festival occurred. Gradually, everybody from the Tape Center became involved. We hired Don Buchla to do the sound system. I wanted to run Big Brother & the Holding Company through the Buchla . . . Well, the Trips Festival certainly wasn't a concert. It was a smorgasbord of all the new happenings around town that were the least bit psychedelic. It was raw material for ceremony. It was dancing and strobe lights and the acid test. When it was over, we had made something like $16,000. None of us had ever seen that much money in our lives and I was so blown away that I packed up my car and went off to the desert to think about it.

By the time of the Trips Festival, the end of the San Francisco Tape Music Center was clearly in sight. Early on, Subotnick had approached the Rockefeller Foundation and received an initial small grant for the 1965–1966 season to be followed by a large grant of $50,000 per year for four years. There was, however, a catch. Oliveros tells it:

In order for us to receive the money, they needed an agent that was fiscally responsible. So the solution was to move the Tape Center to Mills College. This is how large organizations kill small ones. Instead of teaching the small organization how to be fiscally responsible, it gets farmed out to a big one.

Oliveros sat in on the drafting of the contract between Mills College and the Tape Center for the grant. She remembers, "I wanted the studio at Mills to be a public access studio." It was also agreed that, according to Subotnick, "if the Tape Center activities were successful, with good reviews, and so on, that it was probably not fulfilling its purpose."

Subotnick went to New York in 1966 to teach at the New York University School of the Arts. Sender went to Morningstar, Wheeler Ranch, and Star Mountain before he got, as he put it, "communed out." Oliveros and Martin became the transitional co-directors of the Tape Music Center at Mills College which was, according to plan, a public-access as well as educational studio.

And there was some sadness at the end of something wonderful. Thinking back to Divisidero Street, Oliveros reflected, "It was a very amazing time in that city." Looking back, Subotnick comments:

Before the Rockefeller Foundation grant, we had put in every penny ourselves. But by 1965, we knew it was the end because we couldn't go on any longer. And with the 50k per year, the Tape Center could have become a major center as an alternative performance space. It's a shame in a way. The Tape Center did well at Mills, but it's a shame that there was a requirement for major fiscal responsibility. There's nothing more responsible than a group making something happen without any money.

●

Another new center of activity was in Ann Arbor, Michigan. Composers Robert Ashley and Gordon Mumma, with several other artists, formed the Once Group. In 1961, they began to produce the Once Festivals.

Mumma's music through the first festivals became increasingly electronic. His *Sinfonia for 12 Instruments and Magnetic Tape* (1960), performed at the 1961 festival, used taped electronic music only in the third movement and as a transition between the second and third movements. The 1962 festival included his *Meanwhile, a Twopiece* (1962), in which Ashley played piano, Mumma played horn, and they both played percussion, accompanied throughout by taped sounds that, as Mumma recalls, "were often like those we played live, so it was interestingly difficult to tell where the sounds were coming from." In the 1963 festival, his *Medium Size Mograph 1963*, for piano four hands and live electronics, was performed with a circuit that he designed. It was, in his words, "a type of envelope generator that drastically reshaped the amplitude-envelope of the piano sound, so much that it changed the timbre of the instrument." In the 1964 festival, his *Megaton for Wm. Burroughs* (1963) was performed by himself, Ashley, Milton Cohen, and others, with amplified sound sculptures designed by Cohen, six synchronized channels of taped sound, and long steel wires along which objects flew through the performance space. The physical arrangement of the different performers was suggested, following a film that Mumma had seen, by the isolated positions of the crew members of a World War II bomber. As he describes it, "The performers were isolated and illuminated individually, and coordinated with each other by headphones—it made an impressive theater . . ." And he came out of the performance with an interesting reflection:

> Only Ashley and I were musicians. The rest of the performers were visual artists and architects. One of the things I learned from the piece was the different creative sensibility the non-musicians had about the passage of time. I learned an enormous amount about music and time . . .

Much of the Once Festival programming contained theatrical and visual elements. There was performance art, dance, theater, film—the Once Group included composer Robert Sheff, painter Mary Ashley, architects Harold Borkin and Joseph Wehrer, filmmaker George Manupelli, and performance artists Cynthia Lidell and Anne Wehrer—and there was opera. In the 1967 festival, Ashley's opera *That Morning Thing* (1967) was performed twice in its entirety. In the first act, later performed separately as *Frogs*, a background of frog sounds accompanies four men with electronically processed froglike voices who direct the movements of dancers. In the second act, later performed separately as *Purposeful Lady Slow Afternoon*, each of four women's voices describes, to a background of bell sounds and sweet music, a very personal experience that she can't understand except in reminiscence. As Ashley said at the time, "Music has to be *about* something."

There were also performances at different times by guests, among them John Cage, David Tudor, Alvin Lucier and the Brandeis Chamber Chorus, David Behrman, Max Neuhaus, Lukas Foss with the Creative Associates Ensemble, and the Judson Dance Theatre. The Once Festivals, in short, were a focal point for imagination, experimentation, new ideas, new directions, new concepts. In 1993, looking back, Ashley reflected:

> I think that over the last twenty years we've become much more attracted to the idea of music being practical, not just in a social or economic sense, but in the sense that we seem to believe now that we actually want to make "real" music, and I think that thirty or thirty-five years ago that idea was not around. I think that up until around 1970, the most interesting ideas about music were so impractical that they verged on being, well, *imaginary*. There was one British composer who suggested that he was going to tow Iceland from its current position to another location in the Atlantic. And we took that seriously as an idea for a sound. We would not take that seriously now.
>
> Also there were no resources, but there was a great need to make music, which meant that to be practical was to be virtually insane . . . So we did impractical things, and the more impractical the more inspiring it was, the more power the ideas had. The interesting thing was that it made the music available to everybody because, since nobody had anything then, you could have the idea without having anything, so in a sense everybody could have the musical experience, such as it was, by imagining the sound of towing Iceland from its current position to another position in the Atlantic.
>
> It's interesting that you could perform a representation of a piece without performing the piece, that you were simply representing the piece and that the piece did not have any physical, real manifestation. It's an interesting conceptual idea. It was an interesting period of time in music because of this peculiar quality of being imaginary, of being conceptual. At the Once Festival we did wonderful representations of ideas.
>
> We did the first Once Festival in 1961. It was a very, very popular event in Ann Arbor and very unpopular with the University. I think it must have been attractive to the audience and unattractive to the traditionalists because of the increasing weirdness of it, I mean the increasingly rarefied quality of that representation of an idea.

Gradually the Once Festival became the project of the Once Group, of which there were about eight or ten people. These people figured out what we were going to do, planned the pieces, and produced them. The pieces became more and more ambitious. We got into wanting to do big pieces. Even with the notion that they were impractical, there's still a limit, you know, where you need money. We couldn't raise the money. From about 1965 on, it got to be more and more sad and more and more sort of desperate, wanting to do these really grand pieces without any possibility that they would ever happen. And so I think people started to wear out because they were getting tired of being frustrated. It's hard to explain to people now the situation where there isn't anything, no money, no possibility of support. So, there had to be an end to it. The Once Group had to end.

I believe we did the last festival in 1968. Not that I care much about history, but when you're out of it, when you've gone through it, you look back and say, "That was amazing, to be in that situation where everything was imaginary, and where it was valid for being imaginary." It was an incredible thing that happened. The thrill of sitting in your room and hearing Iceland being towed, I'll take it over Elgar any time. They were just incredible pieces, incredible thrills, people thinking up ever more amazing sounds.

●

There were, indeed, incredible pieces done by people who worked in and around these new centers, and in a wide variety of ways, the pieces defined new solutions to the problems of performing with electronics. Ramon Sender's *Desert Ambulance* (1964), for example, called for amplified accordion, a two-track tape, and projections designed by Tony Martin. Martin describes the visual side of it:

> I projected hands at the piano over Pauline's own hands on the accordion keyboard, then a colorful girl on a swing, followed by a black and white sequence of people marching away that filled Pauline's body and accordion as one shape while around her gradually emerged a huge cathedral of abstract light shapes and lines.

Sender solved the tape-performer synchronization problem by using one of the tracks for instructions to the performer. In performance, the instruction track was heard by the performer through headphones while the other track, containing electronic sounds, was heard by the public through loudspeakers. During the summer of 1964, Sender, Morton Subotnick, Pauline Oliveros, and Tony Martin went together on a cross-country concert tour, performing *Desert Ambulance* among other works. At the last concert, in New Hampshire, Sender and Subotnick were operating the tape recorder. But they accidentally switched the channels containing instructions and music so that the audience was hearing the instructions and Oliveros, playing the accordion, was hearing the electronic sounds. As Subotnick remembers, "We didn't hear anything from the loudspeakers, so we turned up the volume—and then we saw Pauline's eyes . . ."

Loudness, however, is relative. Robert Ashley's *Wolfman* (1964), for amplified voice and tape, was generally quite loud in performance. As Pauline Oliveros put it, "All the wax in my ears melted." But *Wolfman* was not about loudness. It was partly about theatrical imagery in the persona of the performer as the Wolfman, a "sinister nightclub vocalist, spotlight and all." Most important, it was about the performer's control of sound by manipulating his/her vocal cavity in pitch, loudness, vowel (tongue placement), and closure (jaw and lip positions). Ashley explains:

> The technical notion of *Wolfman* is that you fill the room with the sound of the resonant relationship between the room and the amplification system. You can adjust and modulate that sound by putting your mouth right next to the microphone. Everybody thinks you yell, but you don't yell at all. You make the softest sounds you can, and by doing manipulations of your vocal cavity you can seem to move the sound around the room. Nowadays, using the very best amplifiers and the very best equalizers, one could do a quiet *Wolfman*. The essence of the piece is to find beautiful sounds out of the relationship between the two systems, the vocal system and the resonance system. It's as simple as that.

In David Behrman's *Players with Circuits* (1967), sounds produced by any combination of electronic guitar, zither, or piano are processed by performers working with electronics. The sounds produced by the instrumental players are coordinated with the processing done by the electronics players such that twenty-six sounds are made by the instrumental ensemble and processed in the course of a performance. In the mid-1960s in general, the music was disciplined but the atmosphere of the concerts was informal. As Will Johnson described one performance of Behrman's work, "The performer no longer controls the sound world, he only initiates it, leaving the work, as it were, to the machines . . . this fact was made all the more obvious by Gordon Mumma, the pianist, who took advantage of the longer pauses in his part to smoke his pipe . . ."

And think, doubtless, about other unusual and technically sophisticated ideas. Mumma, French horn player as well as pianist, designed his own electronic system for *Hornpipe* (1967), in which an electronic box, attached to his belt, analyzed and responded through loudspeakers to the resonances of the performance space. He describes it:

> A musical instrument includes not only the ensemble of performer and instrument, but all of the space in which one performs. I speculated that I could design electronic circuits to extend that process . . . Over several

Gordon Mumma performing Hornpipe at the Metropolitan Museum of Art, New York City, in 1972. Photo by Jumay Chu. Courtesy Gordon Mumma.

years I developed resonant electronic circuits that would change according to the sounds I played and how the space responded to those sounds. The circuits "heard" the space by means of microphones. All of the circuitry, which included eight variable-resonance, gated amplifiers, was in a small metal box that I wore on my belt. Extending to this box was a long umbilical cable that connected the output of the circuits to an amplification system, with loudspeakers, for the performance space . . .

At the start of *Hornpipe*, the repertory of sounds was entirely from the horn (sometimes using a conventional conical mouthpiece, sometimes using double reeds). During this introductory section of the piece, the electronic circuits accumulated information about the acoustical responses of the space, gradually making a resonance "map" . . . At the entrance of the electronic sounds, *Hornpipe* changed from what seemed to be a solo piece. It became an ensemble, a duo, between horn and electronic responses. Eventually one would perceive the ensemble as being a responsive quartet between the performer, horn, electronic circuitry, and performance space . . .

The concluding section of *Hornpipe* was challenging for the performer. I had to complicate the task of the electronic mapping circuits until they could no longer respond with a coherent, audible map . . . Eventually the electronic circuitry ceased to respond, the loudspeakers became silent, and *Hornpipe* reached a conclusion.

•

Alvin Lucier developed more than an incredible piece, he developed a strikingly new concept for music. In *Music for Solo Performer* (1965), the sound of a performer's alpha brain waves were transmitted via amplifiers and loudspeakers to resonate percussion instruments placed around the concert hall. Gordon Mumma describes a performance:

> The soloist seats himself comfortably near the differential amplifier, and the assistant begins the procedure of applying the electrodes to the soloist's head. This operation involves cleaning the scalp with alcohol, applying special conducting electrode paste and gauze pads to secure the electrodes, measuring the electrical resistance between the electrodes (which should be below 10,000 ohms), and adjusting the gain and DC balance of the differential amplifier. The procedure takes several minutes to complete, generally a time of remarkable effect upon the audience . . . the situation is both ambiguous and dynamic. This period of time, before the first tapped brain-waves are directed to their resonant instruments, is really quite mysterious. After the sounds have begun, one comes to recognize the coincidence of the soloist opening his eyes with the stopping of the alpha-articulated sounds . . .

Mystery is not uncommon in performances of electronic works, especially when the musical meaning of a performer's actions is not evident to an audience. But Lucier's piece was the first to use electroencephalic signals, and it was

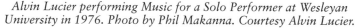

Alvin Lucier performing Music for a Solo Performer at Wesleyan University in 1976. Photo by Phil Makanna. Courtesy Alvin Lucier.

so unusual, so outside of any normal musical context, that it poses another question: How did he think of it? He tells the story:

> I had made the acquaintance of Edmond Dewan, a very imaginative physicist who was on the faculty at Brandeis but who was then working for the Air Force doing experiments with brain waves. They thought that certain pilots who were prone to epilepsy were blacking out when the speed of the spinning propellers got to a crucial point . . . When the sunlight would shine through the spinning props, it would lock onto something visual in the brain of the pilot . . .
>
> Dewan described to me this phenomenon that had to do with visualization, that by putting yourself in a non-visual state . . . you could release the potential of the alpha that is in your head. It's a very small amount, but it would become perceptible, at least to an amplifier . . . Alpha itself is below audibility; it's too low to hear as pitch, but that high energy, those bursts of alpha, would come bumping through the loudspeakers, making the grille cloth on the speakers bump, and I got the idea of using that energy to couple the loudspeakers to instruments. I used gongs, tympani, bass drums . . .
>
> Most people thought the material was too simple . . . but I finally did what I thought was the most honest thing. I tried to be very accurate about what the piece really meant: one person, alone, sitting very, very quietly, releasing a flood of energy which permeates the concert space. And to me, that was a beautiful idea . . .

Lucier often uses sound as part of the performance process. As he puts it, "Most of the time my sounds do some kind of work." In *Music for a Solo Performer*, for example, amplified brain wave sounds were used to resonate percussion instruments placed around the hall. In *The Queen of the South* (1972), a granular substance, such as sand or coffee, is spread on a flat surface; sine waves are then played through that surface, causing it to vibrate; and shapes called *Chladni figures*, which reflect graphically the shapes of the vibrations, appear in the grains. In *Music for Pure Waves, Bass Drums and Acoustic Pendulums* (1980), sine waves vibrate drumheads which in turn cause ping-pong balls to move. It is the way that he uses sound that is the substance of many of his compositions. Lucier continues:

> I use technology for acoustical testing a lot of the time, in much the same way an engineer might. I scan a frequency range with an oscillator, for example, and interface it with some other system, like bass drums, to see what the result is. I use the idea of a task, or a test, in place of structure. And I drive the system in such a way that the result is both unexpected and clear. I've always been interested in cause and effect when the effects are very surprising.

His logical yet surprising effects, indeed, often seem magical. In *Crossings* (1982), for example, the frequency of a sine wave is swept slowly through the ranges of orchestral instruments while the instruments play sustained notes. As the frequency of the sine wave gets closer to and coincides with the frequencies of the instruments, audible *beating* (pulsing changes in loudness) is heard. Lucier also used this idea in pieces for chorus, baritone, soprano, clarinet, accordion, and other instruments. Referring to *Music for Piano with Slow Sweep Pure Wave Oscillators* (1992), he explains:

> I often draw a geometric form such as a diamond and I program the oscillators to sweep in that shape. Starting at the unison, one channel rises as the other channel descends and back again, so they're drawing a diamond shape. And as they draw that object, the instrument, in this case a piano, plays single notes and intervals against the pitches which cause audible beating. And since the waves are sweeping, the beating speeds up and slows down. The result isn't a linear result, it's a complex one.

It's also a subtle result. And to make it clear, as he said, "I've got to reduce the music language to keep the emphasis on the exploration of the acoustics." Occasionally he uses a sophisticated device, as in *Clocker* (1978) where he calls for a digital delay. Occasionally he uses a special device, as in *Bird and Person Dyning* (1975) where he uses an electronic birdcall. He does not use synthesizers: "They just don't appeal to me." He does use oscillators, microphones, and loudspeakers. And he reflects, "It's a simple use of technology, revealing things."

•

In 1952, Merce Cunningham used *Symphonie pour un Homme Seul* as music for his dances *Collage I and II*. It was the first time he had used electronic music. In 1953, David Tudor became one of the Merce Cunningham Dance Company's core musicians. And from the beginning, Tudor built his own electronics. Why? He answers, "Flexibility, portability, and cost, but it was also because I could get the sound I wanted to hear." Tudor's sounds, indeed, were strikingly original.

His approaches to performance were also strikingly original. For *Rainforest*, for example, commissioned by Cunningham in 1958, he attached contact loudspeakers to eight small sculptures and played electronic sounds through the loudspeakers to cause the sculptures to vibrate at their resonant frequencies. Two subsequent versions used Cage's speech and music as sound material. And a fourth version, *Rainforest IV*, called for any objects, any number of objects, and any sounds, with contact microphones (in addition to the contact loudspeakers) attached to the objects to amplify their vibrations. As Tudor explains, "The microphones are releasing the sound of the objects—you put the sound through a physical material, so that the physical material trans-

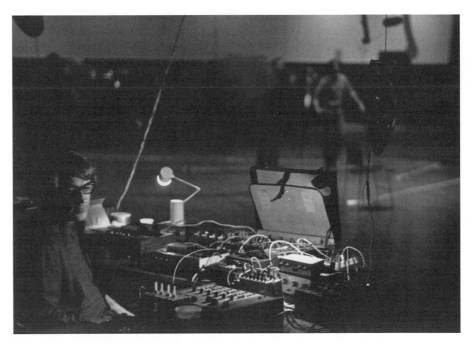

David Tudor with the Merce Cunningham Dance Company in the late 1970s.
Photo by Ben Guthrie. Courtesy The John Cage Trust.

forms the original source which is fed into it, and if you can manage to amplify that sound with a microphone, you release the harmonic content which the
material gives to it." There exists neither written score nor performance directions for *Rainforest IV*, but if there were performance directions, they might
read like this:

> Get some friends together. Each of you identify a suitable object, large or
> small, with an interesting visual appearance (a piece of metal from a junk-
> yard, for example, or something made of wood, or glass, or anything that
> you think will vibrate). Hang the object in the air or place it in such a way
> that it can vibrate. Attach a transducer (contact loudspeaker) to the
> object. Choose sounds, whether recorded on tape or generated from an
> electronic source, and play them "into" the object via the transducer so
> that the sounds vibrate the object at its resonant frequencies. Experiment
> with different sounds for each object. Attach a contact microphone to the
> object. Connect the output from the contact microphone to an amplifier
> and loudspeaker so that the sound picked up by the microphone can be
> clearly heard. In a performance, hang or place all of the chosen objects in
> a gallery or other performance space, arranged so that people can circu-
> late among them. A performance can be of any duration.

*Laetitia Sonami and friend at an installation of David Tudor's
Rainforest as produced at the Espace Pierre Cardin in Paris in 1976.
The artists involved were David Tudor, John Driscoll, Phil Edelstein,
Ralph Jones, Linda Fisher, Martin Kalve, Bill Viola, and Paul
DeMarinis. Photo by Sharon Jones. Courtesy Ralph Jones.*

At the Once Festival in 1965, Tudor had played bandoneon (an
Argentinean accordion-like instrument) in a performance of Mauricio Kagel's
Pandora's Box, and he had invited Mumma to compose a bandoneon piece for
him. Mumma's idea had been to design circuits that would extend the sound
and articulative possibilities of the bandoneon. In general, Mumma was in
complete accord with Tudor on building and experimenting with electronics.
As Mumma put it, "Electronic resources let one explore . . ." He describes the
unfolding of events:

A few months later, in spring 1966, John [Cage] called and asked if I
would be interested in joining the Merce Cunningham Dance Company
for a European tour in summer 1966. I said yes, not really knowing what
I was getting into. Within a few weeks, Merce called and asked if I'd compose a piece for the company. He had heard that I was doing a piece for
David Tudor, and invited that as a possibility. I asked Merce, "When
would you like this?" He said, "Well, we're going to do it on the forth-
coming European tour." I swallowed hard. I wasn't near done. Merce told
me the name of the dance was *Place* and I told him the name of the music
was *Mesa*. I asked him how many dancers there were and how long it
would be. He said there were eight dancers and about twenty minutes. I
asked if there was anything else I needed to know. And he said, "We're

going to perform it at Saint Paul de Vence. You'll like it there. It's very beautiful."

About two weeks before the tour was to begin, I went to Stony Point to work with David, carrying my substantially finished *Mesa* circuitry so that we could rehearse the piece with the bandoneon. I also helped David with technical things for the tour. He oversaw the musical technology for the Cunningham Dance Company. We put *Mesa* together and it worked. David played the bandoneon. I played the circuitry.

Meanwhile, in 1967, Cunningham commissioned David Behrman to compose music for *Walkaround Time*, a repertory dance piece based on Marcel Duchamp's *Large Glass*. Behrman used photocell mixers and recordings of himself walking around Niagra Falls on an icy day, of driving his Volkswagen Beetle, and of all the women in the Cunningham Company reading texts of Marcel Duchamp which described *Large Glass*. The premiere was in Buffalo in March 1968. As Behrman recalls, "Duchamp came up and took a bow onstage, and since I was the young composer who had been commissioned to do the piece, I was up there—it was a very exciting thing . . ." In March 1970, he began to tour with the Cunningham Company. And like Tudor and Mumma, he built his own electronics. Why? He tells us:

> It was Gordon Mumma who pushed me over the edge. We met through the Once Group in Ann Arbor, maybe 1963 or 1964, and Gordon wrote me a series of letters explaining how to build circuits from scratch. A letter would arrive explaining how to build a ring modulator, the cheapest possible, the mother of all ring modulators. It was in a little aluminum box and it cost $10, instead of $300 for a commercial ring modulator, and it wasn't as heavy.
>
> For touring, I needed my synthesizers to weigh only eight pounds, so they would fit into a suitcase. And it was fun to build things, and you could change them, you could do strange things with them. And there was a tradition that came from Tudor and Mumma to build your own electronic music devices. And one could say that there's an American tradition that goes back to Harry Partch about building your own instrument.

●

The world of electronic music was relatively small and closely knit in the 1960s, and people occasionally assembled and reassembled into groups to do particular things. In 1966, for example, David Behrman, Gordon Mumma, Robert Ashley, and Alvin Lucier formed—well, sort of formed—a group, at first calling it the Sonic Arts Group and then the Sonic Arts Union. Ashley tells it:

> Alvin Lucier had a concert at Brandeis University where Gordon Mumma and David Behrman and I came, and afterwards we were having a couple

of drinks, and Alvin said, "That was a successful concert. We should do this someplace else." So we started doing it someplace else . . . Basically, we'd each just play a piece in a concert, and the other guys would help you with your piece if you needed somebody to do something . . .

Ashley's pieces included, for example, *Wolfman, The Entrance, Frogs, Purposeful Lady Slow Afternoon, Fancy Free*, and *Orange Dessert*. Behrman's pieces included *Runthrough, Wavetrain, A New Team Takes Over, Islands in the River of Experience* (with Katharine Morton), and *Sinescreen*. Lucier's pieces included *Music for Solo Performer, Vespers, "I Am Sitting in a Room," The Duke of York*, and *Bird and Person Dyning*. Mumma's pieces included *Mesa, Hornpipe, I Saw Her Dance* (with Barbara Lloyd, a tape by Steven Drews, and slides by Mary Lucier), *Ambivex*, and *Passenger Pigeon*. Mumma reflects, "The variety of those pieces—I still can't believe how different they were . . ." Lucier recalls the 1969 European tour:

We went everywhere, from Rome to Oslo, Helsinki, Switzerland, London. We did almost sixteen performances in thirty days. We'd arrive at a city, maybe the day before a concert, or the same day, and often we didn't know the hotel we were going to stay at. We'd go to the concert hall to meet the engineers so that Bob and David could discuss the technical aspects of the concert. Then we'd work like dogs to set up. And then we'd do the concert. It was exhausting. It was also exciting. We did each other's pieces. We did David's *Runthrough*. Once when he wasn't there, we did Gordon's *Mesa* with mouth organs. We did Bob's *Wolfman* and *Fancy Free*, where each player had an attache case and a cassette machine. We did his *Frogs*, where he had these lights and devices that would sense proximity. Gordon had this wonderful sophisticated electronic circuitry for *Hornpipe*. I think we did such very different work that sometimes it just bypassed people's perceptions. Sometimes the audiences just couldn't process it as music.

By 1976, the people involved had reassembled in different formations. Ashley had become director of the newly named Center for Contemporary Music at Mills College. Lucier had joined the faculty at Wesleyan University. Mumma had joined the faculty at the University of California. And Behrman joined Ashley at Mills College to begin a new and influential line of work with personal computers. Ashley reflects on the last years:

Then Sonic Arts Union went through a kind of crisis of what the music meant to the audience. It was like somebody shut the door, it was like running into furniture in the dark. I don't know if you remember, but you could go to a concert and afterwards somebody would come up to you and say, "I hate your music." You know, I had that happen to me. We went back to Ann Arbor and gave a concert in 1971, and afterwards there was a big party, a lot of people, everybody drinking and having a good time, and I notice this skinny little kid, he's probably a professor of music now. I notice this skinny little kid standing there and I knew he had something to say. He came up to me and said, "You know, I have to tell you that I hate your music." So I said, "You came all the way to this party, you wasted all of that precious time when you could have gone home and written music? What are you doing here at this party? You're wasting your time, don't you understand?" He went home. I had it happen two or three times. I had it happen in Scotland. We gave an amazing concert in Scotland, and I mean amazing in the sense that the concert was so beautiful. And after, a kid came up to me and said, "You know, I gotta tell you I hate your music." I guess, by and large, people liked it. But there was this terrible thing that happened inside all of us around that time. It was really serious, a transformation of ourselves into another set of values to become "practical."

•

Although group improvisation had been one of the activities at the San Francisco Tape Music Center, it had not been thematic to the center's philosophy. Subotnick, Sender, Oliveros, Martin, and company in San Francisco, and for that matter, also the people in the Once Group in Ann Arbor and in the Sonic Arts Union, had come together as groups to pool resources, focus public attention, and cooperate in joint projects. But basically they worked as individuals within the collaborative environments they had formed.

The idea of group improvisation, however, was thematic for Musica Elettronica Viva, or MEV as it came to be called. MEV had gradually formed during the summer and fall of 1966 following a concert of new experimental music organized by Frederic Rzewski and Alvin Curran in the crypt of St. Paul's American Church in Rome. Subsequently, a group of composers and performers living in Rome at the time—among them Richard Teitelbaum, Allan Bryant, Jon Phetteplace, Carol Plantamura, and Ivan Vandor, with Steve Lacy, Jeffrey Levine, and others arriving a few years later—joined Rzewski and Curran with the idea of producing concerts and forming a cooperative electronic music studio. In the fall of 1966, they organized the Avanguardia Musicale festival in Rome. Although Teitelbaum eventually played a Moog synthesizer, the group by and large developed its own equipment with the conviction, according to Rzewski, that "original results could be more easily obtained by using cheap 'home-made' circuitry rather than by following the orthodox procedures observed in the larger studios." Rzewski personally designed and built a photocell-controlled device which functioned as both mixer and sound distributor.

MEV's ideas of group improvisation evolved from *Spacecraft* in 1967—in Rzewski's words, "Form for a music that has no form. We begin with a group of performers and an idea . . . Each performer occupies a part of the space . . . creating a situation in which lines of force are set up between himself and other persons . . ."—to *Zuppa* in 1968 and *Sound Pool* in 1969, which involved audience participation. Frederic Rzewski and Richard Teitelbaum tell the story:

> *FR:* MEV was just a bunch of friends, a more or less chance happening.
>
> *RT:* We were all ivy league dropouts who were denied access to studios. We just decided we'd buy or build our own equipment and make electronic music. And Cage was a big influence too, live electronics and the idea of making music with whatever you can.
>
> *FR:* In the beginning, we didn't do anything collective. We did music by Cage, Behrman, others. We did a lot of concerts in Rome in 1967, and then in the fall of 1967 we started touring. From 1966 to 1969, we did about 200 concerts.
>
> *RT:* I was away for about a year in New York and came back to Europe in September 1967, and we did concerts in Cologne, Munich, a tour in Holland, and Berlin, and Paris in the American Center . . . The year I was in New York, David Behrman taught me to solder.
>
> *FR:* By the grace of God, we didn't get electrocuted.
>
> *RT:* We were already improvising by the fall of 1967. That was the time of *Spacecraft*. The instrumentation included everything from a glass plate, springs, and a large Italian olive oil can, all amplified with contact mikes, to saxophone, trumpet, and synthesizers. The music was very eclectic, open and wild, tending to oscillate between sections of chaotic violence and peaceful calmness. But by 1968, we started feeling, especially Frederic, that what we were doing was too hermetic, too elitist. We were playing in these students' venues, and the radical students would come up and confront us with the elitist character of our work, so we just decided that everybody should play.
>
> *FR:* In early 1968, we did *Zuppa* at the Attico Gallery, with Steve Lacy, Michelangelo Pistoletto, and others. The original idea was "free soup." The idea was that anybody could play, free participation. In February or March 1968, we did a collaboration with members of the Living Theatre and Jean-Jacques Lebel in Parma at an International Theatre Festival, at the Opera House. Jean-Jacques made a speech. I don't remember what he said, but this was the time that the students in Paris were raising hell. They turned off the power. That's a fundamental weakness of electronic music. They can always turn off the power if they don't like you.
>
> *RT:* We had large oil drums on stage, so Jean-Jacques made this speech about coming up and joining us, and it got pretty chaotic. Several hundred college kids came up and started banging on the oil drums, and they turned the power off. Jean-Jacques said, "Alright, everybody let's go out into the square," and that night the students occupied the university.

FR: In the summer of 1968, we rented a studio in the Trastevere section of Rome, in the via Pietro Peretti. We put up posters in the neighborhood. The idea was that we'd play every night. Anybody could come. We had our collection box, but we were lucky if there was enough in it for a pizza.

RT: That was *Sound Pool.* There was a text that was handed out . . .

FR: I wrote a brief text, like program notes, to tell people . . . We said to everyone, "bring a sound." But we were the people with the electronics. The dice were loaded on our side.

RT: Not always. In Oslo, these Viking guys brought a lot of drums and nearly wiped us out.

•

The festivals of the 1960s were the summaries of the era. 9 Evenings: Theatre and Engineering, the first and largest of the festivals, was presented by EAT (Experiments in Art and Technology) in October 1966 at the Twenty-fifth Street Armory in New York City. As Billy Klüver, one of technology and art's principal evangelists at the time and one of EAT's principal organizers, wrote: "This was to be the first major art and technology collaborative event; and it had to take place on a much larger scale than before: by that we meant it had to be widely publicized and that thousands of people had to attend."

The programs included works by John Cage, Lucinda Childs, Oyvind Fahlström, Alex Hay, Deborah Hay, Steve Paxton, Yvonne Rainer, Robert Rauschenberg, Robert Whitman, and David Tudor. And the works included music, dance, and performance art. Cage performed *Variations VII*, picking up sounds from radio, telephone, microphones, "only those sounds which are in the air at the moment of performance . . ." Robert Rauschenberg played tennis with Steve Paxton using wired rackets. Deborah Hay had dancers moving throughout the space on remote-controlled platforms. And David Tudor, in *Bandoneon ! (Bandoneon Factorial)*, controlled the entire sound and light environment of the armory. It was described in the program notes as "a combine incorporating programmed audio circuits, moving loudspeakers, tv images and lighting, instrumentally excited." Tudor, sitting on a sixteen by twenty-four foot platform surrounded by electronic equipment, played his bandoneon, and the sounds of the bandoneon were processed electronically, switched between twelve loudspeakers placed around the space, used to vibrate five sculptures on moving carts, and used to control video images and lights.

Bandoneon ! (Bandoneon Factorial) worked as follows. Contact microphones were placed inside the bandoneon. The sounds from the contact microphones were transformed by a sound-processing system consisting of filters, frequency shifters, and other devices. The sounds were also fed into the *Vochrome*, a control device designed and built for the occasion by Robert Kieronski, which consisted of a set of twelve harmonium reeds vibrated by the signals from the contact microphone, and a twelve-pole double-throw relay.

The relay was mechanically operated by the vibrating harmonium reeds in switching the sound at audio rates between the loudspeakers. As Tudor sums it up, "So according to the pitches that I played, the sounds changed." In other words, the sounds that Tudor played were transformed, but they also controlled how they were transformed and routed to the different loudspeakers.

In addition, Fred Waldhauer contributed a device that he called the Proportional Control, which controlled the loudness of the sound in the loudspeakers and the intensity of eight lights on the performance platform. As Tudor recalls, "I had established discrete switching between loudspeakers through the Vochrome device, and I also wanted smooth control." Tudor also used a switch on the bandoneon to suddenly stop the electronic sound, thereby using the armory's six-second reverberation time as a musical element. He said, "The silence was deafening, because the sound in the armory was extraordinary, so reverberant." Further, the sound from the bandoneon was also sent directly to Lowell Cross' *TV Oscilloscope*, which displayed visual patterns along with the music. Tudor continues:

> And there's more. I had made a number of large sculptures in the manner of *Rainforest*. I think there were five, because Deborah Hay had a piece with dancers on platforms that could be sent around the space, and she wanted to have music, and I agreed to do the music if I could use the platforms for my sculptures. So the sounds from the bandoneon also vibrated the sculptures. My idea was that they would be sent around the room, that their sound would circulate. The audience was on three sides, so they would come close to the loudspeakers. And for that, I had to have five operators, seated on chairs, sending the platforms around. They were really radio-controlled carts . . .

In summary, as Tudor puts it, "There was a lot to take care of during the performance." Indeed, there was a lot to take care of in the entire festival. Billy Klüver, at the time, was a scientist at Bell Telephone Laboratories in Murray Hill, New Jersey, and it was much to the credit of Bell Labs in general, and John Pierce in particular, that Klüver was so well supported in producing the 9 Evenings. Pierce recalls:

> I was Klüver's boss. He got my permission to persuade technical assistants to work on the 9 Evenings on their own time. But then, as the 9 Evenings approached, things weren't getting done, and I arranged for them to work on Bell Labs' time. Some of the people who lost their technical assistants for a few weeks were a little miffed, but no one raised a protest. Well, I liked Billy Klüver and thought there was something in what he was doing.

9 Evenings was the biggest, but there were also other festivals. There was, for example, the First Festival of Live Electronic Music, consisting of five con-

certs presented at Mills College and at the University of California at Davis on December 4, 5, and 6, 1967. The program included some of the Sonic Arts Union and Once Group pieces, among them Robert Ashley's *Wolfman* and *Frogs*, Alvin Lucier's *Whistlers*, Gordon Mumma's *Mesa*, and David Behrman's *Runthrough*. It also included Larry Austin's *Accidents* (1967), composed for David Tudor; Toshi Ichiyanagi's *Activities* (1967), where several electronic, acoustic, and prerecorded sound sources were played simultaneously in the spirit of John Cage; Anthony Gnazzo's *Long Distances* (1966), where sounds were communicated from performers in the hall to performers outside and vice versa; and John Mizelle's *Light Sculpture* and *Radial Energy I* (1967), with a mixture of colors from spotlights and a sound-emitting sculpture activated by the lights.

There was the Cross Talk Intermedia Festival, organized by Roger Reynolds, in February 1969 in Tokyo. The programs included familiar composers and pieces, such as Joji Yuasa's *Icon*, Robert Ashley's *That Morning Thing*, Toru Takemitsu's music for *Kwaidan*, and Salvatore Martirano's *L's G.A.* It also included familiar composers and new pieces, such as Gordon Mumma's *Beam* (1969), for violin, viola, bow-arm coordinate-sleeves, cyber-sonic control console, computer, and nine films by Stan VanDerBeek; Toshi Ichiyanagi's *Tokyo 1969*, for computer-generated sound, rock band, pop music, and electronics, composed at the NHK studio; Alvin Lucier's *Sound Environment Mixtures* (1969), with taped sounds and a film by Takahiko Iimura; and John Cage's *Music for Carillon No. 5* (1967), for two prepared pianos and electronics. It also included David Rosenboom's *"She Loves Me, She Loves Me Not . . ."* (1969), for two musician-actors, two percussionists, witch doctor, visuals, electronics, and fiber optics; and pieces by Takehisa Kosugi, Shuko Mizuno, and Mieko Shiomi, for five musicians, three pianists, six stereo tape decks, CDS relays, transistor radios, RF transmitters, and a fourteen-channel audio system; Yori-Aki Matsudaira's *Electronic Music Assemblage Plus Assemblage for Voice* (1969), for two-channel tape done at the NHK studio, five voices, and ring modulator; and Roger Reynolds' *Ping* (1968), based on a text by Samuel Beckett, for various instruments, electronics including contact microphones and ring modulator, film, other visuals, tape, photocell sound distributor, and fourteen-channel audio system.

Many such festivals were organized during the 1960s. They were also *of* the 1960s. They represented an exuberance that stemmed from what musicians and artists saw as the new musical, artistic, and social opportunities presented by the emergence of electronic technology. They were extravagant, imaginative, expansive, and expensive. They were statements that musicians and artists can lead the way in demonstrating the most creative human uses of technology. They said, in a collective voice, "Technology has liberated us from history. We can remake the world!"

• • •

CHAPTER FIVE

COMPUTER MUSIC

In 1957, while Varèse was composing *Poème Electronique* and while a second group of tape studios was beginning to appear, the first computer-generated sounds were heard at Bell Telephone Laboratories (or Bell Labs, as it was called) in Murray Hill, New Jersey. Max Mathews had joined the acoustic research department at Bell Labs to develop computer equipment to study telephones. With the aim of using listening tests to judge the quality of the sound, he had made a converter to put sound into a computer and a converter to get it back out again, which according to Mathews, "turned out to be a very successful way to do research in telephony." Mathews went further:

> It was immediately apparent that once we could get sound out of a computer, we could write programs to play music on the computer. That interested me a great deal. The computer was an unlimited instrument, and every sound that could be heard could be made this way. And the other thing was that I liked music. I had played the violin for a long time . . .

John Pierce, also at Bell Labs, lent crucial support to the music project. As he explains, "I was executive director of the communication sciences division when Max used the computer to produce musical sounds—I was fascinated."

In 1957, Mathews finished Music I, his first sound-generating computer program. The first music produced with Music I was a seventeen-second composition by Newman Guttman, a linguist and acoustician at Bell Labs. The composition, called *In the Silver Scale*, used a scale slightly different from the diatonic scale so as to have better controlled chords. Mathews said, "It was terrible." Pierce said, "To me, it sounded awful." But, as Mathews continues, "It was the first." In fact, the chords were never heard because Music I was a single-voiced program. As Mathews recalls, "The program was also terrible—it had only one voice, one waveform, a triangular wave, no attack, no decay, and the only expressive parameters you could control were pitch, loudness, and duration."

Music I was the first in a series of sound-generating computer programs collectively referred to as the Music-N series. Music II followed in 1958, with improvements of four voices and arbitrary waveforms, and it introduced the concept of the wavetable oscillator. Music III, which followed in 1960, was, as Mathews puts it, "when things really came together." Music III introduced the concept of modularity, or unit generators, so that one could put together "orchestras" of "instruments." It introduced additional possibilities for shaping sounds and it introduced the concept of a "score," where notes could be listed in the order of their starting times and each note was associated with a timbre, loudness, pitch, and duration.

Mathews and Pierce, both scientists, had early on felt the need to have musicians involved, and they had begun an outreach effort, reading papers at conferences and publishing articles in a variety of magazines. In New York, at an Audio Engineering Society conference in 1959, they had met Milton Babbitt, Vladimir Ussachevsky, Otto Luening, and eventually, Edgard Varèse. In 1960, the publications department at Bell Labs produced a recording called *Music from Mathematics*, a copy of which was sent to Leonard Bernstein, whose secretary acknowledged its receipt with thanks. A copy was sent also to Aaron Copland, who replied, "The implications are dizzying and, if I were twenty, I would be really concerned at the variety of possibilities suggested." David Lewin, Arthur Roberts, and Gerald Strang, all of them older than twenty, did become interested in working with computers. Strang posed an interesting question: "How can we introduce appropriate imperfection in computer music?"

In 1961, Pierce heard that the Illiac computer at the University of Illinois was being used to compose music. But because he didn't know the names of the researchers, he wrote a letter directly to the computer: "Dear computer, I understand that someone has worked with you in composing music . . ." And he received a reply from Lejaren Hiller, inviting him to visit. During the visit, Pierce met Hiller and Leonard Isaacson. He also met Harry Partch, and he observed, with an interesting shift in perspective, that Partch "had built a number of strange musical instruments." He also met James Tenney, whom he hired, "allegedly to do psychoacoustics, but really to do computer music."

Tenney began to work at Bell Labs in 1961 and stayed to 1964. His first composition was *Analog #1: Noise Study*, completed in December 1961. The idea for it was suggested by his commute from New York City via the Holland Tunnel, in his words, "an exhausting, nerve-racking experience, fast, furious, and 'noisy' . . ." Tenney continues:

> One day I found myself *listening* to these sounds . . . When I did, finally, begin to listen, the sounds of the traffic became so interesting that the trip was no longer a thing to be dreaded and gotten through as quickly as possible. From then on, I actually looked forward to it as a source of new perceptual insights. Gradually, I learned to hear these sounds more acutely, to follow the evolution of single elements within the total sonorous 'mass', to feel, kinesthetically, the characteristic rhythmic articulations of the various elements in combination . . .

The composing of the piece was done in stages. First, Tenney created a computer instrument that could generate controllable noise, and then he designed an over-all shape for the composition. Finally, determining the details by a random number method, he realized the sounds. He then began a series of experiments and tests that culminated in PLF 2, a composing program which he used to compose *Four Stochastic Studies* (1962). Other compositions followed, among them *Dialogue* (1963), *Ergodos* I (1963), *Phases* (1963), and *Ergodos II* (1964). By the time Tenney left Bell Labs in March 1964, his work had included six tape compositions, software that had used the computer to make compositional decisions in addition to making sounds, a growing understanding of timbre, and in his words, "a curious history of renunciations of one after another of the traditional attitudes about music . . ."

Meanwhile, in 1962, Mathews and Joan Miller finished Music IV. Music III and Music IV were written for an IBM 7094, one of the first computers to use transistors. Since Princeton University, located conveniently nearby, had also purchased an IBM 7094, Hubert Howe, Godfrey Winham, and Jim Randall at Princeton could run Music IV without difficulty. They also made some improvements, particularly in the program's user-friendliness, and called their new version Music IV-B.

•

In November 1963, an article by Mathews called "The Digital Computer as a Musical Instrument" was published in *Science*. It said, in part:

> There are no theoretical limitations to the performance of the computer as a source of musical sounds, in contrast to the performance of ordinary instruments. At present, the range of computer music is limited principally by cost and by our knowledge of psychoacoustics . . . Computer music appears to be very promising technically. However, the method will become significant only if it is used by serious composers. At present, our goal is to interest and educate such musicians in its use . . .

Jean-Claude Risset was at the time doing graduate work in physics at the Ecole Normale Supérieure in Paris. His professor, Pierre Grivet, read Mathews' *Science* article and passed it on to Risset. A composer at heart, Risset was interested. He recalls: "I decided I wanted to do music and stop all that nonmusical science." With Grivet's help and Pierce's support, Risset received a grant from a French research agency to base his thesis on research at Bell Labs. Risset arrived at Bell Labs in 1964 as research composer in residence, succeeding James Tenney in that position. Risset describes it:

> I was amazed when I got there. It was a fantastic atmosphere. There was an incredible group of researchers, in mathematics, computer science, psychology, acoustics, communications, biology, and they were mixed and woven together. Even the offices were intertwined. There was a lot of openness and generosity and less arrogance and sense of territory than in Europe. A multidisciplinary approach is more difficult in France because you're supposed to belong here or there but not here *and* there. If only for that reason, computer music was more likely to happen in the United States than in France. There was also no pressure of any immediate application. Anything that could be useful in the long term was fostered.

The first professional issue was the specific direction of his work. As Risset recalls, "Max had several ideas for research, including computer composition, but I elected to focus on timbre." He began to study the nature of trumpet tone quality because, as he explains, "The palette of computer sound, potentially boundless, was in fact quite restricted, and one did not know how to generate certain sounds . . ." He continues:

> I recorded trumpet samples, analyzed them with the sound spectrograph and with the computer . . . But the descriptions of the tones were very complex, and varied from one tone to another. I had to try to reduce this information to the essential, that is, to those features that are the most significant to the ear. I checked by synthesis the aural relevance of several aspects, and I found that the most salient characteristic of brass tones was the fact that the spectrum varied with loudness, so as to increase the proportion of high-frequency energy when the loudness increases . . .

What was it like to work there? Risset describes it:

> I came in at about 10 A.M. and usually stayed till 6 or 7 in the evening, sometimes later, and I had lots of interaction with many different people. It was a very exhilarating period. Sometimes I discussed a problem with Max and he would reformulate it. John Pierce occasionally came by, amazingly because he was heading a big part of Bell Labs, but he would come to each researcher and have him explain what he was doing and ask insightful questions.

In 1965, Risset went back to France for military service. Also in 1965, IBM introduced its new Series 360 computers. These computers, based on integrated circuits, led to revised methods of programming based on more widely used languages. The Music-N programs finished prior to 1965 had been written in low-level, machine-specific assembly language and, consequently, could not be run on computers other than the computers on which they were written. After 1965, however, as the computer market opened up and greater numbers of different computers appeared, and as technical improvements occurred with increasing frequency, it become obvious that the Music-N programs could achieve widespread usability only if they were written in high-level, non-machine-specific languages. FORTRAN was one of the leading high-level languages of the mid-1960s, and it could run on virtually any computer. By 1967, Hubert Howe and Godfrey Winham at Princeton University had finished a FORTRAN version of Music IV-B called Music IV-BF.

Also in 1967, F. Richard Moore arrived at Bell Labs, Jean-Claude Risset returned from France, and Vladimir Ussachevsky was a visiting composer. And Mathews, Moore, Risset, and Joan Miller worked on Music V, which was finished in 1968. Music V was organized as a modular system of software-defined unit generators—for example OSC, a waveform generator; AD2, a two-input adder; and RAN, a random number generator—which could be linked together in various ways to make an *instrument*. One simple instrument, for example, might have been the outputs from OSC1 and OSC2 added together in an AD2. Instruments could vary widely in their complexity and operation and consist of any number of unit generators connected in any number of ways. The instruments played discrete sounds called *notes*, each note containing an instrument definition, a set of instructions for the instrument's unit generators, a starting time, and a duration. A complete listing of notes, with their instruments, their data, their starting times, and their durations, was called a *score*. Music V was a definitive statement of the Music-N series, and as such, it provided the basis for a wide range of similar programs written by many composers for a wide range of different computers. Written in FORTRAN, it was easily portable to other computers.

But the word "easily" should be understood relative to the technology of the 1960s. Computer programs were, at the time, disseminated via punched cards. As Moore recalls, "We used to send the Music V program out in two full boxes of punched cards, about 3,500 cards, and a letter saying, 'Good luck!'"

•

Musicians generally like to work intuitively, hearing their music as they perform, trying things out as they compose, occasionally singing a tune. Music V was not intuitive. It wasn't just that a composer's "notation" was in non-singable computer code, it was also that the program did not operate in *real time*. To operate in real time means that the composer hears the music while specifying it, as in playing a piano, for example, where you hear a sound when you press a key. Music V was a multipass program, which meant that a composer's input specifications were processed in successive stages of calculation, which in turn meant that a composer could wait a considerable amount of time before hearing sound. The sound imagined by a composer was in fact generated first by the main computer—which by the time of Music IV was an IBM 7094—as an accumulating and inaudible table of numbers, called *samples*, which were stored on magnetic computer tape. Then, in a separate step, those samples were converted to sound and stored on normal audio tape.

It was primarily F. Richard Moore's job to convert samples to sound, for which he used another computer, an IBM 1620. Moore describes the situation:

> People from Princeton used to drive their tapes up and leave them with us. Then we'd convert them on the 1620 and they'd show up two weeks later and hear their music. A two week turnaround was pretty good, sort of like sending your photos out for developing. Since I was the one who did the conversion, I could get my tapes converted a little faster. I might be able to get up to two runs, which is to say two 30-second segments, a day. Typically, the segments weren't very long, because you had to be sure that they worked.

Barry Vercoe began to work regularly at Princeton in 1968. He recalls, "We were continually driving up to Bell Labs to get bits of tapes converted to sound—it was the only working converter and it was a long trek, sometimes in the middle of heavy traffic." As Jonathan Harvey remembers, "At Princeton, way back in 1969, one had to go to Bell Labs to convert the sound, and drive through this dreadful traffic, and you could only play it when you got back to Princeton and think, 'My God, that's not what I wanted at all,' and then the whole process started again." In 1970, Charles Dodge was finishing his DMA at Columbia University, teaching at Princeton University, and converting his digital tapes at Bell Telephone Laboratories. As he said, "I drove something like 25,000 miles between Columbia, Princeton and Bell Labs." Moore continues:

> Operating under those conditions was incredibly difficult. A simple test could take weeks. Max was a great inspiration to everybody. He was unflappable in these incredibly difficult circumstances of working. He was like a sailor in mid-Atlantic who didn't know how far it was to the other side but knew what to keep doing to get us there.
>
> What kept me going was the puzzlement of why things didn't work. I think everybody who was doing it had a notion of what should work and we were all completely perplexed when it didn't. We thrived on frustration, and the difficulties that occurred were in themselves discoveries.

The early Music-N programs, to be sure, were developed in the spirit of research, learning, and breaking new ground, all of which generated its own excitement. At the same time, however, the composers who worked on them were also interested in the musical possibilities of computers, and these composers seem to have had a dedication sufficiently fanatic to see them through the technical problems. Many compositions were finished, among them, at Bell Labs, James Tenney's *Analog #1: Noise Study*, (1961), *Five Stochastic Studies* (1961), and *Dialogue* (1963); and Jean-Claude Risset's *Little Boy* (1968) and *Mutations* (1969). Jim Randall's *Mudgett: Monologues by a Mass Murderer* (1965) and Charles Dodge's *Changes* (1969) and *Earth's Magnetic Field* (1970) were composed at Princeton University.

Although Ercolino Ferretti at MIT composed *Pipe and Drum* (1963) and *Trio* (1965) with a computer, and although work was begun in various other locations, the first round of formative work was done primarily at and around Bell Labs. By the late 1960s, thanks largely to Max Mathews and his colleagues, the field of computer music was established and growing. Yet it had never been Mathews' or anyone else's job at Bell Labs to do computer music. As Mathews said, "Management tolerated music as part of research, but, on the whole, Bell Labs wanted to downplay it, at least in terms of its cost and whatever commercial possibilities it had, because they weren't supposed to be in that business."

How then could such a significant effort have taken place? The answer is twofold. First, John Pierce played an essential role. As he put it, "Bell Laboratories was in those days a benevolent autocracy—by and large, the management was convinced I was a good guy, so I could slip things in." Management was convinced that Pierce was a good guy surely because of his many significant technical contributions, among them his work on the ECHO and Telstar communications satellites and, as an additional detail, in 1948, his coining of the word *transistor*. (As he tells the story: "Walter Brattain stopped me in the hall and asked me what he should call it, and I thought about it and then suggested 'transistor,' thinking of 'trans-resistance.' And the name stuck.") And his enthusiasm went beyond "slipping things in" to being an active participant. Not only did he work with Mathews in many capacities, he composed many pieces, among them *Stochatta* (1959), *Variations in Timbre and Attack* (1961), *Sea Sounds* (1963), and *Eight-Tone Canon* (1966). As he put it, "I got on the bandwagon."

Second, everyone's enthusiasm led to extra evening hours spent at music. Mathews remembers: "I would typically spend the day doing whatever I had to do at Bell Labs, and about half the night I'd work on musical things—I lived very close to the labs so I could go home for supper and then go back." And Mathews also composed many pieces, among them *Numerology* (1960), *The Second Law* (1961), *Masquerades* (1963), and *International Lullaby* (1966). In 1961, he did the accompaniment and John Kelly and Carol Lochbaum did the vocal lines for a computer rendition of *Bicycle Built for Two* ("Daisy, Daisy, give me your answer true . . ."), which was the subject of an oblique reference in the film *2001*. At the end of the film, as the computer Hal dies and its childhood memories flash past, it remembers its origins in Mathews' work and, expiring, sings the song.

•

In November 1963, when Max Mathews' article was published in *Science*, John Chowning was a graduate student at Stanford University. As Chowning tells it:

> Max's article was passed on to me by a friend. I put it in my pocket and I guess it was a month or so later that I read it. I thought it sounded interesting. So I took a course in computer programming and arranged to meet Max during the summer of 1964. I went to Bell Labs. He explained some of the details of Music IV and gave me a box of cards and said, 'Good luck!'"

Chowning took the cards back to Stanford and, as he recalls, "there I was with this box of cards." He showed Mathews' article and the program to David Poole, a tuba player and student in the computer science department, and by early fall, Chowning and Poole had Music IV running on the computer science department's IBM 7094. Meanwhile, the Stanford artificial intelligence laboratory (or the AI Lab, as it was called) had a PDP-1, which was used by Chowning and Poole to convert the samples into sound. By the end of 1964, the music programs were running and Chowning had begun work, as an unfunded research project within the AI Lab, on the simulation of sounds traveling through space.

In 1966, the AI Lab, with Chowning and Poole, moved to new quarters at the DC Power Laboratory Building, a round wooden building on stilts, suggestive of a flying saucer that had landed in the middle of a large meadow. The meadow was located in the hills above Stanford, about twenty minutes' drive from the main campus. In making the move, the AI Lab abandoned the PDP-1 and acquired a PDP-6, causing a temporary disruption in the music routines. Rising to the occasion, Chowning and Poole wrote Music 10, which was a version of Music IV rewritten for the PDP-6, the predecessor of a soon-to-appear PDP-10. Chowning continued to work on the simulation of sounds traveling through space, and in the summer of 1966, he finished a program with which he could "draw" a single path through a virtual space and the program would figure out the energy distributions between four loudspeakers that would simulate the changes in a sound as it followed the specified path. He then began work on new techniques for sound synthesis. He tells it:

> The sounds we could make with a computer at that time were unbearably dull, not because we couldn't do better but we didn't know a lot. So in 1967, with ears starved for some sound that had the richness of the sounds we hear in nature, I was experimenting with extreme vibrato. I

realized that as I increased the rate and depth of a vibrato, I was no longer hearing it as a change in pitch, but rather as a change in timbre. And that as I changed the frequencies, the sounds would change. And that the sounds had interesting, evolving spectra.

I discussed what I had done with George Gucker, an engineer at the lab, and he explained that it was a form of frequency modulation. I asked him if it was indeed true that certain ratios of frequencies would produce certain kinds of spectra. So we looked at the FM equation and the theory confirmed that what my ear had told me was true.

In 1968, Chowning again visited Bell Labs, and Jean-Claude Risset showed Chowning what he had done in analyzing and simulating trumpet tones, pointing out an essential relationship between loudness and spectrum. Meanwhile, Chowning had joined the music faculty at Stanford University, and Leland Smith, also on the faculty, had developed SCORE, a powerful composing program to be used in conjunction with Music 10. In the summer of 1969 at Stanford University, Chowning and Smith organized the first summer workshop in computer music, taught by Chowning, Smith, Gucker, and, as a visiting professor, Max Mathews. Larry Austin, a participant in that workshop, describes it:

> We'd have at least four hours of classes each morning. There was a class in Music V, with Max Mathews dropping in to elaborate, and we had tutorials. The computer was a PDP-10. I worked at a DECwriter which functioned as a terminal. There was a demonstration program written by Leland Smith. You'd sign on and a menu was printed with a question mark. Then you chose your option—what kind of timbre it was, what pitch—by typing in a number. Then you'd be given another series of options for a sequence of pitches and durations, and you would then enter them one by one. So you'd enter a sequence—I think there was a way to review it in written form so you could correct anything you'd entered wrong—and then there was a Play command. But the Play command didn't mean you'd get the sound back right away. The program would go through the three passes of Music V and the music would be output to digital computer tape. Then you made an appointment to get your digital tape converted to audio tape. The sounds were converted on the main machine down on campus.

In 1971, Chowning resumed his work with frequency modulation (FM) as a synthesis technique and made *the* major breakthrough. He continues:

> I was trying to produce bell-like sounds. Then I remembered what Jean-Claude had said about the relationship between loudness and spectrum, and I did a little experiment. And in a half hour, I had produced some

striking brass-like tones. It was at that moment that I had the thought that someone ought to be interested in this. So I went to the office of technology licensing at Stanford and played some examples and explained that they were done with extreme economy, just two oscillators. We approached a lot of American companies, none of which were interested. Then the office of licensing contacted Yamaha, and Yamaha sent an engineer. I played some examples, and in ten minutes he understood. And in that same period, summer 1971, I went back to Bell Labs. I played the brass tones for Max and he got John Pierce, and John said, "Patent it."

Yamaha licensed Chowning's FM synthesis technique in 1974. The patent was issued in 1977. The striking commercial advantage of FM as a synthesis technique was its "extreme economy," as Chowning had explained in the office of technology licensing. What does that mean for composers? He answers: "It means that you get control over a very large timbral space with a very few knobs."

Meanwhile, Chowning went on sabbatical during the academic year 1972-1973 and wrote an important paper on FM synthesis which was published in the *Journal of the Audio Engineering Society*, September 1973. During the same period, a substantial research effort in psychoacoustics, analysis, digital recording, and the design of synthesis hardware—involving James A. Moorer, Loren Rush, and John Grey—was forming at Stanford. The first major manifestation of the growing research effort was in 1975, when Chowning, Moorer, Rush, and Grey submitted proposals to the National Endowment for the Arts and to the National Science Foundation. The primary goal was to commission the fabrication of a digital synthesizer designed by Peter Samson. As Chowning explains, "Pete had this design for the synthesizer which had been lurking around for years and advancing as the technology had advanced, and we had talked to him continually about the things we were interested in—FM, moving sources, and so on."

The grants were awarded. The Samson Box, as it came to be known, was duly ordered in 1975 and delivered in 1977 and it formed the basis for a variety of research and software projects by Gareth Loy, David Jaffe, Michael McNabb, Bill Shottstaedt, and many others. The Samson Box was programmed via the PDP-10, to which it was linked, and it functioned effectively as a realtime version of Music IV, with all of Music IV's inherent generality. It was used until 1989, at which point CCRMA closed down its PDP-10 facility. As Chowning said, "It was an amazing machine."

As another offshoot of the grants, Chowning had requested and received support from the music department to form CCRMA (Center for Computer Research in Music and Acoustics), as he said, "to have some basis on which we could get more grants." CCRMA was formed, with Leland Smith as founding co-director, in June 1975. Its first home was at the AI Lab in the meadow. Research continued under the auspices of the new center.

In 1979, the AI Lab relocated back to the main campus, abandoning CCRMA to share the meadow with grazing horses. CCRMA was up in the hills until March 1986, when it too moved back to the main campus, specifically to The Knoll, a building that in years past had housed the music department. With financial resources from a National Science Foundation grant in 1980, a five-year grant from the System Development Foundation in 1982, and royalties paid by Yamaha for the FM license, CCRMA grew significantly during the 1980s. Further, John Pierce had left Bell Labs in 1971 for California Institute of Technology, from which he went to Stanford University in 1983 as a research professor associated with CCRMA. In 1987, Max Mathews left Bell Labs, also to become a research professor at Stanford, also associated with CCRMA.

•

In 1969, Jean-Claude Risset went back to France. He started a computer music group at the Institut d'Electronique Fondamental, a research laboratory in Orsay, just outside of Paris. As Risset describes it, "It was a scientific lab, very hostile to music." Nonetheless, he implemented Music V on a Hewlett-Packard computer. It was a modest installation, but it was the first in Europe. In 1971, he moved to Marseilles to become the head of the music department at the Centre Universitaire de Marseille-Luminy and began to raise funds for a computer. He received the funds and finished a piece called *Dialogues* (1975), for four instruments and tape.

During those same years, IRCAM (Institut de Recherche et Coordination Acoustique Musique / Institute for Research and Coordination of Acoustics and Music) was forming in Paris. It had begun in 1970, when Georges Pompidou, then president of France, invited Pierre Boulez to create and direct a music research institute to be associated with the newly forming Centre National d'Art Contemporain; and from 1972 on, Boulez was actively formulating his plans in meetings in Paris with Risset and others. Boulez invited Risset to participate as the *Responsable* for the computer department. As Risset recalls, "Although I had just settled in Marseilles, this was an irresistible call." Gerald Bennett was also invited to participate. As Bennett recalls, "I felt personally engaged in the project—I believed that IRCAM would be a place where research could be carried out." John Chowning stopped by while in Europe on his 1972-1973 sabbatical from Stanford. Chowning tells it:

> In summer 1972, my wife and I bought an old sailboat in Cannes and spent the year sailing with our two children. We just went port-hopping along the Côte d'Azur and the Ligurian coast, day-sailing in and out of little ports. We had left Cannes in September or October, and in December, when the cold weather came, we decided to stay the winter months in Isola d'Ischia. I borrowed a typewriter from the hotel. They let me come in the early morning and work in their office. That's where I

wrote the FM paper. Then, in January 1973, I went to Stockholm for a couple of weeks and gave a course in computer synthesis and FM, and returning from that I stopped in Paris and saw Jean-Claude. IRCAM had started. I spent an hour or so with Pierre Boulez.

By 1973, the construction of IRCAM's new facility, a three-floor underground building, was begun next to the Eglise Saint-Merri in the Place Beaubourg, as part of the new Centre Pompidou, while the first round of musical activities was taking place in an adjoining building. In its initial research approach and equipment, there was continuity from both Bell Labs and Stanford. In 1974, Max Mathews was appointed scientific advisor, in which role, as he recalls, "I would go to Paris three or four times a year and spend a month there each time, and in between do my job at Bell Labs." Risset moved from Marseilles to Paris in 1975. The first computers at IRCAM were a PDP-10 and a PDP-11, and by 1976, sounds were heard from Music V, Music 10, and from a variety of other software that had been developed at Stanford. IRCAM's official opening was in 1977. By 1978, its underground building, with offices, laboratory spaces, recording studios, and an anechoic chamber, was functional—including, at the third level down, the *Espace de Projection*, a black-box concert hall whose space could be rearranged as appropriate for specific musical events and whose acoustics could be changed by reconfiguring the surfaces of the acoustic panels that made up its walls.

IRCAM was at first organized as five departments. In addition to the computer department, there was a department of instrumental performance headed by Vinko Globokar, an electronic music department headed by Luciano Berio, a department of pedagogy headed by Michel Decoust, and a department of the *diagonal* headed by Gerald Bennett (whose job it was to keep the other departments in a cooperative relationship). Risset describes the startup:

> In the initial period, it was very exciting, although I had very little time to do my own research or composition. There were lots of interruptions, lots of visits, pressure to make public appearances. The public relations people didn't understand that you cannot do research and at the same time manage a museum of musical research and show it to everyone. And it became harder and harder as Boulez became more and more demanding for the public concerts. He wanted the research to be the servant of the pieces for the concerts.
>
> So research at IRCAM was often subordinated to the demands of a composer for a specific piece. And those demands were not always reasonable and easy to fulfill. There was a critical mass for musical research—there were enough people and equipment, and it was the official purpose of IRCAM—but the idea of long-term research was not appreciated. My personal frustration was that I couldn't work enough on my own. So I decided to leave. In December 1977, I told Boulez that I

would not stay beyond my four years unless things changed. And in May 1978, I told him, "Ok, I'm going to leave." And I did leave.

In 1979, Risset left IRCAM to accept a post at the University of Aix-Marseille. In 1985, he accepted an appointment to the CNRS (Centre National de la Recherche Scientifique / National Center for Scientific Research) to work in the Laboratoire de Mécanique et d'Acoustique (Laboratory of Mechanics and Acoustics), whose director, Bernard Nayroles, welcomed Risset's computer research projects. Risset's research had been significant. In 1966, he had written *Computer Study of Trumpet Tones*, a Bell Labs publication. His dissertation, submitted in 1967 to the faculty of science at Orsay, had been *On the Analysis, the Synthesis and the Perception of Sounds, Studied with the Aid of Computers*. In 1969, he had written *An Introductory Catalog of Computer Synthesizer Sounds*, another Bell Labs publication. What was the meaning of his research in music? He answers, "It's largely a question of exploration—it's essential to keep posted with new things, to be stimulated by changes in the technology, and to ask for new possibilities from computer science . . ."

The photo on the right shows IRCAM's main entrance hall as it was in 1978, one flight lower than street level, with the stairway at the end of the hall leading up toward the Centre Pompidou. The photo below shows the entrance to an IRCAM workspace, as seen from the main entrance hall. Photos by Joel Chadabe.

•

By the end of the 1970s, CCRMA and IRCAM's computer department had sprung, like two Athenas from the forehead of Zeus, out of the software formulated at Bell Labs. Barry Vercoe also emerged from the Bell Labs environment. He had begun to work at Princeton during the summer of 1967. In 1968, he went back to Princeton for a three-year post-doctoral study, working primarily with Godfrey Winham. Vercoe tells his story:

> I went back to work with Godfrey on the IV-B system, only to find within a few months that Princeton had scheduled the replacement of the IBM 7094 with a newfangled IBM 360. Now the problem for Godfrey, who had written Music IV-B in assembly language, was that all of his work was obsolete, and he vowed he would never write in assembler again. He promptly moved to develop Music IV-BF in combination with Hubert Howe. My attitude was that this very large switch from the 7090 assembler to the 360 assembler was such a major shift that IBM was not likely to do it again soon, and that it was probably quite safe to write in 360 assembly language. So because the computer-time to audio-time ratio was still quite high and made digital synthesis very expensive, there seemed to be a big need for efficient programming of the synthesis algorithms as we understood them. So I set out to develop a language that would enable composers to represent their audio processing ideas as near to the hardware as we could get them. And that was what gave birth to Music 360.

Vercoe worked on Music 360 from 1968 to 1971. He continues:

> During that time, I was exploring what composers found most useful. I got feedback from John Melby, Jonathan Harvey and, later, Charles Dodge. And throughout this period, Godfrey Winham was a model and a sounding board. His instincts were always to push the technology towards more expressive control and I found myself wanting to combine his high standards of control with high standards of efficient and affordable sound production. Music 360 ran about five times faster than Music IV-BF and, ultimately, it could do things that IV-BF wasn't able to do. It became such an efficient sound processing system, by running so close to the hardware, that it has remained in use to this day. That was my gamble. And IBM is still producing mainframes that can run Music 360.

Vercoe taught at Yale during the academic year 1970-1971 and then accepted a position at MIT. As he said, "By that time, the idea of having a computer that was dedicated to music and that had an online digital-to-analog converter was a high-priority goal." Max Mathews had given MIT, his alma mater, an old Honeywell DDP-24, and for Vercoe's first two years at MIT the

Honeywell DDP-24 was the local sound conversion system. MIT proved to be an excellent environment for his work. As he puts it, "Instead of having one big single mainframe computer that everyone on campus shared, at MIT all the professors had their own labs with minicomputers." He, too, was able to establish his own lab with a minicomputer, and in the summer of 1973, Digital Equipment Corporation gave Vercoe a PDP-11. In the fall, he began to write Music 11. He continues:

> Now we had our own computer devoted exclusively to music, nothing else, with online digital-to-analog conversion. That setup invited the development of a Music 360 equivalent on this machine that didn't have to be shared by anybody else. And that became Music 11. It also invited the development of realtime computer music that allowed me to play a computer from a music keyboard and hear the sound back as I played. We got this old organ keyboard from the AI Lab to get the music in and we developed our own converters to get the sound out. We also developed a score editor. There were two modes of performance. One of them was to utilize the realtime software to make simple realtime sounds, which was enough to verify all the notes and rhythms. The other was the full-fidelity complex-timbre careful-envelopes Music 11 mode, which was not realtime—you'd wait around for twenty minutes or so to hear your thirty second fragment. But by 1975, you could play on the keyboard and see the score on the terminal in front of you. It was pretty exciting. By 1976, it was a mature computer music environment.

In 1976, Vercoe wrote *Synapse* (1976) for violist Marcus Thompson. Vercoe described it as "essentially a viola concerto with the orchestra part played by a computer." And he had a problem at the level of note-by-note expressivity: "I was having a problem getting the viola sounds and computer sounds to meld together so that a computer phrase would sound the way Marcus would play—the viola would do something and the computer would do something else." The problem, as it turned out, was in the flexible shaping of a computer-generated sound. And the problem was part of a larger issue involving the balance in the software between performance controls and audio possibilities. He concluded that a system weighted more toward complexity in performance controls, even if that meant simpler audio possibilities, felt more like a musical instrument.

•

In 1979, F. Richard Moore formed CARL (Computer Audio Research Laboratory) within the Center for Music Experiment at UCSD (University of California at San Diego). He thinks back:

> The question that interested me was whether to work for an industrial research lab where we were unofficial but had money, or to go to a uni-

versity where we were official but had no money. In industry, you're guaranteed to make progress but not necessarily in a direction of your choosing. In a university, you're guaranteed that you can choose your direction, but you're not necessarily going to make any progress.

CARL was the last significant Music-N installation, the summary statement, the computer system that could do anything with sound that could be done with computers. CARL research included software synthesis, programming, and the design and development of realtime performance systems. The computer was a VAX, a large minicomputer designed for time sharing, a process by which a single central computer could respond to many users at individual stations by scanning the individual stations and sharing its time between them. The software, written largely by Moore, was called *cmusic*.

Moore's idea was to build a large system and amortize its cost against many users. As he recalls, "At one time, we had as many as sixty-four terminal lines connected to that VAX, and we arranged a sound distribution system so that the sound would be sent only to the location where the person who asked for it was sitting." In other words, the same computer was used to calculate the samples, convert them into sound, and route the sound to different work stations. With CARL, the duration of a single continuous run of sound was up to twenty minutes. As Moore put it, "It's like asking how much music can you put on a record before you have to turn it over."

CARL's responsiveness, as in all time-sharing systems, varied with its workload. It was slowest during peak hours when the largest number of people were using it. When fewer people were using it, things went faster. In Moore's words:

> If you were there late at night, it would take anywhere between ten and 100 seconds to compute one second of sound. That means that if you were a student working alone with the system, you could write a composition and hear it 100 seconds later, or within a few minutes, and then hear it again if you wanted, and then change it if you wanted to. That beats a string quartet by about six months.

•

By the end of the 1970s, although most of the work done in computer music at Stanford, IRCAM, MIT, UCSD, and other places had been done with the Music-N programs, other approaches had also been formulated. Charles Dodge, for example, developed an analysis-synthesis approach to speech synthesis.

Dodge had been a graduate student at Columbia University in the 1960s, and as part of his work, he had studied with Godfrey Winham at Princeton University, converted his digital tapes at Bell Telephone Laboratories, and for a brief time, experimented at IBM's Watson Laboratories. In 1971, partly through his contacts with Max Mathews and John Pierce and partly through his friendship with Joseph Olive, a researcher in speech synthesis, Dodge began to work at Bell Labs. As he recalls, "What Max and I agreed was that I would investigate the feasibility of using the computer for making vocal music." Dodge, however, was not convinced that computer speech and music were compatible, and it took a year's thought, including work at Bell Telephone Laboratories and a trip to Sweden (where he met Bengt Emil Johnson, Lars-Gunnar Bodin, and Sten Hanson, and heard several of their text-sound compositions), to see the potential in computer-generated voice.

In 1972, resolute, Dodge began to compose *Speech Songs*, based on texts by Mark Strand. He recalls, "I asked him if he had any texts and he had these little jottings that he made one summer . . ." Dodge was attracted to the texts in large part because they were surrealistic enough to suggest the unreal voices of the computer settings. His technique was to record the texts on tape and read them into the computer through an analog-to-digital converter. The computer then analyzed the voice sound and resynthesized it based on that analysis, allowing him to edit the analysis to produce altered vocal effects. He describes his procedure:

> The first stage was to reproduce the spoken voice as accurately as I could. I made one run through the poem that way. Then I made another run through the poem making continuous glides through the vowel sounds. Then I made another run where the natural pitch contour of the voice was replaced by a melody. And there were a couple of other runs, one where I replaced the vowel part of the speech with noise so it sounded whispered. In all the runs, I had the text rendered several different ways and the piece went together by cutting between them, which resulted in a fair amount of repetition—which was advantageous because if someone couldn't understood the poem when it was articulated in one way, they understood it better perhaps when it was articulated in another way.

Speech Songs (1972) was followed by other speech-synthesis compositions, among them *The Story of Our Lives* (1974), *In Celebration* (1975), and *Cascando* (1977), based on a radio play by Samuel Beckett. *Cascando* was, in Dodge's words, "a different kettle of fish." The dramatic relationships in Beckett's text led him to compose a synthesized voice and music derived from that synthesized voice and, in performance, to combine the synthesized voice and music with the voice of a live actor.

Meanwhile, he had been listening to Caruso sing on old recordings from which the noise and scratchiness had been removed. Unfortunately, however, as an unintentional side effect of the noise-and-scratchiness removal, the accompaniments had also been removed, which put Dodge in the most uncomfortable situation of listening to Caruso sing a capella. Well, he did what any opera lover would do. He composed *Any Resemblance Is Purely Coincidental*

(1978), processing Caruso's voice itself to make an accompaniment. As he put it, "I surrounded Caruso's voice with a kind of electronic halo."

He finished another speech-synthesis composition—first in Swedish as *Han Motte Henne I Parken* (1981), then in English as *He Met Her in the Park* (1982), both based on words by Richard Kostelanetz—before his vocal work took a turn. In composing *The Waves* (1984) for Joan La Barbara, he first asked her to speak a selection from a Virginia Wolff text and he made taped sounds based on the rises and falls in her speaking voice; then, in performance, she sang the text along with the tape. He recalls, "I got so interested in the vocal contour of Joan's speech that I started writing computer programs that would make contours like her voice, and that got me started in an algorithmic approach with fractals . . ." which led to *Profile* (1984), *Roundalay* (1985), and *Viola Elegy* (1987), among other pieces and other software.

•

Gerald Bennett, at IRCAM, initiated another alternative to the Music-N programs. He begins:

> One day in 1977, Xavier Rodet walked in, introduced himself, and said that he'd devised a computer program that could speak. He invited me to see it at the atomic energy center outside of Paris and, sure enough, this thing talked, very well and fast. You pushed a carriage return and it spoke immediately. And I thought, here is someone who really does stuff. So I hired him to do singing synthesis.

Rodet had been studying engineering in 1969 and 1970 at the Ecole Supérieure de Physique et de Chimie de Paris when he discovered, from reading an article by Jean-Claude Risset, that it was possible to make sounds with a computer. He recalls, "That was a revelation for me because I realized that I could make all the sounds that I had in my head." He began work toward a PhD in speech synthesis, and as part of his degree work, he studied timbre and acoustical analysis at GRM. He reflects, "After a few years of work on my PhD, it was obvious that the more I was working on trying to make speech, the more I understood what was the relationship between speech and music." Rodet then wrote his first realtime speech program: "You just gave a few symbols and you could get a phrase, a sentence."

Bennett and Rodet worked with acoustician Johan Sundberg. Together they measured vocalists' formant frequencies and initiated research toward the idea of generating a singing voice with a computer. The first version of CHANT, as they called it, was finished in 1978. Bennett said: "What interested me in CHANT was the idea of working with a model where I could have a fairly good acoustical image of what I was going to get, and the synthesis was extensible to sounds that weren't vocal at all—more, the sounds from CHANT had a rightness about them that was hard to get otherwise."

CHANT used the human vocal tract, with its immense flexibility in changing the shape and timbre of sounds, as a model for synthesis; and Bennett's and Rodet's first-stage work culminated in a coloratura computer singing the *Queen of the Night* aria from Mozart's *The Magic Flute*. The next stage was the synthesis of non-vocal sounds. And Rodet found that, as he said, "We were able to make any sound we wanted, from Tibetan cymbals to drums, from shakuhachi to Vietnamese koto, and so on, and that was surprising for a program that was aimed mainly at simulating a singing voice."

Rodet worked for several years at modeling different sounds and analyzing other sounds to find just the right values to apply to the CHANT variables. As he explains, "Because CHANT was a physical model, you could make it run and then you could tune the sound—but analysis was a great help to find values to imitate this or that class of instruments." Even with analysis, however, finding the values was a complex problem. For the *Queen of the Night* aria, for example, values for timbre, pitch, loudness, accents, and so on were based on calculations made every ten milliseconds. Consequently, Rodet reasoned that for greater ease and practicality, a new tool was needed. He announced: "We cannot go on with our present style of programming." And in 1981, he and his colleagues began to develop FORMES, a new program based on LISP and object-oriented programming. Jean-Baptiste Barrière used the CHANT/FORMES system to compose *Chreode* (1983). Barrière saw "a window," as he put it, toward sound synthesis and toward the possibility of new compositional structures.

FORMES was based on the concept of a *process*, in this context meaning the evolution of some aspect of music or sound. The evolution of a sound's loudness, for example, could be a process, and that process could be very different from the very quick evolution of the onset of the sound or from the very long evolution of the whole musical passage. Many processes, unfolding at different rates and applying to different aspects of the sounds and music, could unfold together. Further, the processes were interdependent. Loudness that changed over a whole passage, for example, would affect the loudness of every individual sound. FORMES was an important demonstration of the principle that complex control systems are essential to sophisticated sound synthesis.

•

Computer music was created at institutional centers because no one could afford a mainframe computer at home. The Music-N programs required a relatively high level of knowledge of acoustics and computer techniques. And Music-N compositions were disseminated as recordings on tape because the Music-N computers were too large to carry to a concert hall and, in any case, did not function in real time for performance purposes. Yet by the end of the 1980s, a substantial literature of computer-generated music had been created at the various institutional centers. Clearly, computer music, despite the institutionality of the process, despite the technical distance to be traveled to reach sound, and despite the absence of the performance element, had its appeal. Why? What exactly was the allure of using mainframe computers to compose music? How did composers use computers to compose? How did composers deal with the playback of tapes in concert halls?

"Generality," according to John Chowning, "was a great part of the attraction." Generality, as against specificity, meant that any sound-generating algorithm could be tried, tested, tweaked, and perfected in software. F. Richard Moore's words refer directly to CARL, but they apply to all software synthesis approaches:

> There was no limit on the complexity of the sound that could be produced. If you wanted to produce 10,000 sine waves all at the same time, you could do that, no problem. In fact, it gave you time to get a cup of coffee while you waited for it to compute. Another thing is that it very much lent itself to experimentation. It is far easier to prototype a software unit than to prototype a hardware unit, and it doesn't require anything near the technical expertise.

Generality and ease in experimentation were certainly powerful reasons for using mainframes. But for Chowning, there was also something more: "The process of thinking carefully about a problem forces one into a thoughtful, reflective mode of interaction with the machine—I don't think that I would have discovered FM if I had been working with a realtime computer because it was dependent upon my having long spaces of time, where I would reflect upon what I was doing while the computer was cranking the numbers."

What, then, were his reflections? Chowning's idea of computer music was to do things that couldn't otherwise be done. In *Sabelithe* (1971) and *Turenas* (1972), as he recalls, "I experimented with sounds moving in space and with the ambiguity between loudness and distance, something soft and close, loud and distant, of sounds passing through space, and I thought about how sounds could meld from one to the other in ways that were uniquely possible with computer music." His next piece, *Stria* (1977), was in his words, "the piece that I consider the best expression of the unique attributes of a computer." In *Stria*, he used the Golden Section as a basis for relating partials within sounds and creating relationships between sounds. He thinks back to doing it:

> It was an exhilarating experience. It was doing something with the computer that couldn't be done with acoustic instruments. And it was using the power of the computer to manage detail while leaving me in complete control. When I was composing it, it was all night in the lab. It was a kind of weirdness, and I still feel that.

Jean-Claude Risset used a computer because of his interest, as he put it, "in composing sounds as well as composing *with* sounds." Already in *Suite for*

Computer Little Boy (1968), he had composed timbres with unique harmonic qualities. In *Inharmonique* (1977), in his words, "I built the sounds component by component—I developed a fabric based on the overtones of the various notes of a chord, and I controlled how the overtones appeared, like clouds of a given harmony." He also thought of a sound-generating program as a kind of score. As he put it, "I like the idea that a musical score is a tool for a student composer to learn composition—a program is a score of data for the microstructure level of a musical composition, a notation of the sound structure." Different from the traditional musical process of performing by reading from a score, however, Risset's idea was that the score materialized *after* the music was heard. Indeed, one of the reasons to use a computer, in his view, was that a composer could experiment and hear the music before the score was finalized: "Sometimes by mistake, sometimes by exploration, I find inspiration in serendipity—sometimes a failure at finding one thing will lead to a success at finding something else." In fact, at a certain moment in composing *Sud* (1985), he was surprised. He describes it:

> I like many natural sounds. And I like the idea of continuity between different worlds. So the idea of *Sud* was to process natural sounds in such a way that the gulf between natural and synthesized sound would be bridged. And I had a desire to make a musical monument of the area around Marseille. The sea can be so powerful around Marseille that some of the scenes are breathtaking. So I collected the sounds and worked out a plan for transforming them . . .

Even the best of plans, however . . .

> It was a recording of the sea during the mistral, and the sound of the sea was very loud and very rich, so I recorded some sounds and changed their frequencies very slightly, by something like a fiftieth of a semitone, and then I mixed the sounds together—and to my astonishment I got a huge descending glissando!

•

Johannes Goebel was concerned with sound, but he did not seek a continuity between natural and synthesized sounds. He had gotten started with computers at Darmstadt, Germany, in 1972, when he heard John Chowning give a talk about spatialization. He recalls, "John Grey, a researcher at Stanford, had recorded a cowbell in Switzerland and they sent it around the space, right by my nose." Goebel, fascinated, pursued the sound first to Freiburg and then, in 1977, to CCRMA. In his words, "over the next ten years, I spent quite a bit of time at CCRMA, on and off." He was "on" at the right moment in 1988 to welcome a particular group of visitors from Germany, and as a result of that visit, he was invited to form and direct the Institute for Music and Acoustics at

ZKM (Zentrum für Kunst und Medientechnologie / Center for Art and Media Technology) in Karlsruhe.

Working with digital technology, however, was one side of his career. The other side was building nontraditional instruments in wood and metal. And the twain were never intended to meet, as he expressed in a singular statement: "I was interested in working in the digital domain only with things that could only be done in the digital domain." In other words, the sounds that he did with computers could be done only with computers. He continues, "From the digital domain, I took ideas back to the acoustical domain and designed instruments to see if I could produce those ideas, and if that was the case I didn't have to do it with a computer." His reasoning was an elucidation for himself of the particular potential of computers: "We are questioning all the time as to what are the properties of the materials and tools we're using."

As a consequence of this thinking, Goebel intended that his computer music should not be confused with his acoustic instruments. In V*om Ubersetzen über den Fluss* (1988, Of Crossing the River), an example of his computer music, the sounds result from the resonant filtering of fractal noise. His instruments, on the other hand, had physical presence, shape, and size, and often employed innovative tuning and playing methods. His *SubBass-ProtoTone*, for example, approximately six feet square, is in effect a walk-in organ pipe in which someone inside can adjust the tuning. In his words, "one can generate mechanically the transition from low frequencies which can only be felt as impulses to those which one perceives as pitch." His *Extended Tuba*, large conical constructions connected with long hoses to the valves of a tuba, is in his words, "the perfect instrument for playing on top of a mountain into all four directions."

●

The ability to compose sound was, for many composers, *the* fundamental reason to engage in computer music. As Jonathan Harvey put it, "Before the microscope, we never knew what the microworld looked like—and now, because of the tremendous precision in being able to look into sounds and work with them, the whole world of microsound has opened up and we can compose with it." Harvey's *Mortuos Plango, Vivos Voco* (1980), composed at IRCAM, was based largely on the sound of the Winchester Cathedral bell. In his words:

> It's a haunting sound, an ancient bell. It rings out all over Winchester. It has such magisterial qualities. It stands for death, prayer, marriage, visionary transcendence.

But the bell, as he described it, "was superhuman. I also wanted something human." So Harvey recorded a young boy's voice—"the boy is the vivos, the bell is the mortuos"—and electronically transformed it in such a way that the entire composition is a play between the sounds of the bell and the sounds of the boy's voice and their electronic transformations. He transformed acoustically produced sounds also in *Bhakti* (1982): "All my work has been a play on the illusion of a real instrument and an extension of it to something it can't do." Then, in *Ritual Melodies* (1990), also composed at IRCAM, he synthesized the sounds. He reflects, "Computer synthesis had reached a state that people couldn't really tell the difference anymore." And he describes the process of composing *Ritual Melodies*:

> I simulated an Indian oboe, a Vietnamese koto, a Japanese shakuhachi, a Tibetan bell, a plainsong voice, and a Tibetan monk. I wanted to gather together a group of instruments and sounds that were very individualistic. They're not orchestral instruments, meant to blend in the Western sense. They mix and change into each other all the time.

Harvey began by making the melodies, which were sound files that could later be mixed in any order. When that was done, as he tells it, "I was in the marvelous position of starting to mix and combine these melodies with precision so they might be made to interlock into polyphony far more precisely than with human instrumentalists. That was a very exciting day." He made a chain of sixteen melodies, with each melody lasting about fifteen seconds and consisting of two instruments changing into each other. He continues:

> The timbral combinations were very interesting because in each melody the timbres changed—the shakuhachi turned into a oboe, for instance— so mixing melodies was also mixing timbres. I was sitting at a terminal. I would type in the mix specifications, give a file name, start time, the spatial distribution (the panning became very complex), and a loudness factor. The program did a lot of calculations, so I'd give it lots of things to work out, translating the beats into seconds, for example. And then I'd wait a couple of minutes to hear the sound. And it became very musical because we could just mix and try different experiments . . .

For Denis Smalley in England, as for Jonathan Harvey, the primary reason to use a computer is to compose sound, but Smalley thinks of it also in terms of discovery. He uses computers, as he explains, "to make new sonic discoveries which otherwise could not come to light." Smalley began in the early 1970s at the GRM in Paris. He subsequently worked in other studios in France, England, Finland, and Canada. In 1991, he worked at Banff in the Canadian Rockies. He composed *Gradual* (1974), *Vortex* (1982), *Tides* (1984), *Wind Chimes* (1987), *Valley Flow* (1992), and many other pieces in a great diversity of scenery and with a great diversity of sounds. He continues:

> My musical ideas come out of the sounds themselves. I explore their characteristics. I discover. With digital techniques, for example, I can isolate

fragments that the ear can't otherwise hear. So I can pick out surprising elements, and I might say, "Let's play with it," and see if it gives me something. Or I might say, "Now that's a great sound. I have to use it." Or I might think that there are qualities in there which I can harness in building a piece of music.

•

The localization of sound within a concert space became an increasingly important aspect of sound through the 1980s. In 1984, Annea Lockwood came up with an interesting if noncomputer-based approach. She got the idea for the *SoundBall*, essentially a flying loudspeaker. In its final version, it was about eighteen inches in diameter. It contained built-in amplification, six loudspeakers, and an antenna to receive sounds broadcast from elsewhere in a performance space. It was, in fact, a gourmet's soundball, made from two hinged-together colanders purchased at Zabar's, a fine food store in New York. The colanders were covered with foam to smooth the seams and protect the electronics while allowing sound to pass through. Lockwood used it in *Three Short Stories and an Apotheosis* (1985), for SoundBall, performers, and projections. In her words:

> The first story has sounds—a soprano and a wolf howl at the same pitch—coming only from the ball, which is rolling down the center aisle of the performance hall. In the second story, also for ball alone, the ball is suspended on fishline and I swing it over the audience's head while it "sings" a lullaby in Samoan, which I composed. The third story is a Gertrude Stein text from *Many Many Women* about gossiping, which comes from the ball along with the sound of a cat purring. During the second and third stories, a slide of a photograph by Jacques-Henri Lartigue, dated 1904, is projected. It depicts his nurse throwing up a ball which looks just like the SoundBall. There's also a background of women's voices coming from an onstage PA system. Then the ball is passed hand-to-hand through the audience and then, before it ends, I retrieve the ball from the audience and stick it in a backpack and walk off with Gertrude Stein still talking, while the slide is now minus the ball.

Flying loudspeakers, however, were more the exception than the rule. Most composers found it more practical to circulate sounds through space than to circulate loudspeakers. And following many earlier models of multi-loudspeaker "orchestras," in particular François Bayle's Acousmonium, many composers saw the presentation of computer music on tape as best done through a multidirectional sound environment, created by placing many loudspeakers on stage and/or throughout the concert hall. It was, for example, Denis Smalley's solution: "Over a period of years I built up a collection of loudspeakers—in particular, I developed the idea of a tweeter grid over the heads of the audience."

In 1973, Christian Clozier and Françoise Barrière, at GMEB (Groupe de Musique Experimentale de Bourges / Experimental Music Group of Bourges) in France, developed the Gmebaphone, a loudspeaker orchestra with mixing, equalization, and other processing capability. In the mid-1980s, Jonty Harrison and his colleagues at Birmingham University developed an elaborate playback system called BEAST (Birmingham Electro-Acoustic Sound Theatre). In short, by the mid-1980s, multi-loudspeaker facilities for the presentation of tape music had been established in many places. But how did composers think about using such spaces?

François Bayle had begun to work with computers in *Erosphère* (1980), then in *Les Couleurs de la Nuit* (1982), and later in *Son Vitesse-Lumière* (1983), which he said, "was based on the idea that the sound we hear is produced by loudspeakers—the changes go faster than the speed of sound . . ." In composing *Aéroformes* (1984) at IRCAM, as he said, "I made a demonstration of GRM techniques with IRCAM tools." He took particular advantage of l'Espace de Projection, IRCAM's unique concert hall. Bayle knew at the start that the piece would be composed in four tracks and performed via twenty-four loudspeakers, so he recorded the sounds directly onto each of the four tracks with four microphones and then transformed differently each track by transposition, filtering, and other techniques such that each track had a special identity and each sound was dynamically changing in its color, intensity, pitch, and placement in space. The sounds of each of the four tracks were then distributed to groups of six loudspeakers placed throughout the space, "which worked out very well," as Bayle remembers, "because the space was experimental and I could adjust the specific positions of the different loudspeakers." Bayle sums it up: "The idea was to make a form in the air."

In fact, the idea of making a form in the air was in the air, and a major project was launched in Italy. Centro Tempo Reale (Real Time Center), a research and production center in Florence, had been conceived by Luciano Berio and Giuseppe Di Giugno while they were at IRCAM together in the mid-1970s. In 1979, with support from the municipality of Florence and the Tuscany regional government, the new center had become a reality and equipment was installed in the top floor of the Villa Strozzi, which location, incidentally, provided a magnificent view of the beautiful Tuscan hills surrounding Florence. In 1986, there was a second round of funding. In 1987, Peter Otto arrived at Tempo Reale to direct research and development and build a Macintosh- and MIDI-based studio. In 1988, Nicola Bernardini joined Otto to develop a number of research and development projects. Otto and Bernardini then assembled a group of consultants and advisers, among them Zack Settel and Miller Puckette, to define the initial specifications for what became TRAILS (Tempo Reale Audio Interactive Location System), a system to route sounds through space via a multi-loudspeaker network. TRAILS existed in two prototypes: a large configuration with a twenty-four-by-eight spatialization matrix and a smaller and more manageable configuration, called MiniTRAILS, with an eight-by-eight spatialization matrix.

Spatialization systems such as TRAILS presented sophisticated solutions to problems of routing sounds through space, for example routing eight voices independently in different trajectories through eight loudspeakers. And the situation was yet more complex when composers included localization cues, such as Doppler effects, in their sounds. At its most sophisticated, the idea of spatialization was to allow a composer to pinpoint the location from which a sound seemed to originate in a listening space and to trace the way it seemed to move. By the late 1980s, various research projects were in progress, not only at Centro Tempo Reale but also at IRCAM and other places, in spatialization techniques.

•

Given that the synthesis of an interesting sound can be complex, and that localization can be complex, and given the limited capability of current technology to achieve extreme complexity in real time, some composers have preferred to work in the more leisurely, nonrealtime environment of a studio rather than simplify their music to render it suitable for realtime performance. For Curtis Roads, for example, one advantage of studio composing was time and concentration. As he said, "The sound world is infinite, and the labor of sound exploration is sometimes a slow, trial-and-error process, and I'm looking for fluidity, to be able to transform and rearrange at any step of composition."

For Roads, a composition on tape or on compact disc is like a book or a work of art that does not require a performer. Roads argues: "You might ask a painter why he does not paint on stage and he would look at you as if you were crazy, saying 'What does that have to do with making art?'" And, in his view, like the presentation of a painting in a well-lit gallery, the public presentation of music should be managed in a suitable space with suitable equipment. He reports, "I recently had a chance to present *Clang-tint* (1995) with an orchestra of loudspeakers at the auditorium of Radio France, and this type of multi-channel projection makes a great difference in a concert situation."

•

Paul Lansky had other thoughts regarding sound. He said: "I've done a lot of pieces by creating complicated textures or scenarios which allow the listener to use an active imagination while listening—a piece on tape or compact disc has to perplex the listener; it has to have something about it that's puzzling and not completely straightforward." Lansky's compositions into the early 1980s include *Six Fantasies on a Poem by Thomas Campion* (1979) and *As It Grew Dark* (1983), both computer-generated sounds, and *As If* (1982), for computer-generated sounds and string trio. But *Idle Chatter* (1984) was his breakthrough. He describes it:

> The surface of the piece is relatively simple but it's a backdrop to a much more complicated texture. People would talk to me about the piece and nobody would say the same thing. It was as if I was providing them with

an environment in which they could let their ears dance, where there was no particular thing they should be listening to at any point.

Yes, the surface of *Idle Chatter* is simple, with a regular pulse and engaging sounds, and, yes, it is a backdrop to a complicated texture—words spoken by Hannah MacKay were computer processed in multiple tracks of quickly changing rhythmic figures, producing complicated chattering babble in which the words are not understandable, but at the same time, the words' inflections are understandable and imbue the sounds with a feeling of comfort and familiarity. And that idea, of combining confusion and comfort from the processing of spoken words, was so interesting to Lansky that he developed it further in *just_more_idle_chatter* (1987), *Notjustmoreidlechatter* (1988), and *Smalltalk* (1988). But perhaps, for Lansky, the most significant idea to grow out of *Idle Chatter* was that computer-generated sounds should communicate a human quality. As he puts it, "I like to project the feeling that my electronic sounds don't have a supernatural origin, that they have a human origin."

To take that a bit further, Lansky's idea was that the primary meaning of a sound derives from our understanding of its physical origin as well as its context. That thought led him toward using other sounds made by humans, as in *The Sound of Two Hands* (1990), based on clapping, and *Table's Clear* (1992), for which he and his sons hit bottles and plates after dinner one evening. The thought also led him toward using sounds made by environments and machines that were made by humans. Referring to *Night Traffic* (1990), *Quakerbridge* (1992), and *Still Time* (1994), he explains, "I sometimes use the computer as a camera on the sounds of the world and the sounds of the world then color the music." For *Night Traffic*, for example, Lansky recorded cars passing at night and used the chaos of those sounds, with their noise and Doppler-shift elements, as a filter through which to hear the melodies and harmonies that he composed. He said, "The piece has got to do with the way the pitches and harmonies go, but the sounds of the cars themselves are an excitation function of the music and the cars become the inner voice of the music." *Quakerbridge* was based on the sounds of a shopping mall during a pre-Christmas rush. And regarding *Still Time*, Lansky writes:

> *Still Time* was conceived as a kind of film music without images . . . Each of the four overlapping tableaux of the piece rests on an initial realworld sound: wind in the garden, traffic, and groups of people for the last two . . . Turning the tables a bit on film, however, the recorded sounds are used here to color the music that evolves: now the 'images' become the inner voice of the music . . .

●

Dexter Morrill came into computer music as a composer and trumpet player with a background in jazz; and for Morrill, as for many musicians, all instruments including the computer were extensions of the voice. He reiterated a basic truth:

> The human voice is where it all starts. Every good composer, every good musician is a singer, and the trumpet is an extension of that. You don't stop singing. These electronic instruments are really voice extenders in terms of how we do music.

In 1970, shortly after joining the Colgate University faculty in upstate New York, he went to Stanford University to see the computer music system. He was impressed. As he said, "I was simply bowled over by this thing." Leland Smith, on the Stanford faculty, took Morrill in hand and introduced him to Joe Zingheim, a hardware technician at the AI Lab where the music group was located. Colgate had just acquired a PDP-10 computer and Morrill's problem was getting it to make music. He remembers, "I think Joe felt sorry for me, and he said, 'Well, maybe I can build you a converter,' and he did it."

Morrill's lab at Colgate was operational by 1972, his first pieces were finished during 1973, and having finished his *Studies* (1975), for trumpet and computer, as he puts it, "my computer music career began." It wasn't easy going, but he had some significant help, primarily from John Chowning and Leland Smith. Morrill tells it:

> John, Lee, and John Grey, a Stanford graduate student at that time, taught me just about everything I know about computer music programming. Of course it was difficult work, and I gave up a lot of years of my composing life. But I was very excited by it, and I had a lot of energy and the right kind of environment—a liberal arts college and an underused machine.

One of the primary problems in computer music during the 1970s was how to *think about* generating sound. Morrill followed the Stanford model: "The Stanford group had the notion that the point of departure for new sounds should be proven acoustical information, and I thought, 'Well, I play the trumpet,' and so that's why I did it, to start from that point." For his *Studies*, he developed an algorithm which was based on Jean-Claude Risset's earlier acoustical data and Chowning's new FM technique and which generated trumpet sounds. Morrill continues:

> I carried the work very far along with FM synthesis for several years, hacking out single notes. And the end result was that I realized I had exhausted my own potential to work in this area with the resources I had available. I said to Risset, "You know, I'm sick of working on single tones." And then I really felt two things: I was getting older, and I was probably not going to make a significant contribution in systems or in

acoustics. By the late 1970s it was clear to me there were so many more people that had access to equipment and that were so professionally gifted that it was really foolish for a composer to be spending a lot of time in those fields.

Morrill focused on compositions that involved live performers. He said, "It's great to have a highly professional solo player there who takes so much of the burden off the loudspeaker." Following the *Studies*, his compositions included the *Fantasy Quintet* (1978), for piano and tape; *Six Dark Questions* (1979), for soprano and tape; *Tarr* (1982), for four trumpets and tape; and *Getz Variations* (1984), for saxophone and tape. *Getz Variations* was written for jazz saxophonist Stan Getz. Morrill continues:

> I met Stan Getz in Palo Alto in January 1984. And then I went off and did this piece. I was at Stanford a lot that spring. I went back to Getz' famous solo on *Summer Sequence* and used a bit of that material, which I consider to be the most beautiful seven bars in music. I got him to record some more material which I processed in different ways, which drew the piece towards him with saxophone sounds. He was a hard guy to get to know but he said, "Yeah, I think I can do this."

•

For Trevor Wishart, the focus was sound. His *Tongues of Fire* (1994), for example, was based entirely on computer transformations of vocal sounds. As he describes it, "The slightly angry, disgruntled, comic mutterings with which the piece begins are the source of all the sounds which appear in it—sounds suggesting drums, water, metallic resonances, fireworks, or entirely imaginary materials or events, all generated through processes of sound-transformation on the computer . . ." Could this have been done without a computer? In Wishart's view, no. Indeed, he uses computers because, in his words, "You can now treat sound in the same logical way that we treated pitch before."

Wishart, however, had formulated his methods for composing sound before using computers. He had begun in the electronic music studio at the University of York in England, where he worked mainly with tape recorders and mixers. His *Red Bird* (1977) was a breakthrough for him because, as he explained, "I'd figured out a methodology for using realworld sounds—birds, animals, voices, machines." His methodology, as he referred to it, was a way of relating the evocative qualities of sounds with the meanings that might emerge from the ways the sounds were organized and transformed into one another: "I wanted to create a myth in sound." Borrowing concepts from Claude Lévi-Strauss' anthropological study of myth in *The Raw and the Cooked*, and particularly from Lévi-Strauss' idea that the structures of myths are themselves meaningful, Wishart thought in terms of myth and the structure of myth. *Red Bird* was, he wrote, "a journey into an alternative world . . . vibrant with significant sounds and symbols . . . a piece of music and a mythic telling of the world."

The individual sounds in *Red Bird* were thought of as symbols. Wishart divided his primary sound-symbol world into bird songs, machine sounds, animal/body sounds, and words; and he defined a secondary sound-symbol world including the sound of a clock, book, fly ("the sinister Fly, harbinger of death . . ."), and door. Associations of meaning were then derived from the association of sounds, either as juxtapositions or as gradual transformations between sounds. A flock of birds, for example, transforms into the rustling of a book's pages, then into the sound of closing a book, then into a slammed door, into a creaking door, into the vocal sound *rea*, into the sound *reazzzz*, which is heading for *reazzzonable*, while at the same time the buzzing of a fly also transforms into *reazzzzz*.

Wishart worked on *Red Bird* from 1973 to 1977. As one imagines the tasks involved in achieving the sounds, one wonders that it took *only* four years to compose. Merely collecting the sounds was itself a time-consuming effort. After trying to simulate the sound of a fly, for example, with processed vocal sounds and failing, and after trying to generate the sound electronically and failing, the indefatigable Wishart finally decided to record a fly. He tells it:

> I was lucky enough to find a biologist researching the behavior of flies. All the sense-receptors of flies, apart from their eyes, are located on their feet. This means that they can be stuck on the end of a rod without knowing about it, and that if you touch their feet and then let go they receive the message "fly" and begin to do so, creating the characteristic buzzing sound. So I was able to place a microphone very close to a buzzing fly without it actually moving. When the recording session was over, the fly was removed from the end of the rod and it flew off, none the wiser.

In the early 1980s, Wishart, Richard Orton, and Tom Endrich, all composers living in York, formed an electronic music discussion and presentation group called Interface. By 1986, Graham Hearn, Phil Ellis, Chris Fox, and Andrew Bentley had become regular members, and discussions focused on the musical potential of the affordable Atari ST computer, with its sixteen-bit technology and built-in MIDI interface. As Wishart recalls, "There were all those composers with all those crazy ideas thinking, 'You could probably do this with computers,' so we dreamed up a scheme to make it possible and the only machine that we could afford that was fast enough was the Atari." They had support and help from Dave Malham, senior technician at the University of York; from Nigel Roles, who wrote a MIDI recorder and playback program; and especially from Martin Atkins, a graduate student in the computer science department. During the summer of 1986, the group, working on different tasks in pairs, began to port cmusic code acquired from CARL in San Diego to the Atari. It seemed, in Richard Orton's words, "a daunting task," but despite some small degree of mealtime sacrifice, they managed to inspire interest and support from the computer science group. Orton explains:

The computer science crowd always had lunch early . . . so if we had some problem we wanted to get elucidated, we had to go early too . . . We tried to look nonchalant, meeting the others casually, bringing up our latest difficulties as naturally as possible . . . It became apparent that Martin Atkins was getting daily more interested in our struggles . . .

Thanks largely to Atkins, difficult software problems were solved. Thanks largely to Malham, the primary hardware problem, of creating the design for a device that could read sound into and from the computer, was solved. The device was called the SoundStreamer, and it allowed them to hear what was going in and coming out while it was happening. Wishart lent the money to build a prototype SoundStreamer. As he recalls, "We didn't have any capital, so I lent them 100 quid and said, 'Ok, do it.'" There were, of course, more problems, but there were also more solutions, and when it was finished, functioning, and making sound, Andrew Bentley dubbed it the Composers' Desktop Project, or CDP as it came to be known. Then Endrich raised the issue of how the project could continue to develop and become self-sustaining. And, as Orton describes it, "We all began to see in the project the possibility of a national electronic support group for computer music in Britain, and the scope of this excited us all . . ."

As news of the availability of the system spread, the group formulated a three-point policy for disseminating the software: It should be low cost; continued development work should be done on a cooperative basis; and users would access the software by paying a minimal annual subscription fee. A nonprofit corporation was formed with Endrich, Orton, Wishart, and Bentley as directors. Endrich became chief executive officer, in his words, "out of a passion for the intrinsic worth of the enterprise, valuable to me as well as to everyone else."

As the project grew in time, however, there were increasing problems in reconciling CDP's technical and social goals with its goal to be self-sustaining. In 1989, Endrich wrote, "We gradually became aware that even as a non-profit company, the CDP was not earning enough to sustain the endeavor—even if we were in a position to, and willing to, work for nothing full time for the foreseeable future . . ." Endrich sought to resolve the issue by instituting more efficient business practices and by bringing pricing more into line with costs. In *Yearbook 1989*, he concluded, "We believe very strongly in what the CDP can mean to ourselves, to our fellow composers, and to the next generation . . ." And what, indeed, could the CDP mean? Orton, in Yearbook 1989, put it well: "We have been very encouraged . . . There does seem to be a continuing demand for a composer individual workstation which handles real sound in addition to MIDI . . . which increasingly provides, in a number of locations, a forum for on-going compositional activities (and active discussion and seminars) which would otherwise be limited by the long waiting times for access to centres in the United States or in Europe."

The CDP system was the first sustained effort to translate the immense flexibility of mainframe software synthesis into the affordable context of personal computers. Indeed, that it was never intended as a commercial package gave CDP an advantage. It was insulated from dependence upon market forces. And that insulation allowed it to survive and grow into the 1990s. By 1995, close to 200 programs, many of them written by Wishart, had been added to the original set. Endrich brings it up to date: "Now on Atari Falcon 030, PC compatibles, SGI Indy and SGI Indigo . . . with members in twenty countries, extensive reference and tutorial documentation and email help-line access for users, the CDP has come a long way from its initial conception . . ."

Wishart has worked with it consistently. As he said, "I like programming—I find great excitement in making an instrument and changing its specifications to make it do what I want it to do." And again Wishart, these words written in 1994: "You can now do almost anything you could dream of, and more besides, in non-real time—I would argue that this is *the* nonrealtime system for serious composers . . ."

•

All in all, it is surprising how well and how quickly the pioneers solved problems. There was an active community of effort, to be sure, with research results shared through publications such as *Computer Music Journal*, through an annual International Computer Music Conference, and through the ICMA (International Computer Music Association), which disseminates information and publishes a newsletter. As Larry Austin, president of ICMA from 1989 to 1994, puts it, "It turns out that computer music is a very social activity—the inventors worked in teams, interacting with one another, and it continues that way." But it is also surprising how well the pioneers combined technological skills with their musical sensitivities to the extent that they could, individually and collectively, develop the technology and compose music at the same time. As John Pierce said, "It's Billy Klüver's idea that 'isn't it wonderful that the arts will attract the assistance of a lot of engineers,' but the real thing is that it's amazing how many musically talented people become expert with computers."

By the late 1980s, the focus of computer music had moved from mainframe computers to personal computers, synthesizers, and general-purpose digital signal processors. The age of computer music, in the sense of nonrealtime mainframe systems, was fast reaching its end. The lessons learned had been reapplied not only to personal computers but also to the development of digital audio in all its forms, from digital synthesizers to compact discs to digital tape recorders to digital editing software. Indeed, one could say that by the late 1980s the age of computer music was over because *everything* was computer music.

• • •

CHAPTER SIX

SYNTHESIZERS

In 1949, Robert Moog read an article on how to build theremins. Through his following years in high school, as he remembers, "I found myself designing bigger and better theremins." In January 1954, at the age of nineteen, he wrote an article on how to build theremins, published it in *Radio and Television News*, and with his father, started a small business making theremin coils. He continued a business of making theremins, coils, and kits through college (Columbia University) and graduate school (Cornell University). He wrote an article for the January 1961 issue of *Electronics World* which was published as the cover story with, as he recalls, "a big, fat color picture of my instrument on the front cover—we got so busy that I had to drop out of graduate school for six months."

In 1963, he rented a storefront in Trumansburg, a village just north of Ithaca along the west shore of Lake Cayuga in the Finger Lakes region of upstate New York. In December 1963, he went to the annual convention of the New York State School Music Association to sell theremins. It took place at the Concord Hotel in the Catskill Mountains near New York City. "And," as he tells it, "along comes Herb Deutsch—he asked me if I knew anything about electronic music, and he told me that there were some electronic sounds he didn't know how to get and asked if I was interested in that kind of thing." Deutsch, at that time a composer on the music faculty at Hofstra University, remembers: "We talked for an hour about my work, his work, the state of electronic music, and the need for new instrumentation . . ." Moog continues:

> He invited me to a concert of his in New York. He had a percussionist performing along with pre-recorded tape. The concert was held at Jason Seley's studio, and the percussionist played on Seley's sculptures as well as conventional instruments and I thought that was the greatest thing. Playing on the sculptures was a combination of kinetic art, dance and music. I responded to it and the idea of working with Herb to make the sorts of sounds he wanted became a very attractive and fun thing to do—but not for making money because the whole business had the flavor of a hobby. Herb said he wanted sounds that went wooo woo wooo.
>
> The idea of one oscillator controlled by another came to mind. I knew that such a thing as voltage control was possible and the whole idea of making it modular was in an article by Harald Bode in some issue of *Electronics* magazine in 1961, describing a very simple modular system that he had designed. It had a tape delay module, a reverb, a voltage-controlled amplifier. From that I learned what a modular system was.
>
> So I invited Herb to come up the following spring, in 1964. And by the time he came up, I had hand-wired two voltage-controlled oscillators and one voltage-controlled amplifier on a board, with either frequency or amplitude modulation, and it had sawtooth waveforms, square, maybe triangular waveforms, and Herb said, "Oh, wow, that's just what I want." So we set up a little bench for him. He had a Sony home-quality reel-to-reel tape recorder, and he started making music with it.

As Deutsch recalls, "I spent about eight hours a day improvising, composing, and reacting to Moog's experimentation and technical developments." And during the two weeks that Deutsch was there, he composed *Jazz Images*, a short demonstration piece. Moog continues:

> And then it was my turn to say, "Oh, wow!" We didn't have air conditioning so we left the doors open and word got out around town about all the funny noises that were coming out of the place. It was very soon that Herb and I began to talk about the other things we should have. Then Herb went home.
>
> The next thing I did was to build proper working models with knobs. I had some sort of a keyboard with crude envelope generators built in it. When Herb came up again in August, we fooled around a little more. Then we decided we'd take a drive up to Toronto, about four hours, and there we visited the University of Toronto Electronic Music Studio and saw Myron Schaeffer. We showed him the equipment. He got very excited and gave us a lot of encouragement. Now that was the first electronic music studio I had ever been in. Schaeffer had a tremendous amount of

stuff by Hugh Le Caine. Ciamaga was there, Tony Gnazzo, my first introduction to the electronic music establishment.

When we went back to Trumansburg, Herb and I talked some more and at some point then I did the first voltage-controlled filter, maybe in August or early September 1964. And then, I think one day in September, I got a call from Jacqueline Harvey from the AES. She said something to the effect that we hear that you people are doing interesting things up there. What emerged during the conversation was that she was managing the AES convention and one of her exhibitors had paid for a booth but had nothing to exhibit—so she invited us to come at no cost and show whatever it was that we were doing. I was not a member of the AES then. I had never been to an AES convention. I was a shy, awkward nerd. I had a card table with a little box with little modules and paper labels, and on one side of me was Ampex, the other side was Scully, all these hip consoles. I felt out of place. I thought, "What am I doing here?"

One of the things Moog did there was to read his first paper, called "Electronic Music Modules," which was published in 1965 in the *AES Journal*. He also launched a new business:

So there I was. A lot of people came by. Jimmy Seawright came by and said, "Alwin Nikolais should know about this," and later that day Nikolais came by and he was the first one to say the magic words, "I'll take one of these and two of these . . . " And that was the beginning of our being in the synthesizer business. We slipped into it backwards on a banana peel. No thought of the future, no philosophy, no plans. One day we were in the kit business, the next day in the synthesizer business. In those years, I can't ever remember looking into the future, trying to understand what would be best for musicians. Ideas came in from all over the place and what we wound up selling was the sum total of all those ideas . . .

Nikolais' order was for $700 in equipment. Moog's second order came from Eric Siday for $1,400 and as he recalls, "It kept us busy for six months." Then Vladimir Ussachevsky sent Moog the specifications for three devices: a voltage-controlled amplifier, an envelope generator (later called the ADSR), and an amplitude follower. Other early customers included Lejaren Hiller at the University of Illinois, Gustav Ciamaga at the University of Toronto, George Rochberg at the University of Pennsylvania, and Wendy Carlos.

Through the late 1960s, Moog's synthesizers were modular systems with names such as Synthesizer 10, Synthesizer 1c, System 35, System 55, and so on. He used the word *synthesizer* for the first time in 1967: "It was in our 1967 catalog—there was a paragraph or two called *The Synthesizer Concept*." Also through the late 1960s, the mainstream of interest gradually shifted from academic to commercial composers. He continues:

Robert Moog (front) and Jon Weiss (back) working with a Moog modular system in the R. A. Moog studio in Trumansburg, upstate New York, in the late 1960s. Photo courtesy Robert Moog.

In 1967, I got a call from Paul Beaver, who had a very active business in Los Angeles renting out all sorts of electronic instruments. He said he'd like to represent us on the west coast and wanted us to come to the AES convention in Los Angeles. We missed each other at the Los Angeles airport because he was waiting at the first class ramp. He just assumed we were rolling in pure creamery butter. At that time, the west coast AES convention was an outpost, the boonies, a little teeny show at a little hotel. Paul had gotten an exhibit booth on the balcony somewhere, and we had brought out a big modular synthesizer. Paul invited a lot of his friends, "You gotta come down and see this," and the first day a lot of people came down, and "wow, oh, man oh man," and they went back and told their friends. And the second and third day they were four or five people deep for the whole show. We must have gotten half a dozen or a dozen orders out of that show.

Also in 1967, a Moog synthesizer was used in a record called *Zodiac Cosmic Sounds*. And Chris Swanson was beginning to perform concerts in New York. Moog describes one of them:

Chris started with a Bach concert at Riverside Cathedral in New York and after 1968 he was making high quality switched-on jazz. In 1969, we built four systems—small modular systems with presets—for a Jazz in the Garden concert at the Museum of Modern Art. The musicians were Herb

Deutsch, Hank Jones, Chris Swanson, John McLaughlin, Bobby Moses, and there were others. Chris and his group just banged away and wailed away and everybody freaked out. There were 4,000 people there. Well, the whole system—four performance stations, big amplifiers—was plugged into one outlet in the garden, and right when Chris hit an absolute frenzy, someone stood up on the outlet and slipped and knocked the plug out. So Chris got up and said, "Well, that's it folks." And that was the end of the concert.

1969 was a good year for Moog synthesizers. It was not only the Jazz in the Garden concert, which indirectly led to Keith Emerson (Emerson, Lake, and Palmer) buying one. It was also that Wendy Carlos' *Switched on Bach*, which had appeared in November 1968, was becoming extremely successful. As Moog recalls, "It was in *The New York Times*, *Time*, *Newsweek*, it was catapulted into the public consciousness and a ton of record producers decided that this was the gimmick for 1969—with a Moog synthesizer, they could make their hit record."

•

In early 1964, the equipment in the electronic music studio at the American Academy in Rome, which had been specified by Vladimir Ussachevsky, consisted of three oscillators, a couple of Ampex stereo machines, a reverb unit, a mixer, a splicing block, a couple of microphones, and other odds and ends. Larry Austin, as a visiting composer in Rome, used the studio's basement location as an opportunity to compose *Roma, a Theatre Piece in Open Style*. As he recalls, "I made a recording of Italian workers who I couldn't see but could hear through the storm drain—I recorded them and the ambience of Rome as I heard it there."

William O. Smith, John Eaton, Otto Luening, and George Balch Wilson, all American composers connected with the academy, were also in Rome at the time, and they wanted to upgrade the studio. They consulted with Paul Ketoff, a sound engineer for RCA Italiana, and Ketoff took Smith, who at the time was in charge of the studio, to see the *Phonosynth*, a large studio-oriented synthesizer that Ketoff had built a year or so earlier for composer Gino Marinuzzi. Ketoff then proposed that he build a smaller version of the Phonosynth for the American Academy. Smith and the others agreed.

The *Synket* (*Syn*thesizer *Ket*off), as Ketoff called it, was installed at the American Academy in Rome in early 1965. John Eaton, in particular, very quickly saw its possibilities as a performance instrument. As he said, "I started practicing on it." In fact, Eaton started by practicing sounds that invoked the wind and the sea, to be used in his *Songs for RPB* (1965), for soprano, piano, and Synket, first sung by Miciko Hirayama in April 1965 at a concert at the American Academy in Rome. Immediately following the concert, Eaton asked

Ketoff to build a Synket that was optimized for performance. As Eaton recalls, "I wanted the keyboard to be sensitive to velocity and easily tunable, and then Ketoff came up with the idea that I could also wiggle the keys from side to side, as one does on a clavichord, to get a vibrato effect . . ."

The new Synket, delivered several months later, became a major part of Eaton's work in the following years. He composed many pieces that included Synket—among them *Prelude to Myshkin* (1966), *Concert Piece for Synket No. 2* (1966), and *Soliloquy* (1967), for solo Synket; *Thoughts on Rilke* (1966) and *Blind Man's Cry* (1968), for voice and Synket ensemble; *Concert Piece for Synket and Symphony Orchestra* (1967); *Mass* (1970); and an opera called *Myshkin* (1971), which included two Synkets (or tapes of Synkets) in the orchestra—and he concertized. In March 1966, he played at McMillan Theatre at Columbia University in New York. His *Concert Piece for Synket and Symphony Orchestra* was performed at Tanglewood in 1967 and later in Los Angeles. He toured extensively from the 1960s into the 1970s in the United States and Europe. Following a meeting with Robert Moog in 1966, he lived part of the year in Trumansburg, working with Moog on various instrumental concepts, and part of the year in Rome, as a base for his European concerts. In *Duet* (1968) and other pieces, he played both Moog synthesizer and Synket: "You hear the difference between the instruments especially at the beginning . . ." There was also a tour in Latin America and, finally, in 1977, in the Soviet Union. Eaton sums it up:

> Over more than a ten year period, I was really active. I was an electronic troubadour. Have Synket will travel. I gave something like 1,000 concerts with the Synket before finally retiring it.

In the mid-1960s, a group of seven musicians—at first Walter Branchi, Domenico Guaccero, Gino Marinuzzi, Guido Guiducci, Paul Ketoff, Franco Evangelisti, and Egisto Macchi, later to be joined by Ennio Morricone—formed the studio R7 (Roma 7) to improvise and compose for an ensemble of Synkets. In March 1966, Jane Schoonover, an American performer living in Rome, played Synket at an evening's entertainment at the Taverna Margutta, a Roman nightclub. There were a few other musicians who used the Synket, but not very many. Ketoff had not been interested in forming a business to manufacture and promote the Synket, and so it had never become a commercial item. Eaton remained its primary performer and principal evangelist.

Why? What was it about the Synket that Eaton found so appealing? For one thing, as he points out, the Synket was structured as three semi-independent component units (which Ketoff called *sound-combiners*), each controlled by a separate keyboard. And why was this important? He continues:

> It encouraged me to think in terms of independent voices. It allowed for the kind of music that preserved some traditional values. It allowed for

counterpoint, for some focus of attention on more than the main line of the music. So much of electronic music then was so simplistic, with only one line . . .

For another thing, Eaton found it musically challenging. He continues:

> I tried all kinds of different things. And if I found an interesting sound I'd try to figure out how I could do it again. Of course, having a single instrument that I could work with really helped that process because I could spend hours practicing the pieces that I wrote. There was a lot of virtuosity required. I practiced as much as a concert pianist would, seven or eight hours a day, because of all the fine motions involved and the timings of musical gestures and nuances. But I think that instruments should be hard to play. It's very much been my aesthetic that music should be accomplished by a composer mastering with his sensibility a certain range of possibilities.

●

In 1963, at the San Francisco Tape Music Center on Divisidero Street, Morton Subotnick and Ramon Sender had the three-track Ampex, a few old tape recorders, and as Subotnick puts it, "a lot of telephone-type things." They were also accumulating quite a bit of equipment, mostly from junkyards, telephone company surplus, and some creative financing. Subotnick relates one example of equipment acquisition:

> We put an SOS out to a fire insurance company that dealt with hifi stores, and they called us and said that a store had burned down, and they had all the inventory . . . We didn't have any money, but we rented a truck to get the equipment, and we gave them a bad check thinking that we'd find the money before the check bounced. So we sold enough equipment from the inventory, intercoms basically, also microphones, and we finally got enough money to cover the check we'd given them.

Donald Buchla, meanwhile, had been composing tape music at home with a single-track Wollensak (a small, home-quality tape machine) when he heard that the San Francisco Tape Music Center had, as he called it, "this glorious three-track Ampex." He began to work there and observed, "It was a typical studio for those days, with equipment built for other purposes and adapted to music." At about the same time, Subotnick and Sender decided, as Subotnick put it, "that this idea of cutting and splicing was ridiculous," and they came up with some ideas and designs for new equipment, including the idea for an optically controlled "synthesizer."

Buchla designed it and built it. As he recalls, "The first thing I built there was a device that analyzed the shape of a hand to create a waveshape—so that as you moved your hand in an optical path and spread your fingers, you'd get a harmonically rich waveshape, but if you kept your fingers together, you'd get a sine wave, and you could vary the pitch with a footpedal." And after building it, he said: "This is the wrong way to do it."

Buchla's idea was to build a voltage-controlled modular system. His concept included the idea of a *sequencer*, an analog automation device that allowed a composer to set and store a sequence of notes (or a sequence of sounds, or loudnesses, or other musical information) and play it back automatically. As he said, "My first idea was to reduce the labor in splicing tapes, and that was where the sequencer came from, so if I built a sixteen-stage sequencer, I could eliminate sixteen splices." But his main focus was on performance. His concept also included a pressure-sensitive keyboard, actually an array of metallic strips that were sensitive to changes in the pressure with which they were touched. As he explains, "I regarded things that you touch as being a very legitimate input for musical instruments, but I also regarded electronics as freeing us from mechanical linkages so that, in my view, there was no need to adapt a keyboard that was designed to throw hammers and strings." Subotnick continues:

> But this was all on paper. We asked Don how much it would cost to build it. He said, "$500." The Rockefeller Foundation gave us $500. With the $500, suddenly everything got built and the studio became really complete. With Don's absolute brilliance, it was an amazing machine.

Bill Maginnis, the studio's technician, recalls that day in early 1965 when Buchla brought the first synthesizer into the studio:

> I played with it until about 6 in the morning. I programmed the sequencer to play the first eight notes of *Yankee Doodle*. When Pauline [Oliveros] came in later, she turned the power on and it played the first eight notes of *Yankee Doodle*, and she called me and asked, "How do I turn this damn thing off?"

Through 1965, Subotnick and Buchla worked together to refine their ideas, and what became the Series 100 took definitive shape. In 1966, Buchla formed a company called Buchla and Associates and, through the San Francisco Tape Music Center, marketed what he then called *The Modular Electronic Music System*. David Tudor, who had bought an earlier sound-distribution system from Buchla, was quoted in a promotional brochure as saying, "A most remarkable instrument for manipulating sound . . ." In the next years, as Buchla recalls, "I called it the *Electric Music Box*, but everybody else simply called it the 'Buchla Box.'" In 1969, Buchla sold to CBS the rights to manufacture the Series 100. He tells it:

> They thought they wanted to branch into musical instruments. There were quite a few CBS systems sold. They really got into production. But then they dropped the ball. It was too small a market and too narrow a focus. Their Fender guitar business was booming and they wanted the larger market that that represented, and it was clear to them that electronic instruments were designed to be on the fringe.

Meanwhile, in 1966, Subotnick went to New York University and took with him a replica, with a couple of additions, of the first synthesizer that Buchla had built. He set about learning how to use it. Subotnick:

> My method was to go to work at about 8 A.M. and to work until 2 A.M. the next morning, six days a week, and I purposefully did not know what results I was after. I believed that with this new instrument, we were in a new period for composition, that the composer had the potential for being a studio artist, being composer, performer and audience all at once, conceiving the idea, creating and performing the idea, and then stepping back and being critical of the results. I wanted to explore what kind of art I would create in that new circumstance.

Subotnick explored. And beginning in 1966, he received a series of commissions from Nonesuch Records—for *Silver Apples of the Moon* (1967), *The Wild Bull* (1968), and *Touch* (1969)—to compose directly for recordings. He continues:

> When I got the commission for *Silver Apples*, it intrigued me that it would go from living room to living room and that someone listening would re-create my experience for $1.69. I thought three things about the piece. One, it had to be conceived for the medium, without instruments. Two, it had to be something that I really loved, that I'd want to hear again. And three, that the experience had to be a kind of trip, because it was in the living room. What a trip meant to me was that suddenly you'd be experiencing one kind of world, then suddenly another, as if in the desert, and around the bend you're in a jungle, or on the moon, without knowing how you got there, so there's no linearity.
>   But in thinking back on it, I felt I had not done service to the idea of going to someone else's living room. So the vision changed in *The Wild Bull* to become more personal. I found a book of Sumerian poetry, and there was a female poet talking about the loss of her husband in a poem called "The wild bull who was laying down . . ." I decided that her feeling of war and loss would be what the piece was about. I used the record-

*The Buchla Series 200
modular system, late 1960s.
Photo courtesy Donald Buchla.*

ing of my son's voice as a moan. It became the basis of the opening sounds of the piece, and then I decided that on one side of the record would be the woman's feelings, and on the other side would be the man's feelings.

But after *The Wild Bull*, I felt still that I had not come to grips with the living room music of the future and I realized that what I was missing was the raw energy of electronics. I decided that space would become a critical aspect of the gestural quality of the music, and that it had to be raw energy somehow, and I would find a way to take the raw energy of performance in my studio. In *Touch*, the idea was to touch something . . .

In 1969, Subotnick left New York for California Institute of the Arts. His next pieces included *Sidewinder* (1970), *Four Butterflies* (1971), and *Until Spring* (1975), in which he continued to develop ideas of performance, energy, control, and structure. His last early synthesizer composition was *Sky of Cloudless Sulphur* (1978), for eight loudspeakers, commissioned by JBL for the inauguration of a new JBL loudspeaker factory in the San Fernando Valley. And later, thinking back through that first group of pieces, he reflected upon the tight relationship between an instrument and the music that can be composed with it, and he acknowledged that Buchla had been continually responsive and helpful. As he said it, "I was collaborating with Buchla . . ."

•

While Moog, Ketoff, and Buchla were building the first round of synthesizers, Peter Zinovieff in London was deciding what he did not want to do. In his words, "I couldn't stand cutting up tape." By 1966, he had built a sequencer, bought a house in the Putney area of London, overlooking the Thames, and had a shed built in his garden to use as a studio.

During the same period, David Cockerell was earning his living as a technician for the Ministry of Health and developing a strong interest in building electronic music circuits. He remembers, "I'd been messing about at home with voltage-controlled circuits—I'd read an article by Bob Moog in *Radio Electronics*, in 1964, and I thought it was a really interesting thing." Zinovieff and Cockerell met through a mutual friend, and as Cockerell tells it, "I began moonlighting for him, building gadgets, voltage-controlled oscillators, filters, and so on."

In 1967, Zinovieff called Tristram Cary and invited Cary to visit his Putney studio. Cary was living in Fressingfield, in the countryside, but he was also coming to London on a regular basis to put together a studio at the Royal College of Music. He accepted Zinovieff's invitation and observed, "He was into the most complete sequencing you could do short of using a computer." In fact, Cockerell and Zinovieff soon decided that Zinovieff's sequencing should indeed be done with a computer. And Zinovieff moved quickly: "We got in touch with DEC, we sold my wife's tiara, and we bought a PDP-8 with 4k of memory." But there were problems. As Zinovieff put it, "The computer couldn't really do anything but read paper tape." There were also solutions: "So I wrote to a DEC instructor, 'I'll give you a case of whisky if you show me how to load a series of numbers and direct it to an output.'" Zinovieff began to program. He recalls, "I began to take myself seriously as an experimental electronic musician."

Very seriously, indeed, because Zinovieff and Cary then, as Cary tells it, "planned London's first really big electronic music concert and booked Queen Elizabeth Hall for a date in January 1968." Cockerell, meanwhile, was building peripheral equipment, including digitally controlled filters and oscillators, for the computer. By the time of the concert, enough programming had been done and equipment built to perform the concert. All of the equipment was taken to the hall. The program included Zinovieff's *Partita for Computer*. Cary was delighted:

> Believe it or not, we filled the house. We got school children plastering London with little stickers, all over the underground, on the bus stops, wherever the stickers would go, and we actually filled the hall. We claimed it was the first ever appearance of a live performing computer on stage playing an electronic piece without tape.

By 1968, however, Zinovieff's Putney studio had become expensive. He decided, as he put it, "that we should make something to sell." He formed EMS Ltd. with himself, Cary, and Cockerell as founding directors.

The company's first product grew out of a request by composer Don Banks. As Cary remembers, "Don asked if David could put together a package of useful electronic music devices for as little as £50, his budget limit, and this produced the *VCS-1*, built in a standard grey rack-mounting box and containing various synthesizer modules." An expanded version soon followed. The new model became the *VCS-3*, later called the *Putney* for the United States market, and everyone had ideas about how it should be designed. Cary tells us how it happened:

*Peter Zinovieff at the Synthi 100 in his London studio, about 1970.
Photo courtesy of Electronic Music Foundation.*

Peter suggested using pin matrix patching. Having got rid of patchcords, the whole design became elegant and compact. Somewhere along the line, probably on a scrap of paper in a pub, the miniature desk shape seemed a good idea, and having worked out suitable dimensions with David, I took home a patch matrix and spent a weekend at Fressingfield making the box for the prototype. I left the top panel blank for David to drill the holes for the knobs, and within a couple of days it was assembled and working.

Cockerell quit his job with the Ministry of Health to devote himself full time to the new company, and commercial activities began in earnest. Zinovieff decided what was to be designed. According to Cockerell, "He wasn't much interested in tonal music, and neither was Tristram, so the first machines never had a keyboard." The BBC bought one of the first VCS-3s. As Brian Hodgson at the Radiophonic Workshop tells it, "The BBC had decided to buy a Moog, but I said, 'This was madness, we ought to support the British industry,' and so we bought our first synthesizer." The VCS-3 was followed by the *DK-2* keyboard and the portable *Synthi A* (at first called the *Portabella*). In 1970, Peter Grogono began working with Zinovieff as a programmer. Also in 1970, the *Synthi 100*, a large sequencer-based synthesizer in a console, became available. And again, the BBC Radiophonic Workshop bought the first one. As Hodgson

*Tristram Cary working with
VCS-3 synthesizers in his studio
at Fressingfield, Suffolk, in 1972.
Photo courtesy Tristram Cary.*

recalls, "It arrived with David Cockerell but with no manual—so David and I sat up for several days and nights writing one." In 1971, the AKS, a portable synthesizer in a case with a sequencer and touch-sensitive keyboard, was introduced. In December 1971, Tim Orr joined the design group.

By early 1972, EMS was producing not only the VCS-3, the Synthi AKS, the DK-2 keyboard, and the Synthi-100, but also the *256 Sequencer*, a *Random Voltage Generator*, a *Pitch-to-Voltage Converter*, and an *Octave Filter Bank*. In 1973, there was the *Spectrum*, a video synthesizer developed by Richard Monkhouse, who worked under David Cockerell. Cary's job, in his words, "was to raise money with the educational and serious end and write most of the copy for handbooks—Peter insisted I take examples of most of the products down to Fressingfield, and very often I could have personal modules done to order." From Zinovieff's description of the manufacturing operation, however, his personal priorities were clear:

> It was quite big. It employed up to forty people. I hated it. I found it extremely dull. But on the other hand it was our lifeblood. Any money left over went into the studio.

The studio was dedicated to experimentation, developing generally interesting projects, testing ideas and products, creating music, and helping others. As Zinovieff reflected, "That's my gift, as the French say, 'animateur.'" Delia Derbyshire had begun to use the studio in 1963, and through the years, many other composers worked there, among them Brian Hodgson, Don Banks, Justin Connolly, David Lumsdaine, Alan Sutcliffe, Ron Grainer, Annea Lockwood, Tristram Cary, and Jonathan Harvey. Hans Werner Henze did several pieces, among them *Glass Music* (1970), *Prison Song* (1971), and *Tristan* (1973). Zinovieff recounts working with Henze:

He did *Glass Music* by telephone instruction from Italy. I made it and he said, "That's exactly what I wanted you to do," and people said, "That's exactly like Henze." He came to the studio and we'd record bits and analyze them with the filter banks and then synthesize them. We did one piece called *Tristan*. It was terrific. I could set these huge chords up with variable degrees of randomness. That was the time when I had this video camera interface where you could point the camera at something and translate the picture into sounds. I never went further with it, but it was a very interesting idea. You could get even the most straightforward things—a straight line was a glissando, red would be low—and they would make very interesting sounds, and one could say, "Well, I'll work with that."

Harrison Birtwistle was consistently in the studio. His works included *Four Interludes* (1969), *Medusa* (1970), *Signals* (1970), *Chronometer* (1971), *Orpheus* (1976), and many other pieces and sketches. As Zinovieff recalls, "He wasn't interested in programming or in touching the equipment, but he was interested in precise results and would write very specific scores without knowing what the apparatus could do—Birtwistle and I worked on lots of things . . ."

In 1969, making and changing sounds, which involved turning a lot of knobs and making connections between modules, was a major problem in performing with a synthesizer. In Moog and Buchla systems, connections between modules were made with patchcords. But not only did patchcords often lead to an Amazon nightmare of jungle-like visual confusion, it took time to reconnect them, to pull out each patchcord and insert it in a different place. In the EMS synthesizers, connections were made by inserting tiny resistance pins somewhere into a grid of pinholes which connected outputs from the left and inputs to the top. But the pins often broke or got lost on a tabletop, and in any case, it took time to decide where in the grid to insert them. These were not optimal performance-oriented systems.

The *Minimoog*, the first single-unit integrated synthesizer, solved the problem by allowing a musician to push a button or touch a switch to make a module connection. In 1969, the first prototype of the Minimoog, the Model A, was put together by William Hemsath. As Moog recalls, "He put standard modules in it with a little keyboard and hardwired them in back." An improved Model B was built in 1970 as an integrated design, a single panel, with circuit boards in the back. There was then a Model C and, finally, Model D, the production version. In Moog's words:

We all worked on it—myself, Bill Hemsath, Jim Scott, Chad Hunt—and an industrial design firm decided how it would look. The idea was that if we built something that could be carried by one person, a certain number of studio musicians in New York and Los Angeles would buy it.

The Minimoog was first played in public by Dick Hyman at the Eastman School of Music in Rochester in June 1970. It was presented to a far larger public at the AES convention in October in New York. Sales began, slowly at first. Moog remembers, "We had very little luck in interesting music dealers. 'All those knobs?' they would say. 'Are you nuts?'" The large modular systems, meanwhile, were still being manufactured. Moog continues:

> By early 1970, there were a lot of very big systems for sale, and our orders stopped—just like somebody pulled the plug. 1967 was $200k, 1968 was twice that, 1969 was more. We projected more for 1970, and we had ordered the parts. In 1970, we had thirty or forty people sitting there with nothing to build.

During that same period, William Waytena, a businessman in Buffalo, not far from Trumansburg, had formed a company called Musonics and started to produce a portable synthesizer called the *Sonic 5*. Moog continues:

> Bill Waytena watched us slowly die. When we were desperate, he came in—it was March 1971—and bought R. A. Moog Inc. for a promise to pay off our debts. After an interim step of six months or so when the company was called Moog Musonics, he formed Moog Music. I went there as president, but only nominally. I had no control. Waytena had no title, but he had all the power.

Meanwhile, different paths were converging. In 1970, Tom Rhea had gone to Trumansburg to interview Moog for his doctoral dissertation on the history of electronic musical instruments. Rhea remembers, "There was so little room at that facility that Bob and I opened a window and crawled out onto a roof of the first floor so we would have some privacy." In 1971 in Nashville, Rhea met businessman David Van Koevering, and their interests coincided to the extent that they established Electronic Arts Foundation to acquire, preserve, and display historical instruments. In 1972, Van Koevering went to Buffalo to become marketing manager for Moog Music and used Rhea as a consultant to do some technical and educational writing. In 1973, Rhea was hired as head of the studio systems division, which meant modular equipment, and doubled its sales in six months. His success initiated a major career direction. As he observed, "When you can sell stuff, the only thing people want you to do is sell stuff." Then, during Rhea's first year, Moog Music was bought by Norlin Music in Chicago, and Rhea became a Norlin employee. He recalls:

> I worked for six or seven different marketing regimes at Norlin. The marketing people mostly came from Quaker Oats, French's Mustard, Fisher-Price Toys, Gabriel Shock Absorbers, and Beatrice Foods. These men were bright and capable but they had no gut feeling about the music

industry. It was disastrous. The synthesizer industry was not mature. It needed people who could fly by the seat of their pants. And that generally was not the leadership at Norlin.

The Minimoog became successful largely through the efforts and energy of David Van Koevering. As Rhea reflected, "Salespeople can affect history." But there was also some luck. In 1969, shortly after *Switched On Bach* came out, Keith Emerson in London bought a small modular system and played a major synthesizer solo with it. The song was *Lucky Man*. The album was *Emerson Lake & Palmer*. *Lucky Man* got to the top of the charts, and as Moog tells it, "We began hearing things such as, 'You can't get a job as a keyboard player if you don't have a Minimoog,' and once that happened we were selling fifty to 100 every month and by 1973 it got as high as 300 a month." Emerson bought a Minimoog. Stevie Wonder, Blood Sweat and Tears, Mothers of Invention, Todd Rundgren, Yes, Pink Floyd, and numerous other performers and bands in the rock world also bought Minimoogs. Jan Hammer, John McLaughlin, Billy Cobham, Herbie Hancock, and many other performers in the jazz world also bought Minimoogs. As Chick Corea put it, "The only sound I could ever find that I felt comfortable blowing on was the Minimoog." By the time sales declined in the late 1970s and production stopped in 1980, over 12,000 had been sold. Moog had not foreseen that number back in 1970. As he said, "I thought we could sell 100 of them."

●

By the late 1960s, synthesizers were beginning to be used in all forms of commercial music. Eric Siday in New York City used a Moog synthesizer to do the CBS sound logo and many other commercials for television. Pink Floyd used the VCS-3 in *Dark Side of the Moon*. Roxy Music and Brian Eno used the VCS-3. And as other musicians and groups began to play synthesizers, and as electronic sound became increasingly familiar and commercially desirable, the market grew.

And as the market grew, new companies were formed and new synthesizers were developed and improved in quick succession. In 1969, ARP Instruments was established near Boston by Alan R. Pearlman. In 1970, ARP introduced the modular *Model 2500*, and soon after came the portable *Model 2600*, *Pro-Soloist*, *Odyssey*, *Axxe*, and *Omni*.

●

The Minimoog and the portable ARP synthesizers were monophonic instruments, able to generate only one sound at a time. Although they were successful, they were also limited, and there was an increasingly urgent need felt during the early 1970s for the development of a polyphonic synthesizer that could generate several different sounds simultaneously. David Luce had gone to

Moog Music to design what eventually became the *Polymoog*, and other engineers at other companies were working on polyphonic synthesizers.

The *Four Voice*, engineered by Tom Oberheim at Oberheim Electronics, emerged as the first market success. Oberheim had started in the late 1960s building ring modulators and other devices which were marketed by Norlin Music with a Maestro brand name. Then he saw an ARP 2600 in January 1971 at the NAMM (National Association of Music Merchants) show, one of the important trade shows in the field, and said, "I learned what a synthesizer was all about." He became an ARP dealer in Los Angeles. In 1972, drawing upon his experience as a computer engineer, he designed the *DS-2*, a 144-note digital sequencer which sold for $25. But, as he points out, "All the synths at the time were monophonic—if you hooked your sequencer up to a synthesizer, you didn't have anything to play." So he designed a *Synthesizer Expander Module*, an SEM as he called it, which could be played by the digital sequencer at the same time that a musician was playing a keyboard. In 1975, he licensed a keyboard design from E-mu Systems, modified it a bit, and combined it with four SEMs, producing the Four Voice. Oberheim:

> At first, it was a kind of curiosity to a lot of people. But then it started catching on. It was a bear to use. The four voices were completely independent so if you wanted to change the sound you had to patch each SEM separately.

The Four Voice, as Oberheim soon realized, was too complicated. He also realized that the problem of operational complexity could be solved through programmability. In 1976, he designed a synthesizer programmer which, by allowing for the storage of control-voltage parameters, made the SEMs easier to use. In 1977, he produced the *OB-1*, a programmable monophonic synthesizer. Then in 1978, Dave Smith, at Sequential Circuits, designed the *Prophet-5*.

Dave Smith had begun with an electrical engineering profession and a music hobby. In 1972, he had been working in Silicon Valley and, in his words, "not liking it too much, when a friend called and said he'd seen a synthesizer in a music store." Smith bought it. It was a Minimoog, in his words, "right up my alley—technology and music." He then built an analog sequencer and, in 1974, with the thought that other people might want to buy it, formed Sequential Circuits. He sold four sequencers. But, he reasoned, he was working part time.

In 1975, he built a digital sequencer and started getting serious. As he remembers, "*Keyboard Magazine* was just starting up about a half mile from my house—they put in a product announcement and I ended up selling a few hundred of those things." In early 1977, he designed a programmer unit that allowed someone to program sounds on the Minimoog and Arp 2600, "the big two" (as Smith put it) in the market. He began to work full time at Sequential Circuits, at that time with one or two employees. In midsummer 1977, Smith got the idea for the Prophet-5 and made an important decision: "I decided to take a chance and go for the kill and build a real synthesizer."

The Prophet-5, as Smith called it, was more than a real synthesizer. It was fully programmable and polyphonic. It featured microprocessor-based auto-tuning. And it was developed in record time. The first versions were demonstrated at the NAMM show in January 1978. As Smith recalls, "It barely worked, but we got lots of orders—and I got lucky because most people liked the sound a whole lot." The first one was shipped in March 1978. Smith continues:

> We had all kinds of problems, but we had to start shipping what we had or we would have gone out of business. We had trouble getting parts. The synthesizer chips were unreliable. I was trying to get all the bugs out of the instrument. All during the year, we were fighting with bugs and suppliers and listening to musicians and stores yelling at us.

In 1979, the Prophet-5 was redesigned internally, its reliability was significantly improved, and in the next few years, more than 8,000 units were sold. Although Moog, ARP, and Oberheim were dominant forces in the marketplace, and although other interesting synthesizers appeared, such as Crumar's Orchestrator in 1974 and Yamaha's CS-80 in 1976, the Prophet-5 was the hit of the late 1970s.

•

Tuning, in general, was a significant problem with analog technology. Analog synthesizers were neither precise nor impervious to temperature change. Referring to the analog components in the GROOVE system at Bell Labs, F. Richard Moore recalls, "A typical musical evening consisted of sitting down and tuning the equipment for about an hour—then I could use it for a half hour before I had to tune it again."

The solution was digital technology. In 1965 at the University of Toronto, Gustav Ciamaga and doctoral candidate James Gabura began work on what they called *Piper*, a *hybrid* system in which a digital computer was used to control the operations of an analog synthesizer. Piper 0, an initial concept-verification stage, was followed by Piper 1, a working system in the computer laboratory of the department of electrical engineering at the University of Toronto. There were, of course, problems. Gabura wrote:

> The problems associated with Piper 1 were primarily of a physical nature. It was necessary to disassemble certain key portions of the Electronic Music Studio, and to transport the several pieces of heavy and bulky equipment across campus by cab to the Computer Laboratory . . . the reverse procedure had to be followed at the end of each computing session. Yet the need to move equipment was a comparatively minor hard-

ship. Unprotected by its equipment rack, and consisting of many individual units, the apparatus proved extremely vulnerable. High and low-voltage power supply connections . . .

There was yet another problem of a physical nature. As Ciamaga remembers, "We were using computers where the room still had no air conditioner—the room was hot and it contributed to the timing instability of the VCOs." And there was yet another innovation in Piper 1: a tuning program for the unstable analog oscillators which, as Ciamaga explains, "would scan through the oscillators and write a new tuning table."

Piper 2 solved the problems of Piper 1. And as Piper 2 was developed during the next few years, the situation of the computer laboratory itself improved. The analog equipment could be left with the computer and the room was air-conditioned. The room was, in fact, too cool. As Ciamaga said, "I remember wearing a coat in the middle of summer." The computer's output was enlarged from one voice to four. And in 1973, after IBM had taken away the computer, thereby ending the project, Gabura could reflect, "What the 'hybrid computer' method of electronic sound generation does offer electronic composers is an unrivalled combination of control flexibility and immediacy, facilitating the efficient production of electronic music . . ."

•

At Bell Labs, Music V was a hard act to follow, but it was followed. In late 1967, Max Mathews and F. Richard Moore began to develop *GROOVE* (Generated Realtime Operations on Voltage-Controlled Equipment). Its authors described it as follows:

> GROOVE is a hybrid system that interposes a digital computer between a human composer-performer and an electronic sound synthesizer. All of the manual actions of the human being (playing a keyboard, twisting a knob, and so forth) are monitored by the computer and stored in its disk memory . . .

The "manual actions of the human being" were stored on disk and then selectively output to control the variables of a modular analog sound synthesizer, such as pitch, loudness, and timbre. The computer used in GROOVE was a Honeywell DDP224, newly acquired at the time by Bell Labs and dedicated to work in sound. The computer was connected to the analog synthesizer via fourteen independent control lines through which information was updated every hundredth of a second. The analog synthesizer contained a large number of devices, in Mathews' words, "components that I could lay my hands on or build." It also contained a sophisticated patching system consisting of patchboards that plugged into a holder, the effect of which was that users could change connections rapidly. As Moore remembers, "We programmed the patcher by inserting jumper cables into a board, and then dropping the board into a holder that effectively interconnected all of the analog devices—each of us had a personal patchboard or two." GROOVE also had a display system which showed any subset of the fourteen lines of control information as a cursor swept across the monitor's screen, something like a cursor moving across the page of a musical score. Moore: "It provided a control paradigm of continuous control of parameters, rather than event-based control—and that meant that things that were hard to represent, such as a slightly varying vibrato that a violinist might use, could be represented in a very straightforward way, as something varying in time." Laurie Spiegel worked extensively with GROOVE from 1973 to 1978. She describes it:

> In principle, GROOVE was the ultimate hybrid modular synthesizer. It allowed the arbitrary interconnection, via user-programmed logic, of analog and digital input, output, hardware, and software modules, including ever-accumulating numbers of library-resident code modules written by users over the years, and increasing numbers of gizmos built mostly by Max Mathews.

Mathews used GROOVE primarily to develop the first version of his Conductor Program. Moore used GROOVE to compose and develop algorithms. In Moore's words:

> Life in those days was great. I was an applications programmer and I worked mostly on speech and coding theory. I did music at Bell in the evenings and on the weekends, which was the case for everybody there. On a typical night of working on music, my time was divided between improving the GROOVE program itself and writing music with it.

Composers visited. Vladimir Ussachevsky kept in touch and visited from time to time. Pierre Boulez and Gerard Schwartz, as Mathews recalls, "did a little work." Emmanuel Ghent was the most dedicated visiting composer.

Ghent, in fact, had needed GROOVE even before it existed. He had reached a turning point in his own work in 1963. In his *Entelechy*, for viola and piano, the rhythms, as he described them, "were so complex that if I were to go on from there, I needed some kind of external polytempo cueing device." He built what he called the *Polynome*, by which prearranged tempo relationships were coordinated through mechanical gears. He used the Polynome also in *Triality* (1964), for violin, trumpet, bassoon, and (as he called it) "special equipment." The Polynome, however, was limited to the tempos that were represented in its gears.

Ghent wanted something more general, a device that would be capable of representing any rhythmic and tempo relationships. In 1964, he designed the *Coordinome*, a punched paper tape reader in which holes could represent any rhythmic relationships, and had it built. As Ghent recalls, "When Bob Moog saw it, he said, 'Oh my Lord, we could encode the paper tape digitally and then use it to control my equipment up at the Trumansburg studio.'" In composing his *Hex* (1966), for instruments, tape, and "special equipment," Ghent used the Coordinome not only to control Moog's equipment but also, in performance, to coordinate performers with each other and with the electronically generated tape.

In 1967, Ghent felt that his logical next step was to work at Bell Labs. He went to Max Mathews, showed him what he had done, and pointed out that if so much could be done with an eight-track paper tape, imagine what could be done with a computer. Mathews replied, "Well, we had the same idea."

Ghent began to work at Bell Labs just as GROOVE, under Mathews' direction, was moving from conception to realization. From late 1967, Ghent worked extensively with F. Richard Moore, who was writing the GROOVE software. As Ghent recalls, "Dick was writing an endless array of new subroutines for every new idea that came along." Ghent continues:

> The computer was used for speech synthesis during the day. I would come in two or three times a week, usually at 6 or 7 in the evening, and stay there minimum until midnight or 1 A.M. and sometimes much much later. I tried to avoid the morning rush hour into New York City, so it was urgent to get to the highway before 5 A.M.

Emmanuel Ghent in the GROOVE analog room at Bell Labs
in the early 1970s. Photo courtesy Emmanuel Ghent.

Laurie Spiegel in the GROOVE analog room at Bell Labs in the early 1970s. Photo courtesy Emmanuel Ghent.

Ghent's work in those first few years with GROOVE was prolific. His compositions include *Battery Park* (1969), *Molly Bloom's Lament* (1969), an electronic realization of Ben Johnston's *Knocking Piece* (1969), *Danger–High Voltage* (1969), *Helices* (1969), *Innerness* (1970), *Fusion* (1970), *Supernova* (1970), *Phosphones* (1971), and many other pieces. *Phosphones* was especially interesting for two reasons. First, it was used by the Mimi Garrard Dance Company as music and, in conjunction with a custom lighting board designed by James Seawright, as a timebase for synchronized theatrical lighting. Second, the sounds in *Phosphones* were made primarily with special resonator circuits designed and dubbed *Resons* by Max Mathews. And there were other pieces by Ghent for the Mimi Garrard Dance Company, among them *Dualities* (1972) and *Brazen* (1975), in which music, lighting, strobes, projections, and dance were coordinated by digital signals encoded on magnetic tape. In 1972, he used algorithmic methods to compose *Computer Brass* (1972); *Divertimento for Electronic Violin and Computer Brass* (1973); and *Lustrum* (1974), for electronic string quartet, brass quintet and tape. And he often used performance devices, such as a keyboard, a three-dimensional wand, and a variety of switches and other controls to interact with the algorithms while he was composing. He describes it:

> By changing a number here or there, or flipping a switch, I could produce lines of pitches where the voice-leading was at times astonishing and fascinating in its unexpectedness . . . I would create in real time and then

select what I wanted. I remember many occasions working with Laurie all night at this and thinking what the computer was doing was incredible. It would produce lines that were musically so interesting, but who ever would have thought of writing a musical line like that? We had the sense that here we had hired the computer as a musical assistant and it was producing something that we never would have dreamed of.

Laurie Spiegel started to work with GROOVE in 1973, focusing, in her words, "on developing my ideas in compositional logic and realtime interactive processes." Spiegel had met Ghent and Mathews at a concert series at the Kitchen in New York City in 1971. In her words, "I was extremely excited to see what they were doing . . . I called Mannie and asked if I could study with him . . . we worked out an arrangement where I was sort of his apprentice." She continues:

> It was incredibly liberating and exciting, a wonderful breakthrough. I had been working with analog synthesis and tape techniques where extreme limitations were imposed by the technology, so going from hardware to software was a whole new world for me. In contrast to modular hardware systems, GROOVE allowed me to create any number of control modules of any design by simply writing software subroutines and reusing them as I wished. I could define much more complex and abstract musical processes and variables, and hear and see and interact with their output in real time by assigning software variables to physical input devices such as knobs and switches. I could just improvise on and on with more high level musical control than had been possible previously. I also made quite a few fixed form pieces . . .

In those years, she composed *Appalachian Grove* (1974), *Patchwork* (1974), a ballet called *Waves* (1975), *The Expanding Universe* (1975), *Drums* (1975), *Clockworks* (1975), *A Voyage* (1976), and many other compositions. What was it like to work with GROOVE on an everyday basis? She answers:

> We were allowed to use the computers only when they weren't in use for genuine phone company business, so we tended to have access from the late afternoons on. Fridays and Saturdays were best because we could stay all night. I probably spent twenty to thirty hours a week there, always at night, weekends and holidays.
>
> It was noisy. There were loud ventilation sounds that you had to learn to ignore. And it was always freezing in the computer room, so we often wore parkas. A lot of time went into a zillion trips back and forth between the analog and digital parts of the system, which were down a very long hall from each other and connected by 300-foot trunk cables. We used to kid about wanting roller skates.

There was a wonderful synergy among GROOVE's users, who were all both extremely intelligent and doing what they were doing for love of the art. That whole lab complex which Max Mathews ran was full of fascinating projects and people.

Every week, usually on Wednesday or Thursday afternoons, Max and various other scientists would gather in the conference room with their instruments and read string quartets. There was a lot of real love for music in those labs, the kind unfortunately often commoner in amateurs than pros, a very pleasing contrast to the atmosphere of qualification and caution I'd found in academic music and some new music circles.

In 1977, as Ghent's algorithmic thinking progressed, he began a series of twenty-nine studies, from two to twenty-seven minutes each, collectively called *Program Music*. As he said, "They were all studies for what was to come, which was the use of this mode of interaction in such a way that I could create a whole piece . . ." But it was not to be. On November 22, 1978, Bell Labs notification MH-1228-PBD-mm was circulated. It was addressed to DDP224 users and said, in part, "At the end of January we plan to remove from service the DDP224 computer . . ." The GROOVE project, in fact, was terminated at the end of December 1978. Thinking back, Ghent reflects, "It opened opportunities that had been unthinkable—it enabled me to try all kinds of ideas, listen to them in real time, modify them in real time, and thereby get a chance to experiment in ways that would be prohibitive using standard methods like paper and pencil and human musicians."

•

Donald Buchla's systems of the 1970s reflected the trend toward digital technology. In 1971, he developed the *Series 200*, a pre-computer system with digital oscillators. The *Series 500*, which appeared soon after, was as he described it, "a very large and quite elaborate hybrid system, with sixteen oscillators and a gating matrix with which we could interconnect everything . . ." In 1972, he built the *Series 300*, a computer-based controller that interfaced with Series 200 modules. The *Music Easel*, which followed in 1973, was in his words, "an instrument as opposed to a system—it used a touch keyboard and it was pretty small." In 1978, the Buchla 400, a computer-based system, included a computer screen and three programming languages—Midas III, CHOPS, and Patch VI—which allowed composers to program sounds and sequences and define performer interactions. Why did Buchla develop software? What were the important software issues? He answers:

I find commercial synthesizers relatively clumsy in the way the user is given access to important musical relationships. Assumptions are made that are based on the maintenance of the status quo in music and don't

The first Buchla Series 500 hybrid system as installed at California Institute of the Arts in the early 1970s. Note that the computer sits on a table next to the synthesizer and the computer terminal is built into the synthesizer frame. Photo by Joel Chadabe.

allow anyone to deviate very far from the established norms. A user interface includes knobs, pushbuttons and displays, but it also includes the software—and I build software to be general and unassumptive about musical structure to allow myself the freedom to make any relationships between gesture and musical response.

Buchla's software was also easy to learn and use. As he said, "I often hear the comment from users of my systems that they hardly need the instruction manual . . ."

●

By 1970, Zinovieff's studio in London contained two PDP-8s joined together, a 32K hard disk, a DECtape drive, several input/output peripherals, a Synthi 100, various other synthesizers, and a large group of amplifiers, oscillators, envelope generators, filters, switches, clocks, DACs and ADCs, zero-crossing detectors, and a few percussion devices. There were also certain items specified by Zinovieff and built by David Cockerell, among them the so-called *Digital Oscillator Bank*, in fact a sampler to which waveforms were downloaded from the computer; a general-purpose knob, called the *Spinwheel*, with a pushbutton panel to select what the knob was controlling; and a pressure-sensitive keyboard called *Squeeze-Me*—in Cockerell's words, "old hat now, but one couldn't find anything like it then." It was a lot of equipment, some of it very innovative, and Zinovieff's idea was to control his analog equipment with the computers.

By 1970, he and Peter Grogono had finished MUSYS-3, a language for controlling analog synthesis equipment with a PDP-8 computer. MUSYS-3 functioned as a sequencer to record, store, vary, and play back information that had been played into it. It was used as a scheduler to coordinate the operations of the many devices in the studio. And it generated random numbers. As Zinovieff recalls, "We used it to control the 100 or 200 devices that were available . . . it was really a very good language, because you could introduce any degree of randomness."

Zinovieff's primary interest, however, was in a sixty-four channel filter bank that Cockerell had designed and built in 1969. As he said, "My goal was to analyze intelligently any signal and be able to play it back." He used it in working with Harrison Birtwistle to compose Birtwistle's *Chronometer* (1971). In his words:

> It epitomized the way I wanted to work. We went to Big Ben and we went in the clock mechanisms to record the chimes with contact and real microphones. And then I analysed those sounds through the filter bank and made a software archive. Harry wrote a score, a very detailed score, using those sounds but doing transpositions, not very much manipulation, but just putting them together in different pitches and loudnesses on sixteen tracks. And then it was all composed by one program which collected and assembled those sounds and played them. And then varied them. It was a wonderful project. And what came out was a wonderful structured piece made of concrète sounds without a single bit of tape splicing. And without a single touch on any button by Harry. So the score looked like a mixture of graphics and symbols, with pitch notations and written instructions.

As early as 1968, Zinovieff had experimented with digital audio. At a show called Cybernetic Serendipity at the Institute for the Contemporary Arts in London, in his words, "People were invited to whistle into a microphone and the computer would decode it and play it back with variations, percussion accompaniment, and so on—and it was clever enough to anticipate a few tunes, so if someone sang the national anthem it would stop and play the whole thing before they finished."

And so it was a logical next step to develop a digital version of the filter bank. In 1971, Zinovieff hired Peter Eastty, a digital designer. By 1973, the project was called VOCOM (VOice COMmunication) and the digital filter bank was used to analyze voice sounds, store the analysis in data-reduced form, and then resynthesize the sounds on demand. It certainly had musical uses: Tristram

Cary used it for voice transformation in composing his *The Pilgrim's Progress* (1972) and for transforming the sounds of Olivetti typewriters, sixteen singers, and jazz drummer in his *Divertimento* (1973). But the business application was speech compression and transmission. As Cockerell recalls, "We thought we might be able to sell this frequency domain technology for the purpose of compressing speech . . . we found that if you analyzed signals by this filter bank, you could re-create them by playing discrete sine waves, and it was intelligible."

VOCOM represented a big idea with potential major impact. By 1973, however, EMS Ltd. was heavily in debt, and Zinovieff, who had developed more interesting technology than he could sell in the synthesizer market, was looking for a solution to his financial problems in the larger markets addressed by VOCOM. He tells it:

> One of EMS' endeavors was to go public with a speech synthesis project called VOCOM. This was, I think, the beginning of EMS' downfall. The development costs, the cost of people, became very expensive. In the early days, you could do a week's work and finish a new ring modulator, for example. But, later, with digital things, every piece of new machinery would involve a lot of manpower.

Manpower. And capital, Zinovieff might have added. Attempts to raise capital were unsuccessful. EMS was eventually sold and the studio dismantled. And another wonderfully creative enterprise eventually came to an end. As Cockerell reflects, "I enjoyed those years, yes, indeed . . ."

●

In 1964, when Karl Birger Blomdahl was invited to become music director of the Swedish Broadcasting Corporation (the Swedish Radio), he made it one of his conditions for acceptance that the Swedish Radio finance the building of an electronic music studio. As Lars-Gunnar Bodin recalls, "It was almost an ultimatum—'I'll take the job if you establish an electronic music studio,' and the financial situation of the Radio was pretty strong so they said, 'Sure, we need to have a cutting edge.'" At the same time, Fylkingen, a new music organization in Stockholm, had developed a distinctly cutting-edge philosophy—the word *fylkingen*, in Swedish, refers to the arrowhead formation in which the Viking warriors fought—and Knut Wiggen, Fylkingen's chairman, was interested in the design problems of a second generation of electronic music studios. Wiggen was appointed director of the studio project.

The following year, in 1965, Wiggen opened the Sound Workshop, a small, interim tape studio where Lars-Gunnar Bodin composed *Toccata* (1969) and *Traces I* (1970), Sten Hanson composed *Che* (1968) and *How Are You* (1969), and many other composers finished numerous pieces. But his primary activity was the design and building of a fully automated analog studio. In 1970, finally, EMS (Elektronmusikstudion / Electronic Music Studio) opened its doors.

Why did it take six years? Technical difficulties, the sheer magnitude of the project, and Wiggen's refusal to compromise on technical and audio quality were certainly factors. EMS had purchased twenty-four Schlumberger oscillators, for example, and then redesigned them to achieve greater stability and a better signal-to-noise ratio. Extensive simulations and tests with the computer at Upsala University had taken considerable time.

Organizational issues and politics also caused delays. In 1968, Blomdahl died. In 1969, Blomdahl's successor at the Swedish Radio thought the money being used for EMS would be better placed with the orchestra. Wiggen, still Fylkingen's chairman, responded to the crisis with maneuvers that resulted in a new foundation whose trustees included the president of the Swedish Radio and the president of the Royal Academy of Music. Ownership of the studio's equipment was transferred from the Swedish Radio to the new foundation.

At EMS' startup, the analog oscillators were controlled by two digital tape recorders on which control information was recorded via a difficult and cumbersome control panel. In fact, the only composer sufficiently courageous to complete a piece with that system was Jon Appleton, who used it to compose *King's Road #8* (1970). Later in 1970, EMS acquired a PDP-15 computer, and work on a first round of software was begun. Lars-Gunnar Bodin began to use the studio in 1971. As he recalls, "it was very complicated." He elaborates:

> The software was poor. It was complicated and painstaking to program the thing. You had to sit and write on a teletype machine and the code was coming on punched tape which you had to feed into the computer. You could be sure you'd get hundreds of error messages. There wasn't any good editing program, so you had to try and write another punched tape . . .

It was so complicated, in fact, that many Swedish composers worked elsewhere, either in the EMS tape studio or at locations other than EMS. Bodin, for example, though maintaining close contact with EMS, joined the faculty at the State College of Music in 1972, established a studio, and through 1976, developed that studio and in it composed *Clouds* (1976), a major multimedia work involving electronic sounds, projections, singers, and dancers.

Meanwhile, in 1970, Tamas Ungvary was working as an orchestral conductor in Boden, a small town in northern Sweden. He tells the story of his beginnings in electronic music:

> The Swedish Waterfall Company had built a new dam with electrical turbines, and for the opening festivities, when the turbine was started, they wanted the orchestra to play marches and the usual stuff. I had heard about electronic music and I suggested to the director to play electronic music instead of using the orchestra, and he approved. So we borrowed a Moog synthesizer. I thought, "What the hell is that?" but there were some young people in the orchestra and we figured it out. So my first

composition, which sounded like water dropping, was called *Water Drops*. Then I decided to make a one-day open house for electronic music in this little town. Rikskonserter, a Swedish music organization, sent me some material and I chose a couple of pieces. Almost nobody came. But I heard two pieces—they were Morthesson's *Neutron Star* and Norgaard's *Solitaire*—which affected and impressed me as much as traditional music could do. I thought, "Ah, it's possible to make music with electronics."

Spurred by his new interest, Ungvary visited Miklos Maros, a composer working at the time at EMS. Maros showed the studios to Ungvary and, as Ungvary recalls, "I realized that although I had been working more than twenty years as a music professional, I didn't have any idea of what sound was." Ungvary began to work at EMS in 1971. As he put it, "It was some kind of drug for me." Then *Seul* (1972), his first composition, was played at the ISCM World Music Days in Iceland and reviewed by a Swedish critic as a Nordic piece. And that review *really* got him going. He explained, "I was Hungarian, not Nordic, and I had to make *my* music which reflected *my* temperament."

Ungvary was also frustrated by the difficulties: "There was no real computer music course at EMS at that time—EMS-0, the basic software, was under development and there was little documentation and I didn't understand a word, so I took teletype papers from the wastebasket and tried to figure out what they were." Luckily, Gary Lee Nelson, composer at Oberlin College, was visiting EMS and helped Ungvary learn programming. In fact, Ungvary soon became proficient enough to write the first manual for the computer studio.

Other people also made improvements. Erik Nyberg got the system to function in real time, Michael Hinton wrote IMPACT, a realtime control program, and Thomas Sjöland and Ungvary optimized the realtime system. As the software became more accessible, the hardware also became more suitable. Several new input devices were installed, among them joysticks, tablets, and a pen. Ungvary's creative work during the 1970s and into the 1980s developed in parallel with his technical work. Following *Seul*, his computer compositions included *Basic Barrier* (1973), *Traum des Einsamen* (1975), *Les Mouvements Mousseux* (1979), *Ite, Missa Est* (1982), and *L'Aube des Flammes* (1984). But working creatively put him in another frame of mind: "I could not mix technical work with music." He continues:

When I was composing, I couldn't think about technicalities for one moment. I had to develop a stable and sophisticated enough software package beforehand. I always asked myself, "What would you wish for when you're sitting there making music?" So after perhaps three or four years of software development, I said, "Stop, forget the whole thing," and I went back and made a piece and everything I wished for during the compositional process had to be there and had to function. And I needed real time so that I could find the tensions and relaxations in an immediate response to my emotions.

In 1975, in a turn of generations, Knut Wiggen resigned, Per-Olof Strömberg was appointed temporary director, and Jon Appleton was invited to become director. In 1976, Appleton moved to Stockholm and found, to his unpleasant surprise, that EMS was undergoing a governmental evaluation and funds were frozen. In 1977, he left in frustration, and Lars-Gunnar Bodin became temporary director. In 1978, Bodin became director, just in time to deal with another crisis and, eventually, an opportunity. In his words:

> When the evaluation report was finished, it recommended a closedown of EMS. Many people objected, so we started a campaign and we were pretty successful. I remember a protest meeting which was very well attended. All the important people in music life were there. It was a strong showing for keeping EMS, or restarting it, and since there was such an overwhelming response to keep EMS, the government said, "Thank you for the report," and put it in a drawer and it was forgotten. Then EMS was restarted with new money.

In 1979, EMS acquired a twenty-four-track tape recorder and mixer. As Bodin recalls, "For the next year it went day and night, New Year's Eve and Christmas Eve—it was wonderful to be the director at that time; it was like opening a waterfall."

•

In 1961, Stan Tempelaars, a physics student working in the Studio for Electronic Music at the University of Utrecht, was about to launch a project to investigate the loudness and timbral shapes of musical tones and to find a technical solution for synthesizing them. Tempelaars recalls, "I soon discovered that there was no systematic shape to be discovered—the only solution was to build a generator that could generate *any* shape . . ." By 1964, Tempelaars had built a fifty-step *Variable Function Generator*, as he called it, similar in its structure and operation to the analog sequencer developed at about the same time by Donald Buchla in California.

In 1964, Gottfried Michael Koenig was invited to become artistic director of the Utrecht studio. In his words, "Quite naturally, I thought this post would give me more freedom, more possibilities for developing my ideas . . ." He continues:

> It was a rather small studio when I arrived. My commission was to make it into an international studio. And there was money and support. So I could say, "Well, we need more room." And then, when we had two

rooms, I could say, "We need to fill the rooms with equipment." And then, with the equipment there, I could say, "We need people to operate it."

Koenig thought of using the Variable Function Generator as an oscillator. He remembers asking, "Why don't we speed it up a little bit and scan it more quickly, so we can make sounds with it?" Tempelaars then built a larger 100-step version which Koenig described as "a very general device that could be used from one step-per-second to 10,000 per second." And Tempelaars later reflected, "Composers often use your equipment in a different way, often more fanciful, than you imagined in the beginning." Konrad Boehmer used the Variable Function Generator to compose *Aspekte* (1965). Koenig used it to compose his *Funktionen* series of compositions: *Funktion Grün* (1967), *Funktion Gelb* (1968), *Funktion Orange* (1968), *Funktion Rot* (1968), *Funktion Blau* (1969), *Funktion Indigo* (1969), *Funktion Violett* (1969), and *Funktion Grau* (1969).

The Utrecht studio grew. Tempelaars joined the faculty. In October 1967, there was a meeting of the studio personnel. According to Tempelaars, "The group thought that the name 'Studio for Electronic Music' should be more serious, reflecting the idea of research as well as production." *Phonology* was mentioned, but it was rejected because it referred to the study of speech. *Sonology* was proposed, but it was noted that it was "a combination of Greek and Latin." And in the end, perspective prevailed over erudition and the Studio for Electronic Music was renamed the Institute of Sonology. "And eight years later," Tempelaars points out, "'Sonology' was defined in a Dutch dictionary as 'the science of electronic music.'"

By the late 1960s, the composers at the Institute of Sonology needed a computer dedicated to music. Koenig states the problem: "In those days you had to punch in your data with punched tape and take it to the computer center to read in the tapes . . ." Tempelaars continues:

> This was the rich time of the university. Money was no problem. We got a commitment for a PDP-15, the money was given in 1970—250,000 guilders—and the computer itself came in 1971. It was exceptional that we had our own computer just for music, not to be shared with other departments. We suddenly had a device which was at that moment so new that it was difficult to imagine the possibilities. We simulated analog techniques. We used it to control analog equipment. I used it for spectral analysis.

Werner Kaegi, composer and researcher, used the computer to develop a particularly promising voice-simulation approach to sound synthesis. As Tempelaars remembers, "After the first sounds, it was clear that with a small number of controls you had an enormous range of possibilities—speechlike sounds, noiselike sounds." He worked with Kaegi, and by 1973, he had finished a software version of what they called VOSIM (VOice SIMulation).

Between 1975 and 1980, several VOSIM synthesizers were built and tested. By 1980, the system was fully functional, many composers were using it, and Kaegi was trying to commercialize it. But VOSIM never became a commercial product, in large part because it was difficult to understand. As Tempelaars comments, "The weakness of VOSIM, like many other techniques for sound synthesis, was that the relationship between the control parameters and the effect on the sound was not straightforward . . ."

As the Institute of Sonology grew through the 1970s, it became an important center for software development and general experimentation. VOSIM, ultimately unsuccessful commercially, was nonetheless an exceptional research effort. And there were many projects in progress concurrently. Barry Truax developed his POD software. Otto Laske formulated theories of music as a dynamic process. The analog studio, directed by Frits Weiland, composer, and Jaap Vink, technician, became the center of a circle of composers and musical activity. In general, composers and students came to Utrecht from around the world and worked on their own projects, many of which turned out to be innovative and influential. And there was a continual flow of visitors. Koenig looks back: "We got the feeling that there was a large family around the world of people who understood each other, all based on the challenge of using the computer to make music. It was a wonderful time. It was exciting."

•

William Buxton arrived in Utrecht in 1973, just as Barry Truax was about to leave. Truax had been working on probability-based composing software that he called POD (POisson Distribution). He demonstrated the software for Buxton, who thought, as he later said, "that this was pretty cool." Buxton soon made the important observation that the doors at the institute were locked every evening at 8 P.M., an unacceptable condition for someone who liked to work at night. In what was for him an early example of computer-music ingenuity, he approached Koenig and said, "I'm a computer programmer and I've done computer music, and I know Barry Truax is gone, and you've got this wonderful package here, so why don't I teach a course on POD, on computer music?" And Koenig's enthusiastic acceptance of the offer encouraged Buxton to say, "Well, I guess you're going to have to give me a key so I can come in at night and learn the program."

Buxton wrote the manual for POD, and with Jaap Vink, he began writing a manual for the studio. It was a good beginning. As Buxton said, "Writing manuals and teaching, both in analog and computer stuff, really sensitized me to the inadequacies in the technology—the fastest way to find weaknesses in a design is to write a manual." By 1975, he had developed some clear ideas as to how computer systems should feel and operate. He tells it:

> I'd been corresponding with some people in Toronto, among them Leslie Mezie. I had seen Mezie's work in the catalog of Cybernetic Serendipity

and the problems that he was dealing with in computer graphics were similar to what I was struggling with in music composition. He invited me to Toronto and said I could have the run of the laboratory. And so I came back into this really rich milieu of extremely supportive, brilliant people who said, "Well, if you want to do something, do it." They helped make the resources available.

The laboratory was run by Leslie Mezie, K. C. Smith, and Ron Baecker. Buxton continues:

> They asked, "Well, how do you think . . .?" I told them how I thought computer music should work. They said, "Well, build it. There's an electrical engineer." They pointed to K. C. Smith and said, "He'll help you learn what you need to know." There were a few engineers and students that K. C. introduced me to, and they said, "Here are the computers, here are syllabi, write a proposal to make this music system and we'll put our names on it . . ."

In the grant proposal, the project was called the Structured Sound Synthesis Project. As Buxton reflects, "It always struck me as an appropriately pseudo-scientific term for music—it looked good in the proposal." He continues:

> It turned out it was exactly the right place. We had UNIX on a PDP-11/45 and the guys at the lab enabled us to have a really high-resolution, very fast graphics display. It was all set up for interaction. I had a really good programming environment with a state-of-the-art environment for designing graphic user interfaces. So I built a score editor and at the same time started to design a digital synthesizer that we could hook up to that computer.

The synthesizer, which was functioning by 1978, generated sound in several different ways. It could do FM synthesis, waveshaping, additive synthesis, and fixed-waveform synthesis. It was multitimbral. As Buxton remembers, "Every time it played a note, the note object had the synthesis technique embodied in it." He continues:

> The problem was that music is realtime and UNIX is time sharing, so how could we do realtime music on a timesharing minicomputer? The solution was that we got an LSI-11 stuck between the PDP-11/45 and the synthesizer. So UNIX talked to the LSI-11 and the LSI-11 was dedicated to music—it was a mothership arrangement. When you were hooked up to the big computer, you could do composition, authoring scores, and designing timbres. And then we had *Conduct*, a completely separate environment which was optimized for performing. The main thing about this

was that we could take the LSI-11 away when we went on tours. We had a touch tablet, a piano keyboard, slider boxes, four joysticks. We could change articulation, transpose, adjust dynamics. We built a sound distribution system of sixteen channels of computer-controlled mixing. The problem in performances was that we always had trouble setting up. So we built this thing where the computer, synthesizer and everything could stay backstage, and Guy Fedorkow built a multiplexer that put all the control lines in a single coaxial cable that would run down the stage into which everything could plug in—the slider box, the keyboard, and so on.

It was an unusually elegant solution to performance problems. Indeed, the SSSP effort was unusual in three ways. First, Buxton's system embodied a holistic, three-way view of a musical process as scores, timbre, performance:

I figured there were three activities that went into doing music. One of them was writing your score—and for that we had a project doing score editors. The second was sculpting your sound palette—and that's the object editor. It let you sculpt sounds while hearing the music in context, so you could play a score within the timbre editor and hear the sound in the score. And the third was the performance software.

Second, the interface predated the Macintosh interface:

Everything was graphical except for the performance program, and it was, well, sort of graphical. We used a puck and a graphics tablet. The puck looked like a mouse. For editing scores and sounds, we had graphical editors.

Third, there was exceptional teamwork:

I had a strong group of professional musicians to give me feedback, and what I got from them had a major influence on the design and the quality of the final product. In the lab, the computer people and engineers were really enthusiastic to see what these musicians were doing. They went to the concerts. They were really responsive to improving the system.

•

In 1967, Jon Appleton joined the Dartmouth College faculty and established an electronic music studio. In 1969, Gerald Bregman, a graduate of Dartmouth, made a substantial gift to the studio, and the newly named Bregman Studio acquired a large Moog modular system and various other equipment. In 1972, Appleton met Sydney Alonso, at that time faculty at the Thayer School of Engineering at Dartmouth, and Cameron Jones, at that time a student in music and computer science at Dartmouth, and he got an idea for controlling the Moog synthesizer with a computer. As he recalls, "The question was how we could change patching instantly." He discussed his idea with Alonso, who, as Appleton remembers, "made a number of suggestions, one of which was to ignore the Moog synthesizer . . ." As Alonso recalls, "I offered the opinion that we'd be better off starting to build something digital in the first place." Alonso continues:

> We had a little homemade computer in the lab, and so I hooked up a little digital square-wave organ and programmed up some Bach two-part inventions. Then we showed it to John Kemeny, who was President of Dartmouth at that time and a great computer pioneer, having invented Basic, and he said, "Well, if you get rid of that paper tape, I can get you some money to pursue this," by which he meant that we should hook it up to Dartmouth time-sharing.

The next step was Computer-Assisted Instruction (CAI). Alonso tells the story:

> We were aware that we had to do some CAI stuff to get funding, and so we made some files and called them up to a little mini-computer, and we had a system that would give ear-training lessons. Jon wrote a language, a schema of instruction, where kids were given a palette of sound events. At first, they were allowed only to sequence them, then to control more and more, loudness and duration, then the pitch, and so forth. It served one student at a time, and it was always jam-packed. Students loved it. So we said, "Let's apply to the Sloan Foundation for a grant to improve upon this," by which we meant that we should make it independent of time-sharing and available to more than one student at once. And so we built the Dartmouth Digital Synthesizer. We hooked it up to some compiler-type languages which allowed people to get at the synthesizer and program their own sounds and make music, sort of similar to Music V, laborious but satisfying.

Appleton adds, "The idea was that we would have ear training during the day and composing at night." How did composers use the Dartmouth Digital Synthesizer? Cameron Jones wrote two composing languages called KLANG and SING. As Appleton describes them, "They were line numbered files with fields into which one entered envelope, FM ratio, pitch, vibrato, etc.—they were easy to use and since it was the first time I had worked with numbers, it led to some unusual tunings . . ." Among Appleton's pieces were *Georganna's Farewell* (1975) and *In Medias Res* (1978). Other composers also worked with the system, as summarized in a 1976 recording called *The Dartmouth Digital Synthesizer*, which contained *Georganna's Farewell* , Lars-Gunnar Bodin's *Bilder (Images)*, Russell Pinkston's *Emergence*, and William Brunson's *Tapestry I*.

Meanwhile, in 1973, as Alonso tells it, "Kemeny met with Norton Stevens, the head of Norlin Music, and Kemeny said, 'There's something you've got to see.'" Kemeny was referring to the Moog synthesizer. And Stevens, apparently, was quite enthusiastic because, according to Alonso, "The next week, Norlin bought the Moog company." In 1975, Alonso and Jones formed New England Digital Corporation to develop marketing prototypes of the Dartmouth Digital Synthesizer, which, by that time, was controlled with a NOVA minicomputer. Alonso continues:

> Part of the conditions of the Sloan grant was that if it were successful, it should be made accessible. So we said, "Well, why don't we sell this to Norlin?" In spring 1976, we started negotiating with Norlin. It took to about August 1976 till we had a contract.

Expensive and somewhat difficult to operate, however, the Dartmouth Digital Synthesizer was not immediately successful, and Norlin, like many large companies then and now, did not exhibit patience in pursuit of profits. Alonso:

> In April 1977, we got a letter from Norlin saying they were opting for the flameout clause in the contract, that they were no longer interested. But by that time, New England Digital had developed a little very fast 16-bit computer that we called the ABLE, and Cameron Jones had written a compiler for it. So we had a question: Should we go back to Dartmouth, or should we keep trying to sell this technology, or none of the above? Because of our new little computer, we decided to go ahead and make a small synthesizer, and then we added a musical keyboard and a little plastic box which had a zero-seeking knob. By pressing a button on the plastic box, you would say, "I want to control this feature." Then, as you turned the knob to the right a value would increase, to the left it would decrease. When you let it go, the value would stay where you left it. This design is in all commercial synthesizers. I wish we had patented it, but we didn't have any money.

No money, perhaps, but they did have the computer, the synthesizer, the keyboard, and the control panel. In other words, they had the *Synclavier*. Jon Appleton had been in Sweden during 1976. When he returned in 1977, he resumed working with Alonso and Jones. Appleton continues:

> My input was that we should have an instrument for live performance and that the functions of an analog studio and of certain music languages should be hardwired in the form of buttons and knobs on a control panel. So the questions were: How do you specify envelope? How do you specify tracks? Vibrato? What terms do you use? And finally, one question was: What kinds of sounds are acceptable? What techniques of synthesis

are most useful to creative musicians? I discussed these things with Syd and Cameron and I tried to interest other people in what we were doing. I was a kind of publicist for the instrument. I constructed musical examples. And I demonstrated it everywhere—Sweden, Finland, France, Italy, New Zealand, all over the United States. I did a combination of lecture and demonstration and played one or two of the pieces that I'd written.

As Alonso recalls, with some chagrin, "Our first musical sale was to Joel Chadabe who would have none of the control panel or keyboard and insisted on writing his own programs using the XPL compiler." Then, with resignation at the quirks of the particular fate that had delivered a first customer with no regard whatsoever for the hours and months of development time that had gone into the keyboard and control panel, Alonso adds, with a philosophical shrug of the shoulders, "Va bene." In fact, I had been looking for a sixteen-bit digital synthesizer system with floppy disc storage. I had visited New England Digital in Norwich, Vermont, in September 1977, saw some demonstrations, had a brief discussion with Appleton, and ordered a Synclavier, as Alonso said, in a special configuration without the keyboard and control panel.

The next sale, and the first sale of a system with the keyboard, control panel, and software, was in December 1977 to Michel Redolfi for GMEM (Groupe de Musique Expérimentale de Marseille). Redolfi had earlier worked at the Dartmouth College studio and met the Synclavier developers. He was familiar with the Synclavier and knew what he wanted to do. His first finished piece with the Synclavier was *Pacific Tubular Waves* (1979), which he described in terms of imagery: "The flux of the waves, the dance of sea plants, the peace of the depths, all the sound pictures originate from spectral mixes made directly on the instrument—I felt like a painter of sound." He continues:

> I was fascinated by the possibilities of creating complex FM sounds that were full and evocative and far from the coldness of most digital timbres of that time. I could make long, organic, and harmonic sounds that were not like the note-by-note instrumental music of electronic keyboards. And one of the most powerful features of the Synclavier was that you could change values from the infinitely fine to the infinitely large by turning a single big knob. It was a new idea and it remained unique for a long time. There was no patching, no unreadable algorithms. And thanks to this knob, the Synclavier could be thought of not as a super-keyboard but as a machine to create and direct sound.

During the next year, fifteen Synclaviers were sold and work toward a Synclavier II was begun. As Alonso tells it, "A fellow by the name of Denny Jaeger appeared on our doorstep one day and said, 'Look, the Synclavier is nice but you really left some stuff out, and I think if you put the stuff that I tell you in there, you should be able to sell millions of them, and it would be really a

The photo on the top shows Sydney Alonso (left) and Jon Appleton (right) in the offices of New England Digital Corporation in Norwich, Vermont, in 1977. The photo on the bottom shows Jon Appleton playing the Synclavier in 1978, with Cameron Jones standing by. Photos by Joel Chadabe.

hot thing'—and so he talked us into letting him be the product designer." And in 1979, while the Synclavier II was in a design stage, Appleton pulled back a bit. He said:

> I guess they asked me some questions, but I was only marginally involved from that point on. It was already clear that if they were going to make a business of this they were going to have to appeal to the commercial music world and I didn't know that music. I didn't know what kinds of

sounds would appeal to rock groups. So my involvement became increasingly less and after a year or so I resigned all financial interest in the Synclavier. I felt I had nothing more to give. But I remained a friend, both for reasons of self-interest and loyalty. I wanted the Synclavier to become a more sophisticated performance instrument. They kept my tuning option. They did try to make a compromise between the interests of art music and commercial music in the design of the instrument. But there were a thousand systems out there at the end, and of those there were no more than fifty that were used in the art music tradition. It had become a different animal.

Appleton did many compositions for live performance with the Synclavier, among them *Kapingamarangi* (1979), *Sashasonjon* (1981), and *Brush Canyon* (1986), but eventually he stopped using it to perform. He explains, "The instrument had become so large that it became too expensive for me to accept the kind of concert engagements that art musicians are offered, so I would go on a tour and I'd spend every penny that I had earned on shipping the instrument around—and when I started to lose money, I just couldn't afford to do that anymore."

•

By 1977, the Alles Synthesizer, designed and built by Hal Alles at Bell Labs, was up and running. Laurie Spiegel describes it:

It had a glutton's heaven of physical controllers. There were so many sliders and switches and joysticks that you could create as many realtime interactive input parameters as you wanted. I used lots and lots of them, as options and overrides. In addition to all my pitch-time algorithmic variables, I was even able to put the amplitude of each partial of each FM oscillator pair on its own slider and I still had dozens of unused slider pots left over. This was enough to unleash creative mania after four years constrained to GROOVE's bottleneck of just fourteen DAC control channels. I may never see the likes of that hardware interface again!

Bell Labs, having played a part in developing the sync sound process for cinema, was invited to participate in a fiftieth-anniversary celebration of talking pictures, to take place in October 1977 at the Palladium in Hollywood. The Alles Synthesizer was programmed for the occasion to perform several old sounds, including a few words as sung by Al Jolson in his first sound film. And Spiegel was invited by Bell Labs to compose *Concerto for Self-Accompanying Digital Synthesizer* (1977), an interactive process in which whatever was played on the keyboard was continuously recycled into a continually changing accompaniment for what was played next.

There were difficulties in the preparation. As Spiegel describes the routine, "We had six weeks, barely enough time, so we worked around the clock, with Hal working 5 A.M. to 5 P.M. and me working 5 P.M. to 5 A.M., plus some overlapping worktime—I had to switch from FORTRAN on a dedicated computer to working on a UNIX network, writing in C, which was in itself being rewritten and changed constantly while I tried to learn it, and it was hard to tell what were software bugs, compiler changes, or hardware problems or changes." There were difficulties in moving the synthesizer from Bell Labs in Murray Hill, New Jersey, to California. Spiegel recalls, "When we got the thing out of the cargo hold of the plane, all the circuit boards were wet with condensation, so we were backstage using hair dryers on the boards, hoping they'd dry out in time." And as Spiegel tells it, there were difficulties in the performance setup: "The Palladium crew put it on a revolving platform, all glitzy Hollywood style, and when it started turning, the cables began winding up around the platform's base—they caught it just in the nick of time and reversed the direction of the rotation."

•

By the mid-1970s, GRM in Paris was in process of recasting the idea of musique concrète in new technologies. Following GRM's acquisition of a PDP-11/60 computer, Benedict Mailliard had begun to develop sound-processing software modules, collectively called the 123 Programs after the room (Studio 123) in which they were developed, while in parallel, Jean-François Allouis had begun to develop SYTER (SYstème TEmps Réel / Realtime System), a hybrid system consisting of a digital synthesizer controlled by the PDP-11/60. Various prototypes of SYTER were demonstrated during the late 1970s, a first complete version of the system was finished in 1982, and the definitive system was ready in 1984. Its functions included realtime sound transformation and synthesis, direct-to-disk recording, and hard-disk editing, all of it controlled with a graphical screen interface and mouse. Further, SYTER was extensible in that a user could program software modules and incorporate them to operate seamlessly within the system.

SYTER was commercialized in 1985, several systems were sold, and improvements were made through the late 1980s. In 1988, Allouis left GRM to become technical director at IRCAM and Hugues Vinet arrived at GRM to continue Allouis' work. Vinet continued to work on SYTER into 1989, at which time he adapted the SYTER software to the Macintosh, thereby creating the first version of what became GRM Tools, an ensemble of digital signal processing modules including additive synthesis, filters, delays, time stretching, equalization, and Doppler shifts. Following further development, GRM Tools was commercialized in 1993. In 1994, Emmanuel Favreau began to work at GRM and developed a version of GRM Tools compatible with Power PC-based Macintosh computers. By the early 1990s, it had become clear that the recording and processing of acoustically-produced sounds was a well-understood and accepted approach. Indeed, musique concrète had entered the commercial mainstream.

•

In Italy in the mid-1960s, Giuseppe Di Giugno was teaching physics at the University of Naples and conducting nuclear research at the accelerator laboratory in Frascati, near Rome. Music, for Di Giugno, was a hobby. As he said, "I played guitar like a dilettante, I had studied a bit of theory, I could read a classical score." One evening in 1969, at the home of some friends, he heard *Switched on Bach*. He recalls, "I was impressed by this as a curiosity—I didn't know how it had been made." In 1971, he attended a physics conference at Cornell University at which Robert Moog gave a lecture. Di Giugno met Moog: "I talked with him after his lecture and he invited me to his workshop at Trumansburg—he was very charming, *molto simpatico*." Di Giugno continues:

> At that time, at Frascati, we were using our experiment-control computer to make sounds, for fun, as a *divertimento*, as a hobby. And as a hobby, I made a voltage-controlled synthesizer. During that period—1971, 1972—I met many Italian musicians and showed them what I'd done. There was always a problem with tuning because the oscillators weren't stable. You could do something today and it wouldn't be there tomorrow. And I began to wonder if it was possible to produce sound digitally, to make digital oscillators. I didn't know that Max Mathews had already done it. But I had the use of a PDP-15 minicomputer and I did it in real time.

In 1973, Di Giugno founded an electronic music group, the Gruppo Electroacustica di Napoli and, as he put it, "got to know the contemporary electronic music scene." And the contemporary electronic music scene got to know him. In November 1974, Luciano Berio telephoned him and said, "I'd like to meet you." Di Giugno and Berio met, and after much conversation during the following weeks, Berio proposed to Di Giugno that they collaborate in building a digital synthesizer. In Berio's words, "We had had only nine oscillators in Milano, so in a kind of humorous way I said to him, 'We need 1,000 oscillators, not nine.'" And in early 1975, Berio invited Di Giugno to a meeting with Max Mathews at the Rome airport. Di Giugno remembers:

> He had stopped in Rome to meet with me because Luciano had proposed that I come to IRCAM. There had been a proposal for a studio with 1,000 oscillators. So Max asked me, 'What do you think of this project, 1,000 oscillators?' and we began to talk about a future system, and we talked about collaborating at IRCAM in 1976.

During 1975, Di Giugno began building what became known as the *4A* digital synthesizer. He finished it in early 1976 and, in June, went to Paris to begin work at IRCAM. Using the 4A, as David Wessel's *Antony* (1977) demonstrates, a composer could add together many waveforms to make a complex sound. But the 4A's software oscillators could not be made to interact with each other. At that point, Di Giugno met Hal Alles and Alles said, as Di Giugno recalls, "We can do this in another way." By 1977, Di Giugno and Alles had finished building the *4B*, which had sixty-four interconnected oscillators. Di Giugno continues:

> Synthesizers should be made for musicians, not for the people that make them. The 4B was used by very few composers because at that time composers were beginning to have ideas of live performance, with microphones and reverberation. So in 1978, I began to plan the 4C, which was more programmable, the most important concept in my ideology. The 4A was only oscillators, the 4B was oscillators with interconnections, and the 4C didn't have concepts of oscillators but rather of objects with particular algorithms that could be linked. It was much more general and it was used by many composers.

The *4C*, finished in 1979, was used by Tod Machover in *Light* (1979) and *Soft Morning, City!* (1980), among other composers. But the 4C was limited. As Di Giugno explains, "There were many things that were impossible to do with it, and at a certain point I got tired of it because every year there was another machine for something else a musician wanted to do." He continues:

> At that point, after some reflection, I decided we had to do something that was general enough to be independent of any specific composer's needs. I began to study all the things that musicians wanted. I thought of a universal machine that would let every musician construct any particular machine within it. And so I got the idea for the 4X, actually the first digital signal processor ever made.

The *4X*, in a semifinal state of completion, was first used in public at the Donaueschingen Festival in 1981. The occasion was an early performance of Pierre Boulez' *Répons*, for twenty-four musicians and six soloists, in which sounds played by the six soloists (piano, synthesizer, harp, cimbalom, vibraphone, and xylophone) were independently transformed and routed through different loudspeakers placed around the hall.

Even considered retrospectively, *Répons* was the most elaborate composition to utilize the 4X. But it was by no means the only one. The 4X was used by Luciano Berio, Philippe Manoury, Pierre Henry, François Bayle, Jean-Baptiste Barrière, Robert Rowe, Arnaud Petit, Denis Lorrain, George Benjamin, Thierry Lancino, and Marco Stroppa, to mention but a few. Composers Marc Battier and Cort Lippe functioned as tutors to help visiting composers use the technology, and of course, they used the technology themselves in their own compositions. Marc Battier's *Encre sur Polyester* (1984), for example, involved the processing of brass sounds by continual filtering and by microtuning one sound which was played simultaneously by many oscillators. As Battier recalls, "I've never seen another machine that could give as much

Luciano Berio in his IRCAM
workspace in 1978.
Photo by Joel Chadabe.

power and complexity . . . I could do amazing things just by changing a few faders." By 1985, there were four 4X workstations in operation, each consisting of a SUN computer, a VME 68000 computer (developed at IRCAM, based on the Motorola 68000 microprocessor), and a 4X synthesizer. The 4X was, as they say in the American business world, a home run. Di Giugno continues:

> And so in 1983, we thought of commercializing it. The 4X was extremely expensive—it cost approximately $100,000—so it wasn't really accessible to many musicians or conservatories. IRCAM had made four of these machines, and we wanted to sell them to organizations dealing with audio, the military, and other large companies. But at that time, the University of Padua, particularly Luigi Nono and Alvise Vidolin, wanted something. Alvise said, "I want one of these machines."

The 4X was eventually commercialized. Di Giugno responded to Vidolin's request by making a single-module 4X called the 4I (I for Italy) for the University of Padua. And he reasoned that the cost of the 4X could be reduced only through miniaturization and integration. He remembers, "So I said to Boulez, 'We have to go towards microelectronics.'" But IRCAM did not have the necessary funds. Di Giugno did some research at MIT and, in his words, "studied various architectures, various modes of designing, and I thought of a 5A DSP system with floating point mathematics . . ." Then, in 1986, he got a telephone call from Paolo Bontempi in Rome.

Bontempi, a large Italian toy company, had bought Farfisa, an Italian synthesizer company, and Paolo Bontempi made a Faustian proposal. As Di Giugno tells it, "He said, 'For two years, do your research, then you do instruments for me.'" Di Giugno accepted Bontempi's invitation because, in his words, "it let me continue my research in new technology." In May 1987, Di Giugno left Paris for Rome.

•

In 1985, while Di Giugno was still in Paris, Miller Puckette arrived at IRCAM and began to work on 4X-related software with Philippe Manoury. Manoury had earlier composed *Zeitlauf* (1980), for instruments, voices, and tape, in which the instruments and voices were transformed with a Buchla synthesizer, and at the time that Puckette arrived in Paris, he was working with flutist Larry Beauregard on *Jupiter*. Manoury's idea for *Jupiter*, finished in 1987, was that the flute's sound would be transformed in the 4X, pitches played by the flutist would determine how the flute's sounds would be transformed, and at the same time, the flutist would trigger other electronic sounds. The main software problem was how to time musical events independently of one another, measure by measure and beat by beat, so that the 4X could follow the flutist. It wasn't an easy working environment because the computer in the 4X workstation at that time was a PDP-11 controlled with a clumsy RS-232 teletype. But Puckette solved the timing problem by writing a realtime scheduler. He said, "I used ideas that I had learned from Max Mathews and so I ended up calling the program MAX." Manoury continues:

> The idea was to give the flutist the liberty of changing tempo, as against playing with a tape where the player has to follow the tempo of the tape. That for me is something fundamental in music, that flexibility in tempo is fundamental to interpretation. And it became possible with this system. Each time that the flutist played a note, the processing would change in some relation to the note played by the flute. The result was that the spectral evolutions of the electronic sounds were synchronized to the flute in pitch and timbral quality. My idea was to establish a connection between a soloist and a virtual orchestra but the orchestra would keep the characteristics of the soloist. Consequently, perhaps seventy percent of the sounds of the piece were flute sounds. In our experiments with the sounds for this piece, we used frequency shifting, harmonizers, and other kinds of transformations.

Puckette continues:

> In spring 1987, I started thinking about what to do to make the process a little easier. I moved the whole program to the Macintosh because I was sick of the PDP-11 and the teletype. And then, since Philippe was agitating to get started on his next piece, I decided to pull a fast one and just hook a Macintosh up to the 4X with a MIDI line. During August of that year, I figured that we'd need a graphics interface, because the configurations were getting too complicated to visualize in a text file. And so, without really meaning to, I cooked up a graphics interface that I called the

Patcher, which I thought of as a kind of utility. And pretty soon the cart was pulling the horse. It turned out that the graphics interface became a bigger project than the realtime scheduler that I called MAX. So somehow between September 1987 and July 1988, we got a working version of MAX together on the Macintosh and Philippe wrote a thirty-five-minute piece with it.

Manoury's next compositions were *Pluton* (1988) and *Partition du Ciel et de l'Enfer* (1989, Separation of Heaven and Hell). Of *Pluton*, for piano and the 4X, Manoury recalls, "It had been hard and long to do what we'd done with *Jupiter*, mainly because of working with the teletype terminal, and the system in general wasn't very responsive or interactive—so the idea of this piece was to do more easily what we had done with *Jupiter*." He continues:

> In August 1988, Miller and I went to Bordeaux on vacation with our families and we worked for about two weeks, while I put together a lot of ideas for the piece. There was a reciprocal influence while Miller solved my problems and my problems gave Miller ideas for how to make the program easier for musicians to use. So following our experience with *Jupiter*, Miller rewrote the program for the Macintosh with a graphic interface called Patcher. It was more interactive, with sliders, for example, that allowed me to test the elements that I was working with. For me, the graphic interface made a conceptual change in my ways of working because it gave me a way to do more easily what I had done with great difficulty before. This was very important, because with the *Jupiter* system, which was not interactive, I had to formalize every thought in programming terms, and that was not intuitive for me, or for any musician.

The ease with which someone can conceptualize and analyze a problem is an important factor in solving that problem. And conceptual clarity is an important factor in creativity. As MAX's graphic interface was developed, and as MAX therefore became conceptually easier to use, Manoury was able to solve problems more efficiently and, further, think more freely of new dimensions to his ideas. As Manoury said: "What was so good about the new MAX was that it allowed me to think intuitively about my music."

Manoury's thought brings Buchla's words to mind: "A user interface . . . also includes the software." Indeed, software—perhaps even more than the knobs, buttons, displays, and other aspects of a synthesizer's hardware interface—plays an essential role in determining how easy it is to operate a synthesizer.

• • •

CHAPTER SEVEN

THE MIDI WORLD

The first synthesizers appeared in the 1960s. The market grew during the 1970s. By the end of the 1970s and into the 1980s, the market was wide open and exciting, even chaotic. Kraftwerk, Led Zeppelin, Frank Zappa, Herbie Hancock, Moody Blues, Roxy Music, the Beatles, Thomas Dolby, Brian Eno, Depeche Mode, and innumerable other musicians and groups were using technology. Many of the ideas developed at universities and in research centers surfaced in commercial synthesizers. And a wide variety of new synthesizers, keyboards, drum machines, and computer-based systems were becoming commercially available, among them Roland's *Jupiter-4*, the *Chroma* and *PPG Wave* synthesizers, the *Con Brio* synthesizer, Crumar's *Performer*, Rhodes' *Mark III Electronic Piano*, the *Casiotone 301* keyboard, Simmons' *SDS-5 Electronic Drum System*, and the *alphaSyntauri* computer-based music production system.

•

The *Fairlight CMI* (Computer Music Instrument), the first of the so-called *samplers*, sold for about $25,000 when it was introduced in 1980. It was expensive. Like most other new digital systems at the time, it was aimed at a professional market. And it was successful because it applied digital technology to the well-understood idea of keyboard-controlled tape playback. In the 1950s, there had been Hugh Le Caine's Multi-Track Tape Recorder. In the early 1960s, there had been the Chamberlin. And in the mid-1960s, the commercially successful

Mellotron was introduced. A 1975 advertisement listed Larry Fast and Synergy, King Crimson, Isao Tomita, Peter Gabriel and Genesis, and other musicians and groups as Mellotron users. The ad stated: "Only the Mellotron duplicates the real sound of any voice or instrument by means of a series of controlled tape machines—each related to a key on the Mellotron keyboard . . . if you've been wondering how Paul McCartney, Todd Rundgren, The Strawbs, Yes, and many other groups have achieved their distinctive sounds, now you know . . ."

In 1971, Kim Ryrie in Sydney, Australia, was working for *Electronics Today* when the magazine published an article on how to build an analog synthesizer. It set Ryrie thinking that the design of a synthesizer could benefit from a microprocessor. He contacted Peter Vogel, an old school friend, with the proposal that they start a company to build a computer-based instrument. Vogel agreed. In 1973, they were working on a computer-controlled analog synthesizer in the basement of Ryrie's grandmother's house when Vogel's sister, who was working for the Australia Council, put them in touch with Anthony Furse in Canberra. Furse had received an Australia Council grant to build the Qasar II, a hybrid synthesizer. Ryrie and Vogel were enthusiastic. They licensed Furse's technology and formed Fairlight Instruments (after the name of a Sydney harbor ferry) to build a computer-based synthesizer. In fact, they ended with a sampler rather than the hybrid system that Furse had developed. And it had the benefits of a graphic light-pen-based interface to edit or create sounds, automatic sequencing, and keyboard control. By 1979, the Fairlight CMI was ready for production.

•

Meanwhile, the Synclavier II, which at first was based on FM synthesis technology, was beginning to sell. Sydney Alonso recalls, "We sold the first one in July 1979, and between July and December we sold $1 million of them, which for a little company like us made us take notice." Yamaha also noticed. Yamaha had licensed FM technology from Stanford University, and as Alonso tells it, "A couple of austere businessmen-scientists from Yamaha came to us and they gave us some sake and we gave them some maple syrup and they said, 'Why don't you license FM?' and we said, 'Okay.'"

As the Fairlight CMI became successful, however, Alonso began to think along different lines. As he remembers, "They would show up at AES shows, and they'd say, 'Well, let's draw a picture of a Volkswagen on the screen and then we'll play that wave,' and lo and behold, the public bought it, so all of a sudden the idea was that we want to do sampling—and this was a very strong market force, so we were forced to develop the sampling unit." Forced or not, the sampling unit was a great success for New England Digital Corporation. Alonso continues:

> We were a corporation, we had stockholders, we were getting nibbles from more and more investors, and we kept making a profit and growing. The system was getting larger and larger. The prices were going up

and users were being found for very big and expensive systems, for example in the movies. Demand caused us to build a sample-to-disk option that was integrated with the sample-to-RAM. It could do the whole film score, sound effects and music score *and* you could slip in dialog, making it worth millions of dollars to people who had a need to do that in a hurry.

•

Crumar's *General Development System* was also expensive. By the mid-1970s, Crumar, an Italian company known for electronic pianos and keyboards such as the *Compac* and *Orchestrator*, had established close ties with Music Technology Inc. (MTI) in New York. In 1975, through MTI, they acquired Hal Alles' synthesizer technology from Bell Labs and began to design the General Development System. The GDS, as it came to be called, appeared in 1979. Marketed by Digital Keyboards, Inc., an MTI subsidiary, it was described in a 1983 advertisement:

> The General Development System (GDS) was completely developed from digital technology, the result of years of research at Bell Labs and continued by Digital Keyboards, Inc. A $30,000 musical system, the purpose of the GDS is to formulate & pioneer many kinds of digital synthesis techniques, create a library of sounds, and aid musicians in the design of instruments and significant features . . . Included among the GDS users are Wendy Carlos, Klaus Schultz, Billy Cobham, Kansas State University, the University of Oklahoma, Jefferson Research, Leo's Music . . .

•

In 1971, Dave Rossum was a graduate student at the University of California at Santa Cruz when the physics department acquired a Moog synthesizer. Rossum figured out how to use it and then, with several friends, built an analog synthesizer called the *E-mu 25*.

In 1972, Rossum and Scott Wedge formed E-mu Systems. They did consulting and built modules. Eventually, they built modular systems used by, among others, Frank Zappa and Herbie Hancock. They also built digital scanning keyboards which were licensed by Tom Oberheim, Sequential Circuits, and others. And they designed integrated circuits, among them the analog chip licensed by Sequential Circuits for the Prophet-5.

In 1979, they built an oddity called the *Audity*. As Marco Alpert, later E-mu Systems' vice president of marketing, recalls, "We got a commission from Peter Baumann, who had just left Tangerine Dream, to design a computer-controlled synthesizer board—so we designed a board that was a single analog voice that was completely computer controllable, and we decided to use it in a synthesizer." In May 1980, they enthusiastically introduced an Audity prototype at an AES show. Public interest was somewhat moderated by its projected price of around $70,000, and as Alpert mentioned, "We figured it wasn't going to be a commercially viable instrument," but at that same show, Rossum and

E-mu Systems' Emulator, about 1982. Photo courtesy E-mu Systems.

Alpert got their first look at the Fairlight CMI. And it occurred to Rossum that there was an easier way to do sampling.

In January 1981, at the NAMM show, they presented a prototype of the *Emulator I*, a sampler, priced at about $10,000. As Alpert said, "We caused a bit of a stir." The stir was due in part to Stevie Wonder who, as Rossum witnessed, "sort of hugged it to get the feel of it, and then started playing it." Wonder ordered an Emulator. Serial number 001 was shipped to him in May. And in 1982, with the additional features of a sequencer, new sounds, and multisampling, and a lower price of about $8,000, sales of the Emulator I took off. Alpert declared: "That was really the start of sampling." Then, in 1983, E-mu introduced the *Drumulator* which, in Alpert's words, "kicked off the affordable drum machine market." And in 1984, E-mu introduced the Emulator II, with improved sound quality, longer sampling times, full analog processor, hard drive, and in 1985, a CD-ROM drive. Alpert recalls, "It was a phenomenon, it became the instrument to have, everyone understood sampling . . ."

•

More and more companies understood that prices had to come down if they were going to be successful in addressing a growing market. The following words are from a 1983 ad:

> At Digital Keyboards, we realized that very few musicians were in a position to spend $30,000 for a GDS. However, our long years of R&D opened several new doors, allowing us to create a keyboard that offered the most demanding sonic aspects of the GDS—at a fraction of the cost. That keyboard? The Synergy . . .

The *Synergy* sold for about $6,000. And many other new instruments were developed to sell at affordable prices. The story of the *Linn Drum*, for example, began in the late 1970s while Roger Linn was working as a free-lance musician-with-a-computer in Los Angeles. He tells the story:

> I was writing a drum machine program and this guy Moffitt had some money. So in 1979 we started Linn and Moffitt Electronics and that was the origin of the *LM-1*. Before too long, Moffitt parted and I was running out of money. So some of my musician friends got me appointments at the

studios. I had a cardboard box cut out with a bunch of wirewrap boards and I told them that if they gave me half the money up front, I'd finish the product in three months. And I told them the price would be $5,000. So I got a lot of deposits for $2,500, and that helped fund the company and sometime in early 1980 I shipped the first machines. The first machine went to Leon Russell, a songwriter. The second went to Stevie Wonder, who was very excited about it. Then lots of others . . . Anyway, I delivered the machines not in three months, but in eight months, and the first ones had some hardware problems because they were assembled at my house by unemployed musician friends. Altogether, I must have sold eighty-five units. But the LM-1 was the talk of the town, so we were beautifully positioned for the Linn Drum, which came out in 1982—a better machine at $3,000. It had cymbals and three dynamic levels for the snare drum instead of two and better buttons. Oberheim was showing a prototype of the DM-X at shows, and it had a very nice button that I didn't know existed. So I found a source for the button, put the button in my Linn Drum and then beat Oberheim to market and sold a total of about 5,000 units.

Tom Oberheim was adept at dealing with competition. In 1979, he responded to the Prophet-5's success by developing the *OB-X*, a completely programmable, microprocessor-controlled synthesizer which expanded to eight voices. In 1980, the OB-X was improved and became the OB-XA. In 1981, he designed the *DS-X* (digital sequencer) and the *DM-X* (drum machine) and made it possible to synchronize them in what became the Oberheim system. As he said, "It was very crude and expensive, but it worked." But expensive is a relative term. Oberheim's products, in general, were in the few-thousand-dollar range.

•

The breakthrough technologies and growing market of the 1970s attracted many exceptional entrepreneurs, among them Felix Visser in Holland. Around 1970, Visser was working as a free-lance musician when he read an article about EMS (London) in *Tape Recorder* magazine. He remembers, "I wrote to EMS and they followed up with one of those floppy vinyl recordings—I still have it—and that completely blew my mind." Visser bought a Synthi A, in fact the first in Holland, but as he recalls, "After three days the damn machine broke down." Luckily, EMS had given him the circuit diagrams, and as he repaired it he thought, "Why did they do this instead of that?" And then his thoughts took a dangerous turn. As he put it, "I worked myself into a state of believing that I could do a better job."

Visser did the normal thing. He got a loan from a bank and started a company. He established Synton on January 1, 1973. And the plot soon thickened. As he tells it, "Three months, in those days, unhindered as I was by any knowledge or experience, seemed a hell of a lot of time—certainly enough time to design my synthesizer, called the *Syrinx*, a duophonic thing with state variable filters, ADSRs, a ring modulator, noise, random voltage source, everything." So he hired two engineers. The three months flew past and, as he recalls, "of course, still no Syrinx, and then the bank wanted me to make payments." Pressed financially, he went into overdrive. He started to sell a phase shifter, a voltage-controlled filter, somewhat later a mixing console, and various other modules. As Visser said, "We were just beginning to start." He continues:

> We were happily selling our phaser to recording studios when The Golden Earring, a Dutch rock group, brought an Eventide phaser back from a USA tour. We were just trying to close a deal with one of the leading recording studios. All of a sudden they turned around and said, "Sorry, but this thing from the USA sounds a lot better." I spent three seconds sweating. Then I said, "Suppose that by tomorrow we deliver one which is better. Would you buy it or would you be too much of a snob and still go for the Eventide from the USA?" Since the guys didn't want to be snobs, or maybe out of compassion for me, they said that they would buy mine. They probably thought that I'd gone out of my mind. But I spent the whole evening and night building one. Basically, it was eight phase shifters of the type we had, cascaded, crammed into a one-unit nineteen-inch rack, with a front panel done on a 3M photographic aluminum sheet. It had a different model number and it stated the name of the studio. It looked great. They took it. I went to bed.

Visser produced many new devices and systems through the 1970s. A Synton modular series was developed. There were projects done for music conservatories and universities. And there was the Synton hybrid system, a studio driven by a PDP 11/03. But even though the activity increased, Synton remained small, four or five people. And as Visser remembers, they were having a very good time:

> We didn't make a whole lot of money, but it was sufficient and we were having a ball. It was so relaxed that visitors would think we were just having coffee or tea the whole day. It was true. We were enjoying every minute of it. We would just dream something up and then design and build it and we would always find someone to buy it.

The 1970s, however, soon became the 1980s. Visser got tough: "I announced to my Synton pals that we would no longer just do products for fun, but that we would market the hell out of them." The first highly visible product was a vocoder called the *Syntovox 221*, which was exhibited at AES conventions, NAMM shows, the Frankfurt Musik Messe, and, as he remembers, "about a zillion of little local things." He was one of the first European entrepreneurs to understand the importance of the NAMM show in Anaheim each January. In his words, "It marked the beginning of a period in which I started to build a strong worldwide network."

It also marked the beginning of a period when Synton became a distributor as well as a manufacturer. As Visser recalls, "In the early 1980s, the music industry took its first serious dip and we had to compensate for a slack in sales of our own products—so I started to scout for interesting other products." Synton took on products from E-mu, Fairlight, and Linn and expanded its sales territory into Belgium. During the same period, other important distributors and dealers were opening up in Europe, among them Syco in London and Syncrom in Rome. Synton, Syco, and Syncrom kept in such close touch that they were sometimes called "The S-Ociation."

Syco began with Peter Gabriel's interest in the Fairlight CMI. Stephen Paine had worked in stores in London for a year or so selling synthesizers, and then, as he tells it, "My cousin Peter invited me down to Ashcombe Studios in Bath to work on his third album, but when I say work, I mean look at Larry Fast working—I think that ham sandwiches might have been my minor contributions to that album." Coincidentally, Peter Vogel, one of the founders of Fairlight, was in England at the time to promote the Fairlight CMI II. He approached Gabriel as a potential customer. Paine continues:

> Peter was blown away with this thing. So a combination of factors—he wanted to use it, he felt that there would be a lot of interest from other artists, he wanted to be involved with bringing it to the UK, he could buy it less expensively, he felt that he could make some money if other people bought it, and he's always tried to justify his artistic whims with some commercial motivation—led him to persuade me to start a company to sell it.

Gabriel named the company Syco. Operations began in a farmhouse in Bath. Paine made a few sales. And then, after a year or so, Gabriel and Paine decided to move Syco to London. Their concept was to do something very special. As Paine said, "We were determined that it would be entirely different from the sort of normal outfit that sells synthesizers."

In 1982, Syco, located toward the end of an alleyway next to Paddington Station, opened its doors in London. Opening a single large wooden door, in fact, one entered a large foyer, bare except for beautiful paintings, Charles Rennie Mackintosh furniture, and a wooden table off to one side behind which sat a receptionist. There were demonstration areas upstairs ("by appointment only, of course"), and there was a large cafe downstairs, with resident cook and waiter, for staff and customers. In an adjacent building, there was a garage to which selected customers were given automatic door openers so they could privately park their cars. Paine's logic is not untypical of the creative entrepreneur when he reflects, "We didn't always make corporately sensible decisions, but had we been accountants we wouldn't have done it at all." He continues:

> You could buy innovative cutting edge technology in a private, comfortable environment. It was the sort of environment that we wanted to work

in, so the natural assumption was that if we wanted to work there customers would want to come there. And they did. It was immensely successful. It was like nothing before it and probably like nothing ever will be again.

Syco's peak was in 1985 and 1986, with a staff of about thirty people and an expanded product line that included the Emulator, Synclavier, Linn Drum, and PPG Wave synthesizers. The floors were separated, as Paine described it, "into the expensive stuff on the top and the less expensive stuff down below." Syco also sold Fazioli pianos, in Paine's words, "the only handmade pianos in the world, with a purity and depth of sound that no other pianos had—it lent a unique combination of flavors, presentation and ambience, and after all, we were in the business of supplying technology that made beautiful sounds."

Not only supplying technology, Paine also developed technology. Carl Scofield, who had joined Syco in 1984, designed and built several interesting devices, among them the *Sycologic* analog-to-MIDI converter, the *PSP* (Percussion Synthesizer Programmer), and a MIDI patch bay called the *M-16*. Scofield and Paine also developed a digital recording and editing system called *The Tablet*. Paine describes it:

> It was based on transputer technology, which was quite revolutionary in those days. But the interface was the most important element. We wanted to create an interface which would present the user with a set of familiar tools—after all, we were trying to replace tape recorders—but our goal was also to design a reconfigurable interface that would let us change functionality without making things more complex for the user. Like Syco itself, we seemed to have cracked the way to present a radical technology to people who felt they couldn't cope with screens and keyboards. And again, as we designed Syco as a place that we wanted to work in, so we designed The Tablet as a device that we wanted to use. I can't tell you the excitement it caused. We had the BBC Research Department working with us. And there was no lack of orders. We had an order for a quarter-million pounds from the BBC. But the research and development timescale stretched and stretched and stretched, and we weren't able to bring a product to market before the money ran out.

Syncrom began in 1983. At Crumar for several years, Rene Rochat had marketed the General Development System and Synergy, among other products, and then, bit by the entrepreneurial bug in 1981, he had started MIM (Musical Instrument Manufacturers) as a company to distribute the GDS, Synergy, and all E-mu products for Europe. MIM ended in 1982. But the fun began when Rochat started Syncrom, which he referred to as "the first high-tech professional outlet in Italy." Syncrom's opening, with Visser and Paine attending, was in September 1983 in Rome. As Rochat tells it, "We were showing professional performers a completely different way of making music—it was great, there was great enthusiasm for innovative technology." Then, in 1987, Rochat got another idea. He formed Spye. His style was dazzling:

> Spye was located outside of Rome in a villa with four bedrooms and a studio. It was decorated in old Roman Empire decor. I had a painter do a *trompe l'oeil* scene of fallen pillars. And all the tables were glass and the legs were like Roman columns. We had special chairs built, with the bases built like a V-form, like a Roman throne, and covered by soft black leather cushions. I did most of the cooking. There were musicians there a lot. It gave people the opportunity to learn the instruments at their own leisure. Nobody was pressured for time. We selected the musicians. We'd have people who came through for one day, and they'd sometimes stay the night so we had late-night sessions.

It was definitely a silver lining. Rochat continues:

> I had such a lot of fun during those years that it's hard for me to think of doing anything else. I don't think that great fortunes can be made in the industry, but once you've entered into the fun part of it, it's very difficult to get out. The business aspect of it was always a secondary consideration. We created a lot of friendships based on good times, and we were more concerned with having a good time than with anything else. We used to go and meet at trade shows, for example in Paris, and good food was so important that we could think only of going to Lyons on the fast train to have lunch at Paul Bocuse. 300 miles for lunch!

But every silver lining has its cloud. As Rochat recalls, "Spye wasn't really financially viable—we blew a lot of money." Specifically, it wasn't financially viable because one high-end product that Rochat had intended to sell was late in deliveries, and another technology in which he invested never came to market. Generally, it wasn't financially viable because the industry had changed from the exciting breakthrough products of the 1970s to the mass market products of the 1980s. Even as early as the summer of 1984, Visser and Michael Kelly, from Syco, had walked the aisles of the Chicago NAMM show. Visser remembers:

> We couldn't find anything of interest. Just rehashes, more of the same. No more thrill. Michael looked at me and said, "If *we* don't see anything interesting, there *is* nothing interesting. Have we reached the end of this industry?"

Not the end of the industry, but the end of an era. The end of adventure, perhaps, and the beginning of practicality.

●

During the 1960s, Japan had come to represent an important music market, and many Japanese companies had become major developers of musical instruments. One of those companies was Roland. Ikutaro Kakehashi, Roland's founder and president, tells his story:

> I liked classical music, especially Baroque music. I bought many records and I wanted to play myself. I thought that the organ was the best instrument for Baroque music, but in Japan there was no history of the organ. And at that time, no organs. So someone I knew imported a very simple electronic organ from the USA. It was made with tubes. It broke and he asked me to fix it. I was operating a TV store, so I fixed the organ and I liked the sound very much. Then I changed direction, from TV to music. And in 1958, I made an organ.
>
> But then I understood that in Japan there were no organists. So I changed to small keyboards—they were monophonic melody instruments—and in 1959 I started Ace Electronics Industrial Corporation, a company in Osaka. In June 1964, I demonstrated the melody instrument at NAMM. But there were no sales, so I decided to move from melody to rhythm. We developed a rhythm machine called the R1, a small attachment for a home organ, and we found that many organ companies were very interested in a rhythm section. Then we developed the Rhythm Ace, which was an automatic rhythm machine, and Hammond got interested in it. In 1968, we made the rhythm machine as an OEM product and Hammond built my rhythm machine into their organs. We also started to import Hammond organs into Japan and, at the same time, we designed three or four Hammond models for the export market. Also, we worked together with Hammond's engineers to develop the Piper, which was the first single keyboard with rhythm accompaniment. During this growing process, I accepted investment from outside, but after a while I disagreed with the investors, so I sold my shares and, in April 1972, I started Roland . . . My plan was to concentrate in the electronic music area.

In 1973, Roland developed the *SH-1000*, a monophonic synthesizer, which was followed by the SH-2000, both of which had significant sales in the United States. From 1973 to 1983, Roland grew quickly through a succession of innovative products and joint ventures in Australia, North America, and Europe. The products included the *System-700* in 1976, a complete analog synthesizer system; the *GR-500* in 1977, the first commercially-available guitar synthesizer; the *MC-8* in 1977, a stand-alone sequencer and the first musical device containing a microprocessor; the *TR-808* in 1980, a programmable rhythm machine; the *Jupiter-8* in 1980, an eight-voice polyphonic keyboard synthesizer; and the *MC-4* in 1981, a descendant of the MC-8.

By 1981, Kakehashi saw the need for an industry standard. As he put it, "It's wasted energy if people can't communicate, so in the digital era, the question was how to share data, and not to have a standard was not possible." Standards existed in the computer market, where virtually everything, including modems, printers, disks, cables, could be used with everything else regardless of manufacturer. If the music market were to grow, it needed a standard. It needed universal compatibility. "The theory behind MIDI," as Tom Oberheim said, "is that you can hook anything into anything." Kakehashi initiated discussions with American companies:

> I discussed the necessity of a standard with Tom Oberheim. Dave Smith was working in that direction, so we communicated also with him. We discussed what kind of data format to use, what kind of socket, and other issues. We got input from many companies. Yamaha, Korg, and others agreed later, so at the beginning it was mainly the three of us: Roland, Oberheim, and Sequential Circuits. At the beginning, Oberheim wanted it to be a parallel interface. And Tom had a point—the parallel interface was better for a high-end professional market. But I was looking at a consumer market, and a serial interface was fast enough for consumers, even for most professionals.

Dave Smith, as president of Sequential Circuits, played a crucial role. He tells it:

> The very first contact I had with the idea of an interface was when Tom Oberheim approached me at a NAMM show, which must have been in June of 1981. He was approached by Kakehashi from Roland about the possibility of getting a standard digital interface . . . In what must have been October 1981 we had a meeting between the four Japanese Companies—Roland, Yamaha, Korg, and Kawai—Oberheim, and Sequential Circuits. That was just to talk about the idea. We didn't get too specific. The next thing that happened is that I gave a talk in November '81 at the AES convention in New York. I made a proposal for something called the USI (Universal Synthesizer Interface), and described exactly what it would be—a high-speed serial interface. There was some vague interest after that. Next, we called a meeting at the January 1982 NAMM show. We had about ten or fifteen companies come—Oberheim, E-mu, all the Japanese companies, Moog, Fairlight, GDS (Digital Keyboards), just to name a few that come to mind . . . What we found was that nobody really followed up on the ideas except the Japanese, who contacted us later. So we started working with them. They shared the desire to bring out something reasonable . . . No one in the States seemed to be interested anymore, and we lost interest in trying to round everyone up, so we worked with the Japanese companies. At that point we started going back and forth. The Japanese made a lot of suggestions. I think that Roland did most of the work. They did most of the coordinating in Japan . . . We had started with USI, but decided we didn't like the way it sounded . . . Roland came up with UMII, which stood for Universal Musical Instrument Interface or something like that. You were supposed to call it you-me. We came back with Musical Instrument Digital Interface, because that seemed the closest description to what it was . . . By the end of '82 and

beginning of '83, we had a working spec, and Roland and Sequential both brought out instruments with MIDI on them. That's when the fun started . . . at the January '83 NAMM show, when Roland brought down a JP-6 and hooked it to a Prophet 600, and they talked to each other. You could play the keyboard on one and the other would play right along with it. That was the first time you could do that with off-the-shelf products.

We immediately found that there were a lot of subtle differences . . . So we started realizing some of the problems that were going to come up. That was when we sat down with the five companies—Roland, Yamaha, Korg, Kawai and Sequential—and came up with what we called the 1.0 spec. This was in Japan in August 1983. That's the version that we released.

•

Not anyone's idea of perfection, however, MIDI was a multiple compromise between cost, performance, market preferences, and the many different things that many different people wanted to do. As Dave Smith said, "We knew from the start that the interface had to be a compromise." Slower serial communication was chosen instead of faster parallel communication because the necessary hardware was less expensive. MIDI's general keyboard orientation reflected the market's general familiarity with keyboards. Hardly a year later, in 1984, Tom Rhea, at that time director of marketing for Moog Music & Electronics, said, "I think that MIDI has been brought on because of market pressures, not because the *de facto* standard is technically exquisite . . ."

One problem with any de facto standard is that it forces conformity. Manufacturers who disagree with the standard are likely to feel pressured to acquiesce against their better judgment. Carmine Bonanno, for example, then president of Octave-Plateau Electronics, saw MIDI as contrary to his customers' interests. He was lyrical:

> The only thing I won't give in on is this stupid 5-pin DIN plug thing. I can't stand it. To force people to go out and buy a piece of shit connector that they can't use for anything else in their whole rig is insane. It's just totally insane.

Well, maybe the five-pin DIN-connector was an insanity, and maybe there were other insanities, but MIDI solved too many problems and embodied too many benefits to be totally insane. The primary benefit, as intended, was that any number of devices, regardless of their manufacturers, could be linked in a single system to be controlled and synchronized by a single performer, and this flexibility in system design allowed composers to build up systems incrementally, gradually adding or exchanging components according to their pocketbooks and musical needs. Further, the availability of universally compatible components led to a larger and more diverse international market into which any component of the instrument, whether hardware or software, whether made by a large or small company, whether conventional or radical, could be sold.

Organizations were formed to promote MIDI. The Japan MIDI Society Committee functioned, as Kakehashi explained, "to exchange ideas, collect information, form working groups, check future possibilities, keep the standard." In the United States, the IMA (International MIDI Association) was formed to disseminate information, and the MMA (MIDI Manufacturers' Association) was formed to solve technical problems. In 1984, the MMA and the Japan MIDI Society Committee began to develop the *MIDI 1.0 Detailed Specification*, which was published in 1985.

Because of their quick agreement on the MIDI standard, the Japanese manufacturers had an immediate advantage. In June 1983, Yamaha introduced the DX-7, the first MIDI hit, at less than $2,000. As Dominic Milano wrote at the time in *Keyboard Magazine*, "The price is even more remarkable when you consider that the DX-7 has a keyboard that is both velocity- and pressure-sensitive, will produce 16 notes simultaneously, and will store 32 programs [sounds] in its internal memory . . ." Roland developed a line of successful MIDI products, among them the *JUNO-106* in 1984 and the *D-50* in 1987. The D-50, in particular, gave birth to several offspring. By 1990, the D-series devices had sold in excess of 300,000 units, a substantial number for the electronic music market.

•

In hardware development, changes are made from one product to the next product. And because a product design-and-manufacture cycle is so costly, a hardware manufacturer needs to have very good market research or very sensitive intuition to ensure that the product will be welcomed when it arrives in the stores. Manufacture, in particular, is capital intensive. Dave Smith reflects, "At Sequential, we weren't very good at manufacturing and there was always a reliability problem—be it Moog, Arp, whoever, part of it was that they've been real small companies and haven't had the resources to get things right." And everyone makes mistakes. The survival question is whether a company has enough capital to try again. Many companies, not unlike Roland, and not unlike other companies around the world, were started by entrepreneurs, often brilliant engineers with wonderful and potentially winning ideas, who took risks. As Roger Linn puts it:

> What turns me on is innovation, the cutting edge. Guys like me, Tom Oberheim, Dave Smith, we all got in because we wanted to make amazing products. And the NAMM show was fun. Everyone was hungry for new ideas and products, so the demand was looking for the supply. And one crazy guy could do something wonderful.

Dave Smith, like many of the entrepreneurs, had financed Sequential Circuits' new products from revenues, and often with great difficulty and disadvantage. As he explains, "Because we were underfinanced, if a product couldn't hold its own, we would have to drop it because we just couldn't afford to keep putting development into a product line that wasn't producing—whereas if we had had capital, we could have used the first one as a learning curve and developed the next one based on what we learned."

In 1982, Smith developed the Prophet 600, the first MIDI keyboard. In May 1983, he developed the Prophet-T8, also MIDI, with a seventy-six-note wooden keyboard with velocity and polyphonic pressure. He recalls, "Synclavier bought keyboards from us." In 1984, the company's biggest year, Sequential Circuits introduced the 6-Track, the first multi-timbral synthesizer with a built-in sequencer, and the Drum Track, a digital drum machine. Then came the mistake. In 1984, in an effort to enter the personal computer market, Smith began to design sound cards for the Commodore 64 and Apple II. He tells the story:

> We knew we were taking a chance, but we decided to take the chance. It nailed us. The market wasn't ready. We started going downhill quickly in 1985. We were spending too many resources trying to get into the computer market. We made a mad dash to get back into synthesizers. We did the Prophet 2000 in 1985 and shortly afterwards the Prophet VS. But we couldn't adequately market them and we couldn't get parts from our suppliers. There was also the Studio 440, a sampling drum machine with a built-in sequencer. The last product was the Prophet 3000, which was a stereo sampler. That was when we dropped out of sight.
>
> It was towards the end of 1987. We were not having luck finding capital. Then one day Yamaha walked in. We basically told them they could buy the company for nothing. They just had to work things out with our creditors in the next two or three months. And so, in January 1988, we were owned by Yamaha. Well, for the next year and a half, they managed to butcher everything. Nobody quite knew what to do with us and, finally, after a year and a half, they decided to close us down. Everybody was starting to leave when, all of a sudden, in May 1989, Korg called us and said, "We want to get the group together." I said, "Well, you better do it real quick."

Korg did do it quickly. Smith helped Korg start a new division called Korg R&D and then continued to work for Korg as a general consultant. He observes:

> Japanese companies are usually comfortable with long-term thinking, so if the first version doesn't set the world on fire, maybe the next one will. That's what Yamaha did with the DX-7. It was their third FM synthesizer, and they thought they would sell 5,000 of them. It sold a couple hundred thousand.

Following the success of his Linn Drum, Roger Linn also made a mistake. As he remembers, "Well, then I wanted to make something bigger, better, stupendous, so I got the idea for the Linn 9000 and hired some other engineers—I wanted to make the most exciting product I could." But he didn't notice the business-mistake alarm lighting up. And he neglected to calculate the equation of higher expenses + longer than anticipated development time + increasing competition causing sales of existing products to slump = pressure to ship new products before they're ready. He continues:

> I raised my expenses a lot as sales of the Linn Drum dropped off. We shipped the Linn 9000 in 1984, but it had hardware problems. And it had software problems. And although people were very excited about its features, it had reliability problems. So a great buzz at first went down very quickly. We decided to make a redesign of the 9000, so we started on the Linn Drum MIDI Studio. And basically the company closed down before we could ship. Well, I like creating, designing. So I struck a good agreement with Akai in mid-1986. And in a sense the Linn Drum MIDI Studio did eventually come out—in the form of the Akai MPC-60. There was little similarity except for the product concept. But it felt very good to ship it. It was worked out.

Tom Oberheim also faced a crisis and found a solution. In 1983, Oberheim began development of the six-voice Oberheim Xpander, which, as he described it, "combined a lot of MIDI implementation with a complete analog synthesizer voice." In 1985, he finished the Matrix-12, which was two Xpanders with a pressure-sensitive keyboard, and began the Matrix-6. When development costs exceeded sales revenues, he faced a financial crunch, something less than a total crisis. In May 1985, following bad legal advice, the ownership of Oberheim Electronics was transferred to a company called Oberheim/ECC, which was owned by Oberheim's lawyer. As Oberheim said, "My involvement went from being president to being nothing." He worked at Oberheim/ECC for two years. Then his lawyer sold the Oberheim name to Gibson Guitar. Oberheim filed a lawsuit against his lawyer for legal malpractice.

In 1987, Oberheim formed a new company called Marion Systems. From 1987 to 1991, he worked on various products and consulted for Roland and Akai. In 1991, he began the development of the MSR-2, a new synthesizer system with new concepts of modularity at the synthesizer level and with a centralized control of all synthesizer functions.

•

By the mid-1980s, hardware successes were based as much on price, consumer design, and creative marketing as on technology innovation. At the summer NAMM show in 1984, Felix Visser came into contact with Ensoniq and heard that they were about to produce a digital sampler for $1,295. Was it possible? Visser was interested: "I bought a ticket and flew to Philadelphia and I met the Ensoniq people and saw the instrument, which was called the *Mirage*." In 1985, with the consent of Ensoniq, with Rene Rochat as a partner, and with a distribution deal for the United Kingdom with Syco, Visser formed a company called Ensoniq Europe in Brussels. He then began a marketing campaign which included spectacular booths at the Frankfurt Messe, Europe's largest music trade show. In 1987, he commissioned Piet Jan Blauw, a well-known European techno-sculptor, to design a number of headphones resembling wigs, hats, and helmets, all of which hung from an overhead grid, allowing people to put them on and listen to live demonstrations. As Visser said, "We wanted to achieve visibility, we wanted to demonstrate to a lot of people, we wanted to do something playful because I thought that all the usual presentations were boring . . . so we came up with the headphones and we took Polaroid pictures and sent them to people with a card afterwards saying, 'Thank you for coming to the Ensoniq booth.'"

It was very creative marketing. And, in fact, it was recognized: Visser's Ensoniq booth won a press prize from *Backstage*, a prestigious music magazine, for "best product presentation." But as the electronic music market increasingly came to resemble normal big business, the early entrepreneurs, who had been motivated both by the challenge of developing breakthrough products and the enthusiasm of the early users, became a bit discouraged. As Visser put it, "When I was designing booths for our trade shows, I was thinking that people would understand that we were all together in this to find new ways to experiment, to do unorthodox things, but most of the people who visited our booths just came to push buttons."

And the fewer the buttons, he might have added, the more successful the product. E-mu's *Proteus*, in fact, had a few knobs as well as a few buttons, but it offered 256 ready-made sounds with a very easy-to-use interface. As Marco Alpert recalls, "We thought, 'Why not take the sounds that most people want and have a band in a box?'" It was a great idea. Alpert had a winner on his hands: "We showed it at the NAMM show in 1989—it was clearly the right thing at the right time and within days after the show, we had a backlog of 5,000 units ordered, orders of magnitude greater than any other product we had made."

E-mu Systems' Proteus in 1989.
Photo courtesy E-mu Systems.

•

Hardware was only part of the story. As personal computers developed into the 1980s, a new music software industry began to form. To be sure, digital sequencers, far more precise than their analog predecessors, were sometimes built into keyboard synthesizers to allow a player to record a performance and play it back on demand. But software sequencers, modeled after multitrack tape recorders, allowed for serious editing.

The software developers, like their hardware colleagues, came into the field because they enjoyed it, not because they were businesspeople. Dave

Oppenheim, for example, later a founder of Opcode Systems, started in 1977 by building the computer section to a hybrid system for a friend at the Boston School of Electronic Music. The idea was to have an IMSAI, one of the original personal computers, control a Moog modular synthesizer. The hardware engineering was easy, but there was no real precedent for the software. As Oppenheim recalls, "I got this board working, and then I asked, 'Well, what are we going to do for software?'" The question was soon answered. He continues: "So in November 1977, we went to the International Computer Music Conference in San Diego and heard Chadabe's talk on PLAY, and that became the basic language—it was fairly simple but seemed pretty powerful." The PLAY Program, as we called it, was a hybrid-system software sequencer that Roger Meyers and I had written during the previous summer.

Afterward, back at Stanford to complete a degree in electrical engineering, Oppenheim did other projects, mostly with Oberheim equipment. He recalls, "I bought some Oberheim modules and built my own power supply, and it seemed like I was spending lots of time fixing stuff. Then a friend of mine got an Oberheim OB-XA and said, 'Wow, this is interesting, we could make a sequencer for this,' so I made a sequencer . . ." And then:

> I turned thirty and decided it was time to do my own thing, and writing sequencers and being able to record and play stuff on synthesizers was a lot of fun. It was November 1984, and MIDI had been out for almost a year. The DX-7 had come out. I looked at the Macintosh. It was hard to get through to Apple, but I did finally, and I established with Apple that the serial ports could go at the MIDI rate. So the Macintosh could do MIDI, and I was impressed by its level of integration and reliability. I didn't realize at that time that the best reason for choosing a Macintosh was that it was so easy for musicians to use.
>
> I built a little MIDI interface and wrote the first version of the Sequencer program. In February 1985, I came up with the name of Opcode Systems and went to the first Macworld Expo with xeroxed pieces of paper. Then, a few months later, there was MacFest at Stanford, and I set up a little table with synthesizers and Sequencer, and David Zicarelli saw me and came over to my house a week or two later and bought an interface. We went to the NAMM show in June 1985 in New Orleans, the first NAMM show that had anything for the Macintosh. About a week before we went to the NAMM show, David showed me a beta copy of his DX-7 editor, and said, "Sure, you can show it at the NAMM show."

That NAMM show, in June 1985, was the first congregation of the first round of MIDI software developers, among them Mark of the Unicorn, Southworth, Digidesign, Passport Designs, and Dr. T's Music Software. Oppenheim remembers his reaction to seeing the other developers: "I hadn't known that other people were working in the field—it was like the beginning of it all." He continues:

We shipped the first stuff around the last day of July. By that time, there were about six people working at my house. We worked at my house in downtown Palo Alto until December 1985. There was a little bit of investment, from me and from some friends, but basically everything was financed through sales and the usual getting people to work for as little as we could get away with.

There may be a beginning, but there is no end to software. Software is continually developed in small incremental changes, to be periodically relaunched in the market when there are a sufficient number of small incremental changes to merit being called a new version. New versions of Sequencer trickled out through the next months and years with new features, mostly providing more tracks and greater compatibility with other manufacturers' programs. Other programs were developed. Zicarelli's DX-7 editor allowed users of the DX-7 to store, change, and create their own sounds in the easy-to-use graphic programming environment of the Macintosh. Other sound editors were developed. Specific patch librarians, which allowed for the storage of sounds, were created for specific synthesizers. Vision, essentially a new program, was released in 1989 as a major upgrade to Sequencer, and Vision was in turn upgraded with new editing features, compatibility with other programs, notation features, and so on.

Dr. T's Music Software began in 1984. Emile Tobenfeld, in Boston, advertised his software in *Keyboard Magazine*, and Al Hospers, who at the time was working at Alex Music in New York City, saw an ad. As Hospers recalls, "I called him up and we hit it off—but the software was unusable by a normal humanoid, so I started giving him ideas for an interface . . ." Hospers began to sell the software. He continues, "It was an eye-opener because next thing I knew, I was selling everywhere, and making commissions—amazing!" In 1985, Hospers moved to Boston to start a company with Tobenfeld. Hospers remembers:

> There was no music software industry, MIDI had just been invented, and musicians and composers were chomping at the bit. No one had done any software for the truly creative musician yet. There were instruments like the Yamaha DX-7 and Casio CZ-101 that just screamed to be controlled by software. Emile couldn't play, but he had ideas. I could play bass and guitar, but not really keyboards. So we wrote software that would let us do things that we were not able to do on our own. It was a revelation. And as we got known, other programmers approached us with things they had written, or ideas. I jumped into the entrepreneurial swing of things, and by 1990 we were fifteen people, twenty plus products on six platforms, and three million in sales. It was a great time, a terrific ride . . .

In 1982, Karl Steinberg was working as a sound engineer at Delta Studio near Hamburg, Germany, and Manfred Rürup was working as a studio musician. As Rürup recalls, "Karl was fiddling around with a small computer, learning to program, and he wrote a sequencer." In 1983, calling themselves Steinberg Research, Rürup showed the program to a few dealers in music stores. As he remembers, "The feedback was completely lousy—they weren't interested, they couldn't see a home computer becoming a musical instrument." There was, however, positive response form Los Angeles: "A company called Music Data got the idea that music data, whatever that means, would be very important in the future—so they bought the program with a one-time payment." Steinberg then wrote Pro-16, the first of their professional programs. In Rürup's words:

> The funny thing is that because he wasn't a trained programmer, he couldn't do the multiple-page approach that was common, so he put it all on one page. And the one-page graphical interface, which nobody else had at that time, was a breakthrough. So we formed a company. We were funded by the Music Data sale and a credit line at a bank for 5,000 DM, at that time about $2,000. There was enough of a market so that by 1985 we had just enough income to make a living.

In 1986, Steinberg Research introduced the Pro-24 for the newly introduced Atari 520ST computer, and it soon became normal for music dealers to sell software. As Rürup recalls, "They all had Ataris in their shops, and Dire Straights became our first endorser, so things got bigger and bigger—we started writing sound editors and librarians, and making hardware interfaces." In 1989, Cubase, a new sequencer, was released for both Atari and Macintosh, and a marketing company called Steinberg/Jones was formed in the United States. In 1992, a PC version of Cubase was released and diversification began toward professional and entry-level versions and toward versions with audio editing and notation. Rürup observes:

> People often have good musical ideas. But to learn an instrument can be really hard and after you've gone through that process, you've sometimes lost your ideas. With sequencers, people who aren't really professional musicians can do their stuff and put it into a good musical form. And not only amateurs. There were all these groups that couldn't play, and sequencers allowed them to do anything.

•

Not only for MIDI, but personal computer software also became available for editing digital audio. In 1983, Peter Gotcher and Evan Brooks were playing together in a band in the San Francisco area. Gotcher bought a Drumulator. As he tells it, "I was interested in tablas, so Evan opened up this drum machine and we developed a number of alternative sounds, including African and Latin percussion and some electronic drums." In November, they demonstrated what they'd done at E-mu Systems, and as Gotcher recalls, "They loved the sounds—they called Manny's and Sam Ash and got us our first orders on the spot, and before we knew it we had a business." The business was Digidesign, and Gotcher and Brooks, according to Gotcher, "went on to sell 60,000 drum chips for Linn, Oberheim, Simmons, E-mu—we were staying up all night working on them on a home-brew digital audio editing system that Evan had designed and built . . ."

In 1985, when the Macintosh became available, they developed Sound Designer, the first commercial digital audio editor. In 1988, as Gotcher recalls, "We saw the convergence of a lot of technologies, large hard disks, digital-to-analog converters, Macs with slots, and we saw the opportunity to make a hard-disk recording system for the Mac at fairly low cost." The hard-disk recording system was Sound Tools, which sold 8,000 units, and it was the beginning of a new and large market. In the following years, Digidesign developed several professional digital audio editing and recording products, among them Audiomedia, Pro Tools, and Session 8, and the company's products became, by the early 1990s, an industry standard. Gotcher makes his point: "Editing is a really amazing creative tool . . ."

•

By 1985, David Wessel at IRCAM was beginning to feel that IRCAM should become more relevant in a world that was increasingly oriented toward personal computers. As he said, "George Lewis was a big force in this direction because he had come to IRCAM in 1984 and he was already doing interesting things along these lines . . ." At Wessel's instigation, Yamaha donated a MIDI studio, Apple donated six Macintosh computers, and as Wessel recalls, "It quickly became clear that people were interested . . ." He continues:

> My concept was that although equipment and facilities might move into the hands of individual composers, places like IRCAM could provide a meeting ground for experts. I saw it in a social context where free trade could occur between musicians, software developers, and scientists. I saw IRCAM as an institute that facilitated interchange.

In 1986, a new department of personal systems was formed with David Wessel as its director. Its goal was to make available, on small, affordable systems, the expertise developed at IRCAM. And that expertise was considerable. CHANT and FORMES were mainframe examples from the 1970s, but into the 1980s, there was also software written for Macintosh and other personal computers. Some of the software, such as Adrian Freed's MacMix, was straightforward and practical. Some of it, such as MIDI LISP, was aimed at musical experimentation. Wessel begins the story:

> I started the MIDI LISP project with the idea of providing some high level software for a small computer. And the key was that Le LISP was available on the Macintosh. The idea was to show that you could do really serious work on these machines. LISP seemed like a particularly good way to describe musical data structures because it was a programming environment that allowed for a high degree of abstraction. And I wanted

to marry this language with realtime performance. I was interested in making music that had an algorithmic character to it but where the algorithms were guided during performance.

Le LISP, at that time the major version of LISP for the Macintosh, was published by ACT Informatique in Paris. The goal for MIDI LISP was to provide a front-end music language that would allow a composer to write a program in Le LISP to control a MIDI synthesizer. The principal IRCAM developers were Wessel and Lee Boynton, soon to be joined by Pierre Lavoie as a representative of ACT Informatique.

In 1984, Camilio Rueda started work on the first MIDI drivers. In the early spring of 1985, Yann Orlarey, working at Grame, a music research organization in Lyons, finished a program called MIDI LOGO. Why LOGO? Orlarey explains, "LOGO was used quite a bit in France to make programming accessible to children and I thought it would make a good base for composers to begin to program." Orlarey demonstrated MIDI LOGO at IRCAM, and as a result of that presentation, Wessel, Boynton, and Lavoie invited him to join them in the development of MIDI LISP. As Orlarey recalls, "We had many discussions about what we should or shouldn't put in the software—David, for example, didn't like the concept of notes, Lee wanted to use a LISP-based scheduler . . ." In May 1985, Wessel gave a presentation of MIDI LISP at MacWorld Expo in Paris.

Boynton, meanwhile, developed PreFORME, a collection of software objects—*objects*, in this context, are software constructs that send messages to and receive messages from other objects—written in Le LISP. A PreFORME object could be a player that sent messages to another player or a conductor that sent messages to players. Further, PreFORME offered realtime interaction in that the message-passing mechanism had a scheduler that could say, for example, "Send this message at a particular time" or "When this happens, do that."

In February 1986, IRCAM formed a joint venture with ACT Informatique to commercialize MIDI LISP. In Lavoie's words, "We wanted to do things with music outside of the traditional boundaries, and it so happens that all computer literature which has to do with language and intelligence was at the time rooted in LISP, and much of it still is—we had, on a very small scale, a very interesting laboratory with a Macintosh and MIDI . . ."

In 1988, Intelligent Music got into the act, so to speak. Intelligent Music, a software company in upstate New York, entered into an agreement with ACT Informatique to prepare MIDI LISP for publication and then to publish it for the music world. As Lavoie assessed the situation, "It was a good idea, but to get it off the ground we needed to sell Le LISP to the people who wanted MIDI LISP, and Le LISP was a big environment and most musicians didn't know how to use it—so the effort of persuasion was enormous." There were, as it turned out, market realities that could not be ignored. I was president of Intelligent Music at the time, and after about a year, we reluctantly dropped out of the project. MIDI LISP was never commercialized.

•

Yann Orlarey's work with MIDI LISP led him to another significant software project. In 1987, he began work with Hervé Lequay on what they called Atelier Musical (Music Workshop), a software system that, as he put it, "was so complete that it could respond to the diverse needs of all composers." Their idea, as it quickly evolved, was to write a modular system and make the connections between modules in software. Messages, in other words, would be sent between different programs running simultaneously in a multitasking environment. When the first version, called MAK (MIDI Application Kernel), was finished in June 1988, it was obvious to them that the approach was useful for all MIDI software environments, and MAK was then developed to function in a standard MIDI environment.

The new software was called MidiShare. It met a need. There were many specialized programs in the market, among them sequencers (to record music), patch editors and librarians (to create, alter, and store sounds), and notation programs (to see the music in standard notation). Wouldn't it be great, people thought, if these different types of programs could be used simultaneously, if a composer could change a sound, for example, while hearing and seeing the music?

The problem, however, was that the same idea had occurred to other people as well, including software developers at Apple Computer. While Orlarey and Lequay were developing MidiShare, Apple was developing what it called MIDI Manager. Both MidiShare and MIDI Manager were published, and in the opinion of many professionals, MidiShare was superior to MIDI Manager in performance, dependability, and flexibility. But unfortunately for MidiShare's immediate market success, Apple's market clout and commitment to music at the time put MIDI Manager in a favored position. In software development, one might reflect, small organizations can compete with large companies. Marketing, however, is another matter.

•

In 1984, Jean-Baptiste Barrière became director of music research at IRCAM. His goal was the development of software tools for composers, even those not actively engaged in electronic music. He wanted to learn, as he put it, "how using a computer could provoke their imaginations." And because most composers wrote for traditional instruments, the problem was, as he stated it, "How to solve instrumental writing problems with computer techniques." The first solution was CRIME in 1985, a series of LISP functions that allowed a composer to manipulate abstract musical data and present it in musical notation. "It was an experiment," as Barrière described it, "not an IRCAM-sponsored research and development project." And it was not oriented exclusively toward notation. He explains:

> Our concern was to provide conceptual rules about musical structures. It was also to find ways of unifying instrumental writing and synthesis. In

other words, we wanted to make a tool that was comprehensive enough to control data in ways that were not idiomatic and specific to a particular technology. There was the implicit conviction that if we were linked to a specific synthesizer or technology or compositional style, we would never be able to unify the worlds of instrumental writing and synthesis.

By 1988, a team of developers, including Barrière, Pierre-François Baisnée, Marc-André Dalbavie, Magnus Lindberg, Kaija Saariaho, Jacques Duthen, and Yves Potard, had finished Esquisse, a new program written in Le LISP on a Macintosh Plus. Using Esquisse, however, proved to be difficult for composers who did not themselves program. Mikael Laurson took the next step in devising a graphical interface called Patchwork. As Barrière described it, "You might have considered it as a graphical LISP."

Patchwork developed through the years as a series of contributions by different composers at different times, among them Barrière, Laurson, Jacques Duthen, Camilio Rueda, Andrew Gerzso, Pierre-François Baisnée, Yves Potard, Magnus Lindberg, Marc-André Dalbavie, Tristan Murail, Xavier Chabot, Kaija Saariaho, and Lee Boynton. By the early 1990s, it had become a substantial and complex program. In 1992, it became an official IRCAM project. In 1993, Version 2 was finished as a collaboration between Camilio Rueda, Mikhail Malt, Tristan Murail, Xavier Chabot, Gérard Assayag, and Antoine Bonnet. Barrière describes it:

> It's an aid-to-composition system, written in Common LISP and Clos on the Macintosh. It provides you with about twenty libraries of functions— you have libraries of stochastic functions, libraries of spectral functions which use analysis of natural models to build structural models, some serial functions, and all kinds of libraries describing various personal worlds of composition. And there are all kinds of editors for editing traditional music notation. It's a fully graphical language. A composer can work at a graphical level without knowing that he's doing programming. And there are all kind of filters that allow you to convert data to MIDI files, or send data to synthesizers, or to other software such as Finale, Csound, CHANT, MAX . . .

•

By 1988, Intelligent Music had published several unconventional programs, among them M and Jam Factory, both of which had been written by David Zicarelli. And since the software had achieved some notoriety, Zicarelli, director of software development at Intelligent Music, had become widely known as an expert and interesting Macintosh programmer.

In 1988, Zicarelli was invited to lecture at IRCAM. Shortly before he left California for Paris, he attended a demonstration of MAX given by David Wessel at CCRMA. Zicarelli was impressed: "It seemed clearly superior to the project I was working on at the time . . ." Then, in Paris, following one of his lectures, Miller Puckette invited him for a drink at l'Excelsior, a nearby cafe, and asked him how he thought MAX could be commercialized. Zicarelli was interested. As he reflected, "Miller solved the problem of collaborating with a composer brilliantly . . ."

As the basic elements—Puckette's desire to commercialize MAX, Zicarelli's interest, and the beginning of a professional rapport between them—fell into place, I began discussions with Jean-François Allouis, then technical director at IRCAM. In July 1989, as president of Intelligent Music, I signed an agreement with IRCAM whereby Intelligent Music would publish MAX. Zicarelli began work. He remembers, "My interest in actually furthering MAX's development technically arose out of my role with Intelligent Music which had made an agreement with IRCAM to publish the program."

What did Zicarelli actually do to turn MAX from a program into a product? First, in his words, "I took a program which was being used in a situation in which the programmer was always there to a situation in which the programmer did not have to be there." He continues:

> It was also necessary to modify the scheduler so that we could have the program play music while the user was doing other things to the computer's interface. Seeing the need for this came directly out of my experience with M and Jam Factory, where it was an essential requirement that music play smoothly while a person operated the interface to change what was going on.

Zicarelli also extended MAX: "Over the last five years, I believe I've written about seventy-five objects, some very elaborate." He wrote software that made it possible for others to write objects. He also introduced some practical professional functions: "There's also a set of five objects I worked on to duplicate the functions of an Opcode style patch librarian and editor system so that people could construct editors for their MIDI synthesizers."

In early 1990, however, while MAX was still in preparation for publication, Intelligent Music faced a financial crisis. A considerable investment in software development had been made during the previous few years. The company's products, in addition to the Macintosh M and Jam Factory, included: UpBeat, a rhythm-oriented sequencer, developed for the Macintosh by John Offenhartz; M ported to the Atari by Eric Ameres and to the Amiga by Darrienn Fitzgerald; RealTime, an enlargement of UpBeat, developed by Eric Ameres for the Atari; MidiDraw, a drawing-input music program, developed by Frank Balde for the Atari; and OvalTune, an algorithmic graphics-and-music program written by Zicarelli for the Macintosh. Further, the Axxess Mapper, a hardware device that converted any MIDI message into any other MIDI message, was distributed by Intelligent Music for a brief time, and Cartographer, a software editor for the Mapper, was developed by Mark Brown for the Atari. Ameres and Brown had also developed MIDI multitasking software for the Atari. Other experiments, upgrades, and software ideas had been developed and discussed. It had been a lot to do. In fact, it had been too much.

It was noted, first, that unconventional software could be better sustained within the framework of a company that was publishing a wider range of software and, second, that David Asher, Intelligent Music's hardware engineer, was at the time developing a touch-and-pressure-sensitive control device that was applicable to consumer markets. Following further discussions within the company and with other companies, it was decided, in March 1990, to sell most of the major software products to Dr. T's Music Software and to concentrate on the development of the control device. It was agreed with Zicarelli that Opcode Systems would be the best alternative to support his preparation of MAX and its eventual publication. In May 1990, I went to Paris to facilitate an agreement between IRCAM and Opcode Systems whereby Opcode would publish MAX.

MAX was published in late 1990 and quickly became an almost universal solution for problems that required customized software. As Carter Scholz put it in *Keyboard Magazine*, "MAX is simply the most exciting MIDI technology I've seen this year—or any other." Christopher Dobrian, who wrote the operating manual, observed that MAX was "accessible to a lot of people who might not otherwise have had access to computer music programming . . ." MAX also let composers work at a musically meaningful level of objects and actions. As Zicarelli put it, "There's a sharp conceptual division between the MAX level and the C level." In summary, MAX provided relatively easy-to-learn, high-level, and efficient access to writing software. As Richard Zvonar, composer, consultant, and programmer, wrote:

> My work includes editing and control software for signal processors and MIDI tone modules . . . I have done custom house effects and stage monitor control software for Ultra Sound (the Grateful Dead's sound company), interactive sound installation control software for sound artist Max Neuhaus (mostly built around a neural net object custom made for us by David Roach and Frank Kurzawa), and with Steve Ellison have co-designed the Yamaha DMP-7 automated mixer control software and the MediaBand sequencer. I find MAX easy to work with . . . An especially useful feature is the capacity to edit a patch while it is running . . . Extensibility is another strong point. Even if one is not a C programmer one can accumulate a personal library of subpatchers, or one can download from several ftp sites any of the libraries created by a global community of MAX developers . . .

In 1992, Antony Widoff worked with U2 at the Zoo TV Outside Broadcast in Hershey, Pennsylvania. As he tells it, "They were running Vision on two rack-mounted Macintosh computers, and they had a bunch of samplers and synthesizers that played various background parts and sound effects during some of the songs—my job was to set up a system to trigger sequences from the stage and at the same time send time-code information to the video crew so

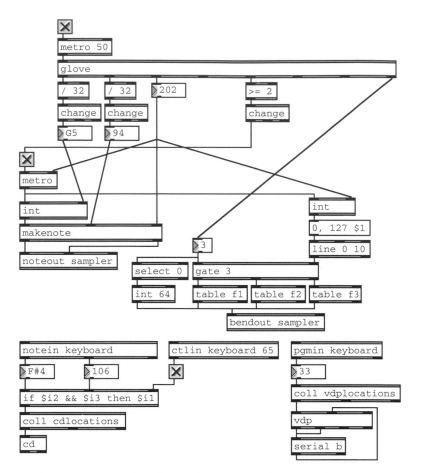

An example MAX program by Chris Dobrian. He explains: "In the upper portion of the program, input from a Mattel Power Glove game controller attached to the Macintosh computer's ADB port is polled every fifty milliseconds, and position data from the glove is used to play notes on a MIDI sampler. The horizontal and vertical coordinates of the glove are used to provide pitch and velocity data, and the distance of the glove from the computer screen is used to determine the duration and inter-onset interval of the notes . . . In the lower portion of the program, note, footswitch, and program change messages from a MIDI keyboard are used to control playback of an audio compact disc player and a video laser disc player."

that there wouldn't have to be a guy anticipating when Edge would start a song." He wrote a program in MAX to solve the problem. He continues:

One of the other things I did was to reorganize their MIDI system so that the backup system was always on line. Their method of switching from computer A to computer B was to take the large multi-bin connectors for system A, disconnect them, and reconnect them into system B. I just redesigned it so it wasn't necessary to change hardware connections, so that if A went down you could simply switch over to B by calling up the appropriate MAX patch.

Widoff worked with U2 again in 1993 in Ireland, where the basic problem was to be able to control a laser disc player from a software sequencer. As he explained, "They had to make sure that Lou Reed starts singing at the right time in the middle of *Satellite of Love.*" He wrote a short program with MAX to control the laser disc. He then continued with U2 for a few weeks in Holland. He describes the concerts:

> They're stadium shows. You're talking about audiences of up to 50,000 people a night. The stage is a huge steel girder construction on which are mounted three huge projection screens. There are four video walls on the stage itself, and then scattered about the stage are roughly ten to twenty television monitors. Each song has recorded and live video material that's thrown about from screen to screen in various manipulations, and there's a handheld camera which Bono throws around and uses on himself and other band members. There's a satellite dish that they lug around from show to show, and there's a part of the show where Bono has a remote control and he switches channels to whatever he can pick up on the satellite disk. Basically, he flips through them quickly and rejects each program as being ridiculous in some way or another. Sometimes he'll say something like, "Did you people come all the way out here and pay $50 to watch television?" And the audience will scream. There's a runway to the B-stage in the middle of the audience, and there's a camera on a dolly that goes up and down that stage. There's the mixing tower which stands about a third of the way into the stadium, which is the location from which the whole show is mixed and the video portion is directed. Each of the band members has his own separate monitor mix. Underneath the stage, which is where most of the equipment is, there are four different mixing consoles which provide different mixes for each of the band members, and all the band members have onstage monitors and, in addition, have wireless monitors. The wireless monitors have earplugs formed to the contours of their ears, which enable the band to perform on the B-stage. If they didn't have these monitors, the distance between the band and the house PA system would make it impossible to play because of the delay time involved.

•

By the early 1990s, everyone needed technology. And technology was available to everyone. A wide range of synthesizers, samplers, effects generators, controllers, and other hardware items were available at prices roughly between $500 and $5,000. In 1991, for example, the new names that appeared in magazine ads included the Akai *S1100*, Alesis *Quadraverb*, Cheetah *MS6*, Ensoniq *SQ-11*, Kawai *K4*, Korg *01/W*, Korg *Wavestation*, Kurzweil *K2000*, Oberheim

Matrix-12, Peavey *DPM 3*, Roland *D-70*, *Waldorf Microwave*, Yamaha *SY99*, and *Zeta MIDI Guitar*. A new vocabulary—as in "Just got an SQ-11," "My D-50's better than your SY99," "The K2000's cool, but the Matrix-12 is baaad"—was one of the positive literary byproducts of the growing market. And software—mostly sequencers such as Opcode's Vision, Mark of the Unicorn's Performer, Steinberg's Cubase, C-Lab's Notator, Passport Design's Master Tracks Pro, Voyetyra's Sequencer Plus, and Twelve Tone Systems' Cakewalk—was widely used to record and edit sounds and music. With perhaps a few exceptions here and there, every musician and every performing group used electronics, every film was scored with electronics, every television jingle was done with electronics. In fact, virtually all new music, except for music in the classical chamber music and orchestral tradition, used electronics in one way or another. As Robert Ashley said, "Electronic music is all over the place, it's ubiquitous—what do you hear that isn't electronic music?"

● ● ●

Chapter Eight

Inputs and Controls

Iannis Xenakis, as early as 1953, had devised a notation based on graphic designs rather than conventional musical symbols. As he tells it, "I was doing designs for *Metastasis* and *Pithoprakta* because it was easier for me to control large numbers of events by designing them instead of by writing them on staves, which was cumbersome, so I linked one pitch with another pitch through lines, and I thought, 'Why should I write them as notes instead of as these lines?'— we are used to seeing things in visual shapes, it's natural." In 1972, he formed CEMAMu (Centre d'Etudes de Mathématiques et Automatiques Musicales / Center for Studies in Mathematics and Automated Music) in Issy les Moulineaux, just outside Paris. Within a few years he had sufficient funding, largely from the French Ministry of Culture, to purchase equipment and hire technicians and programmers, and he began to develop UPIC (Unité Polyagogique Informatique du CEMAMu), a computer-based system which allowed him to draw a shape on a tablet and interpret the shape as a control for some aspect of sound or music. He used it to compose parts of the sound material for *La Légende d'Eer* (1977) and *Mycenae–Alpha* (1978). As he said, "How would you relate probabilities to shapes? Well, look at the clouds."

Other composers also worked with UPIC in those early days, among them Pierre Barbaud, a pioneer in algorithmic composition, François-Bernard Mâche, Cornelia Colyer, and Jean-Claude Eloy. In 1978, UPIC was shown to the public at a UNESCO-sponsored show on art and technology in Paris. Shortly thereafter, demonstrations were organized throughout France, in Holland, Germany, Portugal, Greece, and Japan, and schoolchildren were invited to make music with it. Xenakis said:

> Anybody, even myself or you, or children, can draw lines or graphics with an electromagnetic ballpoint, and they are transformed by computer directly into sound . . . You can compose or do any training or pedagogy for the ear or for writing, because the writing is not the usual musical writing. It's a much more universal one, because it is with lines. For instance, a note that is held is just a horizontal line . . . The vertical aspect is for the pitches, exactly like when you write for an instrument: when you go up it's higher; when you go down, it's a lower sound . . . Polyphony, yes of course. Hundreds of lines at the same time . . . The interesting thing is that you can design, listen, and then start again . . . correct or throw away what you don't want . . . it's like a game. I noticed with children of five or six, they have imagination, but they have no milestones, structures on their mind, in order to organize things . . . In the beginning they try to do designs, nice designs . . . the imagery of houses, or cats, or suns. But then they have this immediate response from the machine and they start listening more carefully to what they design . . .

A production model was then developed by CEMAMu engineers Jean-Michel Raczinski and Gerard Marino. In the new UPIC, a graphic shape, called an *arc*, could represent virtually any aspect of a musical sound; up to 4,000 arcs could be drawn on the same *page*; and a page could be played back in any direction, backward, forward, and with any changes in speed, including abrupt motions. In 1985, Les Ateliers UPIC (UPIC Workshops) was formed in Massy, just south of Paris, to house the new UPIC and to function as a CEMAMu satellite for pedagogy and production. In 1991, Gerard Pape became director. As he reflected, "Composing with a graphic score, using graphic notation, seems to open doors to new possibilities . . ." And Les Ateliers UPIC opened its doors to many composers, among them Bernard Parmegiani, Jean-Claude Eloy, François-Bernard Mâche, Julio Estrada, Cort Lippe, Jean-Claude Risset, and Joji Yuasa.

Yuasa, in particular, had composed graphic scores before working at Les Ateliers UPIC. He had earlier worked at IRCAM, where he had composed *Nine Levels by Ze-Ami* (1988), for computer-generated quadraphonic tape and chamber ensemble; and in the process of its composition, he had drawn a graphic score with frequency indicated on an up-and-down axis, time indicated from left to right, and loudness shown as a graph on the bottom of each page. Marc Battier had assisted Yuasa in realizing the score with IRCAM's technology. As Yuasa remembers, "I didn't find it a problem to work through someone else, but I started with very basic things, using band-limited white noise, and it took time." He continues:

I could imagine what would happen. I had a lot of experience with graphic scores. All the shapes, the character of the shapes are changing through the piece. Many of the lines are curves, smooth gradual curves, with diverging and converging bandwidths. I designed all the frequencies quite precisely, as well as some bands where there's a random distribution of fragments.

So when Yuasa composed *Eye on Genesis I* (1991) at Les Ateliers UPIC, it was a natural step. He continues:

It was easy for me because I was so acquainted with working on graphic compositions that I knew what shapes would produce which sounds. At UPIC, however, the approach was a little different because the graphics weren't just graphic road maps through a piece. They were sketches, drawings, freehand graphics that were then interpreted as music. The graphic fragments were made independently and then mixed in any order. In designing the sounds, I used several voices of different timbres as well as various envelope shapes that I could orchestrate by combining different timbres at the same time. For example, I made a bright timbre and then, like a shadow, a soft timbre remaining on the same pitch.

Yuasa's words—"sketches, drawings, freehand graphics"—pose a question: Can UPIC translate the graphic beauty of the *Mona Lisa*, for example, into music? And Pape's answer is sobering: "Sometimes the pages that are the most attractive visually don't sound well—beauty on a visual level does not necessarily correspond to interest on a sonic or musical level."

Yet the idea of composing by drawing (remember Xenakis' words, "Anybody can draw . . .") was seductive. In April 1993, at the Université de Paris VIII à Saint-Denis, with Giuseppe Englert's encouragement, Vincent Lesbros began to work on Phonogramme. As Lesbros explained, "I tried to find an input structure that would produce both image and sound so I could import pictures and use the visual information to make music . . ." Marc Battier used Phonogramme in composing *Toca* (1993), for marimba and tape. He began with the idea of deriving sounds, as he tells it, "from wooden bells that I had originally recorded twenty years earlier in a monastery in Romania—the bells were descendents from a very old Central Asian music and the rhythm was for me very haunting." He first analyzed the bell sounds, then used the shapes resulting from his analysis to draw a melodic line for the marimba, and then drew the melodic line into Phonogramme to specify the electric sounds.

•

An electronic musical instrument can look like modules in a rack, or like a computer, or like a lot of little gray boxes on a table, or like a violin, or for that matter, like virtually anything. But whatever its size, shape, or other physical attributes, an electronic musical instrument, like any musical instrument, contains a performance device, a sound generator, and a link between them. The performance device is what a player touches or manipulates to control the sound, for example the strings and bow of a violin. The sound generator, for example the body of a violin, produces the sound. And the link connects the performance device to the sound generator, as does the bridge on a violin.

In a violin, as in all acoustic instruments, the sound generator colorizes and projects the sound initiated by the performance device. The sound of a Stradivarius violin, for example, starts with the vibrating string, but its tone quality and projection result from the resonant qualities of the materials, shape, and size of its body. Further, because the performance device of an acoustic instrument initiates the sound of the instrument, the performance device is an intrinsic part of the instrument to which it is attached.

In a typical electronic musical instrument, on the other hand, the performance device does not initiate a sound and it is not, consequently, an intrinsic part of the instrument to which it is attached. Because it triggers or controls the sound of the instrument, as against initiating the sound, any electronic performance device—as Max Mathews put it, "from traditional keys and knobs to microphones, breath-pressure sensors, eye trackers, TV cameras, and even EEG electrodes"—can be attached to any instrument. And an electronic sound generator can produce any sound in response to any performance device. An electronic keyboard, for example, can be used to play a trumpet sound. Or a duck sound. Or the sound of 42nd Street at noon.

How, then, does a performer choose a device? The answer is: according to the musical context and the musical role the performer wants to play. Playing a keyboard, for example, with one's fingers is musically different from playing a theremin and moving one's arms and hands through the air. And because making a particular physical gesture will cause a performer to feel in a particular way about the music that's being performed, certain devices are more appropriate than others to certain musical situations. Morton Subotnick agrees:

> I can imagine a number of different kinds of input devices for different kinds of pieces. For instance, for a piano piece I'd want to use my fingers, to some extent my wrists and arms. For other kinds of music, for things that were timbrally rich, I'd want to sculpt the air with my palms, shoulders, my head. I could imagine, if I were a different person, tap-dancing a piece, shuffling my feet across the floor . . .

Further, because a performance device is connected to the rest of the instrument via software, it can be used to control any aspect of the music as well as any sound. Playing a note on a MIDI keyboard, for example, can trigger a sequence of notes as easily as it can trigger a single note. Consequently, if an instrument is intended for public performance, the performer needs to be sure that the connection between a performance gesture and its musical effects will be evident to the audience. Composer and performer Neil Rolnick elaborates:

One extreme is pushing a button and having the whole piece come out, the other is playing all the notes individually—the real problem is to find the right middle ground. When working with an ensemble, I need the flexibility of playing from the keyboard to be able to adjust tempi and coordinate the music with other players. In a solo or improvisational situation, I can make more thorough use of the power of the computer as a controller.

But there has to be some correlation between a performer's physical movement and the sound. In one piece, I trigger sequences from the keyboard but the sequences are so fast that each triggering of a sequence becomes an arpeggiated individual note, and I can be seen playing it. In other pieces, I try to use a sequencer actively, to perform with it, to make the process visible. For example, I change the sequence in real time and react to it. In a recent performance, I was using the sequencer to build a huge orchestral sound with lots of movement, something clearly beyond the capability of ten fingers to play. I was bringing in tracks of sequences, altering the sounds, altering the combinations, the pitch levels, all of this in real time, and the reactions that I got from the public included people listening and being impressed that I sounded like the orchestra and people who watched and were disturbed by the lack of virtuoso keyboard work . . .

•

Traditional instruments are traditional precisely because people have played them through the ages. So, as many composers have thought, why throw away the tradition? Why not use traditional instruments to control electronics and, thereby, combine traditional virtuosity with imaginative sounds? And further, why not integrate electronic music into the context and performance practices of traditional music?

In his orchestral pieces *Two Butterflies* (1974) and *Before the Butterfly* (1975), Morton Subotnick used muted violins to control electronic devices. In his so-called "ghost" pieces, he used the sound of a "ghost" instrument, recorded on tape but not itself present, to control electronics. In *After the Butterfly* (1979), as he explains, "I was the ghost—I encoded my voice as a ghost performer and put it onto a tape which was sent to the performer with a ghost box which contained a frequency shifter, left and right panner, and a voltage-controlled amplifier for volume." He composed *Ascent into Air* (1981), for amplified instrument ensemble, at IRCAM, and he used two unmuted and audible cellos as controls for Di Giugno's 4C synthesizer.

By the early 1980s, however, Subotnick's techniques were becoming complicated. In fact, too complicated. As he described it, "We had twenty contact mikes all over the stage, with wires to the envelope followers . . ." He concluded, "I decided it was time for me to get serious about this." He got serious in 1984. He did a residency at MIT. As he tells it, "I thought we could get a computer to respond properly as if it were a musician following a conductor, so I went to MIT, I played a bit with Barry Vercoe's program . . ."

In fact, Barry Vercoe had been serious for some time. In 1982, he had gone to IRCAM on the first of several visits to develop techniques for synchronizing a computer-generated accompaniment with a performer playing an acoustic instrument. By 1984, he could report that he had the computer "able to listen to a flute performance of a Handel flute sonata, say, or the Boulez *Sonatine*, and synchronize a realtime accompaniment to what it was hearing" and that the system had "a high degree of sensitivity to tempo, so that the player could speed up and slow down at will and the computer accompaniment was always with him."

Although Subotnick and Vercoe were both serious about deriving control information from an acoustic instrument, they approached the problem in different ways. Vercoe had concentrated on what he called *score following*. Subotnick focused on relating events, as in "if an instrument does this, then the electronics do that," and during the next few years, he composed several pieces in which a computer tracked a performer's actions and controlled something accordingly. By the time of his *Hungers* (1986), an electronic opera done in collaboration with video artist Ed Emshwiller, Subotnick was working with Mark Coniglio to develop Interactor, a new program developed specifically to track a performer's actions, or several performers' actions, and control all aspects of a performance as certain things happened. As Subotnick explains, "For example, when the players are at measure 72 on the third beat and when Joan moves her right hand down, the lights are going to go off when the keyboard player releases the longest chord." In *Jacob's Room* (1993), a chamber opera for live soprano, recorded baritone voice, live solo cello, video projections by Woody and Steina Vasulka, and loudspeakers placed around the performance space, Subotnick used Interactor to follow the soprano's and cellist's performances and control video laser discs (start time, frame number, speed, direction forward or backward, and duration) accordingly.

In her *Events in the Elsewhere* (1990), a music-theater-video piece inspired by Stephen Hawking, Joan La Barbara used Interactor to track her voice and control video imagery. She describes it:

> I was imagining that if one were trapped in a minimally functioning body, one might imagine life in another reality. In my piece, unlike Hawking, I allowed my character to make vocal sounds, and the character was controlling certain elements of the environment by the voice. And so using a pitch follower and a program that Mark Coniglio and Mort Subotnick had developed, I was using the voice to control video imagery. I was also controlling the movement of a camera which had 360-degree pan, tilt, and rotation, and so I could use the voice to control the directionality and speed of movement of the robot camera.

Tod Machover at MIT was also interested in deriving information from an acoustic instrument. In 1986 and 1987 at IRCAM, he had composed *Valis*, an opera based on Philip K. Dick's science fiction novel, and he had used Di Giugno's 4X system to process the voices. In the spirit of practicality, he had decided, as he said, "to score the piece for just two players, keyboard and percussion, and to figure out a way to extend their performance into many layers of sounds and complexity." It foreshadowed his concept of the *hyperinstrument*, which, he explains, "means taking more and more sophisticated measurements—of the cello, for instance, we know a lot about the bowing and about the wrist movements, but for me what's important are all the extra things that the performer's putting into the performance." The idea was to get a complete picture of what a performer was doing and use that knowledge to control some musical result. Machover continues:

> You need to get detailed information, but the problem with details is that it's very hard to have them add up to the total picture again. There's a real danger of measuring every little tick on the instrument and losing the sense of the instrument. So the best thing I know how to do right now is to measure the details while always trying to put them back into the larger picture of whatever it is we call "expression."

Machover's *Begin Again Again . . .* (1991), composed for Yo-Yo Ma, is for a *hypercello*, which is to say a cello-based system with sensors and computer. Wrist measurements, bow pressure-and-position sensors, left-hand fingering-position indicators, and direct sound analysis enabled the computer to measure, evaluate, and respond to what the cellist did, and then to affect the sounds directly, and sometimes to affect the way the cellist affected the sounds. He continues:

> In *Begin Again Again . . .*, instead of measuring bow position and sending that out as a parameter, I measured types of bowing—pressure, position of the bow, how much bow is being used, how often the bow is changing direction—which is a collection of a bunch of variables together. If you can measure type or style of bowing, that's already much closer to what a musician can feel than if you say, "Play at this part of the bow to trigger such and such an event."
>
> What I measure has a lot to do with what the music is. If there are times where the music is particularly complex, I would just as soon have the performer think in the most general terms, like a kind of scale of tension from one to ten. Since my music has a variety of layers, I quite often change the layer of detail that I have the performer working at. It's all built into my compositions. In fact, in *Begin Again Again . . .*, the performer acts more and more like a conductor as the piece goes along, dealing less with details than with large structural or timbral shapes.
>
> I've often thought about the model of the one-man band on stage and been a bit scared of that as a comic image. But it should be possible to extract that amount of information from a single player on a single instrument.

•

Traditional instruments—pianos, violins, clarinets, drums, and so on—have indeed become traditional largely because they are enjoyable to play, because they are musically rewarding extensions of our physical selves. Keyboards, for example, extend our hands and fingers. Violin bows and drumsticks extend our arms. A clarinet extends its player's voice. Traditional instruments, consequently, have been widely imitated in electronic instruments.

Electronic keyboards, in particular, have been popular. Virtually every manufacturer has made them, and some manufacturers have gone to great lengths to make them feel like their acoustic progenitors. Kurzweil, for example, developed a wooden-key keyboard for its Model 250. On the other hand, some performers have looked for ways to extend their keyboard skills by developing new functionality in keyboard designs. As John Chowning said, "It would be silly to throw away the keyboard simply because it's related to an older music—you can apply people's keyboard facility in new and different ways." And that was exactly what John Eaton had in mind.

Eaton's experience with the Synket had led him to think about how the functionality of electronic keyboards might be improved. The Synket, for one thing, had not been entirely stable. As Eaton said, "I'd take a trip and something would jiggle loose . . ." But Eaton's ideas went further: "I also wanted to make the instrument more sensitive to slight inflections of touch—my ideal became to localize the control in the fingertips as much as possible . . ." Later in 1967, he began to discuss those issues with Robert Moog:

> So Bob and I started talking and I asked him to have on the keyboard the sensitivity that it should be able to read out the precise degree to which the key is depressed, so that if it were applied to volume you could make crescendos or diminuendos. I also asked for the sensitivity of the front-back position and the side-to-side position at which the key is touched. I also asked for applying hard pressure to a completely depressed key. And I asked that each one of these sensitivities could be applied to any aspect of the music that you could control through a synthesizer or a sound-generating program on a computer. And then Bob, at one point, discovered that you could read out the amount of area that your finger would cover.

Eaton joined the faculty of the University of Indiana and, in 1972, received a grant to commission Moog to build the *Multiple-Touch-Sensitive Keyboard*. In 1977, Moog left Buffalo, moved to North Carolina, built a house, and started Big Briar, a new company specializing in unusual controllers such as touchplates, theremins, ribbon controllers, and ultrasonic sensors, and one of his first projects was Eaton's keyboard. As he said, "It was just so complicated—but it's general enough so you can learn a great deal from it and there's so much you can do with it, compared to ordinary keyboards, that a guy like John will significantly expand our notion of what performance on electronic instruments can be."

Robert Moog (left) and John Eaton (right) at the first public showing of the Multiple-Touch-Sensitive Keyboard at the University of Chicago in 1992. Photo by Renee Moog.

Gregory Kramer also ordered a keyboard. After graduating from California Institute of the Arts in 1972, Kramer was living outside of Los Angeles, performing with a few groups and scoring a few films, when he felt an impulse to invent things. He formed Electron Farm, a manufacturing company for synthesizers and controllers. He tells it:

> I went to CBS because I heard they had some Buchla 100s on the shelf and I bought the whole inventory, faceplates, parts, schematics, circuit boards. So I had synthesizers in my home and I started getting people to build synthesizers in exchange for synthesizers. We sold a number of synthesizers to universities, but what I really got out of it was technicians to build stuff for me. I would customize modules, add features, I would get new modules designed, and I could try all kinds of weird things. At that time, if you wanted a new sound, you had to make the ability to create that sound. Or if you wanted a new way of controlling things, you had to make that.

Kramer moved to New York in 1975 with much of the Electron Farm parts inventory. In 1977, he founded PASS (Public Access Synthesizer Studio). PASS eventually grew into Harvestworks, an organization that supported PASS and the Electronic Art Ensemble as well as recording and residency programs. In 1981, he formed Clarity, through which he developed technologies that were licensed to Lexicon and other companies. In general, Kramer was interested in human control issues: "I was looking for that link with electronics where the very feel and nature of my physical gestures would come through the sound." And so, in 1982, he went to visit Moog. He saw the Multiple-Touch-Sensitive Keyboard as an extension of a piano into the electronic world. As Kramer put it, "I could control the signal processing on the keyboard, not even striking notes, just massaging different dimensions—I saw it as a hybrid instrument that would be analog, digital and electro-acoustic, that would let me play a music that would be a hybrid of pure sound and rhythms and pitches."

The building of the Multiple-Touch-Sensitive Keyboard was interrupted by the professional demands of Moog's positions at Kurzweil Music Systems in Boston from 1984 to 1989 and then at the University of North Carolina in Asheville. But finally, it was finished. In 1991, Eaton received the first one. He used it to compose *Genesis* (1992). And he found that it was more sensitive than MIDI sound generators could handle:

> I was very excited about it. But I also felt like someone threshing wheat with a surgeon's scalpel—because the keyboard was so sensitive while the commercial synthesizers were so crude in the way that a performer could really affect the sound. The next thing that needed to be done was a different kind of sound production apparatus . . .

•

Not only keyboards, but virtually all traditional instruments, including saxophones, guitars, drums, wind instruments, violins, even the harp, have been reconceived as electronic instruments. In general, these "traditional" electronic instruments appeal to musicians who have instrumental skills. They are comfortable and familiar. And because they typically offer an expanded range of sounds, they are often fun. Dorothy Martirano, for example, plays a Zeta MIDI violin. Asked what she thinks about hearing a nonviolin sound coming out, she answers, "Well, it's exciting—I like doing it."

Martin Hurni reconceived the saxophone. In 1974 in Berne, Switzerland, he began to build things, as he said, "because commercial equipment was so expensive, and at the same time I was actively playing the saxophone—so I decided to combine the saxophone world with electronic music production and build an electronic saxophone that I could play." In 1978, he built a small wooden controller with simple keys on it and an approximate Boehm fingering, but as he said, "The more I looked for an optimized key positioning, the closer I got to the real saxophone—so my next logical step was in experimenting with an alto saxophone and putting microswitches under each key." In 1981, he disassembled a saxophone, inserted sensors and microprocessor hardware, equipped the mouthpiece with sensors for lip and breath pressure, and thereby finished a prototype *Synthophone*, as he called it. In 1984, he played it at Ars Electronica, and he recalls, "Bob Moog gave me the idea of making the Synthophone accessible to others, so I concentrated on making the instrument manufacturable . . ." In 1986, he finished the first commercial model. In 1987, he went to the Frankfurt Music Messe, distributed pamphlets at the Sequential Circuits booth and, encouraged by people's interest, formed a company called Softwind Instruments and began to make Synthophones.

Peter Beyls playing the IR-violin in Brussels, 1987.
Photo courtesy Peter Beyls.

Peter Beyls reconceived a violin. In 1990, at the artificial intelligence laboratory at Brussels University in Belgium, he turned a normal violin into an infrared violin—an *IR-violin*, as he called it—by fitting each string and the bow with an infrared transmitter and receiver. As each string and/or the bow was pressed, the distance between its transmitter and receiver changed, and consequently, the intensity of its infrared light changed, and the intensity information was then used to control sound.

Nicolas Collins mounted an optical sensor in the crook of a trombone, and a keypad on the slide, and he used what he called his *trombone-propelled electronics* to control a digital signal-processing system. He said, "It was my entry point to the world of improvised music—I made instantaneous transformations of other players' sounds." His pieces included *Real Electronic Music* (1986), *Tobabo Fonio* (1986), and *100 of the World's Most Beautiful Melodies* (1989). He observed: "to the uninitiated there is something baffling about a movement that changes pitch at one time and loudness the next . . . Nonetheless, the apparently quixotic relationship between physical action and sonic response fascinates . . ."

Paul DeMarinis did it in reverse. Rather than start with a traditional instrument and turn it into an electronic performance device, he started with an electronic performance device and evolved it toward a traditional instrument. In 1978, he made a sort-of guitar, actually a touch-sensitive device with sensors instead of frets. In 1980, he added a microprocessor which made it possible to start something with one fret, for example, then hold that and play another fret, and then capture that with the microprocessor and move to another area of the fret-board to do something else. He then made a proposal

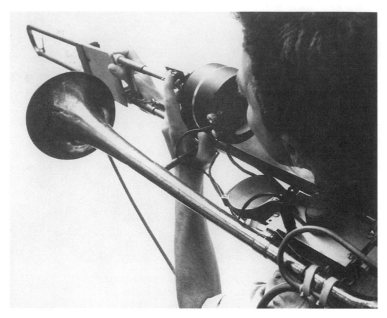

*Nicolas Collins performing with his trombone-propelled electronics in
the late 1980s. Photo courtesy Nicolas Collins.*

to the Exploratorium in San Francisco for an installation in 1981 and 1982
that would involve people playing together on several of his "guitars." He tells
the story:

> The process of making interactive art needs to be interactive. When
> you're making an interactive piece, you have to test it out, to continu-
> ously interact with the people who'll be using it interactively. And the
> process of doing the piece at the Exploratorium was, for me, learning
> about how technology socializes, and how sociology technologizes, and
> about the human dimension that makes interaction. And how slight
> changes will totally change the interaction. I started out as Mister Weirdo
> with people on the staff telling me that my sticks didn't look like guitars.
> Then I met someone on the staff who had previously worked for
> Alembic—they did guitars for The Grateful Dead—and he agreed to
> make guitar-style bodies for my electronics, patterned after standard elec-
> tric guitar types. There were five guitars, one was a Gibson, one a
> Stratocaster, one a Flying V, and so on, all standard styles, and it was
> amazing how they played into everyone's musical fantasies. The reality of
> the guitar, the weight, the finish, the leather straps, the smell of the leather
> straps, all of these were intangible but socially meaningful qualities that
> affected the way people played together. Suddenly, everybody knew they
> were making music, and their actions were reinforced by the actual expe-
> rience they were having. The fantasy of the rock-and-roll guitarist, that
> was music making. Holding these objects meant music to them.

•

Some composers built electronic controllers that were not traditional instruments but resembled traditional instruments in the way they were played. In the mid-1960s, for example, Gary Lee Nelson was a tuba player in the Netherlands Philharmonic in Amsterdam. Curiosity led him to attend Gottfried Michael Koenig's course at the Institute of Sonology, and it launched him in a direction that eventually took him through graduate school and two teaching positions and ultimately, in 1974, to join the faculty at Oberlin College in Ohio. Being in Ohio clearly made a difference. As he put it: "Got rid of the tuba. Did mostly mainframe software synthesis and tape composition." In 1983, however, he began again, in his words, "to feel the need for using my brass player's chops." So he talked with John Talbert, engineer, about making an electronic wind instrument. In two months, Talbert had finished a prototype. As Nelson recalls, "It was pretty smooth, easier to play than a tuba."

The *MIDI Horn*, as Nelson called it, contained controls for pitch and sound changes, a breath-pressure sensor, and a slider operated with his thumb. In 1986, he began performing with it and developing software that connected its outputs to a musical result. Some of it was straightforward. As he put it, "What the audience saw was a fairly traditional kind of soloist in the middle of the stage, playing in an engaging way." But some of it was a more-than-meets-the-eye algorithmic approach: "I'd play a note with the pedal down and the computer would generate a sequence from a pitch-generating algorithm— or the pitch and velocity of a single note would determine the tune or lick that was played." In his *Fractal Mountains* (1988), for example, the accompani-

Gary Lee Nelson playing his
MIDI Horn in the mid-1980s.
Photo courtesy Gary Lee Nelson.

Above: Dexter Morrill in 1990 and his MIDI Trumpet with pitch detection software by Perry Cook. Photo courtesy Dexter Morrill.

Left: Chris Chafe playing his Celletto in the late 1980s. Photo courtesy Chris Chafe.

ment figures were generated by fractal interpolation between the time, key, and velocity of the the first note and the time, key, and velocity of the second note.

In 1987, Chris Chafe built the *Celletto*, as he called it, a bodiless cello designed to send audio signals to a pitch-to-MIDI converter. He describes it:

> It's a single block of maple, as long as the length of the strings, as thin as the fingerboard, and as deep as a cello is deep. The intent was to make it feel like a cello. There are some extensions that are screwed onto it for my knees and chest so that all the points of contact for my body are in the right place. I use a normal cello bow. The bridge was designed by Max Mathews in a new idea that he had just had about a specific type of transducer called the piezo ceramic bi-morph transducer. So in the bridge there's a transducer aligned with each of the four strings. It's a wooden bridge with saw cuts that eliminate the crosstalk between strings. You can look at it as four fingers supporting the strings, each with a separate output. It's heavy enough but not as heavy as a standard instrument. It collapses into a case about like a trombone case.
>
> I've spent some time trying to put a transducer in the bow to read bow speed and pressure. The first time out was a combination of accelerometer and strain gauge to measure the flex in the bow. The second time was the Lightning used to track position—the transmitter is on my wrist and the receiver directly in front. The Celletto is an unfinished project. It's going to keep evolving.

It's likely to keep evolving, in fact, in two different directions simultaneously. Chafe is interested in controlling sound: "I'd like to apply the string player's natural control parameters to bowed string synthesis in real time." He is also interested in higher level compositional control. In *El Zorro* (1991), for example, he called for a Lightning to be attached to the bell of Dexter Morrill's trumpet: "When he blows a note, he moves—so I gave him a kind of steering wheel to steer an algorithm through a performance." And he is using the Celletto to expand that approach: "I want to get out of this division between accompanist and soloist and create an improvisation environment for myself . . ."

•

In the mid-1980s, Donald Buchla designed the last of his synthesizers. As he tells it, "I assumed that with a MIDI standard there would be a proliferation of interesting controllers, so I designed the 700 with three MIDI inputs thinking that someone could have several kinds of MIDI controllers playing this one system, and that isn't what happened . . . all one could buy for controllers were the usual organ keyboards and very crude imitations of guitars with MIDI outputs, and that was it—so after I designed the 700, I thought, 'Well, I guess it's mine to design some new controllers.'"

In 1990, Buchla finished *Thunder*, a tactile surface broken up into several areas arranged in the shape of a hand. The areas functioned something like nonmechanical keys, with each key sensitive to impact, pressure, and position. Bruno Spoerri, among many others, has performed extensively with Thunder. As

Donald Buchla playing Thunder
at Stanford University in 1991.
Photo by Renee Moog.

he describes it, "It has twenty-five keys of different sizes and shapes that can be used for different MIDI functions and the keys are oriented in such a way that you don't have to move your arms—your hands basically stay in the same place." How does it feel to use it? Spoerri answers: "It feels good—it's a way of playing that is very near to my idea of how to play a keyboard instrument."

In 1991, Buchla finished *Lightning* which, as he put it, "allows you to create instruments in space." A performer moves a wand or a ring in the air, which acts as a transmitter. A distant receiver translates the movement into MIDI information and knows whether a particular gesture was made by the performer's left or right hand. Warren Burt, Bruno Spoerri, Chris Chafe, Dexter Morrill, and many other composers and performers have used Lightning. And Buchla has used it in two of his own compositions. In *En Plein Vol* (1991), a percussionist uses Lightning to play percussion instruments, even after two onstage thieves have removed them, and the audience, of course, continues to hear sound. In his *Trajectories* (1992), two jugglers are juggling six clubs which are, in fact, Lightning transmitters. As Buchla explains, "When the clubs flip, the sound flips."

●

Michel Waisvisz in Amsterdam, Holland, explained, "It's not that I like technology so much—my work has been trying to bring back a unity between physical and mental activities." By physical activities, Waisvisz meant the effort of working with an instrument in performance. As he said, "I'm afraid it's true one has to suffer a bit while playing; the physical effort you make is what is perceived by listeners as the cause and manifestation of the musical tension . . ." By mental activities, he meant formal structure: "Once one takes formal structure as a synonym for the beauty of patterns, cold reasoning, a law-abiding mind, and dogmatic thinking, and one interprets physicality as wild emotion . . . The composer who can handle these extremities is bound to create a lively piece of music."

Waisvisz' *Hands*, built first at STEIM by Johan den Biggelaar in 1984, then further developed by Wim Rijnsburger, are two aluminum plates, formed to be comfortably strapped under his hands. The plates contain keys that respond to finger touch and sensors that respond to thumb pressure, tilt, and the relative distance between the Hands. Waisvisz, for example, can hold his arms out sideways and play the keys, simultaneously tilting the Hands while moving a potentiometer with his thumb, and then move his arms closer to each other so that the Hands sense their increasing proximity. As Waisvisz describes his feelings during a performance, "There is a kind of physical excitement—I make moves that I just feel like making and, you know, for example, moving my hands apart is definitely showing that things are going bigger and wilder." Waisvisz' compositions for the Hands include *Beat Concert* (1984), *Touch Monkeys* (1987), *Archaic Symphony* (1989), *The Scream Lines* (1990), *Songs from the Hands* (1991), and *Faustos Schrei* (1994). As he said, "It really became my instrument."

•

Mattel Toys developed the Power Glove during the mid-1980s as a videogame controller. It was not a successful product, but it did interest many musicians, among them Paul DeMarinis: "I got a Power Glove in 1989, I cut off everything but the finger-flex sensors—it looked like a gardening glove." DeMarinis continues:

> I used the recorded text of a new-age hypnotist and resynthesized it with changes. In performance, using the glove, I could change the pitch of the voice with one finger. With a gesture of a combination of fingers, I could stop the speech or start it, and there were many pauses in the speech. It was kind of slow and hypnotic, and with the other fingers I could change the orchestration of the accompanying music. And then, with a thumb gesture, I could "take a snapshot" and freeze it. So with a series of hand gestures, I could manipulate the speech and the glove was the image of manipulation, the hand of authority.

In 1991, Laetitia Sonami performed with DeMarinis and got an idea. As she tells it, "In my part of the piece, I used rubber kitchen gloves with magnetic sensors to trigger things—one glove had the sensors in the fingertips and the other had a magnet on top of the hand." In May 1992, for her *Story Road*, she designed a glove with five microswitches and the magnet in the thumb, so that she had a complete controller for her left hand and she could use her right hand for turning knobs. Then, in Amsterdam during that summer, she went to a concert with Joel Ryan and heard an Indian singer. The singer was using his hands for counting and keeping the beat. She recalls, "There was a beauty of expression in the way he was using his hands—it was very appealing, and I thought that it would really fit my way of performing, so I turned to Joel and said, 'Wouldn't it be nice to control electronic music with the same kind of subtleties that he was expressing in the singing.'"

She then composed *What Happened II* and, at STEIM, built a new version of what she called the *Lady's Glove*. It was an arm-length glove made of soft cloth. The fingertips contained microswitches, which were the only visible controls. Flex sensors responded to bending in the wrist and in the three middle fingers. Each of the finger sensors reported two values, one for bending the lower and one for bending the upper finger joints. Inside the fingertips, there were magnetic sensors with the magnet in the opposing thumb, so that they responded to the distance of each fingertip from the thumb. There was a pressure pad between index finger and thumb, so that the thumb could press against the inside of the index finger. There was an ultrasound emitter in the palm with a receiver in the belt and in the shoe.

The idea was to allow a performer to control music by finger and wrist bending, by moving fingers at relative distances to the thumb-tip, by touching the thumb to the upper joint of the index finger, and by activating the microswitches on top of the fingertips while moving the hand in relative dis-

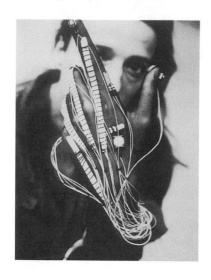

Laetitia Sonami showing the sensors and wiring in the Lady's Glove. Photo by Andre Hoekzema. Courtesy Laetitia Sonami.

tance from the body as measured by the ultrasound. As Sonami said, "This is for me the ultimate instrument in dealing with expressivity in electronic music—if you move one finger, everything else moves. It's multiple controls to multiple variables in the sound . . ." After she had built it with all of the sensors hidden within the glove, STEIM commissioned Bert Bongers, an electronic music instrument builder in The Hague, to copy the design and improve it. He did. And he added an accelerometer.

•

Max Mathews said: "One has to think of overall systems to get a musically useful thing—you can't really develop a sensor without relating it to the programs that you're going to use it with." Mathews' *Radio Baton* grew out of his Conductor Program, begun in 1976 while he was at Bell Labs and GROOVE was up and running and when Pierre Boulez, at that time music director of the New York Philharmonic, made a request. Mathews tells it:

> By that time there were a lot of pieces for tape and live instruments, and they were always unpleasant for the performers because they were unyielding, and the performer carried the burden for the ensemble. Boulez wanted to conduct the tape. I never did figure out how to conduct a tape because speeding and slowing produces unpleasant effects on the sound, but it did lead me to think about a synthesizer, and that led me to write the Conductor Program.

The Conductor Program functioned in three stages. First, in the score-entry stage, notes were input to the computer's memory. Second, in the rehearsal stage, phrasing, accents, and other articulation were added to each voice. Third, in the performance stage, all of the voices were played back together. Different devices were used to "conduct" different aspects of the music during the performance stage. There was a joystick, built by Michael Noll at Bell Labs, large enough that a performer could use full arm motions to control continuous variables such as dynamics and balance. There was a keyboard which had some special keys that could be tapped. And there was a mechanical drum with strain gauges built into it to measure the hardness and point of impact. Paul Zukofsky, violinist and conductor, and Gerard Schwartz, trumpetist and conductor, were invited to conduct parts of Ravel's *String Quartet* to demonstrate, quite successfully as it turned out, that the program allowed for expressive individuality.

The Radio Baton grew out of those performance devices. The first version, called the Sequential Drum, was developed at IRCAM in 1980 as a surface with a gridwork of wires and a contact microphone underneath. When the surface was hit with a mallet, the gridwork sensed where the surface had been hit, and the microphone sensed how hard it had been hit. The mechanical design, however, was problematic. As Mathews remembers, "The wires were always breaking—it was a completely impractical instrument." A subsequently improved version of the Sequential Drum used strain gauges, which were more reliable than the wires. But the problem remained that the device could not register continuous motion and, consequently, could not be used as the controller for the Conductor Program. Mathews said: "I needed continuous information for expressive controls."

In 1987, Robert Boie at Bell Labs solved Mathews' problem by building the Radio Baton, essentially two wands that are waved over a surface about the size of a breakfast tray. The wands contain low-frequency radio-signal transmitters. The surface contains the receivers. The Radio Baton has attracted the attention of a number of composers, among them Jon Appleton, Larry Austin, Joanne Cary, Amy Radunskaya, Sergio Marin, Dexter Morrill, David Jaffe, Richard Boulanger, and Andrew Schloss.

Max Mathews with the Radio Baton in 1992.
Photo by Patte Wood.

Richard Boulanger was one of the first people to compose for the Radio Baton. In 1985, Mathews had showed up at UCSD to do a demonstration, and Boulanger was impressed by the performance possibilities. He said, "Max, I'd love to write a piece for your Baton." And the opportunity came the following year. In November 1986, with a commitment to perform at the MIT Media Lab in February 1987, Boulanger went to Bell Labs and began to compose. He recalls:

> I'd spend pretty much every weekend there and stay around the clock, fig-uring out the Baton, writing for it, entering scores, asking for changes, asking questions. Can it do this? Can it do that? Max was incredibly responsive to my needs. It was wonderful.

Since 1986, Boulanger has used the Radio Baton in solo works, improvi-sational works, duets for acoustic instruments and baton, chamber music, vocal music, as a solo instrument with symphony orchestra, and on several occasions he and Mathews performed together. His works include *Shadows* (1987), for electronic violin and Radio Baton; *I Know of No Geometry* (1990), for Radio Baton; *Concerto for Virtual Orchestra* (1991), for two Radio Batons; *Solemn Song for Evening* (1992), for voice and Radio Baton; *Virtual Encounters* (1992), for chamber ensemble and Radio Baton; *Three Symphonic States* (1993), for orchestra, Radio Baton, and PowerGlove; *The Dark Wind* (1994), for bass clarinet and Radio Baton; and *OutCries* (1995), for voice and Radio Baton.

Andrew Schloss, because of the way he used it, called it the Radio Drum. In 1973, he was studying electronic music and percussion at Bennington College. He took a leave of absence to join the Peter Brook Centre for International Theatre Research in France. As he recalls, "Brook forbade me to do anything with electronics, so I played drums a lot." After a year, he returned to Bennington to finish his degree, following which he studied ethnomusicolo-gy and mathematics at the University of Washington. In 1978, he began work in computer music at CCRMA, where he composed *The Towers of Hanoi* (1980). Also in 1980, during a visit to Cuba, he became interested in Afro-Cuban music. In 1986, he went to Bell Telephone Laboratories—"I heard that they had some sort of Radio Drum and I was hoping to merge Cuban and com-puter music"—and he convinced Mathews and Boie to lend him a Radio Baton. In 1988, he went to IRCAM and met Miller Puckette. Puckette wrote a MAX object that allowed Schloss to use his Radio Baton with a Macintosh. Then Schloss met Jeff Gardner, an American pianist who was living in Paris. Gardner was interested in Brazilian and Cuban music, and during the next few years, Schloss and Gardner played several concerts together. As Schloss recalls, "I started to think of the Radio Drum as a really serious instrument."

Meanwhile, in 1986, David Jaffe, with Julius Smith at CCRMA, began to design a sound and music system for the NeXT computer. The result was Music Kit, a superset of tools which, in Jaffe's words, "combined the flexibility of the Music V approach with the realtime interactivity of MIDI." Jaffe, also a graduate of Bennington College, and Schloss decided to combine their skills in a collaborative improvisation. They worked together for two weeks. Jaffe describes it:

> Andy had been working with the Radio Drum and an early version of MAX, and he had a NeXT machine. I brought a Zeta MIDI violin with an IVL pitch detector. We hooked things up in series. The Drum and violin info went into a Macintosh which did various mappings in MAX, and then it went into the NeXT machine, running Michael McNabb's version of the Music Kit application called Ensemble. On the NeXT, we had fractal music generators and other higher-level algorithms that were listening to the pitches and materials. We started improvising. Our goal was to write a more or less improvised piece with a shape that had some similarity from performance to performance. We experimented.

The result was called *Wildlife* (1992), completely improvised, with the music resulting from shared control. A pitch played by the violin, for example, would trigger a chord, but which chord and in which register would be determined by the positioning of the mallets on the Radio Baton. Jaffe's next piece, *Terra Non Firma* (1992), for four cellos and Radio Baton, was completely notated using Max Mathews' Conductor Program. How did it work? Well, how does an orchestra interpret a conductor's gestures in playing the first four notes, for example, of Beethoven's *Fifth Symphony*? To answer the second question first, there is a visual link, taught to the orchestra by the conductor in rehearsal, between the conductor's gesture and the way that every player is expected to respond to it. In the Conductor Program, there is a software link, "taught" to the program in "rehearsal," that interprets a performer's gestures as controls for the music. Jaffe, in using the Conductor Program, created a score that said, in effect, "when this is done with a baton, then the musical result is . . ." As Jaffe said, "I found it responded very quickly, so I built the piece around the idea of constantly and abruptly changing tempos, suggesting the cataclysmic changes of an earthquake."

Jaffe's third and largest Radio Baton piece was *The Seven Wonders of the Ancient World* (1995), a seven-movement, seventy-minute concerto with improvisation for Radio-Baton-controlled Disklavier grand piano, harpsichord, harp, mandolin, guitar, bass, harmonium, and two percussionists, with the Radio Baton part composed for Schloss. As Jaffe describes it, "The coupling of the piano with the Radio Drum [Jaffe calls it the Radio Drum when referring to Schloss' performances] was particularly exciting—sometimes you'd feel like you're banging on mud, and then you make a slight modification and suddenly it becomes like Paganini."

Meanwhile, Schloss' primary focus remained on developing the Radio Baton as a drum: "We need controllers that refer to physical experience and, yes, I want to make a drum, but I want to be able to do things that you can't do with a physical drum." Schloss' aim was to extend what can be done with a drum, particularly in modifying sounds. He differentiated, for example, between hitting the surface of the Radio Baton and moving a mallet continuously through space, which he called *whack mode* and *continuous mode*, respectively, and he used one mode to modify the other, "like a generalization of a hand drum where one hand hits the drum and the other modifies it." His approach represented an unlikely combination of cultural traditions. He reflected, "What's great for me is that the different threads in my music, Cuban music and computer music, have merged."

•

Many technologies have been developed to sense a performer's movements in space. Gordon Mumma, for example, used accelerometers in his *Ambivex* (1971). As he describes it, "I played solo cornet with live modification—I was wired with accelerometers and every move I made triggered sound modifications." He made similar accelerometer circuits for his *Telepos* (1972), a commission for Merce Cunningham's dance *TV Rerun* (1972):

> I made a set of accelerometer belts that measured changes in the dancers' acceleration as they moved through the performance space. Those measurements were converted into frequency-modulated signals. Each belt had an FM oscillator made from a common Signetics integrated-circuit function generator used for touch-tone telephones. The changes in pitch from the FM oscillators were transmitted by miniature UHF radios on each belt to receivers in the orchestra pit. I mixed and distributed the received FM signals through loudspeakers around the audience.
>
> My original idea was that each of the eight dancers would have a belt, but the expense was too great—each belt cost between $500 and $1,000. The dancers didn't get paid enough to justify such extravagance. So I made only three belts, and designed them so that each belt produced a different set of pitches when worn upside down. The dancers exchanged and inverted belts when they were offstage between their exits and entrances. The accelerometers were little glass things. Just a few weeks before the premiere, when the belts were being sewn, I thought, "What if these things break?" But the dancers were always in the air and we never broke an accelerometer.

In 1989, Mark Coniglio designed *MidiDancer*, a set of sensors that monitored the movements of a dancer's body and transmitted that information via wireless link to a computer. The computer interpreted the information and sent commands to a synthesizer. Coniglio recalls, "I had been writing a lot of dance music, and had simultaneously become very interested in live interaction—the combination of these two interests resulted in my desire to have the dancers directly generating music from their movement . . ."

Neil Rolnick played air drums in performances of his *Macedonian Air Drumming* (1990) and *The Persistence of the Clave* (1992). The air drums, built by Palm Tree Instruments in San Diego, were two "claves," each of which contained three mercury switches, one to sense pitch, one to sense roll, and one to sense yaw. A performer held one in each hand and moved them in the air. Rolnick describes it: "You have two hands, each with three switches and two directions for each switch, so you have basically twelve MIDI signals that can be sent at any one time—getting up there and waving your arms around and getting music to happen is perfectly natural, and the really interesting part of composing for something like this is to figure out ways of moving that will somehow make sense with the music."

•

As a space sensor, the theremin, invented in 1920, was elegant, even magical, because the performer did not need to hold any object, and it was playable in a wide range of musical contexts. Lenin could play it as an amateur in his office. Clara Rockmore could play it as a virtuoso in a concert hall. John Cage used theremins to sense Merce Cunningham's dancers' movements in *Variations V* (1965). And many other performers and composers have used theremins in different ways. In 1992 at Big Briar, Robert Moog resumed making theremins according to Theremin's design principles, which means, in Moog's words, "what waveform is produced and what the responses of the antennas are—as a violin maker would shape the neck, I shape the response of the antennas." On August 14, 1994, Moog hosted a celebration for the opening of a new Big Briar facility in Asheville, with Marylee DiLorenzo banishing evil spirits by performing a smudging ceremony based on North and South American Indian ceremonial traditions. It was an unusual approach to the beginning of a business venture. But appropriate, one might reflect, because the theremin represents such an unusual approach to musical performance.

Paul DeMarinis also developed an unusual approach, so to speak, in *The Pigmy Gamelan* (1973). In 1969, encouraged by David Behrman, David Tudor, and Gordon Mumma, DeMarinis had started to build circuits. As he said, "I really took it on, maybe more than other people, really building pieces—it occurred to me that instead of building a synthesizer, it was more economical to actually build the piece that I wanted." He observed further, "We were the first generation of artists who learned electronics from artists—at that point, technology became a real tool of artists." *The Pigmy Gamelan* was among his first pieces. He describes it:

> It was like an untuned radio that was hooked up to a music synthesizer— it was a small box with loudspeakers playing very softly . . . It ran by itself, but it was influenced by people coming close to it. People could move around it, touch it. They disturbed the electrical field around it. It was based on an automatic circuit that produces agreeable changes in sound. It was making people aware that they're electrical creatures, that we're swimming in electricity, that all the radio stations and microwave stations in the world are making signals that are going through us all the

time. The collapse of a distant galaxy produces electromagnetic waves that pass through us. We're in an electrical world.

In 1972, Godfried-Willem Raes in Belgium began to work with ultrasound technology. In 1983, Raes and Moniek Darge, known together as the Logos Duo, finished *Holosound*, a concert piece where Darge's movements in a three-dimensional space were sensed by ultrasound devices and used to control aspects of sound and music. Raes continued to develop and improve his ultrasound technology, and in 1992, he finished the first version of *A Book of Moves*, an evening-length group of multimedia compositions wherein each composition is based on a unique relationship between movement and sound. Raes thought of each situation as an "instrument." The idea was, as he put it, "to design a series of very different, yet invisible, musical instruments" where specific types of movements would be used as controllers for different aspects of a musical activity. In *Tempi*, a simple example, movements are used to control the tempos of three independent voices. In *Topoi*, a more complex example, movements are used to feed a simple neural network that attempts to map relations between a topological analysis of the performer's moving body and the structures of chords.

David Rokeby in Toronto was also interested in developing an instrument that allowed for a programmable relationship between a performer's physical motion in space and a particular musical result. He developed the *Very Nervous System*, an electronic system that analyzes images from a video camera to track a performer's movements and translate them into musical controls. When Bruno Spoerri saw the system in 1989 in Brussels, he was immediately interested. As he recalls, "It was the first movement-driven system that I had seen that had a musical flair, so I invited Rokeby to Zurich, to the Ericsson Gallery where I was organizing some workshop evenings, and he did an installation that stayed there for two months or so—and at the end of the exhibition I urged him to sell the system to me instead of taking it back." Spoerri tried to work with dancers, but as he reflects, "They had the impression that they could do a *pas de deux* and Tchaikovsky would come out—they weren't used to making music themselves." He continues:

> There's always a performer in front of the camera, and the performer's gestures trigger or control an existing musical process, like conducting. They influence the system. The system senses motion, not absolute position, so the nature of the performer's motions is what matters. And since the space can be divided into regions, control motions can be very complex. You can move one way in a high region, for example, to do one thing, and another way in a low region to do another.

Spoerri's first piece with the Very Nervous System was *In and Out* (1991). As he described it, "With big movements you can bring out very heavy masses of sound that stay until you stop them with new movements, so the performer is performing in two separate ways, by playing his instrument and by moving

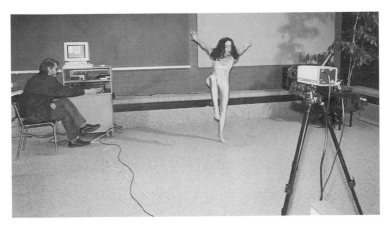

Bruno Spoerri (seated) with a dancer controlling a MIDI system through David Rockeby's Very Nervous System in 1991. Photo courtesy Bruno Spoerri.

his body . . ." His next piece was *Shake, Shuttle, and Blow* (1991), which he described as "a kind of drum duo where I'm playing by moving." Then there was *Did You Do?* (1993), in which a singer's motions control the accompanying sounds. And Spoerri programmed *Spiegelei* (1992) so that, as he put it, "the smaller the movement, the more excited the system becomes." But large movements in large spaces, he might have added, were more problematic. The Very Nervous System required that a performer's movements were made relative to a single camera which, not so incidentally, could not be very far from the performer.

In the early 1980s, Simon Veitch in Melbourne, Australia, developed a multicamera video-based control system which allowed for large-area motion detection from afar. 3DIS (3 Dimensional Interactive Space), as it was called, consisted of one to twelve video cameras, a video monitor, a computer, and electronics. A user could draw rectangles on the computer's screen to define contiguous, overlapping, or separate spatial zones which were watched by the video cameras. When the system saw a significant change within a defined zone, it sent a control signal to an external device, such as a synthesizer. Warren Burt used 3DIS in Expo '88 in Brisbane. He describes the situations:

> It was a fairground installation, definitely general public . . . There was a series of fountains, for example, triggered to spray water as people passed. And there was a sonic fun park. When people put their hands through an empty window frame, they would hear the sound of breaking glass. And there was an optical illusion which made a telephone seem to be where it wasn't. As people approached the telephone, it would ring. And as they reached for it, it would disappear . . .

Burt's next 3DIS project, in Melbourne in March 1989, was *Hear the Dance, See the Music!*, a collaboration with composer Ros Bandt and dancers

Sylvia Staehli, Shona Innes, and Jane Refshauge, in which the dancers triggered words, or danced notes from a musical scale, or affected the statistical likelihood that more or fewer notes would appear. He used 3DIS in *Jazzmaze*, at a show called *Les Images en Folie* in Martigny, Switzerland, May through October 1991. As he recalls, "One guy said, 'It's very nice but I don't like jazz.'" And he used 3DIS in other shows, exhibitions, and installations, among them a show at the Technorama in Winterthur, Switzerland, celebrating the 150th anniversary of the Laufen Ceramics Company. As Burt describes it, "An outer ring of spaces triggered the sounds of smashing ceramics . . . the children, of course, would be running around the outer ring playing bulls in a china shop and having a wonderful time, as if it were magic." But after working with 3DIS for several years, as he reflects, "I never found it magical because I knew how the technology worked . . . when I saw looks of utter amazement and magical delight on people's faces, I was bewildered—I asked myself, 'Why are they looking at this in amazement?'"

In 1993, at the third Australian Sculpture Triennial in Melbourne, Burt deployed 3DIS in Joan Brassil's *Sine Waves, Harbour Waves*. It was a large installation with wooden beams, piles, seaweed, and plexiglass constructions, with a video monitor playing scenes of the waves in Sydney harbor which were reflected in the molded plexiglass. Necessarily for the video, there was low ambient light, so infrared cameras were used. The movement of the public triggered sounds of water and of sine waves played with tuning forks, which seemed to emanate softly from random locations within the space. As Burt said, "I wanted to be fascinated and, finally, I think I achieved it."

•

Designers and/or musicians who view electronic music as developing seamlessly from past musical practice into the future are likely to build or play instruments that call for traditional skills. As Neil Rolnick puts it, "as musicians we've spent years and years developing finely-tuned reflexes and skills in playing instruments, and those skills, which our minds and bodies relate to music and how we make music, provide access to electronic as well as traditional instruments." On the other hand, designers and/or musicians who view electronic music as radically different from the past are likely to call for new types of physical movements and skills. Again, Rolnick: "If you're dealing with a new paradigm for making sounds, you'd want to have something that doesn't tie you to old kinds of gestures, something which kind of unfetters you from traditional ways of thinking so that you can take a more exploratory approach." It is the designer's and/or musician's understanding of music, in other words, that drives the design of an electronic performance device. For Peter Otto and Michel Waisvisz, who viewed electronic music as radically different from the past, the musical problem was how to control complexity.

In 1988, as the audio industry was completing its conversion to digital technology, Otto designed what he called *Contact*. In his view, "What was lost in digital technology was the gestural, tactile immediacy of the analog world, so here you were with this incredible computing power and just a mouse to control it with." Contact is a desktop control surface containing ninety-one knobs, switches, and faders, each of which can be assigned to control any musical or audio variable, or group of variables, in any system to which it is connected. Otto's solution, in other words, was a large number of independent performance controls that could be flexibly applied to a large number of musical variables.

In 1976, Michel Waisvisz had designed the Crackle Box, a hand-size wooden box containing electronics, loudspeaker, and touch-sensitive metal strips, which "crackled" as one touched it. As he described it, "You just touched the technology, the instrument went wild, and you learned to control it." Years later, Waisvisz had a related idea: "I thought, 'How could I, with a single finger movement, create an incredible amount of coordinated and related changes in an electronic system?'" And one morning in 1989, he looked out of a window, and as he tells it, "I saw a spider web, and I realized that if each thread in the web were related to a variable in a system, touching the web at some place would create related changes everywhere—so I imagined that grabbing several strands of the web would change an incredible number of things."

•

Xavier Chabot in Paris understood the depth of the problem—of relating the old to the new, relating acquired skills to skills yet to be acquired, relating the bodyless complexity of software to the physicality of human movement—and he searched for a solution. He began by exploring the connection of physical gestures with sound in the context of musical and theatrical performance: "I was never a dancer, but at the same time I'd done some sport, some judo . . ." Chabot went to San Diego in 1984. He reflects, "California was an enormous influence, an opening of ideas—the nature, and Harry Partch, and Kiva, it was all very important for me." Kiva was an improvisational performance group formed by percussionist-composer Jean-Charles François, trombonist John Silber, both faculty at the University of California at San Diego, and Keith Humble, visiting professor from Australia. Chabot played with the group. He tells it:

> In the context of Kiva, I began to use electronics because electronics allowed me to deal with the problems of finding a rapport between making a gesture and hearing a sound. First, it was instrumental gestures. I tried to find the gestures that were not in a traditional playing mode and that produced new sounds . . . We tried all sorts of things. We experimented with fuzzy logic. We used electronic instruments. I used my pitch detector for the flute and saxophone. We used Jam Factory. It was a complex development. We used ultrasound to sense distance, and we used the air drum. Pat Downes developed various things for us, including a detector that I attached to my arm to know whether it was horizontal or vertical. I had an accelerometer on my foot and in my hand. I did *Futurity* with Joji Yuasa where I was using space, moving up/down, left/right . . .

In 1989, Chabot went to Japan for two years.

> I went to Japan specifically to study Noh music. I played also with a Gagaku ensemble. Why? The problem was relating the body, the voice, and the space and the sound, and Noh music was a very particular and effective solution . . . Zeami, the founder of Noh in the 14th century, said the sound comes before the gesture. So I ask: how can I control an electronic process?

In Robert Moog's words, "It's long-term research."

• • •

CHAPTER NINE

MAKING SOUND

"MIDI?" as Bruno Spoerri said, "At the moment, it's the only way to live."
Even if, as he might have added, it's not the best of all possible worlds.

In the MIDI protocol, notes are specified by one group of numbers, loudness by another, vibrato by another, and so on. MIDI sound is divided into separate and independently controllable parameters. When someone plays middle-C on a MIDI keyboard, a note-on message is sent from the keyboard to a synthesizer saying, for example, "Play note number 60 with a loudness value of 77 on channel 12." And to bend the pitch a little bit, the player turns a pitchwheel, located at the side of the keyboard. As Joel Ryan, composer and programmer, puts it:

> Engineers are interested in keeping parameters separated, keeping them from influencing each other. For example, if an engineer were going to design a saxophone, he would try to separate all the influences, say, that embouchure has on the sound. It wouldn't occur to an engineer that they would be interdependent. Engineers are not attracted to ambiguity.

Ryan had started at Mills College in the late 1970s and then worked at IRCAM, STEIM, and the Institute of Sonology in the 1980s. In his words, "I began to realize that logic was not the basis for making music, so I was trying to find ways to make the computer act as if it were a physical thing, with the complexity of a physical object rather than the simplicity of a logical one." Engineers, according to Ryan, see things differently than musicians. As he puts it, "The rules of thumb of engineering are basically antithetical to the development of instruments." Engineers, for one thing, are concerned with simplicity and what they call "elegant" design. But simplicity, in Ryan's view, "eliminates all the contingencies of the real world that make musical instruments interesting."

Sound, in other words, is complex—for one thing because different levels of change and control are interrelated in so many different ways. Stan Tempelaars, faculty at the Institute for Sonology, puts it well:

> Nature gave us vocal chords which vibrate fast enough so that we can communicate acoustically. But we shape words by controlling changes in the sounds produced by those vibrations. We *modulate* the sounds we make. Speech is a modulated signal. So are musical sounds.

To modulate a sound is to control the way it changes. And the way a sound is made to change is what conveys the information, whether musical or verbal, carried by that sound. Tempelaars distinguishes between *global* modulation, which affects aspects of the entire sound, such as pitch and general loudness, and *micro*-modulation, which causes change instant by instant. Further, Tempelaars distinguishes between *internally generated* micro-modulation, which results from the properties of the instrument itself, and *externally generated* micro-modulation, which results from a performer's input. *Micro-modulation*, as Tempelaars calls it, is essential to an interesting sound. Without internal complexity and without instantaneous sensitivity to a performer's controls, an instrument is crude and unmusical. Tempelaars said: "We need an intelligent sound generator, intelligent in the sense that it simulates truly complex physical systems like musical instruments so that we can produce new sounds with the same degree of complexity as the sounds of traditional instruments—we can learn a lot from traditional instruments."

In fact, in 1978 in Grenoble, France, Claude Cadoz, Annie Luciani, and Jean-Loup Florens founded ACROE (Association pour la Création et la Recherche sur les Outils d'Expression / Association for the Creation of and Research into Tools for Expression) to study traditional instruments, and their work led to what they called the *Cordis-Anima* environment for the modeling of physical systems. The concept behind Cordis-Anima was that an isolated analysis of sound structure yields meaningless acoustic information because acoustic information is meaningful to a musician only in the context of playing an instrument. Their procedure, consequently, was to analyze the types of physical gestures required of a performer in playing traditional instruments, to relate that analysis to the way the instrument responds, and to derive a definition of timbre as everything in the sound that the instrument thereby produces. Their questions were: What does the performer do? What does the instrument do? What do they both do? Their immediate purpose was, in their words, "to research the equilibrium between what, in a sound event, proceeds from the gesture and what proceeds from the instrument . . ." and, in so doing, to be able to build sophisticated and meaningful electronic instruments. Their long-term purpose is "the possibility of creating innovative and unheard-of sound structures loaded with meaning . . ."

•

We can also learn a lot from the human voice. With its expressivity and its complexity of sound modulation in changing from vowels to fricatives to sibilants, and in the immediacy of its translating human intentions into actual sound, the human voice has been viewed by many as the model for an ideal synthesizer. Xavier Rodet's CHANT software, developed at IRCAM, and Perry Cook's Spasm software, developed at CCRMA, used the human vocal tract as a model for electronically-produced sound. As poet Chris Mann put it, "Speech is portable synthesis." In *Anticredos* (1980), Trevor Wishart used the human voice to produce primarily nonverbal sounds. As he said, "Before writing the piece, I spent four years exploring the possibilities of the voice for producing sounds."

Joan La Barbara, soprano and composer, had the same goal: "I was always very interested in using my voice as an instrument, not just to deliver a text . . ." This was not, however, an easy matter. In the mid-1970s in New York, she worked with the New Wilderness Preservation Band, musicians, poets, and writers, improvising soundscapes. She set up exercises with other musicians: "I asked the musicians to play long tones and I thought about the timbre and about the sound coming out of me and adjusted the timbre each time I made a new sound in imitation of the instrumental sound." She created performance situations—for example, a performance piece called *Hear What I Feel*—that extended her own vocal awareness. And she set up exercises for herself: "In work sessions, I would tape all the time, because sometimes I found I would emit a sound and I didn't know how I had done it, and I would have to listen to the tape and figure out how I made the sounds, so I could do it again." She continues:

> I found that you could extend the voice without damaging it. I made it a kind of manifesto that I could do very weird things and still come back and "sing" in the traditional sense. When you sing as a western classically-trained singer, you tend to blend resonance areas. There's a triangle of resonance areas that includes the nose and the mouth, and you manipulate it to produce what's called in bel canto "the golden tone," and what I found fascinating was to isolate the resonance areas so that you begin to explore the beautiful in strangeness, you begin to explore what might be, say, more strident. For example, in Chinese opera, the timbre that's considered beautiful is harsh, brittle, strident to our ears. It's a higher placement, at the bridge of the nose.

As an instrumentalist becomes familiar with an instrument, so La Barbara points out, "You become very familiar with the inside of the front of your face as a singer." She continues:

> There are so many factors and qualities involved in making a sound human. You have breath, the fluctuations of breath, you have a myriad of resonance cavities and minute fluctuations of how the voice sounds in those resonating cavities. And to move from one pitch to another, sometimes you adjust the pitch or the speed and distance of a vibrato because you want to give more or less tension to the linear movement. Or if you want the line to be a comfortable, lyrical line, or if you want to create a certain anxiety, you adjust the breath flow or the pitch to accomplish it. And to synthesize all of that is so very complex, so complicated. You'd have to instruct a computer how to think about how to make a musical phrase and how to accomplish that musical phrase according to what you want to do.

•

Human voices and acoustic instruments offer controllability and complexity as well as a reasonable variety of sound. But a voice is limited to what a voice can do. A violin sounds like a violin. And most vocal and instrumental sounds are familiar. So some musicians have thought that, well, if a human voice sounds like a human voice and a violin sounds like a violin, then perhaps the sound of a voice or a violin, or for that matter, any instrument or object, could be extended with electronics, thereby giving a composer or performer the combined benefits of controllability, complexity, and an expanded range of sounds.

Ivan Tcherepnin, for example, based his *Santur Opera* (1976) on the idea of expanding the sound of an acoustic instrument. In 1971, just before returning home, an Iranian student at Stanford University presented Tcherepnin with a santur, an Iranian lute. Moved by the generosity in the gesture, and at the same time interested in the sound of the santur, Tcherepnin began to write *Santur Opera*. As he tells it, "My vision of a very romantic plot became a series of pieces that linked to each other . . ." He began by using filters and modulators designed by Serge Tcherepnin, his brother and well-known equipment designer, to transform the sound of the santur. He describes it:

> The whole box was a resonating chamber so it was a wonderful sound source for processing. That was one factor, the acoustic signal being picked up, and there, as a performer, I simply played the santur. But the other aspect of it was that I was using the sound also as a control. I detected the envelope of each attack, and there was some frequency following. I set it up so I could be like a janitor in the sense that I could adjust the temperature, the knobs. If something started to go wrong, I knew where the shutoff valve was. Basically, it was as automated as it could be, but there was always a large human component of adjustment.

*Ivan Tcherepnin performing his Santur Opera at State University
of New York at Albany in 1979. He is using a Serge modular
system to modify the sounds of the santur. Note the complexity
of the patchcord connections. Photo by Joel Chadabe.*

And why use the santur for controls as well as sound?

> I was trying to use the santur like a miraculous producer of everything
> and give the feeling that it was all integrated. It's unsatisfying for some-
> body who's thinking holistically to say that the controls are here and the
> instrument there. I wanted to think that everything was connected and
> integrated, that it was one whole, one organism.

In 1976, Simon Emmerson joined the faculty of City University in
London and established a studio. He had earlier worked with Roger Smalley
and Tim Souster in Intermodulation, an electronics performance group in
Cambridge, and so the City University studio was, as he described it, "a seamless transition to similar equipment." And his interests remained in performance. In *Ophelia's Dream II* (1979), he transformed singers' vocal sounds to
create an inner world of dreamlike unreality. When the studio acquired a
Fairlight CMI in the early 1980s, he carried tapes to concerts, but his ideas
remained the same: "I was interested in extending the timbral world of live performers' voices and their acoustic instruments." For *Time Past IV* (1984), he
used transformed vocal sounds, on tape, as echoes of a soprano's voice: "It was
a different sort of live music . . ." In 1987, when the studio acquired Macintosh
computers, samplers, and a new generation of portable MIDI equipment, he
again moved equipment into the concert hall and developed an approach based
on what he called the *second performer*, someone seated in the hall to manipulate the electronics while hearing the sounds from the audience's perspective.
In his *Sentences* (1990), for soprano and live electronics, the second performer

plays an active role in processing the soprano's voice and distributing the sound to loudspeakers around the hall.

In 1963, while Alcides Lanza was working at the newly formed CLAEM, Bruno Maderna visited Buenos Aires. As he recalls, "Maderna mentioned that there were more than 5,000 tape music compositions in the world, and he thought that was too many . . ." In 1965, Lanza went to New York, studied with Vladimir Ussachevsky, and experimented with ways of extending the human voice with electronics. In *Ekphonesis II* (1968), as he describes it, "I was using a Putney synthesizer to do realtime modifications on the voice— there were two, actually three levels, one frozen on tape, one done in real time on the stage, and the 'influence' of electronics in having performers make unusual sounds." In 1971, he joined the faculty at McGill University in Montreal and finished *Trilogy*, a composite voice/theater composition made up of *Ekphonesis V* (1979), *Penetrations VII* (1972), and *Ekphonesis VI* (1988). Based on multilingual texts and invented languages, *Trilogy* was composed as a full-evening solo opera for singer/actress Meg Sheppard, who also chose some of the texts. As Lanza said, "My main intention in writing this vocal piece was to be able to create a situation where the singer will be accompanied only by the tape and digital signal processing . . ." He used the digital signal processing, what he calls the *electronic extensions*, to grade the comprehensibility of the text between clear semantic meaning and abstract sound. As he reflects, "I always saw that I wanted an electric voice."

•

In the mid-1960s, Pauline Oliveros conceived of the *Expanded Instrument System*, the EIS as she calls it, as an extension of her improvisations and performances with accordion. Developed further with Panaiotis in the late 1980s and yet further with David Gamper in the 1990s, the EIS allows improvising musicians to play acoustic instruments and, by manipulating foot pedals and switches to control various digital signal-processing devices, to enhance and transform their sounds. In Oliveros' Deep Listening Band, for example, she plays accordion, Gamper plays keyboards and other instruments, and Stuart Dempster plays trombone and didjeridoo, and they all play the EIS, sometimes independently, sometimes by combining their sounds and controlling aspects of each other's processing.

For his video opera *Perfect Lives* (1977–1983), Robert Ashley needed a special piano sound. The music for *Perfect Lives* consists of several rhythmic and quasi-melodic tracks, some of them done with electronic sounds, with Ashley speaking and "Blue" Gene Tyranny playing the piano throughout. So how did he do the piano sound? Ashley answers:

> I couldn't find an electronic piano that I could afford with the sound resources that were necessary for the character of Buddy, the world's greatest piano player, to develop over a course of three and a half hours.

The Deep Listening Band performing in 1996 in Kingston, upstate New York.
From left to right, David Gamper (keyboard), Pauline Oliveros (accordion),
Stuart Dempster (trombone), Joe Giardullo (soprano saxophone), and
Thomas Buckner (voice). Photo by Joel Chadabe.

If it did exist, I didn't have the money for it. So finally, Blue and I decided together that it had to be an acoustic piano because that's all there was. We used contact microphones, PZMs, we used those tiny little AKGs which we kept buried in the piano, we used three or four different kinds of microphone techniques. We transformed the piano into an electronic instrument. And when we finally recorded it, we rented a piano from Steinway, we brought it up to my studio, and we just totally buried it in acoustic blankets and mattresses so there's no acoustic presence to the piano at all. It sounds like a synthesizer. But it's got all the attack qualities of a piano, which are generally very hard to get in a synthesizer.

According to Antony Widoff, U2's lead guitarist has a particular and distinctive sound: "Edge's guitar sound is certainly one of the best guitar sounds in the rock and roll business—he has an exciting timbral palette, a mixture of high- and low-end technology." How does he do it? Widoff describes it:

The source signal is a magnetic pickup producing waveforms from a metallic string. Then there's vast processing through an extremely complicated matrix of signal routing. He's got some of his own custom effects devices and a wide range of both high- and low-end digital processing. Then he has at least a half dozen vintage tube amplifiers. You have these

Robert Ashley (center) performing Perfect Lives in London, 1983.
Photo by Barbara Mayfield. Courtesy Performing Artservices.

30-year-old tube amplifiers that are receiving signals from devices invented yesterday.

Performing with distinctive and original sounds was the reason that Karlheinz Stockhausen used ring modulators, that Pierre Boulez used Di Giugno's 4X synthesizer, that countless composers and performers have used modulators, frequency shifters, harmonizers, filters, equalizers, flangers, delay lines, reverberation units, digital signal processors, and all manner of other equipment and techniques to transform sound. Referring to his *String Quartet No. 1: In Memoriam . . .* (1993), Stephen Montague said:

> Now, with electronics, for the first time in a century, there are new orchestration possibilities. It's like creating some kind of super instrument. But I mean "super" in the sense of beyond, not big, but beyond what the instruments could normally do. The simplest effect is amplification so that you can hear sounds that would be ordinarily inaudible to anyone but the fiddle player—for example, sul ponticello right on top of the bridge, as in the very opening of the string quartet. If that weren't amplified, you couldn't hear it. At a later point in the quartet, I add a prerecorded tape of white noise sounds which are perceived as emanating from the strings. I like this kind of sleight-of-hand. Is this the strings? What is the string sound and what is the electronic sound?

As Joan La Barbara puts it, referring to her *Vocal Extensions* (1975): "Without the electronics, I had only my voice, and the sound I could make depended upon what I could physically do—but with electronics, I could extend this . . ." In *Autumn Signal* (1978), La Barbara used Buchla equipment to process her vocal sounds and move them in space. In composing *73 Poems* (1993), she worked with Michael Hoenig in Los Angeles to transform the sounds of her voice to delineate the structure in Kenneth Goldsmith's poems which, as she explains, "are actually double texts, a light one and a dark one, superimposed." She remembers, "I thought about the kind of electronic treatment that I wanted to use to differentiate these texts—I would come up with verbal descriptions of what I wanted a particular line to sound like, and we'd try out different electronic devices and treatments until we got the sound we wanted."

As Kaija Saariaho said, "I use the computer to extend my instrumental writing—when I do sound synthesis, it's to realize certain ideas that I cannot realize with the instruments alone." She had begun at IRCAM in 1982 by using CHANT to generate sounds for *Vers le Blanc* (1982) and *Jardin Secret I* (1984). And she composed *Stilleben* (1988) at the Finnish Radio Experimental Studio in Helsinki by transforming, as she called them, "environmental and singing and orchestral sounds." She describes it:

> I processed the sounds with a variety of tools and I transformed the instrumental sounds into environmental sounds—well, the piece was about communication, so I used different travelling tools, like trains and airplanes, and different means of communication like typewriters and telephones. So an instrumental sound evolved, for example, into a train which passes by. It was really interesting working with these noises in a musical way, while at the same time being conscious of the associations they were giving to people and being aware of the point at which you don't recognize their origins.

But her focus was on extending instrumental sounds. In composing *Nymphea* (1987), for string quartet and electronics, she processed independently and differently the sound of each instrument and then used the resulting electronic sounds as the basis of the harmonic structure of the composition. Her *Amers* (1992) calls for an electronically transformed solo cello, synthesizer, sampler, various amplified acoustic instruments, and prerecorded electronic sounds. For the solo cello sound, she places four microphones on or near the cello, one for each string, and transforms the sound of each string separately from the others. In composing *Io* (1987), for chamber ensemble and electronic sounds, she used an analysis of a double-bass sound as a starting point. As she said, "I was interested in the contrabass playing in different manners, like increasing the bow pressure so that the pitched sound becomes inharmonic noise . . ."

•

Whereas most composers transformed the sounds of existing instruments, Hugh Davies, in 1968 in London, built an instrument specifically so that he could transform its sounds. It was, as he tells it, "built between the covers of an encyclopedia volume from which the pages had been torn out—I happened to use a final volume covering words that began with SHO-ZYG, and for lack of any other title . . ." *Shozyg* contained small objects that were amplified with contact microphones.

Davies continued to develop the idea by experimenting with mechanical sound generators and magnetic pickups: "I began to use small coiled springs as the basis for an instrument that used these magnetic pickups . . ." In 1972, he finished the first version of *Concert Aeolian Harp*, made of amplified jigsaw blades which were struck, bowed, plucked, and blown: "Typically for my microsonic world, bowing is done with a feather, blowing by the human breath, and so on . . ." And during the next years, he built different versions, improvements, and expansions. By 1986, its components included springs and wires, steel balls of various sizes mounted above ball bearings, wire rods of different lengths and thicknesses fixed at one end in a row, a plastic wheel that can be spun, a cut from a forty-five-rpm disc, a section of "rainbow" computer cable, and microphones and pickups, all mounted on a wooden board with wires running underneath. It was a universe of sound on a tabletop, animated by a single performer with feathers, superball mallets, paintbrushes of various sizes, a toothbrush, lengths of nylon wire, hairs from a violin bow, and plastic straws and tubes for blowing air, all of it extended with electronics. It reflected, as Davies said, "many of my ideas about sound, not only delicate and beautiful sounds, but also gutsy ugly sounds, sounds that have strong personalities." And he adds, "I get totally absorbed in it . . ."

•

Yasuhiko Mori, an engineer at Korg in Japan, also had the idea for an instrument built specifically to be processed with electronics. As Dave Smith tells it, "Korg had started a new engineering division to look into future technologies . . . they looked at the SynthKit, a Macintosh-based software algorithm development system which we developed here . . . and came up with the idea of the Wavedrum." In 1995, the *Wavedrum*, as it was called, became commercially available. It was basically an acoustic hand drum with its sounds extended and transformed by an internal digital signal-processing system. As Greg Rule wrote in *Keyboard Magazine*, "What makes this instrument so impressive is the accurate and sensitive way that it captures the player's performance, and how its internal synth engine responds to that information . . ."

•

A violinist does not need to know that sound is variation in air pressure, graphed as a waveform; that congruent and anticongruent soundwaves produced by multiple sources, such as instruments in an orchestra, mix in the air with each other and with themselves as they bounce off walls; that soundwaves are analyzed as spectrums, which are collections of partials that add together at their respective and continually changing amplitudes and frequencies to give us a sense of timbre; or that we recognize sounds largely by their onset transients, such as the noise of putting a bow on a string, which give us clues as to how the sound is made. A violinist needs to know how to play Tchaikovsky.

On the other hand, a musician playing a DX-7 or SY-99, or any other Yamaha synthesizer developed between 1983 and 1995, would be well advised to learn something about frequency modulation. Here is a brief explanation:

> In *frequency modulation*, the instantaneous frequency of one waveform, called the *carrier*, is varied by another waveform, called the *modulator*. The extent to which the carrier frequency varies, called *peak deviation*, is determined by the amplitude of the modulator. The rate at which the carrier frequency varies is determined by the frequency of the modulator.
>
> When carrier and modulator are at audio frequencies, audible extra partials, called *sidebands*, appear in the carrier spectrum. These sidebands are located symmetrically above and below the carrier at intervals equal to the modulator frequency. If, as an example, a carrier at 100Hz is modulated by a 100Hz modulator, the first four sidebands in a positive direction will be 200Hz, 300Hz, 400Hz, and 500Hz, and the first four sidebands in a negative direction will be 0Hz, -100Hz, -200Hz, and -300Hz. The negative frequencies are phase-reversed in relation to their complements in the positive domain.
>
> The series of sidebands extends in theory to infinity, but in practice the sidebands can be at such infinitesimal amplitudes as to be insignificant. The number of sidebands with significant amplitude is determined by the *modulation index*, which is the ratio between the peak deviation and the modulator frequency (index = peak deviation / modulator frequency). As the modulation index increases, energy is diverted from the carrier and distributed among an increasing number of sidebands. Because the amplitudes of the individual sidebands are, however, different for every index (they are determined by Bessel functions of the first kind and *n*th order), various degrees of phase cancellation occur between the negative and positive frequencies, and energy is distributed nonlinearly throughout the spectrum.
>
> In summary, there are two important variables in frequency modulation: (1) the carrier/modulator ratio, called the *c:m ratio*, which determines the placement of the sidebands in the modulated carrier spectrum, and (2) the modulation index, which determines the number of sidebands with significant amplitude.

Confronted with such an explanation, the aspiring musician might ask, "Do I *really* need to understand all of this technology?" And the old pro might answer, "Yes, if you want to create sounds with Yamaha synthesizers," adding afterward, softly, to offer comfort and encouragement, "But don't worry too much about the Bessel functions."

The point is that playing an instrument is more intuitive than creating a sound. In the heat of performance, a musician should be thinking only about playing the music, and that means playing an instrument intuitively, naturally, without conscious thought. As Julius Smith, professor at CCRMA, points out, "Most people that play have a lifetime of rehearsal in their bones and they really understand instruments and know how to make music with them—all you need to say is that it's a piano, for example, and you've said a lot because people know what to do with it." By contrast, even after understanding the theory of frequency modulation, the problem, he continues, "is understanding how to do what you want to do."

Smith's idea, consequently, is to design an electronic instrument as a model of a familiar instrument and let it evolve. And software, which is inherently more malleable than hardware, will evolve faster and more easily than hardware. A traditional wood-and-metal piano, for example, is heavy, expensive, difficult to keep in perfect adjustment, sensitive to climate, and relatively inflexible in its tuning, sound generation, and mode of performance, whereas a software piano has none of those problems. Smith and his students have been building a software piano:

> Ultimately, we'll build a high-quality physical device, an instrument, that feels exactly right to the performer. And I can give my best performance on it because it feels just right, and the fact that the sounds are generated in twenty-four bits by an algorithm should not be of concern to the performer.

Smith adds, "And when you lift the hood, there are no strings." It brings to mind the episode of a popular 1950s television show in which a car without an engine is propelled by crouching pushers, unseen by the attendant, into a gas station. The woman sitting in the driver's seat says, "Check the oil, please," and *Candid Camera* records the attendant's expression as he opens the hood and exclaims, "There's no engine here!"

Smith's point, however, goes beyond mechanical advantages. He is saying that a software piano is a more flexible instrument than a hardware piano. He continues:

> There are no limits as to how you can change that instrument. You can use a different scale. You can, in the blink of an eye, change it to any other instrument, and you don't have to file or hammer or hack—you just change a line or two of code and it's done. You're not restricted by the real world any more, not by the physical construction, not by physics. You can do anything that you can conceive of. It's a little like movie cartoons in the 1950s, where you can stretch a character's neck to fourteen feet, or you can hit a guitar over someone's head and have it wrap around their heads fourteen times and still be ready to play. It's whatever your imagination wants.

"Whatever," however, is hyperbole. "Whatever," in this reference to the physical model of a piano, means that one can change string length and mass to physically impossible limits. One can make a "piano" with 100-foot strings, for example. But one cannot make a clarinet sound using the physical model of a piano.

•

Composer David Jaffe agrees with Smith. He reflects: "How do you create a sound you've never heard before? You could come up with a mathematical formula that will produce an unknown effect, and you're intrigued, it has potential, and you're basically surprised . . . but another possibility is to start with the known and then extend it in some direction." For Jaffe, starting with the known and extending it seemed a natural approach. In 1981 at CCRMA, he was in pursuit of a computer-generated guitar sound to use in his *May All Your Children Be Acrobats*, for eight guitars, soprano, and tape. At a string quartet reading one evening, he happened to mention his research problems to Alex Strong, a graduate student in computer science at Stanford University and fellow string quartet reader. As Jaffe recalls:

> He got real excited and said that he'd just discovered a new way to do a guitar sound. So I went to the computer science building and, after signing a nondisclosure agreement, he showed me the technique. I thought it was pretty good but I immediately came up against roadblocks. For example, it was hard to tune, although Alex's partner Kevin Karplus had come up with a probabilistic method to work around this limitation, and it had no effective dynamics control. In any case, I was very interested. I started working on the technique with Julius Smith and we explored it from every angle.

Jaffe and Smith developed what became known as the Extended Karplus-Strong Algorithm. Jaffe went on to compose *Silicon Valley Breakdown* (1982), which explored a wide range of computer-generated plucked string sounds. As he said, "I liked the possibilities, like changing the size of the body of a virtua instrument, the thickness of the string . . ." And Smith went on to formulat the waveguide approach to physical modelling.

A *sound*, as Gertrude Stein might have said, is a sound. A sound *alg rithm*, such as physical modeling, is a method for generating sound. Physi modeling (more specifically *waveguide synthesis*, as Smith is doing it), quency modulation, additive synthesis, and granular synthesis are a few of sound-generating algorithms available in the 1990s. And every algorithm its advantages and disadvantages.

Perry Cook began to work on physical modeling as a doctoral can at Stanford University. His adviser suggested that modeling the voice, recalls, "would probably be the path of least resistance towards finis degree, so I went in the voice direction." At the same time, he develope els for trombone, flute, and clarinet, in his words, "as fun hacks for class demonstrations." He discovered something from those models:

> It was one of the first revealing things about these three instrument models to realize that they're differentiated by very small things. There's a minute difference between a clarinet and a flute, and a minute difference between a trombone and a clarinet. There are many ambiguous cases where a clarinet can sound like a flute, where one of these instruments can sound like another. So I tried to make a metamodel that includes all of them.

Cook's metamodel—which embodied lip (trombone), jet (flute), and reed (clarinet) excitation, and in which pitch was controllable by simulations of tube length, embouchure, register hole, and jet length—was appropriately called *Whirlwind*; and he went further to develop the HIRN (German for "brain") Meta-Wind Instrument Controller, which sensed bite and breath pressure and contained control keys, a linear slide, and different rotation controls for varying a player's blowing angle. The metamodel, however, worked within the same family of wind instruments.

The problem with physical modeling is in bridging between different families of instruments where the physical systems that generate the sounds are based on different principles. Cook explains:

> What physical models do is let you go from a big-bodied cello to a little-bodied cello to a viola da gamba to a double bass because you're playing around within the family. I've made a flute that turns into a Charlie Sullivan rock-and-roll guitar with complete continuity, but it's not completely generic. There is no generic model for interpolating between physical models yet, and I'm not sure that we'll ever have one. There are some bridges over which we can't walk.

•

David Wessel at CNMAT (Center for New Music and Audio Technology) at the University of California at Berkeley disagrees with the physical modeling approach. He asks: "Why tie yourself to the physical world?—art is about making artifacts, it's about the new." And Jean-Claude Risset agrees:

> The point of physical systems, it seems to me, is that they create a world of sound that is virtual and illusory, but where the parameters of control are the parameters of the physical world. But they are not acoustic parameters and it's very hard to do things like paradoxes or illusions, because these are things that do not exist in the physical world. You can't explore the whole world of sound with physical models.

Wessel views additive synthesis as the solution to electronic sound:

Trying to speak more directly to the ear is a sensible way to go. Even with a good model of a clarinet or a generalized wind instrument, it's usually very hard to make that model adapt to some other sound fantasy. You work with one class of sound material and it's difficult to move to another sound domain. I often have fantasies about sounds that are quite different from what is plausibly produced by physical systems. The real bottom line is that with spectral modelling, with the proper structures for control, one can implement the kinds of behavior that you find in physical models and yet achieve complete freedom in the actual sounds you produce.

Complete freedom? Effectively, yes. The basic component of a sound is a *partial*, a single sine wave, sometimes called an *overtone*. Additive synthesis controls the way every partial changes in time and then adds them together to make the total sound. The problem is that there's a lot of detail to control. If, for example, a sound is made up of twenty partials (a modest number) and each partial is changed ten times each second (also modest), then for every second of sound a performer will need to specify 200 items of control information. That's a lot for a human performer with fingers, toes, and a nose.

The solution lies in defining a meaningful control system. A *variable* is a part of a system that changes. A *control* tells a variable how to change. If a system has but one variable, it can be controlled only in that one respect. As the number of variables in a system increases, the number of ways in which the system can be controlled increases. A system with a large number of variables is clearly more malleable than a system with a few variables. Yet as the number of variables increases, the system becomes harder to steer because each control affects a smaller part of the whole. If a system contains 200 independent variables, for example, then each control will affect only 1/200th of the whole. The question is: What is a meaningful control? Julius Smith states the problem well:

> So here I give you 200 inputs and I say, "Play!" You're lost. If you pick up a signal processing algorithm at random and hook up to its possible inputs, the probability is that you'll be lost in that parameter space. You'll have no idea where to go or what to do in that space.

The solution is to conceptualize a multivariable electronic musical instrument as an extremely maneuverable airplane, one that has, say, 200 control surfaces, and to play that instrument with what pilots call a *fly-by-wire* control system. F. Richard Moore, also a pilot, explains: "In fly-by-wire systems, the pilot's controls are connected to a computer—the computer interprets what the pilot wants to do by sensing the pilot's gestures, and then manipulates the control surfaces of the airplane." In a group effort with Xavier Rodet, Adrian Freed, and Marc Goldstein, Wessel created a fly-by-wire system to control the variables of additive synthesis. Specifically, he defined a neural network to function as an adaptive system. He explains:

An *adaptive* system somehow adjusts itself by some kind of optimization algorithm to stay within the boundaries specified by a control problem or to produce an appropriate input-output relationship. In other words, we're faced with a control problem when we want to speak a word, for example the word "music." We have an intention. And then we have to send a rather complex sequence of commands to the different parts of our vocal tract to make that word come out. We adapt in the course of speaking by adjusting the controllers of our vocal tract to match the output, which is to say the word, that we would like to produce. If the output is somehow erroneous, we adjust the way our controllers operate to do a better job . . .

The adaptive-system control model applies to the problem of controlling musical sound. Given knowledge of a performer's intention to make a particular sound, Wessel's software generates and coordinates controls and applies them appropriately to the variables of additive synthesis. But how does Wessel know how to coordinate the controls? Or what the values are? He answers, "We analyze sounds and observe correlations . . ."

•

Gottfried Michael Koenig said: "I'm very annoyed with composers . . . trying to imitate existing instruments." Around 1970 at the Institute for Sonology, Koenig developed a sound-generating program at first called CSP (Computer Sound Program), later called SSP (Sound Synthesis Program). The program functioned, as he described it, "not referring to a given acoustic model but rather describing the waveform in terms of amplitude values and time values . . . My first intention was to go away from the classical instrumental definitions of sound . . ." He continues:

You could generate with it not only a more or less aleatoric waveform but practically all steps between stationary and random-controlled waveforms. We did it in real time with the PDP-15. This came from the idea of making sounds that don't imitate other sounds. The computer should be an instrument, like a violin which doesn't make a sound like any other instrument.

In 1972, Herbert Brun at the University of Illinois began a series of explorations collectively called *Sawdust*. It was an approach to generating sound that, as Brun said, "allows me to work with the smallest parts of waveforms, to link them and to mingle or merge them with one another . . ." The pieces composed with Sawdust began to appear in 1976, among them *Dust* (1976), *More Dust* (1977), *More Dust with Percussion* (1977), *Dustiny* (1978), *A Mere Ripple* (1979), *U-Turn-To* (1980), and *I toLD YOU so!* (1981). Brun's results were rich, granular sounds, difficult to produce with other techniques, controllable with probabilistic "handles" that let him vary waveform shapes anywhere from randomness to periodicity. His idea was to make sounds not modeled on existing sounds.

•

In 1963 in *Musiques Formelles*, Iannis Xenakis wrote: "All sound is an integration of grains, of elementary sonic particles, of sonic quanta . . . All sound, even all continuous sonic variation, is conceived as an assemblage of a large number of elementary grains adequately disposed in time . . ." Xenakis proposed, in other words, what came to be called *granular synthesis*. But he did not develop it further in a significant way.

Although Curtis Roads and others subsequently worked with granular methods, it was Barry Truax who most consistently developed granular techniques into a sound-generating algorithm. The grains, for Truax, were small *quanta*, tiny waveform fragments that were connected one after the other to define the shape of a waveform. In his words, "the grains did for my sounds what pixels do for graphics: they were building blocks." The number of grains per unit time, their individual shapes, their uniformity, and their distribution were all factors in determining the nature of a resultant sound.

In 1973, Truax returned to Vancouver from Utrecht to join the faculty at Simon Fraser University. His compositions through the 1970s and into the 1980s included *Sonic Landscape No. 3* (1977), *Androgyny* (1978), and *Arras* (1980), and through that period, as he tells it, "One of my goals was to integrate timbre into the piece itself, which eventually led to the granulation idea where sound and structure were no longer separate." In 1982, Simon Fraser University acquired a DMX-1000 digital signal-processing system, and by 1983, Truax had turned his POD software, which he had begun earlier in Utrecht, into the realtime PODX software, optimized for composing sound with the DMX-1000. *Wave Edge* (1983) and *Solar Ellipse* (1985) were his first compositions with it, and *Solar Ellipse* was, as he called it, "a landmark piece which would have been impossible without POD . . ." *Riverrun* (1986) was done in real time entirely with granular synthesis techniques. As he said, "I had the wonderful experience of breaking into a new territory." And *Riverrun* was based on a suitable poetic idea, as he put it, "on the flow of a river from the smallest droplets or grains, to the magnificence, particularly in British Columbia, of rivers . . ."

He then applied granulation techniques to recorded sounds. In composing *The Wings of Nike* (1987), based on phoneme sequences spoken by a man and a woman, and *Pacific* (1990), based on Pacific sounds such as seagulls and a Chinese New Year dragon dance, he used granulation techniques to change the time scales of the sounds. As he explains, "You can repeat or magnify instants and slowly move through the sound because you're dealing at the micro level of the grains . . ."

•

Although the basic approaches to sound synthesis—physical models, spectrum-based synthesis, and waveform techniques—are available in different specific manifestations in commercial synthesizers, most synthesizers are sold with a collection of easily accessed ready-made sounds, colloquially called "factory sounds," which are created (the process is called *voicing*) by a synthesizer company's experts. The advantages of ready-made sounds are obvious. As Julius Smith said, "If you have a good orchestra on the shelf, you can pull it out and create music very efficiently." Indeed, the commercial trend through the 1990s has been toward continually easier access to greater numbers of ready-made sounds. The success of E-mu's *Proteus*-series synthesizers, for example, has been due not only to the simplicity of its interface (a few knobs, clear menus) but also to the number (256) of excellent sounds available at the turn of one of its knobs. Dave Smith, consultant to Korg, puts it very clearly:

> In general, nobody programs synthesizers. I noticed in machines coming back for servicing that nobody had changed the sounds. Other companies noticed that too. And as synthesizers become more complex, it's even harder to change the sounds. Korg has a team of voicing experts to make sounds for the new instruments and someone who buys a synthesizer is better off, in a sense, using the factory-provided sounds. Obviously, there's a group of computer musicians who will get in there and change things, and we try to provide a top-level macro control surface for them, but to think that somebody that buys this thing will sit down and program it is a fallacy.

Further, most people do not want distinctive sounds. Dave Smith continues:

> We've determined that what people have always wanted in a synthesizer is an emulative sound capability. They want to be able to play standard instruments—pianos, saxophones, drums, brass instruments—from a keyboard. The ability to come up with new sounds is not all that important to the average player. So if we came out with a new sound, we'd be limited to 20,000 people in the world who would want to buy that as opposed to the 200,000 people who would buy a familiar sound.

Yet one of the historical dreams of electronic music has been to compose sound as well as music. Edgard Varèse said it in 1939: " I need an entirely new medium of expression: a sound-producing machine (not a sound-reproducing one)." Other composers, at different times and in different contexts, have concurred. As Jean-Claude Risset observes, "The easier a system is to use, the more limited are its possibilities." Barry Truax said, "I've never used any software except my own, but nowadays, I suspect, most people are the opposite, that they'll never use their own—I don't think that most people are aware of how commercial software colors their musical process and causes standardization." As Paul Lanksy puts it, "The most interesting music is generally going to be by people who have taken the design of their instruments into their own hands." And Robert Ashley states: "If we're composers, we've got to be serious about the idea of sound." Risset continues:

With electronic sound, we're in a completely new era of music. Electronic sound is completely different in its nature from instrumental sound. I know that there are many people that are just asking for a computer to make normal sounds. But with all the possibilities of crafting things, I don't think that normal sounds are the most exciting part of it. With electronic sound, you can navigate from island to island and in between. You have very few intrinsic constraints.

So if, as Ashley puts it, we've got to be serious about the idea of sound, the question becomes one of time and expertise. At what level does a composer need to invent a sound? Are factory sounds acceptable? Can they be customized? Ashley speaks to the issue:

> I love factory sounds. I actually change them a little bit, but I love them. It's like hiring a wonderful clarinet player in the old days, or like hiring a wonderful piano player. Those factory sounds are not to be sneered at. The only problem that I have with factory sounds is that so many of them are made in the abstract by guys who are making up sounds at 4 A.M. on the twenty-fifth cup of coffee. So it's not exactly as if they're making a sound specifically for me. When you play a pop record, you hear extremely expensive invented sounds, like the rimshot in the second verse of a Michael Jackson song. A bunch of guys worked on that, and they made this beautiful rimshot. That's a tailored sound; it's an expensive tailored sound. When you listen to pop music, the best pop music, you hear very expensive sounds, like designer sounds, Gucci sounds. But for guys like me, I'm operating at the off-the-rack level, so I like factory sounds. I would love to just be able to plug in a factory sound and use it, but for the most part it doesn't quite fit because the guy who made it was not making it for me. He was just making it, and he expects me to do something to make it useful.

Making a sound useful means customizing the sound. And customizing a sound is not very far from making a sound. To be sure, most commercial synthesizers offer capabilities in designing sounds, but the range of any single algorithm is obviously limited to what can be done within the constraints of that algorithm. Is it possible to design a system that is truly flexible and easy to use, and that any composer can use to make any sound?

The current wisdom is that generality requires a system that offers access to a variety of different sound algorithms. And although it was the basis of Tom Oberheim's new modular approach at Marion Systems, for most composers generality usually means software. Larry Austin, for example, uses his personal computer as a synthesizer and creates his sounds in software. As he said, "The only constraints that affect my work are those that I define—I have several very powerful software synthesis packages, including Csound and Cmix and several processing and editing packages . . ."

In 1985, as a translation of the Music-N programs to personal computers, Barry Vercoe finished the first version of Csound. He comments, "Csound started as a non-realtime synthesis medium but now desktop machines are fast enough to do Csound in real time—once software synthesis gets into real time, you've got all the control you want, and realtime interactions . . ." Composer Richard Karpen is a Csound user. In his words:

> I had previously used Moog modular synthesizers, so I immediately saw Music 11 in terms of inputs and outputs as with the Moog. I could see how things like oscillators and filters were patched together. I then used Music 360 in Padua, Italy, at the Centro di Sonologia Computazionale where I spent a year in the early 1980s. Music 360 was identical in many ways to Music 11, at least on the surface, so it wasn't like learning a new system. After leaving Italy, I spent four years at Stanford using the Samson Box. I spent nearly a year at IRCAM and then went back to Stanford. When I left Stanford in 1989 and got a NeXT computer, I immediately made a port of Csound for it and since then it's been my primary sound synthesis and sound processing tool.
>
> There are not many things that can't be done using Csound. But suppose there is some process that Csound doesn't contain. A person with only moderate C programming skills can very easily learn how to add their own processing routines into Csound. I have done this on a number of occasions and it has recently become a very common thing for Csound users to do. Once one starts to add their own functionality to Csound, the only limit to what it can do is one's imagination. So it's easily extensible, which to me is an essential ingredient of any composer's tools.

Other composers and programmers have also contributed to the available software resources, some of it free, some of it shareware, some for sale. Paul Lansky, for example, wrote Cmix in 1986, in his words, "as a toolkit which makes it easy to design instruments," and Lansky and Kenneth Steiglitz wrote EIN in 1991, a "scratchpad" for filter design and general digital signal processing. In 1991, Tom Erbe began work on SoundHack, a general digital signal-processing sound-transformation program. Is software synthesis the future? Dave Smith thinks so:

> The ideal is for everything to be soft so you're not fixed on any one synthesis method. The problem in the past has been that synthesizers have been limited to one synthesis technology. It was a necessity in the past because specialization is cheaper, but, in the future, in a machine that's software based, a person will be able to start by implementing any of the historic previous synthesis methods, like FM or waveguide, in any combination that they want. And as synthesis methods are discovered in the future, they can be implemented on the same system because it's soft. All voicing will be upwards compatible in the future. There'll be continuity.

Dave Smith is speaking from the perspective of a synthesizer manufacturer when he concludes, "It's what's going to happen; it has to be done—it has to be done because it's the only plausible way for the industry to go . . ."

•

As microprocessors become faster through the next several years, increasing levels of complexity will become achievable in real time. One can foresee that eventually both controls and audio will be able to function in the same hardware environment, which means that a composer will need nothing more to control and process sound than a single computer. Meanwhile, however, a computer is typically used to generate and process controls, and a synthesizer or digital signal processor (DSP) is typically used to generate or process audio, and both computer and DSP are typically used together in functional symbiosis to comprise an electronic music system.

By way of illustrating the concept of the two-device system, the first version of Adrian Freed's MacMix, written in 1985 at IRCAM, was entirely software, but it required two computers. As Freed said, "The best tool at that time for the graphical user interface was the Macintosh; the best tool for sound editing was IRCAM's VAX 11/780." He tells the story:

> My intention was to work on a user interface for a sound editor. David Wessel suggested that editing is just part of a musically more interesting process: mixing. I studied the features of Robert Gross's batch mode UNIX mixing program and queried IRCAM musicians about how they used such tools. The important thing I learned was that you can do interesting things musically by mixing at all time scales, from microsurgery at the microseconds scale, musique concrète at the seconds scale, and composing and ordering at the minutes scale.
>
> The major goal of MacMix was to smoothly integrate mixing at all these time scales and leverage the use of disk storage to allow for efficient mixing of an arbitrary number of channels (David routinely used hundreds for layering). The major innovations in MacMix to achieve this include multiresolution sound representation for rapid display at all time scales, event logging by timing mouse clicks relative to played back audio, disk access and CPU optimal mix scheduling. An interesting feature of the optimized scheduling is that editing operations were optimized to the point that they operated in real time since sound playback operated from play lists. Cross-fade edits were almost realtime since only the fades needed to be computed.

In 1986, Freed rewrote MacMix and commissioned IMS, a small company, to build a specialized hardware device to replace the VAX 11/780 and connect to the Macintosh so that MacMix could run as a Macintosh-based system with a peripheral signal processor and disk-based recorder. The system was called *Dyaxsis*. It was successful. IMS was subsequently bought by Studer and renamed Studer Editech. Dyaxsis eventually became Dyaxsis II, still a Macintosh-based system with a peripheral signal processor and disk-based recorder.

And, incidentally, how would a composer work with Dyaxsis? Curtis Roads used it to compose *Clang-tint* (1995), which encompassed a wide palette of recorded sounds, including musical instruments at the museum of Kunitachi

College of Music in Tokyo, industrial noises, sounds from nature, and computer-generated sounds. He describes his approach:

> Some sampled sounds trigger semantic associations. When the timbre is beautiful in itself one has the choice of using it in a "neutral" way—for its color alone, removed from associations—or more directly, associations and all. There are various techniques for neutralizing associations. One method is to introduce such materials in bursts with other semantically loaded sounds. All of these associations are triggered so fast that they cancel each other out. You hear them as expressive timbres rather than as "animal cry" followed by "human sigh." Other times I use such sounds more directly to evoke a mood. For example, there is one moment in *Clang-tint* where I insert a texture from a recording of whales in the ocean. Due to the way it is cut, the original source is obscured. But there remains an evocative sense of depth and space in that sample.

Clang-tint is in several sections. How are the sounds organized? He continues:

> I did not conceive the sections in terms of the resultant forms but rather in terms of their materials and the strategies I used to organize the materials. In the section called *Purity*, for example, I was interested in very simple sinusoidal waveforms and harmonic relationships in pure ratios. Whereas in the section called *Filth*, the emphasis is on "dirty" sounds: distortions, inharmonic clusters, stochastic globules, and exploding grains. In the section *Organic*, I began with an expressive way of playing a synthesizer. This is spliced into phrases with animal and insect cries, bird calls, and whale samples. The section called *Robotic* starts from a recording I made in Tokyo of a nineteenth-century mechanical musical instrument, which I controlled manually rather than having it play automatically. In the studio I interpolated the sounds of other machines . . .

●

James Dashow had gone to Rome in 1969 and, as he put it, "just decided to stay—I had gotten involved in the musical life." At about that time, Giovanni De Poli and Alvise Vidolin, engineering students at the University of Padua, began working with composer Teresa Rampazzi in her private electronic music studio. Through the next few years, they gradually formed what eventually became CSC (Centro di Sonologia Computazionale / Center for Computer Sonology) at the University of Padua.

In 1974, Dashow met Graziano Tisato, and together they implemented Music IV-BF on the CSC computer. Dashow began to work there, unofficially but regularly. As CSC developed through the years, it grew to include not only De Poli, Vidolin, Tisato, and Dashow, but also Roberto Doati, Marco Stroppa, Mauro Graziani, Sylviane Sapir, and others. In 1984, CSC acquired a 4I synthesizer from IRCAM.

LIMB (Laboratorio permanente per l'Informatica Musicale della Biennale di Venezia / Computer Music Laboratory of the Venice Biennale), directed by Alvise Vidolin, grew out of CSC's activities to provide a vehicle for organizing major events. In 1982, LIMB organized the International Computer Music Conference. In 1986, in conjunction with the Venice Biennale, LIMB organized *Nuova Atlantide* (New Atlantis), a major exhibition of electronic music technology. LIMB organized workshops, commissions of musical works, concerts, the publication of a newsletter, and festivals that focused on the inter-action between traditional instruments and electronics. As Vidolin tells it, "The important thing was that whereas computer music had always been heard in concerts for specialists, in these events it was presented to the public in festi-vals." CSC, in short, became a lively center for a wide range of research, pro-duction, and outreach initiatives.

It also provided a starting point from which Dashow could design and build a personal DSP system. In 1988, he set up a studio at Poggio San Lorenzo and began work on Music 30 for the 320-C30 Texas Instruments DSP chip. The chip was available, mounted on the Spirit 30 circuit board from Sonitech, a company located near Boston, and his hardware system consisted of two Sonitech boards and a computer. He used it to compose, among other pieces, *Reconstructions* (1992), for harp and computer, and *Morfologie* (1993), for trumpet and computer. Throughout the process, Sonitech had been very help-ful. As Dashow reports, "In 1990, they made a technician available to me for several days to help do some basic development . . ." But why take the time? Why not use a commercial synthesizer? Because, he answers, "My software was more flexible—for example, I could have the clarinetist play in a different hall for every note."

•

In 1988, Jean-François Allouis became technical director at IRCAM, and Eric Lindemann arrived from the United States to design a successor to the 4X syn-thesizer. Miller Puckette tells the story:

> Several of us got together as a group—there was me, Eric, Bennett Smith, Patrick Potascek, Michel Starkier—and we started planning. We were all in agreement that we were going to do a DSP solution and we were look-ing for a suitable host computer. We chose NeXT because it had a back-plane that we could put a synthesizer on, it was more extensible to add a serious amount of hardware, and it was also attractive that the NeXT people were talking a lot about music. We thought very seriously about the software structure before we designed the hardware, and that told us what the hardware capabilities had to be. Well, the hardware came off exactly as planned, and the software came out totally different. What we ended up with was a machine that ran MAX.

The ISPW (IRCAM Signal Processing Workstation), as it was called, was an electronics board that ran inside a NeXT computer. It was used in many compositions at IRCAM, among them Kaija Saariaho's *NoaNoa* (1991), for ISPW and flute; Saariaho's *Près* (1992), for ISPW and cello; Philippe Manoury's

En Echo (1994), for ISPW and soprano solo; and Pierre Boulez' ...*explosante-fixe*... (1994), for ISPW, flute solos, and instrument ensemble. Many other composers also used it, among them José Campana, Frédéric Durieux, Joshua Fineberg, Philippe Hurel, Alessandro Melchiorre, François Nicolas, Ichiro Nodaira, and Zack Settel. Peter Otto and Rick Bidlack, in the United States, used it as the hardware platform for MixNet, an integrated audio recording, synthesis, and processing environment. Cort Lippe, who was working at IRCAM during the development period, tested early prototypes, ported most of the 4X repertory to the ISPW, used the ISPW in many compositions, among them his *Music for Clarinet and ISPW* (1992), and continued to use a prototype ISPW even after he left IRCAM in 1994. He said: "It was everything I was looking for . . ."

In fact, it was everything many people were looking for, but unfortunately, it never became available. Shortly after the ISPW was finished, NeXT stopped making computers.

•

Soon after Giuseppe Di Giugno left IRCAM in 1987, Paolo Bontempi founded IRIS (Istituto di Ricerca per l'Industria dello Spettacolo / Research Institute for the Entertainment Industry) on the grounds of a park for exotic birds in a small town just south of Rome. With flamingos and ostriches fluttering in the background, Di Giugno began to form an electronics design center:

> I invited everyone I knew—among collaborators, students, and others that I had met and knew of—that was expert in the relevant fields. I assembled an interdisciplinary group. We had two years to advance with my ideas for the new machine. We took a 4X and began to simplify it. And then we conceived a completely new machine. We made a fairly large chip—400,000 transistors—and we began to develop the MARS workstation.

In 1979, Sylviane Sapir was working at the CNRS Laboratory in Marseilles toward a doctorate in solid state physics, specifically wave propagation in rubber, when Jean-Claude Risset returned to Marseilles from Paris. Risset's lab, happily as it turned out, was next to hers. She had studied music. She became interested in his sounds, and as she put it, "I left rubber for computer music." She finished her thesis with Risset. She then received a grant to continue her work in Toronto. But before leaving for Toronto, she went to Venice to attend the International Computer Music Conference. It changed everything. As she said, "I fell in love with Venice." And she requested a change in her grant, as she put it, "to go to Venice by train instead of Toronto by plane."

Actually, she worked in Padua, near Venice. She developed particular skills in realtime software. She assisted musicians, collaborated with LIMB and the Biennale di Venezia, and taught a course in computer music for engineers at the University of Padua. When IRIS was created, Di Giugno invited her to join the group, and she soon became manager of the software development team for the MARS (Musical Audio Research Station) project.

Thinking of the project, she said, "There's an enormous distance between the bits and the musician." And she meant two things. First, that there is a conceptual distance to be covered in software by developing an interface that will allow a musician to use the system intuitively. Second, that software development takes time. To keep the MARS project on schedule, the software was developed as the chip was designed. There were problems, of course. The chip and the software were continually modified. But in general, the process worked so well that the software was ready before the chip was produced by the foundry. And lo and behold, as she said with rightful pride, "When the chip arrived, the software worked."

When the system was finished, she reports, "We gave examples of the MARS to Tempo Reale and the University of Padua—it worked well, and it was used right away by several composers." Karlheinz Stockhausen in Germany and Thomas Kessler in Switzerland used it. Salvatore Sciarrino used it in *Perseo et Andromeda*, an opera. André Richard used it in *Glidif*, for contrabass, clarinet, and electronics. Luciano Berio used it in *Ofanim* because, in his words, "I wanted to have a hybridization of things—a voice becomes a clarinet, a clarinet becomes a voice . . ."

●

Alvise Vidolin at Tempo Reale saw in the MARS workstation the solution for a generic electronic music problem. As he explains, "The problem is to perform with the machines of today the music that was conceived for the machines of yesterday, and there's a problem of transcription, for example from analog machines to digital machines." He had earlier worked with Luigi Nono on Nono's live electronics pieces. He reflected, "Our work together in the 1980s, with live electronics, was a collaborative friendship . . ." Vidolin decided to re-create those pieces. He explains:

> In the 1980s, Nono worked in live electronics at the Experimentalstudio der Heinrich Strobel Stiftung des Sudwestfunks in Freiburg. There was a hybrid system at that studio at the time, with analog sound processors and various digital connection and sound-distribution devices and delays. There were a lot of specialized machines. For example, in Nono's score for *Post-prae Ludium Donau*, there are specifications for delays, spatialization, reverberation time, filtering, and pitch transpositions for harmonizer effects, and since the score specifies all that, we could realize it all on the MARS . . . I thought of transcribing to the MARS the many things that Nono had done at Freiburg.

●

As a graduate student at the University of Illinois at Urbana in the late 1970s, Carla Scaletti worked with Buchla and Moog synthesizers. She recalls, "What was so much fun about the analog studio was to be working directly with the sound itself in such a concrete way." She also worked with Music IV-BF and Music 360. She remembers, "When I started doing software synthesis, it felt almost like a step backwards, because it was less direct and it wasn't real time. On the other hand, the computer let me do algorithmic things and build structures in a way that I could not do in the analog studio."

In 1980, while a student in Chicago, Kurt Hebel heard about CERL (Computer-based Education Research Laboratory) at the University of Illinois at Urbana. He transferred to Urbana, and as he tells it, "I just showed up at CERL and started programming . . . and after about three weeks, they hired me." In 1981, with others, he began to work on the IMS (Interactive Music System). As Scaletti remembers it, "They had microprocessors in the terminals that would actually control the synthesizers and put music notation graphics up on the screen." Hebel continues:

> CERL was a unique situation because it was run completely by undergraduate students. We had a budget, and we could build things. There was never any central control. It was a fun place because you could do anything you wanted. There was always an underlying goal but it was never explicit. We never really knew what we were working together towards, but it ended up as the IMS for synthesis, timbre design and performance. CERL was sort of like a clubhouse, and people would bring the things that were important with them, like aquariums, gerbils, lizards, hamsters . . .

Scaletti and Hebel met at CERL in 1981. Scaletti describes it:

> Nobody took the CERL group very seriously because it was a bunch of undergraduate engineers who looked as though they were just playing around. But I saw things there that were better than the "official" state-of-the-art. Also it was the atmosphere. People were comfortable with computers. It was a little chaotic, but things were happening fast. Kurt got interested in what I was working on in software synthesis and said, "You don't have to wait. You can do this in real time."

Scaletti was working at the time with the Synclavier at the university. But she was a bit troubled because, in her words, "It was difficult to get in and control the low-level sound synthesis and sound design." Hebel saw the opportunity and made his move. She tells it:

> One night Kurt showed up at Studio D, where the Synclavier was. I was mildly annoyed that someone was interrupting my studio time (scarce resources at that time) but Kurt insisted that he had an idea of how to control the hardware directly, without the note language. He started typing in hex, trying to poke around and see if he could stumble upon some real machine instructions. Suddenly the disks all started spinning and the terminal started beeping like mad and my entire disk was wiped out. So there was nothing left to do but go next door to Treno's and have a drink.

Well, it must have been a very good drink because many good things followed, among them the *Platypus*, marriage, and a company. In 1984, Hebel and Lippold Haken built the Platypus, a RAM-based microprogrammable dig-

Carla Scaletti (left) and Kurt Hebel (right) in 1995 in front of the Cabybara, the hardware component of the Kyma System. Photo courtesy Symbolic Sound.

ital signal processor. Scaletti finished her doctorate and began to teach classes in computer music. As she tells it, "I was teaching people how to use the programs that existed and I started to feel I wanted to learn more about how to make programs rather than just use them, so I went back to school and I got a masters degree in computer science, and I had an assistantship in CERL because I wanted to work on this Platypus—I wanted to write software for it."

In 1985, she began to work on what she called *Kyma*, after the Greek word for "wave." "At that time," she remembers, "Kyma was completely software synthesis on a Mac Plus—it took five minutes to compute a sine wave." Also at that time, funding for music hardware at CERL dried up, causing Scaletti and Hebel to fund their work personally. As she remembers, "We bought the components and assembled our own Platypus, and by May 1987 we had a version of Kyma that was using our Platypus to do synthesis in real time."

In 1987, Apple gave her a grant to design a graphical interface for Kyma. In 1988, Scaletti and Hebel formed a company called Kymatics whose principal business location was a spare bedroom in their apartment. She adds, "And that's when we redid the interface to show the hierarchy as a tree graph, and when variables were added, and score language, and user defined classes." Then, on June 6, 1989, the day after defending a doctoral dissertation on digital filtering, Hebel started to design the *Capybara* (named after a South American aquatic rodent that looks like a large guinea pig), which became the hardware component of what became the Kyma System. Hebel remembers, "The design took from June to August . . . we first had Kyma making sounds on New Years' eve that year, although it was around midnight so the first sounds were probably made in the first minutes of 1990."

In March 1990, Scaletti and Hebel incorporated Symbolic Sound. Their first orders, which came in the fall of 1990 from Richard Robinson in Atlanta and Francesco Guerra, a physicist at the University of Rome, were shipped in January 1991. Scaletti thinks back:

> Kyma was born out of a kind of greediness. I wanted the immediacy of working with tape, of working with sound in a concrete way, and I liked the voltage-control idea that some signals could be controlling others, and the software synthesis idea of composing timbre as well as events. But I was greedy enough to want to do all of it in real time.

• • •

CHAPTER TEN

AUTOMATA

In 1644 in France, Salomon de Caus described an organ in which a pegged cylinder, turned by a water wheel, activated levers which triggered bellows to force air through pipes. In the 1780s, a certain Mr. Merlin in London advertised "Morning and Evening Amusements," including a "Mechanical Garden"; a barrel harpsichord, "similar to a Hand-Organ, which plays seven tunes"; a barrel organ "which plays eight tunes by clockwork"; and "A Curious Hand-Organ, which plays eight tunes for the Ladies and Gentlemen to dance by, accompanied by a Kettle-Drum." In early nineteenth-century England, Charles Babbage developed an "Analytical Engine," essentially a mechanical computer, and Ada Lovelace, mathematician, speculated that it could be used for music: "Supposing, for instance, that the fundamental relations of pitched sound in the signs of harmony and of musical composition were susceptible of such expression and adaptations, the engine might compose elaborate and scientific pieces of music of any degree of complexity or extent." In early nineteenth-century Germany, Johann Maelzel invented the metronome and, among numerous other automata, built the *Panharmonicon*, an orchestra of forty-two robot musicians for which Beethoven composed *Wellington's Victory*.

Musical automata, in short, have been with us for quite a while. Indeed, innumerable water organs, music boxes, musical clocks, and barrel organs of all shapes and sizes were built through the eighteenth and nineteenth centuries. These early automata generally behaved in predictable ways. But the idea of an unpredictable automaton seems also to have had a certain charm, at least in the following passage from a story by E.T.A. Hoffmann:

The Talking Turk was attracting universal attention, and setting the town in commotion . . . It was, in fact, a very remarkable automaton . . . "You must have put an extraordinary question," Lewis answered . . . "Chance, I should imagine, has educed something which by accident is appropriate to your question . . ."

•

The use of chance and randomness in the arts had an eighteenth-century precedent in Mozart's *Musical Dice Game*. And there were a few early twentieth-century precedents. Marcel Duchamp's *The Bride Stripped Bare by Her Bachelors, Even. Musical Erratum, 1913*, for example, calls for a vase (with a funnel, we assume), a toy train with open cars, and lots of little balls, the exact number to be determined by the range of the instrument that will play the music. Each ball has a number, representing a note, printed on it. The balls are put in the vase such that they fall (through the funnel) into the toy train passing below, from which the balls are taken by the musicians and played. Duchamp's description of this is, in part, as follows:

Vase containing the 89 notes (or more: 1/4 tone) figures among numbers on each ball Opening A letting the balls drop into a series of little wagons B, C, D, E, F, etc. Wagons B, D, E, F, going at a variable speed, each one receiving one or several balls . . . can be performed by a designated instrument . . . (to be developed).

In making his *Collage with Squares Arranged According to the Laws of Chance* (1917), Hans Arp let pieces of colored paper fall randomly to the floor to suggest patterns. Tristan Tzara cut single words out of a newspaper, shook them in a bag, and took them out one by one to write a poem.

But it was John Cage, in about 1950, who first began to use chance procedures with consistency. His focus was discovery. As he said in 1952, "It is thus possible to make a musical composition the continuity of which is free of individual taste and memory (psychology) and also of the literature and 'traditions' of the art . . ." In freeing himself from "individual taste and memory," chance made possible the discovery of new combinations of things, new events that would not have occurred had he relied on what he already knew, had already experienced, and already found pleasing. The composer, for Cage, was properly an explorer, an inventor, and the proper questions for the composer to ask were: How can I get beyond myself? How can I find things that I would otherwise not have thought of? Further, Cage found that chance methods changed his awareness of what was pleasing. In 1961, he said:

What actually happened was that when things happened that were not in line with my views as to what would be pleasing, I discovered that they altered my awareness. That is to say, I saw that things which I didn't think would be pleasing were in fact pleasing, and so my views gradually changed from particular ideas as to what would be pleasing, toward no ideas as to what would be pleasing.

In the eyes of many, however, Cage's methods raised a few questions. One of them had to do with the composer's responsibility. Was Cage abdicating that responsibility? Was he, further, abandoning his talent, expertise, and control by throwing coins that, after all, anyone could throw? One might have asked Cage, "If all you do is throw coins, could I be a composer as important as you?" And Cage, exercising both his mischievousness and his good-natured inclination to encourage, might have and occasionally did answer, "Yes." It was a provocative answer.

But it was the wrong question. It's obvious that Cage was bringing a lot to the table. His music could not have been composed by anyone else. The question should have been: "*How*, exactly, do you use random numbers?" And the answer is in the way that Cage composed. In 1972, for example, Cage composed *Birdcage* in the electronic music studio at the State University of New York at Albany. I worked with him. Here is my account of it:

Cage arrived in Albany on a Monday night with Hans Helms, a German music critic and film director, and a film and audio crew of three people from the WDR. Hans had been commissioned to do a film of John composing the piece. John also brought three groups of prerecorded tapes: Group "A," we'll call it, was of singing birds that he had recorded in aviaries during the previous two weeks. Group "B" was recordings of John singing his own *Mureau* (an earlier piece based on Thoreau's writings) in a chanting voice (as he observed: "It makes the birds seem less ridiculous"). And Group "C" was environmental sounds (the "wild-track," as filmmakers call it).

On Tuesday, we put the tapes in piles—A1, A2, A3 . . . and B1, B2, B3 . . . and so on—and set up eight source tape recorders, continually playing, routed through a mixer to one destination tape recorder. John was sitting in the center of the studio, looking at the studio's digital clock. According to a timing chart that he had prepared Monday evening, he would say, for example, at a particular time: "Put tape C3 on tape recorder 7," and we would do it; and he would say, for example, at a particular time: "Now switch to tape recorder 5," and we would get ready, he would give a hand signal at the very instant that this was to be done, and we would at that signal change the settings on the mixer so that whatever sound was at that moment being played on tape recorder 5 was routed to the destination tape recorder. At different times throughout the day, according to his instructions, we would change the tapes being played on the source tape recorders; and at random time intervals measured in seconds—an interval of approximately five seconds, for example, might be followed by an interval of seventy-two seconds—we would change the settings on the mixer to route a new sound group to the destination tape recorder. In this way all of the Group A, B and C tapes were sampled, in random order and in random durations, onto what turned out to be twelve single tapes. Those tapes functioned as "submasters." They were yet subject to another series of operations, scheduled for the following day.

Wednesday, however, was wasted because of misunderstandings between myself and John as to what was technically possible in the studio and what we needed to do. After a frustrating work session, everyone came to my home for a dinner party, which was jovial and funny. I thought to myself, "What happens when we have a *good* day?"

On Thursday, we processed the sounds from the submasters. The tapes were in turn played back through filters, ring modulators, and other audio processing devices, according to a time chart that John had prepared after dinner the previous night. We set up a routing system such that each submaster tape, played back on one source tape recorder, could be routed by switching through any of the various processing devices to a single destination tape recorder. One after another we played the submasters and processed them. Again, John was sitting in the center of the studio, watching the digital clock as he followed his time chart, this time calling out, for example, "Now, ring modulation," and we would switch from whatever processing device was currently being used to the ring modulator. Since the audio processing and the amount of time that each type of audio processing was used were determined by chance, the processing was completely independent of the sounds that were being processed. We had no idea as to results until we heard them. Sometimes John would say something like, "That's absurd." Sometimes we would all laugh. Sometimes we were delighted.

In summary, the art of Cage's composing was, first, in the sounds of the piece—who else would have thought of combining birds with *Mureau*?—and, second, in the formulation of the questions that determined how the piece would be composed. Who else would have asked: Which sound should be on which submaster and for what duration? Which type of processing will be used and for what duration? Cage could not and did not use randomness in a completely unconstrained free-for-all where anything was possible anytime in any composition. Indeed, if he had, if anything had been possible anytime, then every composition would have been the same as every other. Cage differentiated and defined his compositions by the questions he asked. For each composition, he defined a unique array of sounds and procedures. He then used random numbers to select from those arrays.

Further, Cage explored indeterminacy not only through random numbers. He also set up performance situations based on underlying complexities that produced *seemingly* random results. *Reunion*, for example, an event first performed in Toronto in 1968, was a five-hour series of chess games played by Cage against Marcel and Teeny Duchamp. Lowell Cross had designed and built an electronically wired chessboard in which electrical contacts were made by the movements of the chess pieces. Whenever a contact was made, music produced by any of Cross, David Tudor, David Behrman, or Gordon Mumma was gated through to the loudspeakers.

•

Cage opened the door in the early 1950s, and others walked through, not always with the same methods but certainly with the same delight at the surprising and unpredictable. Larry Austin's *Accidents* (1967), for example, came about while Austin was working with David Tudor in 1967 at the University of California at Davis, performing pieces for live electronics. Austin tells it:

> One evening, he fixed a meal for me—it was Indian food—and he said, "Larry, write a piece for me." I said, "David, but you don't play the piano any more." And he said, "Oh, you'll think of something . . ." So I composed a piece where David would not play the piano on purpose, but only accidentally.

Tamas Ungvary worked at EMS in Stockholm in 1972, just as the EMS hybrid system began to function. Were the oscillators stable? Ungvary answers:

> Yes and no. Yes, they were made in 1968 and they were extremely stable for their time. No, they were not really stable by later standards. But it's fantastic if they are not stable. It's fantastic if at a certain time one of them gets crazy, because those are the creative moments and possibilities in your life, the surprise, something which you would never do, which you would never think of. Life was giving you some random result—if you were not a creative person you wouldn't see possibilities in that, but if you were, you would thank God who gave you a new idea. I got some very very good suggestions from those oscillators.

And Charles Dodge must have gotten some very good suggestions from the Kp indices for earth's magnetic field from January 1 to March 4, 1961, as depicted in a chart in "Bulletin No. 18" of the International Association for Geomagnetism and Aeronomy, because he based the pitches and rhythms of *Earth's Magnetic Field* (1970) on them. In 1969, Dodge had received a call from the Goddard Institute for Space Studies at Columbia University:

> The geophysicists at Goddard had a way of recording the effects of the radiation of the sun on the magnetic field that resembled, in its notation, music. They wanted to try playing it because they had some ideas that it might be interesting. They had tried doing such things—one of them played the flute, I believe—and it sounded pleasant . . .

Even the reticent may be open to suggestions. Michel Waisvisz' physicality in performance requires that he remain in control of a musical process. Consequently, he does not use computer programs that compose—in his words, "The logic stuff, I hate it"—but he does use algorithms to explore:

They produce a hell of a lot of nonsense and sometimes they just produce a little jewel of notes or sounds. I use these programs to produce things that I might not otherwise have thought of. I can't use the programs in performance, but I sometimes use some of the results.

In 1972, Cage and David Tudor performed together in a concert tour in Europe. There were two programs. One consisted of simultaneous performances of Cage's *Mureau* with Tudor's *Rainforest III*. Tudor recalls:

> The last performance was in Spain, in Pamplona. It was outdoors, poor John, that was the very last performance on that tour . . . Our last parting shot was to do the other collaboration which was John singing his *Mesostics Re Merce Cunningham* together with my work called *Untitled*.
> That was actually one of the high points of my electronic career, that piece called *Untitled*. Even for me it was unimaginably wild. *Untitled* was an electronic hookup designed in such a way that it had no beginning, no point in my thinking where the sound originated. The manner of making the hookup was to connect the end of every chain to the beginning in a complete feedback loop. But highly involved. There were . . . I counted them at one time, there were sixty feedback loops in the electronic hookup . . . So it really came out wild. It was so unpredictable, it was just wonderful. It's the kind of thing that couldn't be done again.

●

In 1955 at the University of Illinois at Urbana, Lejaren Hiller and Leonard Isaacson began a series of experiments toward using a computer to automate musical composition. Their work culminated in 1957 in the *Illiac Suite for String Quartet* which was, in Hiller's words, "the first substantial piece of music produced with a computer." He explains the idea:

> I had been working in the Chemistry Department of the University of Illinois on some problems in statistical mechanics that involved the solution of what we call "restricted random walks." A very crude example of such a walk would arise if I were to walk through a city and flip a coin at each corner to tell me whether to turn right or left. Since it is a cumbersome process to obtain solutions to these problems whenever they are at all subtle or complex, we used Illiac I to help out. Since I had also been composing music for years, I observed that if we could program a computer to simulate a "walk" through, say, ordinary space, we could also simulate a "walk" through a grid defined to represent musical elements such as pitch, rhythmic durations, and timbre choices. Leonard Isaacson and I thus assembled enough material to form the *Illiac Suite* . . .

Hiller's method was based on a generate-and-test principle. Large quantities of random numbers were generated, and each number was tested and accepted or rejected according to specific criteria. The numbers representing pitches, for example, could produce no tritones, the melody had to start and end on middle-C, and the range of the melody from its lowest to its highest note could not exceed one octave. Once a number was accepted, it was placed in a note list that was eventually printed out and converted by hand into musical notation to be played by acoustic instruments.

The generate part of the generate-and-test method, as Hiller saw it, produced the richness of possibilities that flows from chance. The test part extracted coherence and intelligibility from those possibilities. Hiller's handle on chance was Information Theory, which relates the information content of a sequence of symbols, such as words or musical notes, to the number of different symbols that could possibly appear in the sequence. As the logic goes, the number of different words, for example, that could possibly appear in a message is evidenced in the predictability with which word follows word; the less predictably word follows word, the greater, it is assumed, are the possibilities, and consequently, the more informative the message. As Norbert Wiener put it, "Messages are themselves a form of pattern and organization . . . the more probable the message, the less information it gives. Clichés, for example, are less illuminating than great poems."

Randomness, the logic continues, because of its complete unpredictability, represents the highest level of information content and is consequently associated with qualities such as newness and originality—and incoherence. Repetition, at the opposite extreme, because it is completely predictable, represents the lowest level of information content and is consequently associated with qualities such as banality and boredom—and intelligibility. The idea, of course, is to strike somewhere within the range between utter chaos and falling asleep. *Meaning* is somewhere within that range; but after all, the idea of *information*, as discussed in the theory, is not so much in what you say as in what you could possibly say.

Information Theory's association of randomness with originality provided common ground between Cage's and Hiller's work, and retrospectively, it seems almost inevitable that Cage and Hiller should have eventually collaborated. Following the *Illiac Suite*, Hiller finished, among many compositions, *Computer Cantata* (a collaboration with Robert Baker, 1963) and *An Avalanche for Pitchman, Prima Donna, Player Piano, Percussionist and Prerecorded Tape* (based on a script by Frank Parman, 1968). His collaboration with Cage was *HPSCHD*, begun in the fall of 1967 and finished in early 1969. As Cage said, "Jerry Hiller called me from Urbana and said he could arrange for me to do a piece using computer facilities . . . and, since he's had so much experience in the field, the piece has become a collaboration between us . . ." Cage described his concept for the piece:

> The original idea came from a notion I had about Mozart's music and how it differed from Bach's music. In the case of Bach, if one looked at a few measures and at the different voices, they would all be observing

more or less the same scalar movement . . . Whereas, in the case of Mozart . . . one would see the chromatic scale, the diatonic scale, and a use of chords melodically . . . I thought to extend this "moving-away-from-unity" and "moving-towards-multiplicity" . . .

The name *HPSCHD* (HarPSiCHorD, written in upper-case letters as was normal at the time for a computer file name) came about through a commission to Cage from Antoinette Vischer in Switzerland to write a harpsichord piece. It was merely the starting point, however, as the piece grew to something far beyond a harpsichord composition. Cage confessed:

> I must admit I've never particularly liked the instrument. It sounded to me like a sewing machine . . . We have tried—Jerry Hiller and I—to give a quality of fine division not only to the pitches but to the durations and also to the timbre, which will be, in general, imitative of harpsichord sound . . .

In composing the piece, Hiller started by writing a subroutine called ICHING, which generated random numbers between 1 and 64 according to the rules in the *I Ching*. He then wrote three programs. The first was called DICEGAME, which called for random numbers to be generated by ICHING and which was used to produce seven harpsichord scores, or "versions." He explains the process of composing the first five versions:

> The simplest —"Version 1"—is Mozart's *Musical Dice Game* . . . Then there are four versions in which a number of bars of the music were replaced . . . Since the *Musical Dice Game* is 64 bars long—a neat coincidence—we used the ICHING values to designate those bars of the dice game which were to be replaced by other music. For this we selected two sets of compositions. One set provides replacement of Mozart by Mozart. These are passages from sections of his piano sonatas. John went through one of the regular editions of the Mozart piano sonatas and used the *I Ching* to choose which sonata and which movement . . . The two "Mozart versions" differ only in that, in one case, both treble and bass clefs are replaced simultaneously. This is our "hands-together" version. In the more complex version the hands are treated independently, so that it is highly probable . . . that the right hand will be required to play a passage from a different composition than the left hand. Finally, there are the two historical versions. These differ also in that one is "hands-together" and the other is "hands-independent." This time, we replace Mozart's *Musical Dice Game* with music that originates more and more recently in history. This time, the process piles up at the end in a piece which is a combination of Cage and Hiller. John picked his *Winter Music*, and I picked a passage out of an old piano sonata of mine . . . We end up with roughly a 50/50 mixture of the two compositions plus residual material from earlier pieces . . . Beethoven's the *Appassionata Sonata*; the Chopin

Prelude in D minor, Op. 28, No. 24; Schumann's *Reconnaissance* from *Carnival*; Gottschalk's *Banjo*; Ives' *Three-Page Sonata*; Schönberg's *Op. 11, No. 1* . . .

The second program was called HPSCHD, which incorporated subroutines Hiller had devised for *Computer Cantata* and *Algorithms I*, still in progress as of the time he was working on *HPSCHD*. The program HPSCHD was used to define equal-tempered scales of from five to fifty-six notes per octave, then choose pitches and durations in those scales, and then produce the sounds for fifty-one audio tapes, each of twenty minutes' duration, which were to be played back simultaneously, in all or in part, in performance. One of these scales was the normal twelve-note scale which was used once for a tape and then that tape was transcribed for keyboard as *Version 6. Version 7* consisted of the instruction to the performer: "Play anything you desire for 20 minutes."

A performance of *HPSCHD* is the ultimate discotheque. It's not just that any or all of the seven keyboard parts are played simultaneously with as many of the fifty-one tapes as is manageable. It's also the visuals. A performance includes projections of over 5,000 slides of spaceship and rocket technology and abstract designs and films of space technology. The whole thing comes together as an ongoing process with no sections, no structured beginning, and no structured end, as Cage put it, "like the weather." Performances have been typically in the four-hour range, with the musicians and tapes overlapping,

Lejaren Hiller (front, seated) and John Cage (standing between the computer racks, ready to push a button on the tape recorder) composing HPSCHD at the University of Illinois at Urbana in 1968. Photo courtesy The John Cage Trust.

with continual visuals, and with members of the public coming in, staying awhile, going out, coming back, and so on, with the performance decisions made by the performers themselves. Hiller wrote:

> Each tape, once it is started, must run through to its end. Meanwhile, other tapes might be started. Each keyboard performer should select and play through one of the seven versions for keyboard to the end . . . Then he can get up, go out, smoke a cigarette, have a drink—whatever he wants—and, if he feels like it, come back and play the same version again or play another . . .

HPSCHD was first performed in the Assembly Hall at the University of Illinois at Urbana on May 16, 1969, with all seven harpsichord solos, all fifty-one computer-generated tapes, eighty slide projectors, seven film projectors, and 9,000 people in attendance. A twenty-minute version was then recorded and became available commercially, and Hiller's third program, called KNOBS, supplied directions to the listener as to how to manipulate the balance and volume controls of the listener's stereo system. As Hiller said, "It's the first piece that I know of where the home listener's hifi set is integral to the composition." Cage, in general, endorsed the idea of performer collaboration:

> When you get right down to it, a composer is simply someone who tells other people what to do. I find this an unattractive way of getting things done. I'd like our activities to be more social and anarchically so . . .

•

Herbert Brun began to work with electronics in the 1950s. He composed *Anepigraphe* (1958) at the WDR in Cologne and *Klänge unterwegs* (1962, Wayfaring Sounds) at the Siemens studio in Munich. In 1962, he lectured throughout the United States, visiting universities. At his last lecture, at MIT, he met some executives from IBM who took him to the Playboy Club in New York, as he put it, "entertaining a suspicious character." They asked him to write them a letter describing his ideas for using computers to assist composers. He complied. They forwarded the letter to Lejaren Hiller at the University of Illinois. Hiller had just received a grant from the National Science Foundation. He invited Brun to come as a research associate during 1963.

As Brun recalls, "When I arrived at the University of Illinois, Hiller already had a software package for the IBM 7094 which offered algorithms that according to Hiller were the daily fare of thinking composers—algorithms for pitches, durations, timbres, proportions and percentages of events." The package was MUSICOMP. Brun continues, "It was extremely intelligent, far beyond the technology of the time—you could apply it to today's machines and it would not be boring, so I got stuck and thirty years later I'm still a member of the University of Illinois."

Brun composed *Futility 1964*, for tape, in the electronic music studio, and he composed many pieces with MUSICOMP, among them *Sonoriferous Loops* (1964) and *Non Sequitur VI* (1966), both for instruments and electronic sounds on tape. Of *Sonoriferous Loops*, he said:

> My desire was to prove to myself and to Hiller and to other colleagues that I could program a computer with their software so they would recognize it as a piece by Brun. It was a polemic. The idea was in response to rumors that personality can't get through, that you can't compose with a machine. I wanted to show that that's bullshit.

In 1967 and 1968, he studied FORTRAN, experimented in programming, and began to work with the Illiac II computer, built at the University of Illinois. The Illiac II was meant as a transitional device between the Illiac I, which was basically an imitation of the IBM, and the Illiac III, which as he puts it, "could recognize patterns before they happened." He tells it:

> Due to the preoccupation of the engineering department with the Illiac III, we had full use of the Illiac II. And then we joined forces with Gary Grossman, a graduate student in computer science and mathematics and a clarinetist in the music department. I could design something on a piece of paper, and he went home and three days later he came back with a program. I can tell you we had a brilliant year together. It was a festivity. That was for me the first time I practically approached my goal. *Infraudibles* are the traces left by a well-considered universe that I could construct and in which I could connect beginning states to end states without having to specify the in-betweens.
>
> 1968 was the beginning of *Infraudibles* in music and *Mutatis Mutandis* in graphics. *Infraudibles* means "infra-audibles," but also "infraudulent," and *Mutatis Mutandis* is considered a pattern for anybody who would like to use it as a pattern for a composition in whatever medium.

Both *Infraudibles* (1968) and *Mutatis Mutandis* (1968) focus on the process of making music rather than a particular musical result. Of *Infraudibles* Brun writes, "Instead of approaching again the aesthetic question: 'Which process will generate the desired audible event and thus music?' it attempts to deal with the political question: 'What audible events would be generated by desirable processes, and thus music?'" Of *Mutatis Mutandis* he writes:

> A FORTRAN program written by the composer and run on an IBM 7094 generates instructions for the Calcomp plotter to draw various sets of figures. The program simulates a process by which different shapes, each created independently and randomly somewhere on the page, appear to be mutations of one another . . . The graphic displays turn into scores as soon as an interpreter translates their structural characteristics . . . and following the translation re-creates the simulated process by analogy.

Thinking of the 1960s, Brun reflects, "It may be well to remind people today that storage was cumbersome, and you had to punch cards, and these cards were frequently victims of mutilation, and before you corrected a mistake you had to find the card, and this took enormous amounts of time—but it also gave occasion to think a lot."

•

In 1956, Iannis Xenakis coined the term *stochastic music* to describe music based on the laws of probabilities and the laws of large numbers. In his orchestral composition *Achorripsis* (1957), the occurrences and characters of musical elements such as timbre, pitch, loudness, and duration were scattered throughout the composition according to a Poisson distribution. He wrote:

> The laws of the calculus of probabilities entered composition through musical necessity. But other paths also led to the same stochastic crossroads—first of all, natural events such as the collision of hail and rain with hard surfaces, or the song of cicadas in a summer field. These sonic events are made out of thousands of isolated sounds; this multitude of sounds, seen as a totality, is a new sonic event. This mass event is articulated and forms a plastic mold of time, which itself follows aleatory and stochastic laws.

Xenakis' examples of "the collision of hail and rain with hard surfaces, or the song of cicadas in a summer field" depict situations in which there is such a complexity of underlying causalities that our ability to track and analyze individual causalities is overwhelmed and our only recourse is to understand events in terms of likelihoods and distributions within a statistical whole. For Xenakis, the "calculus of probabilities" was a tool for controlling a complexity of musical events. By specifying a certain distribution, for example, he could cause any number of events to fall into place.

In 1961, through friends in Paris, he made contact with IBM-France, which gave him a place and the tools to continue his work. As he said, "I was interested in automating what I had done before, mass events like *Metastasis*— so I saw the computer as a tool, a machine that could make easier the things I was working with, and I thought perhaps I could discover new things." He wrote:

> In most human relations it is rarely pure logical persuasion which is important; usually the paramount consideration is material interest. Now in this case it was not logic, much less self-interest, that arranged the betrothal, but purely experiment for experiment's sake . . . Yet the doors were opened, and at the end of a year and a half of contacts and hard work "the most unusual event witnessed by the firm or by this musical season [in Paris]" took place on 24 May 1962 at the headquarters of IBM-France.

The "most unusual event" was a concert, performed by the Ensemble de Musique Contemporaine de Paris and conducted by Konstantin Simonovic ("brilliantly," according to Xenakis), of the music that Xenakis had composed at IBM-France. Among his computer-generated compositions of that period were *ST/48-1,240162* (1962), for forty-eight instruments; *Amorsima-Morsima* (1962), for ten instruments; and *Atrées* (1962), for ten instruments. And was it necessary to use a computer? Xenakis answers:

> Freed from tedious calculations the composer is able to devote himself to the general problems that the new musical form poses and to explore the nooks and crannies of this form while modifying the values of the input data. For example, he may test all instrumental combinations from soloists to chamber orchestras, to large orchestras. With the aid of electronic computers the composer becomes a sort of pilot: he presses the buttons, introduces coordinates, and supervises the controls of a cosmic vessel sailing in the space of sound, across sonic constellations and galaxies that he could formerly glimpse only as a distant dream. Now he can explore them all at his ease, seated in an armchair.

•

In the early 1960s, while working at the WDR studio in Cologne, Gottfried Michael Koenig began to study computer programming. He started to write PR1 (Project 1) because, in his words, "I needed to make a program, and so I thought it would be good to do it in music." When he moved to Utrecht in 1964, he brought the software with him. He recalls:

> I worked on it continuously. By 1967, PR1 was finished in its first version and could be used. I had invented a structure which I could have written out as a piece of music. For me, PR1 was a composition, a structure, based on rules—but where the rules could be used to create another piece. In fact, I realized that I could write at the same time many other pieces.

In fact, Koenig used PR1 to compose instrumental solos and chamber music as well as electronic music, including a large orchestra piece called *Beitrag* (1986, Contribution). Meanwhile, in 1968, he began to work on a second program called PR2 (Project 2). He describes it:

> Actually . . . this was a testing environment, not a composing machine, but of course I could only test it by composing music with it. I did about three pieces with PR2. But I made most of my pieces with PR1, because PR2 was a long complicated program and PR1 was easier to use.

PR1 grew out of serialist ideas. As Koenig said, "The model was intended to carry on from serial technique, based on my own experience as a composer . . ." Serialism was based on a *parametric* description of sound, where a parameter was an attribute of sound such as pitch, loudness, duration, or timbre. Koenig began to design PR1 by identifying the parameters with which he wanted to work. As he said, "I took only the most basic elementary parameters, like something about the instrument, the pitch, the octave position of the pitch, the loudness, and time, and restricted myself to the time between the attacks of notes, what I called *entry delay*." In other words, the aspects of a musical process that were of concern to him were timbre ("something about the instrument"), pitch (chosen from the twelve pitches), the octave in which the pitch was played, the loudness with which the pitch was played, and the timings between the beginnings of the notes ("what I called *entry delay*") which determined rhythm. Rhythm did not include the durations of notes. If a note was longer than an entry delay, it overlapped the following sounds, forming a chord.

He then began to devise methods for changing the parameters' values during the course of a composition. In serialism, each parameter's value at any point in time was determined by the series on which the composition was based. Koenig continues:

> PR1 was meant to replace the very strict idea of a series, a preset order of musical values, by a space in which the potential of any parameter was to change in any way. Suppose I wanted to fill the space of an octave with notes. I could have done it with a preset series—and I realized that any series could be read in any order—but I discarded the idea of one series because I realized that what comes first is not necessarily the cause of that which follows. And I realized I could replace a series with random numbers.

Koenig's problem, then, was defining a general principle for organizing values. He began to think in terms of regular and irregular patterns. *Regular* patterns were repetitive. *Irregular* patterns were nonrepetitive. As he said, "I made regularity and irregularity as extremes with five steps in between." Koenig, in other words, devised a pattern scale based on ascending degrees of unpredictability. Step 1 was nonrepetitive and unpredictable. Step 7 was repetitive. Step 4 was in the middle. As he said, "In step 4, I invented a kind of bridging function which brought it together, so there's a balanced mixture between regular and irregular events." Regular and irregular patterns could be applied simultaneously to different parameters and interchanged: "You could have an irregular structure in pitch and a regular structure in rhythm, so each was completely interchangeable."

In summary, Koenig defined parameters and specified rules. As an output from the program, he received a numerical printout that contained a series of values for each of the parameters. He then evaluated the patterns and applied them to the specific musical composition he was working on at the time, whether electronic or instrumental.

Through the late 1960s and into the 1970s, the program went through various changes and developments. In Koenig's words, "I opened it up more and more to give the composer more influence in the input data, and to give room for the way parameter values are selected before they're put into that score." In 1978, Koenig extended the program so that it could be used in conjunction with the VOSIM oscillators, at which point the output was sound. The extended program was called PR1X. Then, following a composers' workshop in the summer of 1978, he made further modifications resulting in PR1XM, finished in 1979. He used PR1XM and VOSIM to compose *Output* (1979) which, in fact, grew directly from his experiments. He explains:

> Although I was not trying to compose a piece of music, I was intrigued by a particular result (=output). I took a closer look at it, adjusting the input data slightly and finally arrived at a sonic structure which was both typical and aesthetically satisfying.

•

In 1970 at Koenig's invitation, Otto Laske went to work in Utrecht. He began by working with PR1 and using the analog studio. At that time, there were no rules, no customs, no textbooks, no guidelines for linking sounds, and certain questions occurred to him. Are there rules that apply to linking sounds? How do these new musical tools affect the way we think about music? Laske continues:

> I started being interested in generative grammars for music. Pierre Schaeffer had investigated how sound was structured by and in itself and suggested a taxonomy of *objets sonores*. He also said that what really was needed was a treatise on how musical objects are linked to one another. That's what I wanted to do. I wanted to investigate linkages between sounds by investigation into the musical process, because that's where the linkage occurred.
>
> For me, then, there were three notions that took on equal relevance: *competence*, *performance*, and *task environment*. Competence is knowledge of musical grammar, a knowledge of sound linkages. Performance is doing, it's observable activity, the expression of competence. The task environment is the environment in which performance is done. It structures our thinking, our doing. We are interacting with it so we cannot help but be inspired by it, constrained by it. In electronic music, it is something that can be designed to a composer's liking. When I choose a program to work with, I'm designing my task environment. The electronic music studio's relevance is not in its physical configuration but in the fact that it was an environment that one could redesign and choose and be aware of as a set of constraints that informed one's work.

As Laske developed his theory through the 1970s and 1980s, in experiments, articles, and papers, he focused increasingly on enlarging his concept of performance to include what he called *biography*, by which he meant the wide range of experiential influences that cause a composer to make a particular set of musical decisions. His work is distinctive because it represents the first substantial investigation into the process of composing. As Laske said in the mid-1990s, "With hindsight, I realize that my main interest was always in creativity . . ."

•

As Barry Truax put it, referring to the beginning of his electronic music studies at the University of British Columbia, "I walked in as a refugee from physics and math." According to Truax, electronic music was not yet a well-established field of endeavor in western Canada, and as he added, "It wasn't that obvious that you could be interested in music and science and technology and not be a candidate for a psychiatrist's couch." He finished a graduate degree and, in 1971, went to Utrecht for further study. He arrived just when the PDP-15 arrived. He describes the environment:

> It was a wonderful opportunity. Koenig was teaching us programming almost as fast as he was learning it himself. And there was the concept of real time, the idea that you could sit at a clunky old teletype and program a single-user system where in menu fashion you'd be asked a series of questions, you'd provide some data, and you could try some algorithmic approaches.

At the time, Gottfried Michael Koenig was teaching programming and compositional theory, Stan Tempelaars was teaching psychoacoustics, Frits Weiland and Jaap Vink were teaching analog studio techniques, and Otto Laske was developing a theory of music as a dynamic creative process. Laske's work was particularly influential. As Truax said, "Laske was seeing music as an activity, as something that people did, and he was saying that we should be studying musical behavior, as against musical artifacts."

Truax began to develop the POD (POisson Distribution) programs. As he recalls, "The original printouts were tiny little subroutines where I used Poisson distributions to create two-dimensional frequency-time scores." Then, in 1973, John Chowning visited Utrecht. He played *Turenas*, visited the computer facility, and said, as Truax recalls, "There's a better way—it's called FM." And that encounter led Truax to introduce dynamically changing sounds into the POD system. As he recalls, "A couple of months later, I had a realtime version of FM worked out." During that period, he finished *She, a Solo* (1973), for mezzo-soprano and tape, in the analog studio, and *Gilgamesh* (1974), a major work involving singers, chorus, narrator, instruments, and twelve tapes, one of which was done with the POD system.

As the POD programs developed, it became increasingly clear to Truax that they offered the distinctive advantage of powerful controls. He referred to it as "top down" composing:

> I could say, "I want five sounds per second in this frequency range," and I could do that without having to specify every event. I could suddenly

create something from the top down. And this is one of the beauties of algorithmic composition. After all, if you get out only what you put in, why do it? Why bother with the computer if it just produces the specification that you've given it?

Indeed, *algorithmic composition*, as computer-automated composition came to be called, was a process- rather than result-oriented way to compose. A composer specified an algorithm and the algorithm composed the piece, and it was a reasonable expectation that the result would exceed what the composer could have done without the computer.

•

Algorithmic approaches to composition were in the air. And algorithms, in the sense of procedures that automatically generate information, were not always written in software. Hugh Le Caine's *Serial Structure Sound Generator*, designed in collaboration with Gustav Ciamaga and built in 1968, was as Ciamaga describes it, "a huge collection of sequencers and associated custom-designed modules for pitch, amplitude, filtering, speed, modulation, control of the multi-track tape recorder, control of any analog sound source, sound rotation in space—the concept was to link an entire studio to one variable time structure through several clocks." The concept was also that the modules

The Serial Structure Sound Generator, built by Hugh Le Caine with Gustav Ciamaga's collaboration in 1968, as installed at the University of Toronto Electronic Music Studio. Photo courtesy Gustav Ciamaga.

could be interconnected in any particular way, forming thereby an "analog algorithm" that would automatically generate information.

Larry Austin, along with many other composers at the time, had similar thoughts. He remembers:

> Through the late 1960s, I was fascinated by process. The process itself was more important than the compositional content. These were unending forms, automatons, unending music, music without a beginning and music without an end, and music without a denouement, music that was of the moment . . .

In 1969, Austin bought a Buchla synthesizer and began to create a series of pieces which incorporated automated analog synthesizer processes. The pieces included *Quartet Three* (1971) and *Primal Hybrid* (1972), both of which were performed onto tape and edited, and several performance and theatrical pieces including *Walter* (1971), for viola, viola d'amore, tape, and films; *Prelude and Postlude to Plastic Surgery* (1971), for keyboards, film, and tape; and *First Fantasy on Ives' Universe Symphony—The Earth* (1975), for double brass quintet, narrator, and tape. Austin continues:

> I made music that was unpredictable in its event and timbral characteristics. I used the sequencer, and interrupted it with the touch controller so that the rate at which it was sequencing could be controlled by my performance. I also used Buchla's pink noise generator at control frequencies. I called the whole thing "the composing machine," although it was actually an improvising machine. What I wanted to do was to have a whole bunch of sequencers and automated processes going at once and at different speeds, and I wanted these to interact, so that each process would interact with another process. My model was improvisation. I had gotten the machine to improvise.

• • •

Chapter Eleven

Interaction

In 1966, I got an idea. I drew up a plan for a completely automated synthesizer system, discussed its feasibility with Robert Moog, described it in an article in *Perspectives of New Music*, and got the funding to have it built. That system, which I called the CEMS (Coordinated Electronic Music Studio) System, was ordered from Moog in 1967 and installed in the electronic music studio at the State University of New York at Albany in December 1969. In addition to an extended array of sound-generating and processing modules, an automated matrix mixer, and a digital clock, the system contained a bank of eight analog sequencers with customized logic hardware for running them synchronously, asynchronously, in succession, or in any combination. A distinction of sorts, it was the world's largest concentration of Moog sequencers under a single roof, and after a few months, I was able to program a pseudo-random process sufficiently complex to automate an entire composition. In *Drift* (1970), for example, icy electronic sounds swooped automatically through a virtual space without my intervention or control. It was the realtime equivalent of algorithmic composition. I simply listened while the system was producing sound and while it was deciding what sounds to produce.

In a performance of *Ideas of Movement at Bolton Landing* (1971) a few months later, I was using joysticks to control oscillators, filters, modulators, amplifiers, and several sequencers. The sequencers, configured to generate pseudo-random patterns, were also controlling the oscillators, filters, modulators, and amplifiers. And I was also controlling the sequencers. It was a com-

Joel Chadabe working with the CEMS (Coordinated Electronic Music Studio) System at State University of New York at Albany in 1970. Photo by Carl Howard.

plex network of modular interconnections which, as intended, caused a certain balance between predictability and surprise. Because I was sharing control of the music with the sequencers, I was only partially controlling the music, and the music, consequently, contained surprising as well as predictable elements. The surprising elements made me react. The predictable elements made me feel that I was exerting some control. It was like conversing with a clever friend who was never boring but always responsive. I was, in effect, conversing with a musical instrument that seemed to have its own interesting personality.

Echoes (1972) was a different specific instance of the same general approach. In a performance of *Echoes*, sounds played by an instrumentalist—at different times percussionist Jan Williams, violinist Paul Zukofsky, cellist David Gibson, and trombonist James Fulkerson—were delayed for a few seconds in a tape delay system, then randomly transformed through electronic processing, and then randomly routed to four loudspeakers around the performance space. Williams, for example, would play something, and a few seconds later, a transformed echo from somewhere in the space would provide him with a cue for how to play the next sound. What was it like to perform *Echoes*? Williams describes it:

> It demanded a new performance technique, attaching the microphone to a stick and holding the stick under my arm so I had both hands free. And

it was a whole new thing, a whole new way of thinking about what I was going to play. I wasn't sure what was actually going to come back to me in the performance. So it wasn't a kind of thing I could really rehearse. I remember that we developed strategies for a performance, rather than specific musical results. And it came naturally, deciding which sounds to play next. It was deciding on the spot what I was going to do. Sometimes I got in trouble and sometimes something didn't happen so I tried something else. It was a very dynamic performance situation.

In the following few years, the hardware systems I used in performance became smaller and more portable thanks in large part to *Daisy*, a compact pseudo-random signal generator built for me in 1972 by visual artist and electronics designer John Roy. We carried Daisy instead of the sequencers to concerts. In 1976, the studio acquired a small PDP-11 computer, and Roger Meyers, a student in electronic music, joined me as a partner in developing software. Meyers and I set up a hybrid system, and in the summer of 1977, we wrote the PLAY Program, basically a software sequencer that we could run on the PDP-11 to control the analog synthesizer.

Meanwhile, years earlier and at my request, soprano Irene Oliver had recorded a tape of spirituals. I played her tape through the computer system. Meyers wrote software that tracked the pitches that she sang. I configured the equipment so that the software would control the analog equipment in transforming the vocal sounds to produce, if not exactly an accompaniment, perhaps, a *setting*. The result, which I called *Settings for Spirituals* (1977), was an unusual combination of tradition and technology.

In traditional composition, music is typically composed before it is performed. *Drift, Ideas of Movement at Bolton Landing, Echoes*, and *Settings for Spirituals* grew out of a very untraditional approach to using technology. They were different examples of what I referred to at the time as a *design-then-do* process. The design stage was the specification of the system that would produce the music, which included a definition of the nature of the performer's interactions. Working with the CEMS System, the design stage was a matter of configuring module settings and interconnections and deciding what a performer would do. The do stage was the functioning of the system to compose and simultaneously perform the music.

•

Meanwhile, in the mid-1960s at the University of Illinois, Salvatore Martirano was building his own instruments, first because there was so much electronic building and designing going on in Urbana and, second, because in his words, "My father was a builder of public buildings, so building was part of my growing up—building instruments was a normal idea for me." Martirano had built a spatialization system to use in *Underworld* (1965), for actors, instruments, and tape. During that same period in 1964 and 1965, he had also been working with a piano technician at the University of Illinois to build a piano-harp in which each string would have a dedicated magnetic pickup. The harp was vertical so that it could be played on the piano keys or plucked on the strings from a sitting position. As Martirano explained, "I always thought that the pianist's behind from a standing position leaning over a normal grand to pluck the strings was most unattractive and distracting for the listener—the idea behind this instrument was, once we had the string sound electronically amplified, to go through signal processing of some kind."

At the same time that Martirano was beginning to build instruments, his sense of musical structure was evolving. As he put it, "Serialism was in the air, it was all around," and his early interest in serialism had evolved, by the time of *Cocktail Music* (1962), for solo piano, into a system of underlying patterns and permutations. Martirano explains:

> There's the presentation of an idea and then the complement of that idea. Sometimes the complement is presented later, and at a certain point the complement is implied and not presented at all. So the question comes up of how far you are going to be able to trace the pattern. It's almost like a test.

In 1966, he saw a demonstration of the Heathkit Analog/Digital Designer, a device designed to help someone learn digital logic. He read Malmstadt and Enke's *Digital Electronics for Scientists*. In 1967, he built *The Malmstadt Enke Blues*, an instrument based on algorithms and pattern manipulation and, with video artist Steve Beck, performed several concerts. He then got in touch with James Divilbiss, principal engineer for the Illiac II, a parallel-processing computer built at the University of Illinois. Divilbiss, who was at the time developing a computerized machine to punch holes in player piano rolls, had a strong interest in music.

In 1968, Martirano and Divilbiss built the *Marvil Construction*, a real-time performance instrument, a sketch of what was to come. In 1969, they began work on the *SalMar Construction*. One of Martirano's concerns was how it would be played. He discussed the issue with Divilbiss: "I was talking with him and said, 'You know, it'd be really good to have a touch-sensitive switch.'" Divilbiss developed a touch-sensitive switch, and as Martirano recalls, "the interesting thing was that it could be both manually and logically driven—that was very important because it placed the performer in the loop allowing user-machine interaction."

Divilbiss then recommended that they expand the collaboration to include Sergio Franco, who eventually based his PhD dissertation on it. The team quickly grew to become Martirano, Divilbiss, Franco, Richard Borovec (who had been chief engineer for the Illiac II), and Jay Barr (technician for Bell Telephone). Everyone made contributions. Divilbiss designed, sketched, donated salvaged electronic components from a computer fire at the University of Illinois digital computer lab, and had the switches built in the computer shop. Franco designed the analog cards. Barr wire-wrapped the digital logic boards. Martirano designed the data-generating circuits. And Borovec designed the multiplexer for the distribution of sound through twenty-four loudspeakers. Eventually Josef Sekon and Terry Mohn, both composers, came into the project.

All of the circuits of the SalMar Construction were mounted in a large two-section metal frame. The lower section was a control console that contained a large plasterboard surface of touch-sensitive switches, lights which indicated whether the switches were on or off, and digital control circuits. Martirano describes the logical process: "A data base, consisting of a programmable-width shift register whose parallel output fed a programmable-width Exclusive Or gate, whose output fed the serial input of the shift register, produced number sequences—this was organized such that sequences controlled sequences in a tree from macro to micro." The top section contained the analog cards (oscillators, filters, amplifiers) for sound generation and shaping, and there was a patching matrix which connected the digital control circuits on the bottom to the sound-generating electronics on top. Emanating outward from the body of the instrument were audio connections to twenty-four polyplanar loudspeakers—thin and light, typically hanging from the ceiling of the performance space about fifteen feet apart—and four large loudspeakers to boost the bass.

The SalMar Construction was finished in 1972. In performance, Martirano stood or sat in front of the control console and moved a finger over the switches. There were 291 switches multiplexed to control four concurrently running programs. The programs controlled the four voices in any of four

This photo of the SalMar Construction was taken in Salvatore Martirano's studio in Urbana, Illinois, in 1977. Note the complexity of patchcord connections between the performance panel and the synthesizer circuit boards in the top racks. Photo by Joel Chadabe.

different tuning modes. Some switches were dedicated to cause change in all four programs, while others affected change in only one program depending upon the level of control Martirano had selected. The control system had a "zoom-lens" characteristic in that Martirano could move from level to level throughout the control hierarchy, from macrostructure to microstructure. "In performance," he said, "I can change my relationship to the sound by zooming in on a microprocess, fiddle around, change the process or not, remain there or turn my attention to another process . . ." And the sounds whizzed through the network of loudspeakers in four simultaneous paths. How did it feel to perform? He answers:

> It was too complex to analyze. But it was possible to predict what sound would result, and this caused me to lightly touch or slam a switch as if this had an effect. Control was an illusion. But I was in the loop. I was trading swaps with the logic. I enabled paths. Or better, I steered. It was like driving a bus.

●

The CEMS System and the SalMar Construction were the first interactive composing instruments, which is to say that they made musical decisions, or at least *seemed* to make musical decisions, as they produced sound and as they responded to a performer. These instruments were interactive in the sense that performer and instrument were mutually influential. The performer was influenced by the music produced by the instrument, and the instrument was influenced by the performer's controls. These instruments introduced the concept of shared, symbiotic control of a musical process wherein the instrument's generation of ideas and the performer's musical judgment worked together to shape the overall flow of the music.

The CEMS System was a general-purpose system of modules that was configured into a specific instrument for a specific composition. The SalMar Construction was always a specific instrument producing a specific composition. But the idea was the same. When an instrument is configured or built to play one composition, however the details of that composition might change from performance to performance, and when that music is interactively composed while it is being performed, distinctions fade between instrument and music, composer and performer. The instrument is the music. The composer is the performer. The thought brings to mind the words from a Yeats poem: "How can we know the dancer from the dance?"

●

In November 1977, I drove to New England Digital Corporation in Norwich, Vermont, and drove away with a Synclavier. It was not, however, a normal Synclavier. It was a computer-and-synthesizer system which allowed for developing original software and connecting a wide variety of performance devices. In early 1978, Roger Meyers designed a software structure for the flexible and interactive scheduling of musical events. I began to compose *Solo* (1978), which meant writing a specific program within Meyers' structure. Here is my description of the way it worked:

> My software automatically composed the notes of a melody. The melodic concept was based on a clarinet improvisation by J. D. Parran that I had heard in New York, notes scurrying through wide register and tempo changes. In *Solo*, eight electronic voices—two clarinet sounds, two flute sounds, and four vibraphone sounds—converged and diverged around the melody.
>
> I performed with two proximity-sensitive antennas, actually theremins modified to communicate with the computer without themselves making sounds. The first antennas, built for me by Robert Moog, were about five feet in height and a half inch in diameter. Later, I used Volkswagen car antennas, which could be collapsed into an equipment case for carrying to concerts. In a performance, the antennas were placed on the stage about three feet apart. As I moved my right hand towards or away from the right antenna, I controlled tempo by increasing or decreasing the duration of each note. As I moved my left hand towards or away from the left antenna, I controlled timbre by bringing in or fading out the different sounds. The gestures of moving my arms in the air to control tempo and cue instruments in or out reinforced the performance metaphor of conducting an orchestra. It was, in fact, an "improvising" orchestra. I would cue two "clarinets" to play slowly, for example, but I could not foresee what chord they would play. I was always performing the *next* note on the basis of the last note. And because I could not predict the instrument's contribution, I could not completely predict the result, so I would be

Joel Chadabe performing Solo (1978) in 1979 at The Kitchen in New York City. The antennas were modified theremins made for Chadabe by Robert Moog, and Chadabe is using them to "conduct" the musical processes generated by the Synclavier system on the table behind him. Photo by Carlo Carnevali.

reacting to what I heard in deciding how to perform yet the next event. It was like a conversation with a clever friend.

I did several other compositions with the Synclavier system, among them *Playthings* (1978), an interactive installation where the public was invited to play with the antennas; *Scenes from Stevens* (1979), a reference to Wallace Stevens' poetry; *Several Views of an Elusive Lady* (1985), for soprano and tape; and *Bar Music* (1985), played on a keyboard with some of the keys used as control keys. I worked extensively in performance with Jan Williams, percussionist, in *Rhythms* (1980) and *Follow Me Softly* (1984). But it was *Solo* that most closely followed from the interactive concepts of the earlier *Ideas of Movement at Bolton Landing* and *Echoes*. It was *Solo*, consequently, that best represented the idea of interactive composing. In 1981, I was invited to deliver a keynote address at the International Music and Technology Conference in Melbourne, Australia. In preparing for that conference, I coined the term *interactive composing* to describe a performance process wherein a performer shares control of the music by interacting with a musical instrument.

•

GAIV (Groupe Arts et Informatique de Vincennes / Computer Arts Group of Vincennes) was founded in 1969 by Patrick Greussay, composer, and Hervé Huitric, painter, at the Université de Paris VIII à Vincennes. They were soon joined by several others, among them painters, poets, a filmmaker, and musicians, and GAIV became a loose association of several people linked by their interest in using computers in the arts. The members of GAIV produced events, exchanged ideas, and in general worked together. Giuseppe Englert joined in the spring of 1974. As he remembers, "The equipment was terribly primitive—the only output was a line printer, so the painters made graphs which were later painted by hand and the musicians printed schemes for improvisation."

In 1974, GAIV was given an Intel 8008, one of the early small computers. It was programmed at first by toggling switches to input machine code. Then an old teletype was acquired, and Patrick Greussay wrote an assembly language called *Intelgreu* (*Intel* + the beginning of *Greu*ssay). DACS were built so that the system could be used to control analog synthesizers. As Englert recalls, "We had four or five VCS-3s, and we could hook them together and control them with the Intel, which allowed us to travel and do live performances—we did group concerts in France, Italy, Germany, and Switzerland from 1974 to 1977." Englert had bought a VCS-3 as early as 1970 and in collaboration with his students at the university had composed several pieces, among them *Exemple* (1970, Example) and *Expérience pour Como* (1970, Experiment for Como). And his collaborations with other GAIV composers—which by the mid-1970s included, in addition to Englert and Greussay, Jacques Arveiller, Marc Battier, Gilbert Dalmasso, and Didier Roncin—moved him closer toward automated, interactive, and collaborative systems, culminating in a group performance on January 10, 1978 at the Porte de la Suisse in Paris, called *Sept heures d'activités continues autour de mini-ordinateurs . . .* (Seven hours of continuous activity involving mini-computers . . .) to which Englert contributed *Girolles et Autres Champignons* (1978, Girolles and Other Mushrooms). Englert's pieces during this period were largely based on ideas developed in four programs—called *Melanzane, Fragola, Basil 2,* and *Girolle,* referring respectively to eggplant and strawberry in Italian and basil and a type of mushroom in French—doubtless finished and named late at night after a dinnerless evening and/or, as Englert points out, named according to his sense of "time definition referring to the season's fruits or mushrooms."

There was a major advance in 1978. As Englert tells it, "I bought a Synclavier and put it at the disposition of the group, and, of course, that stimulated the activity of the group enormously, both in the quality and quantity of the compositions done—there have been periods that the Synclavier was working twenty-four hours a day, seven days a week, including Christmas Eve and New Year's Eve, and for some of my colleagues, this opened up a new world of possibility for them to express their musical thoughts." Didier Roncin then built a sixteen-channel control device consisting of two joysticks and twelve sliders, which was, as Englert described it, "the ideal tool for realtime performance for all members of GAIV." Englert wrote his own software for the Synclavier, which allowed him great freedom in making unusual sounds: "I could invent even sounds that could not exist in nature, sounds that live, that are never static, that are constantly moving—I wanted to hear sounds that I had never heard before and that did not imitate any sound that I had heard before."

But he had equal concerns for performance interaction: "When I wrote software for electronic music, I reserved the necessary space for realtime interaction because I knew that I would be the performer of the composition." Englert, in other words, saw a composition as an interactive system. He said: "We can, then, describe composition as the realization of a network of interactive processes that engender other, equally interactive processes such that the musician is just a link in the chain of processes." In performing his *Juralpyroc* (1981), the software made choices for sound contours, durations, timbre structures, and pitches according to probabilistic algorithms, and Englert, performing at a computer terminal, interactively weighted the probabilities, causing the program to produce *more probably* certain specific results. He continues:

> They are neither musical sequences nor sound events that I formulate in my computer programs. I program algorithms, criteria for decision, scales of priorities in case of conflict, choices within a determined field of possibilities. The computer can act autonomously to compose my music, but only up to a point. At that point, I intervene . . .

And as time went on, Englert's thoughts and music evolved. His electronic compositions during the period included *Quatuor 'S'* (1979), *Les Dits d'Amenhotep XIX* (1980), *Suite Ocre* (1984), and *Model 'S'* (1984). He continues:

> Pretty soon I had the feeling that manual intervention from my side corresponded to a weak point in the program. In other words, that I was nec-

essary to optimize the program's decisions and operations. If the program were perfect, it should be capable of making all decisions during a performance without me being there. A utopia, of course. But my ultimate goal was utopian. It was to write the perfect program. I am the beneficiary of a western music education to such an extent that the feeling of right proportions concerning density, time and sound in a musical discourse has become part of my being. Now, if I want to write the perfect program, I have to be able to formulate what I have almost unconsciously inside me as rules that the computer can follow.

In Englert's reasoning, a computer can follow those rules to their logical ends and think of things that the composer has not thought of or remembered or experienced. He concludes: "The perfect program will think as I think but it will be more original because it will not be constrained by the limitations imposed on me by my memory."

•

Meanwhile, at Mills College in the mid-1970s, the League of Automatic Music Composers, and then The Hub, developed ideas of interactivity in the context of networked computers. The League, as it was often called, came together at first through the mutual interests of Jim Horton, John Bischoff, and Rich Gold, all of whom had been graduate students at Mills during the early 1970s. Horton was the ringleader. His first public appearance with a KIM-1 computer was in October 1976 at the Exploratorium in San Francisco. Jim Horton and John Bischoff tell the story:

JH: I had seen an ad in an electronics magazine for a computer on a board for $250. I borrowed the money and sent off for it, with a coupon. And, sure enough, UPS showed up with this little computer.

JB: I remember seeing Jim's computer on his table. It was like science fiction.

JH: It was like an underground frenzy. There was a huge number of people interested in this kind of music, and it all seemed to fit in with the Mills scene. So in 1977, Rich Gold had his system set up and I had my system set up, and we started hooking them up together. And then, within a couple of months, John Bischoff and I had interconnected computers.

JB: I'd gotten my KIM-1 through my contact with Jim, and I made a piece making sounds and pitches based on random numbers. It was all automatic.

JH: When John wasn't playing, my system would play just-intoned melodies, and then when I received something from John's system, I would use that as the tonic tone for a system of harmonies. And then we'd steer it around a little bit with the keyboards, trying to trick the system into being well behaved . . .

In early 1978, Horton and Bischoff played a concert at Saint John's Church in Berkeley. In May 1978, they played separately at the Blind Lemon,

The League of Automatic Music Composers in concert at Fort Mason,
San Francisco, 1980. Left to right: Tim Perkis, Jim Horton, John
Bischoff. Photo by Peter Abramowitsch. Courtesy John Bischoff.

an old blues place in Berkeley that had been turned into a new music spot. On
July 2, 1978, Horton, Bischoff, and Rich Gold played a concert together and
for the first time called themselves the League of Automatic Music Composers.
In February 1979, they began to present concerts every other Sunday afternoon
at the Finnish Hall in Berkeley. As Horton describes it, "They used to have
communist party meetings in the back of the hall, but they were elderly com-
munists—they were doing posters on how bad the health care system was, and
so on, so we would set our equipment up on a table, and people would come
in and sit around, and we'd talk, and we'd demonstrate what we were doing."
Rich Gold dropped out after the first few weeks, and Tim Perkis, a video artist,
joined the group.

During the period 1979 to 1983, the League concertized extensively in
the Bay Area. One memorable concert was at the New Music America Festival
in 1981 at Japan Center in San Francisco. Perkis begins the tale of woe: "We
went out on stage and turned up the volume and nothing happened—the guy
in the sound booth couldn't believe that it was what he should be hearing, so
he refused to turn up the sound." And Horton continues, "He just couldn't
believe that anyone would play music like this, so he thought he was helping
us—oh, what a disaster!"

The group ended its activities in 1983, partly because Jim Horton
dropped out for reasons of health and partly because, as Bischoff reflects,
"We'd played for quite a while, and it was time to move on." Perkis observes,
"It had just run its course." In 1982, shortly before the group disbanded, Chris
Brown was driving up Franklin Street in San Francisco listening to the League
play on KPFA. "It just knocked me out," he said later, "it was electronic, but it

had this feeling of improvised music, that everyone was talking at the same time and everyone was listening at the same time, and I thought, 'How did they do this?'" They had done it, in fact, with great difficulty. Connecting their computers together for a concert had been a wire-by-wire matter. As Perkis remembers, "It took hours to set up."

The idea of computer-network music, however, remained so compelling even after the official dissolution of the League that they all continued to think about how to make connectivity easier. And then Perkis got an idea. In 1984, he and Bischoff built a connecting box and called it *The Hub*. They used it in a concert in August 1985 at The Lab in San Francisco. And it gave rise to a new group, also called The Hub, formed by Tim Perkis, John Bischoff, Scot Gresham-Lancaster, Phil Stone, Chris Brown, and Mark Trayle.

As a matter of normal procedure, each member of The Hub would design a piece that would be played cooperatively by everyone. In Phil Stone's *Is It Borrowing or Stealing?* (1987), each player played a melody of his own choosing and electronically reported to the group what he was playing, whereupon the other players were free to borrow or steal this melodic information and use it in some way. In Tim Perkis' *The Minister of Pitch* (1988), one player was responsible for making rhythmic decisions, another for pitch relationships, and yet another for different aspects of the timbre. As Bischoff sums it up, "The emphasis was on the network being a shared instrument." Brown adds, "Pieces done by The Hub defined ways of interacting." And Gresham-Lancaster devised a MIDI interface system that served to coordinate the group's communications, allowing everyone in the group to write his own software and use his own computer and synthesizer.

The group's interactions, in short, were modeled not on a normal music improvisation group but on a shared, interactive network. It was a particularly appealing idea that metaphorically suggested a global-village method for bringing individuals, even individuals with different personalities and ways of working, together in an active collaboration.

•

In 1975, the Merce Cunningham Dance Company commissioned David Behrman to compose *Voice with Melody-Driven Electronics*. Behrman had been a touring musician with the company since 1970 and, like David Tudor, had been designing and building his own instruments. For *Voice with Melody-Driven Electronics*, he built an array of pitch sensors that controlled special circuits which switched chords from one preset tuning to another, so that when an instrumentalist or singer hit a preset pitch, the chords would change in pitch and loudness. As Behrman put it, "Very simple, minimal music." There were three specific pieces based on this idea: *Voice with Melody-Driven Electronics*, for Joan La Barbara; *Cello with Melody-Driven Electronics*, for David Gibson; and *Trumpet with Melody-Driven Electronics*, for Gordon Mumma. Merce Cunningham, incidentally, supported his musicians. As Behrman recalls, "Occasionally, the Cunningham musicians would give concerts produced by the company in conjunction with a tour—I remember in early 1975 they flew David Gibson out to Chicago to perform cello in a performance of my *Cello with Melody-Driven Electronics*."

Then Behrman started to work with a computer. As he tells it, "I went to work at Mills College in 1975, and in 1976 these little computer kits came out and you could actually buy one and experiment with it—the Bay Area atmosphere was very supportive of the idea of using small, inexpensive new micro-

The photo on the left shows David Behrman in his studio in 1977 with a KIM-1 computer and his system of sound modules.
The photo below is a closer view of the sound modules.
Photos by Joel Chadabe.

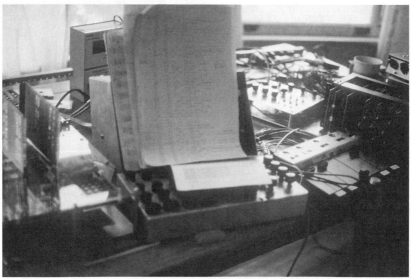

computers, and there were people around who knew about them, like Paul DeMarinis, Jim Horton, John Bishoff, Bob Gonsalves, and Frankie Mann, and so I got a KIM-1 computer and started learning how to program it."

The benefit of the KIM-1 was greater musical flexibility and ease in trying things out. As Behrman said, "I had a strong interest in the changing states of networks of logic gates and overlapping events—my musical interest was in harmonic changes that were made partially by willful actions and partly by automatic circuits, so now I could easily change in software the processes that I'd developed in earlier pieces in hardware, like melody-driven electronics." His *On the Other Ocean* (1977), for computer, six pitch sensors, homemade synthesizer, flute, and bassoon, was a full-fledged example of interactive composing. The computer interpreted the order and timing of pitches played by the instrumentalists and, in response to certain patterns, chose which sound to generate from a wide range of chords. As he later wrote, "The relationship between the two musicians and the computer is an interactive one, with the computer changing the electronically-produced harmonies in response to what the musicians play, and the musicians being influenced in their improvising by what the computer does."

•

In 1976, George Lewis, trombonist and composer, visited Mills College, and so to speak, the small-computer bug bit him as well. As he said, "It was the first time I saw composers working with small computers." He continues:

> The deciding moment was at David Behrman's house, and there was this network going on with KIM-1s, and they had them all hooked up, and it sounded like improvisors. I had no idea you could get computers to do anything like that. Behrman and the others were encouraging. It's really important to encourage people. I remember that my experience with technology was very discouraging until I met these people, and so I got a KIM-1 and started to learn how to program it. David Behrman was my mentor. I'd call him up and ask him these stupid questions. I looked at the programmer's manual. My first question was, "Why do I have to read this book?" It was frustrating, tedious. So I got something to work. I typed in a sample program and it gave me the right answer, and I asked, "Well, what have I done?" Then I asked, "Well, how do you make music with it?" It was like learning how to represent things symbolically, and what I remember was trying to figure out how to get it to play notes. I spent all my rent money on this KIM-1 computer. I had to figure things out about timing from the programming book. I said, "Look, I don't understand a damn thing about this book," and David said, "I had to read it eight times." So I developed a personal technology. I realized that there was this idea in my head and I was figuring out how to represent it, like score paper or whatever.

Many of Lewis' compositions involved electronics, among them *Trio by Candlelight* (1977) and *Chicago Slow Dance* (1977), for electronic ensembles;

Atlantic (1978), for amplified trombones with resonant filters; and *The Imaginary Suite* (1978), for tape and instruments. His first piece with a computer was *The KIM and I* (1979), for microcomputer, synthesizer, and improvising musician. As he recalls, "It was a simple bass player, like a jazz bass player, and it would concatenate little melodic cells—no notion of making melodies, just little sequences switched around, and I just played around with that." In *The KIM and I*, the computer did not react to him. It just played and he played along with it. But by that time, David Behrman had finished *On the Other Ocean*. As Lewis remembers, "He had made pieces that were listening, and I started to think about how to get that to work."

Lewis' electronic compositions during the next few years included *Chamber Music for Humans and Non-Humans* (1980), for computers and improvising musicians; *Minds in Flux* (1980), for tape; *A Friend* (1980), for dance and tape; *Homage to Charles Parker* (1980), for electronics and instruments; and *Unison* (1978, revised 1982), for soloist and score-following interactive computer program. In 1984, he finished *Rainbow Family*, an interactive composition for computer with pitch sensor, synthesizer, and acoustic melody instrument, in which the computer listened and improvised. He described the basis for his idea:

> In performance, musical decision-making is much more immediate than it is in traditional composing. Many snap judgements are made. Some kind of context control is necessary, and I'm trying to help my machines understand musical context. Since good improvisors can't listen to everything, they have to keep track of the context in which they place the sounds they're making and hearing. You have to find the structure in what you've just played and heard or, if necessary, posit it or another structure as a point of departure. Improvisors often work in terms of rather loosely defined "shapes," which can be defined in terms of characteristics such as volume direction, pitch direction, duration, rhythm regularity, pitch or duration transposition, time between major changes in output or input, pattern-finding, and frequency of silence. You don't need or want an exhaustive transcription, but instead a fast, general analysis of what's happening at any given moment and what's been happening. This requires massive, but musically important, data reductions.

He carried the idea of an improvising computer further in *Voyager* (1987), for soloist and, as he put it, "interactive computer music composer-listener." The software for *Voyager* analyzes aspects of the soloist's performance while the soloist is playing and decides accordingly what music it will generate. The result is two independent musical streams of activity, one played by the soloist, one played by the computer, each influencing the other. Lewis explains:

> When you're playing with someone else, you're finding out what they know about music and where they're going. Some players ask, "What happens if I do this?" and if the machine doesn't respond the way it's sup-

posed to, they worry. It's supposed to be instantaneous response to the do-what-I-mean principle. But if everything is going along with the performer all the time, it can get boring, because the performer is then completely responsible for everything that's happening. So I try to get the computer to do its own thing as well as follow a performer. And as soon as the computer generates something independent, a performer can react to that and go with it.

The idea is to get the machine to pay attention to the performer as it composes. So there's an analysis of what's going on, and the analysis informs the composition. Let's say it's the pitch you have to analyze first. First you're looking for low and high. Then you map it onto the MIDI space, by register or by octave. Then you get a second pitch and you map that to intervals, averaging the pitches over time, so there's an idea of where someone is playing. Then the whole thing is mapped to stability over time, to see if it changes much or doesn't. Then we get to intervals. What's the average interval, the instantaneous interval? Then it's time, the duration between onsets. It's like the accumulation of a lot of details.

My big thing is averages. So we're talking about analyzing basics like high-low, fast-slow, dense-sparse, soft-loud. We're talking about pitch, which goes into register or octave. Then volume, then average volume or range. And interval width, average width, and a notion of stability in interval width. Then you can map all of that to the output.

•

In 1979, David Rosenboom joined the faculty at Mills College. But his work had begun in the mid-1960s in New York. He describes the starting point:

I felt that we needed more broadly applicable theoretical models for music. The well-developed theories were so limited in their stylistic focus, and there were so few theories, that it seemed interesting to me to start by looking inside the brain and work outward toward musical experience. What this led me to was an exploration of ways in which we could look at brain activity in relation to musical experience and try to come up with some models that we could use to create algorithms to put in instruments.

In 1968, Rosenboom began to work in the lab of Les Fehmi, a biofeedback researcher at State University of New York at Stony Brook. In 1970, he went to work at York University in Toronto. His *Ecology of the Skin* (1970) was based on the idea that a listener's psychological state, as reflected by alpharhythm brain waves detected by EEG sensors, could be used to control music. He soon developed a situation where a listener could, by controlling his or her psychological state through biofeedback processes, steer the music: "I was looking for an extended musical interface with the human nervous system." In 1972, he formed the Laboratory of Experimental Aesthetics at York. His next works—among them *Portable Gold and Philosophers' Stones* (1972), where the sound was controlled by brain waves, galvanic skin response, and body temperature; and *Chilean Drought* (1972), where the performer's state of mind was affected by the emotionally charged content of the piece—were based on biofeedback. As he said, "It was very stimulating because the cybernetic feedback model provided a means to stabilize or develop control over internal processes, and I was interested in investigating those processes."

The most elaborate of Rosenboom's feedback pieces was *On Being Invisible* (1977), a music-theater composition first finished in the mid-1970s and then revised as *On Being Invisible II* (1995). In *On Being Invisible*, the underlying feedback process was based on detecting ERPs (Event-Related Potentials), very "soft," difficult-to-sense transient brain waves that are related to very specific perceptual and information-processing events. As Rosenboom explains, "Evoked responses are very tiny, and in order to extract them from background information, you need to use a lot of complex signal-processing techniques, and you can't tell the computer when to start these processes unless you know where and when to look." He continues:

> The computer generates some starting musical structure. Embedded in the computer software is a partial model of perception with which the computer is analyzing its own output, the purpose of which is to allow the computer to make predictions about which events or changes in the sound are likely to be perceived by an attentive listener as perceptually or structurally significant.

His computer model, in other words, was based upon his assumptions regarding, first, the ways in which musical events are parsed (divided into groupings like phrases, gestures, patterns) and, second, which of the musical events would be perceived by an attentive listener as landmarks in this process. If his assumptions were correct, then what the computer perceived as an important change in the music would probably match what the attentive listener perceived as well, and the computer would then know when to search for ERPs in the listener's response. He continues:

> So to predict when to look, the computer analyzes its own output and then records a performer's reaction and, provided the performer is paying attention, it looks to see if ERPs are present. If they are, the computer says, "Yes, my prediction was correct. That moment was structurally significant." Then the composition algorithms take over and decide how to make the music evolve in relation to this feedback. So what happens is that from any starting point, the music will organize itself and evolve according to its feedback. When the computer analyzes higher-level pattern groupings, it says, "Given what's happened in recent history, what's the most likely thing that will happen next?" It looks for evoked responses when new things like surprises or anomalies in the patterns occur. And if it fails, it tries again.

And are there any special qualifications for a performer of this music? Rosenboom answers:

> I look for performers who can control their attention. It's harder than it may seem. Performers of this music have to ride a fine line that divides the two states of volitional control and passive involvement. They have to find ways to gain control of their intentional focus and then make subtle shifts in their attention. They have to make careful decisions about when to be an initiator of action and when to remain part of a larger, ongoing process. It's very tricky and it's sometimes hard for them to know when they've been successful. It's a very interesting state of mind for a performer to be in. And, in fact, not so unrelated to improvisation. I've found many useful spin-offs of this work in non-feedback-based music.

•

In 1979, shortly after arriving at Mills College, Rosenboom began work with Donald Buchla on Buchla's Touché synthesizer. As Rosenboom recalls, "First we designed the front panel, which meant deciding what someone would want to do and how someone would want to interact with it, and then Don designed the circuits and I designed the software." Rosenboom developed a language that he called FOIL (Far Out Instrument Language). In 1981, he became director of the Center for Contemporary Music (CCM) and set a direction: "It seemed to me we were best equipped to work on input devices and algorithmic approaches to composition and performance—I wanted to design a language that was based on a cognitive modeling approach to musical structures, and so I called Larry Polansky to see if he'd be interested in getting started on what became HMSL." Polansky was indeed interested, and he agreed with Rosenboom that CCM was the place to do it. As Polansky said, "There was a strong sense at CCM that one of its missions was to develop and be in the forefront of live interactive ideas."

HMSL (Hierarchical Music Specification Language) is an extensible object-oriented programming language that had its roots in the 1970s in discussions between Rosenboom, Polansky, and James Tenney in Toronto. Both Polansky and Rosenboom were interested in moving their ideas from the 1970s to the increased power and speed of the new chips of the 1980s, and as Polansky remembers, "We were also interested in the aesthetics of writing a language." When Polansky showed up at Mills College, as Rosenboom recalls, "We started working on the idea and scoped out an architecture for it."

In 1979, Polansky and Rosenboom began to discuss ideas. By 1980, they were designing and writing code. By 1981, the first version of HMSL was up and running on a home-built computer at CCM. Polansky later wrote: "No musical idea is deemed too outlandish, strange, or peculiar to be precluded by HMSL's design. Our unofficial motto has always been 'Everything is possible, but some things may not be easy.'" Phil Burke began to work on the project shortly after it began, and in 1985, when the group received a grant from The

Inter-University Consortium on Educational Computing, Burke was able to join in as a full-time software developer. He transformed HMSL into an object-oriented language and rewrote it for Macintosh and Amiga computers.

The development of HMSL had been and continued to be an immense effort. Yet the three developers remained consistently noncommercial in their orientation. Their goal was more to encourage a community for experimentation than to develop a commercial package. As Polansky put it, "Often your software will influence other people's work and that synergy is very interesting." He elaborates:

> I don't distinguish between the idea and the piece. It's part of the same synergy to me. The sound of the piece is not simply confined to the particular things that hit my ear at a particular time. The sound of the piece includes the interaction of the programmers working with HMSL, the intent, the sincerity, the place in the experimental tradition, the goals of the piece, and the process by which the composer and performer worked, and the new doors that are opened up or new ideas that are explored. I love to collapse the distinctions between the idea, the software, the hardware. That was clearly a part of the community process of HMSL. We encouraged as many forms of activity as we could, from pure research to making a piece for MIDI instruments. It all seems to me to be part of the same process, and we felt, the three of us, that we had some kind of collaborative role in the big piece where everyone's working.

Rosenboom used an early version of HMSL (and FOIL) in his *Zones of Influence* (1986), for percussion soloist and the Touché, in which a percussionist's sounds and performance patterns were analyzed and transformed. As MIDI became ubiquitous, he designed a program called HFG (Hierarchical Form Generator), written in HMSL, that listens to MIDI input from a performer. He describes it:

> Using ideas about musical perception from *On Being Invisible*, it identifies and captures musical phrases and stores them in memory. It then remaps these phrases onto the MIDI input device, so I can call them back and use them with a library of transformation routines. It captures spontaneously generated material and I can push it in different directions to make musical structures, just by how I play. I've been really excited by it because it's the first improvising program I've made that really sounds like me when I'm playing with it.

Polansky used HMSL extensively. In his *B'rey'sheet* (1984, subsequently revised, the title transliterated from the Hebrew for *In the Beginning*), based on eleventh- and twelfth-century cantillation melodies for singing the Torah, the tropes were sung unadorned by a singer whose pitches were captured by HMSL and transformed. *17 Simple Melodies* (1987) was an HMSL program defined only by its fundamental structure and given to a performer with an invitation to collaborate by specifying the details. *Simple Actions* (1987) gave a single performer at a single computer controls for modifying automatic and chaotic processes. As Polansky explains, "There are hundreds of possible simple interacting processes, or 'critters,' and it is often nearly impossible to tell what is causing certain effects—the performer often becomes an observer, trying to figure out what is going on and how to shape it toward something else." He carried the idea further in *Cocks crow, dogs bark, this all men know, but even the wisest, cannot tell, why cocks crow, dogs bark, when they do* (1988). As he explains, "The title is from a Thomas Mertin translation of a Chang Tzu poem. It describes my intent in the piece: things happen, and they happen for some reason, but there is really no way to predict or know when or why they happen." *Cocks crow* . . . also contains a complex schema for shared control of a central process by three improvisors, somewhat along the lines of The Hub's network model, but guaranteeing unfathomable results.

There were other Polansky HMSL pieces as well, among them *Horn* (1990), *3 Studies* (1990), *There is more headroom, but one's feet are forced into slippers of steel* (1991), and *The World's Longest Melody* (1993). There were notable collaborations: *The Birth of Peace* (1989), with Chris Mann, Alistair Riddell, Simon Veitch, and others, a live goldfish-controlled HMSL system with texts and other materials, at the Australian Center for Contemporary Art, Melbourne; and *Dear John* (1986), with Pauline Oliveros for a John Cage birthday celebration at the West German Radio in Cologne. And there were many other pieces by many other composers, among them David Rosenboom, John Bischoff, Chris Bobrowski, Phil Burk, Philip Corner, Nick Didkovsky, Ann LaBerge, David Mahler, Robert Marsanyi, Jeane Parson, Carter Scholz, Phil Stone, Peter Yadlowsky, and Peter Beyls, who used HMSL to create *Oscar*.

•

Peter Beyls brought together many elements of a varied background. At different times through the 1970s and into the 1980s, he had studied electrical engineering, music history, computer science, computer graphics, and music composition. His compositions included *Tea for Two* (1975), for two electronics performers; *Heartbeat* (1976), which used electrocardiogram signals from a performer's body; *Crosstalk* (1980), for live electronics; and *The Hollow Man* (1980), *Painted Words* (1981), and *Heading into the Storm* (1985), all performances with a computer. In the mid-1980s, at the artificial intelligence laboratory at Brussels University in Belgium, Beyls began to focus on issues involving interactive and intelligent systems. As he put it, "I made musical discovery machines—I used computers as vehicles for what I call 'conceptual navigation,' the exploration of the potential in ideas." His work led him to the development of a knowledge-based model, which he personified in 1985 as software called *Oscar* (*Os*cillator *ar*tist). He describes the project:

> Oscar was designed to be a companion in live performance, to listen to a single human performer and react in a musically coherent way. This

research is specifically performance oriented—the audience is a witness of the behavior of both the human (myself) and the digital performer (Oscar) and how they interact and exchange musical ideas. It is important to note that responsibilities are shared and shifting back and forth between man and machine . . .

To understand how Oscar works, one might imagine a simple if-then input-output relationship: if Oscar perceives (input) that something happens, then it responds (output) by doing something. One might also imagine greater complexity and ask: Can Oscar's inputs have filters? In other words, can Oscar have culture, or knowledge, or memory that might supply a context for an understanding of what it hears? Can Oscar generate new information? To what extent can Oscar express its own identity in its response? To what extent can Oscar be social and sensitive to others? Can Oscar be bored if its inputs are not sufficiently varied? Can it become overly excited by too much variation in input?

The answer is yes. Beyls' anthropomorphic explanation that "Oscar wanted to express its personality while at the same time it wanted to integrate itself into a larger, social whole," translates into a range of software responses from a close relationship between input and output to no relationship. Oscar was social in the sense that it remembered the melodic intervals and patterns that it heard, and it expressed its personality by transforming them. When input was slow, Oscar was bored and produced very little output. When input was fast, Oscar became arbitrary and agitated, producing disjointed ideas. Oscar's functioning, in short, simulated human characteristics such as ego, social instinct, and emotional reactions to the outside world. Further, as Beyls continued to work on Oscar, and as Oscar "grew up" to become more complex, Beyls noted that the relationship between Oscar's inputs and outputs became harder to understand. As Beyls observed in August 1995, "Oscar is approaching the complexity barrier, so it becomes very difficult to debug its behavior." Beyls also observed, however, that as Oscar approaches the complexity barrier, it becomes more independent, more original, and more interesting.

•

Felix Hess in Holland wrote his dissertation between 1975 and 1979 while he was working at Adelaide University in Australia. His subject was the aerodynamics of boomerangs. But his attention was turned in another direction. He tells it:

I lived in the hills just outside Adelaide. I was immediately struck by the sound of frogs. They were in my backyard, in my garden. There was a little creek in the garden, very beautiful, and each night I would hear magnificent concerts which people told me were the sounds of frogs. Well, I couldn't believe it at first, because these were very different from Dutch frogs. They sounded like insects to me, but I spent many hours in the nights listening. There were perhaps hundreds or thousands of little frogs working together in such a way that the sound seemed to move in waves. I really found it wonderful.

I started to record them. I heard some frogs in the distance, so I went there to set up the microphones. But then I found that the frogs were farther away than I thought and I had to walk more, and then suddenly I heard them behind me. The frogs were everywhere in the area, I realized, and they would stop calling whenever they heard me. But once I sat down and didn't move and made no sound whatsoever, just silent, then the frogs started to call. First the ones further away, then the ones closer. It was an incoming wave of sound. I learned to sit still and listen to three-dimensional sound patterns. This is exactly what the frogs do. They listen to each other and they call on the basis of what they hear. Each individual frog may react in a very simplistic manner, yet all of them together produce something that's very complex.

Back in Holland, I played the recordings. But then I thought I should make live concerts myself using machines that react more or less to sounds the way frogs do. For me it was a synthetic model of animal communication. Other people told me it was art.

In 1983, at STEIM in Amsterdam, Hess finished building his first group of forty machines. He called them *Electronic Sound Creatures*. As he described them, "Each machine had a microphone to listen, a little speaker to call, a battery for food, so to speak, and some electronics." They were packaged in little aluminum boxes and hung from the ceiling over the audience. What did they do? He answers, "The machines listened, and when they heard another machine calling, they recognized the sound so they tended to answer." It was an interesting idea, but as he recalls, "that was a rough design, it didn't work very well."

Felix Hess' Moving Sound Creatures in the late 1980s.
Photo by John Stoel. Courtesy Felix Hess.

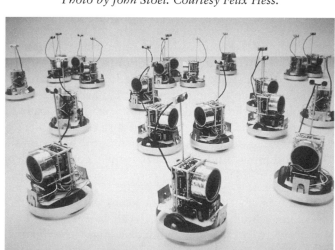

In 1986, he finished a second generation of Electronic Sound Creatures. He said, "I'm interested in machines which communicate with each other." Then in 1987, he made twenty-four *Moving Sound Creatures*, each about nine inches high and about five inches across, with two wheels, a little bumper, and two microphones on a shaft coming out of the top like a little head. They were, well, cute. Hess continues:

> I gave these machines stereo hearing so they would know from which direction another machine called. And I gave them wheels so they could move on a floor and try to find each other. They give a live concert combined with a very simple kind of live dance. The machines have two calls. One means "come here." The other, which they use when they get stuck somewhere, means "go away."

He did not always use sound as the vehicle for communication. *Air Flows* (1989) was a group of fifteen machines that communicated through wind, turning their fans on and off as they sensed air currents. *Parrots* (1990) were machines that copied, without understanding, what they heard. *Kazebotaru* (1991, Wind Fireflies), created for a festival in Japan, consisted of many little lights that were sensitive to the wind. As Hess said, "They're very silent but to me this multitude of very small lights seemed to be like a silent concert."

•

Roger Dannenberg started to work on score-following programs in 1983. As he explained, "Playing with ensembles taught me that it's very important to listen to other players and synchronize with them, so I made the computer into another player." But to actually use that computer in performance meant, in those pre-Macintosh days, building a realtime portable music system. So Dannenberg built a system. In his words, "The sound was very crude but it was adequate and the whole thing fit into a little case that fit under an airline seat."

Storing it under his airline seat, Dannenberg took his computer to Paris in 1984, where he demonstrated the first version of his score-following program at the International Computer Music Conference. As he recalls, "It really did a good job." The computer could follow a soloist while keeping the soloist synchronized with a score, something like a conductor following a soloist while conducting an orchestral accompaniment. The system, in fact, anticipated the soloist to eliminate delays, and it made musically appropriate tempo adjustments. In 1985, Dannenberg and Josh Bloch implemented a new system that incorporated additional rules for musical behavior and handled polyphonic keyboard input. And at about that time, composer Georges Bloch (no relation to Josh) heard Dannenberg's demonstrations and reflected:

> The problem was what to do with the accompaniment idea. What were the musical implications? And I came to a concept which I called "composing improvisation." The thing about a computer, compared to normal

improvisation, is that the computer has memory, and so the computer can use what the improvisor has done to create in real time a new variety of form. The computer listens to what the instrumentalist is playing, and since it can remember what was played, and analyze what was done, it can create a form in electronic sounds that has some dependence on the material that was played.

In 1985, Georges Bloch and Dannenberg began work on Bloch's *Jimmy Durante Boulevard*. In Dannenberg's words, "Our idea was to use a computer as a composer's agent to lead improvisors into more structured, composed performances." *Jimmy Durante Boulevard* was a composition involving three improvisers (in this case Bloch playing keyboard, Dannenberg playing trumpet, and Xavier Chabot playing flute), each of whom would control a different aspect of the music. The first performance was at STEIM in Amsterdam, in 1986. Putting it together had involved exceptional teamwork considering that the three musicians lived far apart: Bloch in Paris, Dannenberg in Pittsburgh (Pennsylvania), and Chabot in San Diego (California). As Dannenberg recalls, "We put the first concert together by email." Georges Bloch describes the performance:

> Melodic material was analyzed from the trumpet part through a pitch tracker whenever Roger pushed a pedal—it was an interesting part of the system that a musician could decide when what he was playing was analyzed—and the analysis decided which electronic sounds would play. We used the texture of the keyboard part to analyze and set some order into the electronic sounds. And there was a sort of overall form, which was breaking things into pieces and getting towards a climax, either with things getting shorter or longer. You could also have several forms going on, some going in one direction and some going in another direction. The system was pretty complex. But we had a pretty good feeling for it, so we knew what to do and we did performances which worked out fine. What was great about it was that what came out of the loudspeakers really had a lot to do with what was just played.

•

Richard Teitelbaum had been working with MEV in Rome. In 1966, he returned to New York to build a synthesizer and study biofeedback techniques. He assembled his synthesizer partly from modules he built (with David Behrman's help) and partly from modules he bought from Moog. It had no keyboard. So how did he perform? He answers: "I used to twirl knobs and change patch cords."

He stayed in New York for one year, as he tells it, "working in the brain wave lab at Queens College, learning how to attach electrodes and earning enough money to buy a used Moog synthesizer." But still without a keyboard. While in New York, he was invited by Steve Lacy to work on an improvisational setting of Lao Tzu's *The Way*. He spent most of the summer of 1967 rehearsing with Lacy and vocalist Irene Aebi. As he remembers, "It was the first extensive improvising with a synthesizer that I'd done." In the fall of 1967, he returned to Rome to rejoin MEV. He describes his performance techniques: "I used to play my synthesizer with my toes, using spring-loaded rocker switches to trigger the envelope generators so I could keep my hands free to twirl knobs."

He also continued his experiments in biofeedback music. In 1968, he performed *Organ Music*, in which he used Lacy's brain waves and Aebi's heartbeats while he controlled the synthesizer and mixer. Later that year, he created *In Tune*, in which Barbara Mayfield's brain waves controlled the synthesizer while her heartbeat and breath sounds were processed electronically. Into the 1970s, his pieces included *Alpha Bean Lima Brain* (1971), done with Serge Tcherepnin's considerable technical assistance, in which brain waves were transmitted via telephone lines from California Institute of the Arts near Los Angeles to make a solenoid-driven pot of beans jump at Charlotte Moorman's Avant Garde Festival in New York. And he did *Tai Chi Alpha Tala* (1974) using brain waves transmitted by radio from a Tai Chi performer to control a raga-playing sequencer accompanied by a live Indian drummer.

He eventually got a keyboard for his synthesizer and, through the 1970s, played it in concerts with a number of musicians, first with Anthony Braxton, later with George Lewis, Roscoe Mitchell, Leo Smith, Andrew Cyrille, Carlos Zingaro, and others. Braxton and Teitelbaum had first met during the Actuel Festival at Amougies, Belgium, in 1969. Given the technology of that time, it was a most unlikely idea to combine saxophones and synthesizer. Yet they played many wonderful improvisations, among them *Open Aspects (Duo)* (1974) and *Time Zones* (1976). How did they work together? Teitelbaum tells us:

> Sometimes I tried to match and approximate his sound, and sometimes what I did was very different. I was more like an accompanist, a drummer, not in the sense that I imitated standard drum sounds, but I made more noise, my sounds were less pitched. He could do noise things on his horn, so we did matching and not matching. We both go for the broadest possible inclusiveness and range of expressive extremes, very loud/very soft, very smooth/very harsh, peaceful/aggressive, pitch/noise, space/density, unity/contrast, and have a similar sense of form.

Teitelbaum went to Japan in 1977, where he studied traditional Japanese music and composed *Blends*, for shakuhachi, percussion, and synthesizers, performed in Tokyo by Teitelbaum, shakuhachi master Katsuya Yokoyama, composer Toshi Ichiyanagi, and percussionist Michael Ranta. At about that time in the late 1970s, he added a microcomputer to process control voltages to make delays, loops, and other more quirky transformations, all of which led to his *"Colorless Green Ideas Sleep Furiously"* (1979), the title being a sentence that

Noam Chomsky made up to demonstrate that grammar did not necessarily generate meaning.

He was, during this period, developing an increasingly powerful improvisational instrument. He asks, "How is an electronic instrument different from an acoustic instrument?" and answers: "You don't have the subtlety of response you can get from an acoustic instrument but on the other hand you can make much more complex musical structures." Given that thought, it is not surprising that his next project, begun in 1980, was the computer control of an acoustic instrument. As he tells it, "I wanted to do something in which the sound was acoustic but the control possibilities went beyond what normal human capabilities could be."

By chance, he saw a Marantz Pianocorder in Baldwin's showroom in New York. As he recalls, "I'd already been very much inspired by Nancarrow's stuff, so I immediately had the idea that if I replaced the cassette player on the Pianocorder with a computer that could respond to what I played on another piano keyboard, transform it and play it back all in real time, I could make a sort-of 'live Nancarrow.'" The Vorsetzer version of the Pianocorder was a device with an array of solenoid-controlled mechanical "fingers," metal rods with felt tips that fit over the keys of the piano in such a way that each mechanical finger could depress a note when instructed electronically to do so. Teitelbaum convinced Marantz to lend him a Pianocorder Vorsetzer on a long-term basis. He attached it to a piano. He eventually added another Pianocorder to a second piano. He installed velocity sensor switches under the keys of yet another piano and began work on his computer-extended piano system. He wrote:

> The computer functions as an extension of the pianist-composer's body and mind—affording him, for example, direct control over as many as eighty "fingers" per piano, and the ability to program an infinite variety of instantaneous musical responses and transformations of what he plays, as he plays it.

Teitelbaum developed—at first with engineer Mark Bernard in Woodstock in upstate New York and later with Stefan Tiedje in Berlin—what he called the Patch Control Language (PCL). PCL was an object-oriented language made up of some thirty software modules performing a variety of arithmetic, logical, and musical functions that could be patched together in any configuration. Teitelbaum's first PCL composition was *Solo for Three Pianos* (1982). He explained how the software worked:

> As my system is presently configured, music played live by the pianist on one piano keyboard is sensed and instantly read into computer memory where it can be stored, overlayed, delayed, transposed, inverted, randomized, and otherwise manipulated before being passed on to the other two pianos for playback at the performer's behest. This may be done

either simultaneously, or at a selectable delay time, or stored for future recall. Any section of material may also be looped to form an ostinato; foot pedals controlling the power to the solenoids for each of the remote pianos allow the performer to balance and fade them in or out . . .

The largest PCL composition was *Concerto Grosso* (1985), combining the three-piano system with MIDI synthesizers and samplers. It was performed by Teitelbaum playing the "master" acoustic piano and an electronic keyboard with Anthony Braxton playing wind instruments and George Lewis playing trombone, both sharing control of various synthesizers and two Pianocorders with Teitelbaum. It was a complex network of controls and audio signals, rich, exuberant, and wild in its sounds. Teitelbaum describes it:

> We did five days of soldering and programming in the Grosser Sendesaal WDR in Cologne and we finally got it to work. The human-played acoustic instruments—one piano, wind instruments, and trombone— were the concertino, the small solo group, and the synthesizers and the two slave pianos were like the orchestra. My software was doing various kinds of delays, transpositions, switching between various instrumental voices and timbres, looping, retrogrades, inversions, etc., and George's was performing different kinds of algorithmic processes, so there were multiple logics and processes that I could switch between or let go on simultaneously.

In its complexity of activities and relationships, *Concerto Grosso* was on the borderline between order and chaos. At what point can a system be thought of as out of control? Teitelbaum's series of compositions on the *Golem* theme, from *Golem I* (1987) to *Golem: An Interactive Opera* (1995), posed the question by evoking a centuries-old legend. In Jewish folklore, the Golem was a supernatural creature, imbued with life by Rabbi Loew in Prague. The Golem was created to aid the community. But as the legend goes, it then became a monster and had to be destroyed. Teitelbaum said, "I thought of a system that gets out of control, that first obeys you and then becomes increasingly chaotic and unpredictable."

And from that perspective, the question might be rephrased: At what point can a system be thought of as so complex that the connection between the composer's intention and the system's behavior becomes obscure? And when is that bad? Well, there's only one sensible answer. It becomes bad when, like Rabbi Loew's Golem, it makes bad music.

•

In 1986, following from his earlier work with the SalMar Construction, Salvatore Martirano began work on the first version of his SAL (Sound And Logic) software in Le LISP. Then David Tcheng, a graduate student, improved the code, and as Martirano recalls, "it really worked well in 1987." Martirano describes it:

It was a performance program. A three-voice canon in which voices 2 and 3 answered my performance. I seeded the program with a 320-byte stream of improv. The program extracted and transformed phrases. One of the criteria for extracting a phrase was to look for a two-second rest. It would extract two to four phrases that were six to fifteen seconds in length. It executed transformations, such as contour inversion, note skipping, orchestration, retrograde, and transposition, within a network of probability ladders with min and max values. While it played back phrases, it prepared the current performance for the next playback.

SAL was the software basis of the *YahaSALmaMAC Orchestra* (1986), a "realtime answering service" consisting of a Macintosh II computer, a variety of synthesizers, and a drum machine. Martirano performed with a MIDI keyboard. Dorothy Martirano, his wife, performed with a Zeta violin.

By 1992, Martirano had purchased a Kyma system, William Walker had translated SAL into SAL80 for use with the Kyma system, and SAL80 had become a collaborative project including Martirano, Walker, Kurt Hebel, and Carla Scaletti, called *ImprovisationBuilder*. ImprovisationBuilder contained three activity types: Listeners which extracted phrases from incoming music; Players which took phrases from the Listeners and transformed them; and Realizers which played back the transformed phrases through the Kyma system and MIDI synthesizers. These activities occurred at different levels, which created further complexity. Martirano continues:

> There were fifteen orchestras. Each orchestra consisted of five MIDI synths assigned to voice 2 and five MIDI synths assigned to voice 3. Combos from one to five synths for each voice could change on a MIDI event. Orchestration in real time was executed by dialing one of five ranges from one to 233 MIDI events. This resulted in an explosion of timbre change. When I played solo into the system, there were voices extracted and the voice 2 orchestra played them back. Then, phrases were extracted from the extracted phrases at a second level and voice 3 orchestra got those. Voice 3 orchestra was dependent upon the voice 2 orchestra for its material. When Dorothy and I played together, we'd have to depend upon our heads connecting. Phrases extracted from my stream went to one orchestra and phrases extracted from her stream were sent to the second orchestra.

The players' sensitivities had to be extended in every direction as they interacted with each other and with the software, and it was sometimes true that the software was not the most intelligent improvising partner. As Martirano and others later reflected, "Musicality emerges when the human performer learns to adapt to an improvisation partner who interrupts rather often and sometimes focuses on insignificant parts of the human's performance."

•

In 1987, Robert Rowe began work on *Cypher*, a listening program. Rowe's idea was to create an interactive instrument that understood what it heard and, based on what it heard, produced an interesting response. He personified the basic functions of the program as Listener and Player. As he described it, "The Listener was sensing a MIDI information stream, analyzing it, then sending messages over to the Player saying, 'this is what I think is going on in the music.'" The Player then generated its response. The need for such a program had become evident to Rowe earlier, at IRCAM in Paris, when his *Hall of Mirrors* (1986) was played by Harry Spaarney, bass clarinetist. Rowe explains:

> Spaarney could hear what the computer was doing and react to it. But it became apparent that the only musical intelligence was his own. He was deciding, based upon what the computer was doing, what he'd do next—but the computer was always doing the same thing. It made me want to write a program that behaved more on the same level as a human player, making decisions based on musical criteria.

Consequently, Rowe focused primarily on the Listener because in his view the Listener presented the central musical problem: "I was trying to make a model of certain ideas about music cognition because the more a program knows about music, the better a program it will be."

But how, one might ask, could the software learn about music? Cypher's Listener paid attention to register, dynamics, vertical density, horizontal density, and articulation, and analyzed their characteristics. When it was listening to register, it decided what was high and what was low. When it was listening to dynamics, it decided whether the loudness value was over a threshold, which was loud, or under a threshold, which was soft. Listening to vertical density, it decided how many notes there were and whether the voicing was wide or narrow. Horizontal density was a measure of speed, looking at the number of attacks that occurred within a period of time. Articulation was a question of whether the notes were short or long.

Once the basic inputs were analyzed, the Listener identified the beginnings and endings of phrases by noting discontinuities, for example, sudden changes in register, loudness, and density. And once it decided where the phrases were, it decided to what extent the activity of the music within each phrase was irregular or regular, with or without discontinuous elements. The Listener also did a neural-network-based harmonic analysis to provide a picture of harmonic context and key. As Rowe summed it up, "I programmed the Listener to find out how the music is changing over time."

Once the Listener understood how the music changed in time, it passed the information to the Player for action, and the Player could react to the information in different ways. As Rowe explains, "For example, you could tell the program, 'if you're hearing loud, fast single notes in a high register, I want you to take that material and invert it, and make chords out of it, and add accelerando.'" The Player consisted of many transformation types linked in series. A composer could instruct the Player, for example, to take the input, invert it, then slow it down, then change its register . . . Rowe continues:

> I took the approach of making a Listener because of my motivation to base the program's responses on musical concepts. If the software did indeed embody the same musical concepts that underlie human music cognition, then what it was doing should have been comprehensible to both performers working with it and an audience. I've used the program a lot with improvisors like Steve Coleman, Muhal Richard Abrams, and Roscoe Mitchell, and it's been exciting to see how they interact with the program.
>
> Actually, the program has two Listeners, one that's analyzing what's coming in from the outside world, the other that's analyzing what the Player is about to play. I call that second one the Critic. You can program the system's personality directly. For instance, you could have the Critic looking at what's about to be played and have a rule, like "if I'm about to play twenty dense chords in the low register, I don't want to do that . . .," then give it some combination of processes to move it to a higher register.

Rowe used Cypher in *Flood Gate* (1989), *Sun and Ice* (1990), *Banff Sketches* (1991), *Maritime* (1992), and *Shells* (1993). Through these compositions, Cypher was a working model of an idea continually in development—as Rowe puts it, "a working model of my ideas"—and after *Maritime*, Rowe went on to develop the idea of the Listener in other contexts. He developed specific Listeners for specific pieces of music, as in *Not About Water* (1994), for various instruments and interactive computer system, and *A Flock of Words* (1995), for instruments, animation, video, holography, and interactive computer system, in which the player was controlling the animation and lighting along with the musical environment. Rowe also developed improvisational environments: "We wanted it to look at more than one Player at once, for example one Listener for each Player and a super-Listener looking at the combination, so that Cypher would become part of an ensemble."

•

In 1983, I thought that the idea of an interactive musical instrument was an idea whose time had come. In November, Thomas E. Bezanson, a musically visionary attorney, arranged for the necessary legal work and together we signed Intelligent Music into existence. Our mission was the development of an interactive instrument for the home entertainment market.

But as it turned out, the idea was both ahead of its time and capital intensive, and like many companies, Intelligent Music was founded with abundant vision and no capital. A few software models of an interactive instrument were developed during 1984 and 1985, mostly with the Synclavier II at Bennington College. Progress was minimal. In 1985, however, things began to happen, although in an unexpected direction. Here is the story of M:

> I was working with Tony Widoff and John Offenhartz during the summer in the Bennington College electronic music studio. David Zicarelli, who had recently graduated from Bennington, was teaching electronic music in the college's summer program. He came by to see what we were doing and showed us the DX-7 editor he'd written for Opcode. David then offered to help me transport my software from the Synclavier to the Macintosh.
>
> Writing software for the Synclavier had become frustrating for me. I would program an algorithm, then have to run the program to hear its result. This required going through a compile cycle. I would push the red button and wait thirty seconds or so before I could hear what I'd done. What I needed was a realtime environment where I could change the variables and hear the results immediately, without compiling. I also needed a lighter system. I was traveling a lot and I thought I should take advantage of smaller and lighter equipment becoming available. I accepted David's offer.
>
> On New Year's Day, 1986, David arrived in Albany to begin work. His first question was: "What do you want to do?" Well, I'd bought a Macintosh about a year earlier. I'd also bought a flight simulator for my son in which the plane's joystick was controlled with the mouse. Since I had often conceptualized the realtime control of an interactive instrument as flying a plane through a musical space, I said, "I want to fly a plane through a musical space." So David designed a joystick in the form of a conductor's hand, controllable with the mouse. And to define what the conductor's hand was conducting, we began to incorporate some of the algorithms I'd been using in my Synclavier software. After a day or two, two things became clear to me. I was not going to be a Macintosh programmer. And we were, in fact, creating a program that other composers might want to use.
>
> During the next few months, Tony and John came into the project with many ideas. David divided his time between his responsibilities at Stanford—he was a graduate student and teaching assistant—and writing software. In addition to the program we had begun together, he was developing another idea, based on transition tables, which became Jam Factory. In April, we decided that Intelligent Music would temporarily become a software company and publish these programs.

The names M and Jam Factory were the result of a brainstorming session with Curtis Roads and Christopher Yavelow during the summer of 1986. The first version of M was finished on New Year's Eve, 1986—its initial development from start to finish had taken exactly one year—and Jam Factory was fin-

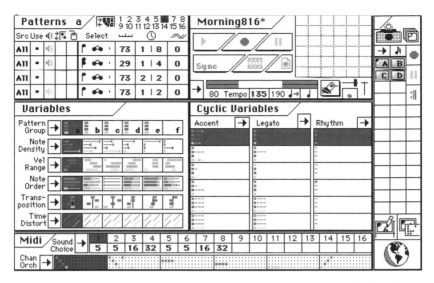

The main screen of Intelligent Music's M as configured by Joel Chadabe for Many Mornings, Many Moods (1989). The screen, designed by David Zicarelli, functions as a realtime control panel for musical performance.

ished at about the same time. Jam Factory consisted of four Players, each of which independently transformed the musical material that had been recorded into it.

M was a collection of algorithms, portrayed graphically on the computer screen and manipulated with particular graphic controls—range bars, numericals, grids, sliders, and of course, the conductor's hand—designed by Zicarelli with musicians in mind. A composer could record some basic material through a MIDI keyboard, for example, and then use the graphic controls to transform the pitches, rhythms, and timbres of that material in a wide variety of ways. Any combination of cyclic, random, and performed change, applied to virtually any aspect of the music, was possible. And a composer would hear the results immediately. The goal had been to provide an environment in which composers could create interactive compositions quickly and effortlessly. In 1989, Zicarelli extended his interactive concepts in a graphics-and-music program called OvalTune. In short, he was interested in computer-based interactive processes. In his words:

> Most computer tools are rendering tools. By drawing more precisely than you could with a pencil and paper, you're able to realize an idea. The interesting thing in M and Jam Factory, and particularly OvalTune, is the idea of tools which affect the process of creativity. You can start with little or no concept—and with immediate feedback you can decide in what direction to go next. This seems to me to be one of the most novel things

that computers offer to the field of music. Certainly they can make new and unusual sounds and play more notes than any human being could within a certain space or time, but somehow those things are not as exciting to me as the possibility of aiding the process of musical creativity.

Antony Widoff puts M in the context of the professional music market:

> M suggests a way of working with musical material that's outside of the mainstream. Music has become a business and that business is either writing songs, or writing music for some other medium such as film, or TV, and there's a prevailing form in commercial music which M does not really address. But that's where the money is. And professionals may buy things that don't reasonably lead to making money, and they may say, "Well, that's really cool," but they put them on a shelf.

I found M to be excellent, however, at creating interactive compositions. Between 1987 and 1994, I used M to compose *After Some Songs*, a group of short improvisational pieces based primarily on jazz classics. I thought of the group as a solo concert for percussionist Jan Williams, in which his playing would be enlarged and extended by electronic sounds which so closely resembled the acoustic percussion sounds that it would seem as if he were playing a larger-than-life instrument. I described the performance process in the liner notes:

> The electronic sounds also function as a kind of interactive accompaniment. In performance, I'm sitting at a computer, manipulating screen controls, while the computer is generating variations on the basic material and controlling a synthesizer. Jan plays along with what he hears. At the same time, I'm following what he does. It's as if I'm conducting an improvising orchestra which is accompanying an improvising soloist. We're following each other in performance, matching sounds and gestures, letting the music unfold as the result of that mutually influential process.

•

In 1979, Carl Stone had an equipment problem. "The only resources I had available to me," he explains, "were at the radio station where I worked, tape recorders and so on, and so the question was: How can I make my pieces with this material?" The station was KPFK in Los Angeles, and the first piece he did, with a phonograph and two stereo tape recorders, was *Sukothai* (1979), named as were all of his pieces after Los Angeles restaurants, mostly Thai and Korean. He describes his technique as "layering," which in this particular piece meant taking a short instrumental interlude from a Purcell opera and building up multiple layers of it by bouncing it from tape channel to tape channel while mixing it with playback from the phonograph. He noted that layering in this fashion caused what began as recognizable sounds to become progressively more abstract and unrecognizable. As he said, "I became interested in the continuous transformation of recognizable musical material, and especially in exploring the middle states somewhere between the recognizable and the abstract."

In 1980, feeling alienated from his audience, he adapted his ideas to performance. At first he used multiple tape recorders and mixers. Then he used a stereo Publison digital-delay harmonizer. As he recalls, "I could freeze a moment of sound, then dynamically compress or expand the endpoints, and still preserve the whole sample." He began to develop a body of works, the first of which was *Kuk Il Kwan* (1981), which he performed on tour in Europe during the fall of 1981. As he tells it, "I would make urban recordings of the soundscape and incorporate them into the next performance." He also used recordings, mainly of baroque or prebaroque classical music, Asian and African music, and Motown: "Through practice, I turned it into pretty interesting collage work."

How did Stone perform these collages? In performing *Dong Il Jang* (1982), for example, he sat at a table on stage facing the audience. On the table were the Publison, a microphone, a phonograph, and a pile of records. He began by saying, "Testing one, two, three," and recorded that into the Publison. He then played back a few milliseconds of his voice, gradually enlarging the playback duration so that the audience would recognize that it was the words that he recorded at the beginning. During the rest of the performance, he inserted material from the records, changed pitch, changed the playback direction, and in general, created on-the-spot sound transformations. Then in 1985, he executed the well-known maneuver called "the upgrade-through-insurance-reimbursement play." He tells it:

> A day or two before Christmas, my Publison was stolen along with the rest of my studio, allowing me to collect a jolly insurance check. I took a look around and asked, "Do I want to turn this into another Publison, or might not it be wiser to try something new?" So I bought a Prophet 2000 and a TX-816. The software was the real problem. There were a couple of sequencers on the market, but they weren't really very interesting as live performance vehicles. So I was very glad when, on tour in late 1986, I chanced by Albany and was given a beta copy of M. It changed my life.

Stone became an M musician, composing and performing, among many other pieces, *Hop Ken* (1987), *Wall Me Do* (1987), *Amatersau* (1988), *Jang Toh* (1988), *Nekai* (1988), and *Gadberry's* (1989). As he put it, "I considered M to be my instrument."

•

Giuseppe Englert bought a Macintosh in 1986 and used it with his colleagues at GAIV. As he recalls, "At first, we used Intelligent Music's M—all of the members of the group were enthusiastic about it, so we all used it." Englert composed many pieces with M, among them *'Mus Est Syllaba'* (1987), *Basilico*

(1988), *Dodeca* (1989), and *Plusieurs Multiples* (1990). But he was also inspired to go further into software development, especially given the presence and interest in GAIV of Vincent Lesbros, an unusually gifted Macintosh programmer. Following Lesbros' suggestion and Englert's proposal of certain musical algorithms, they began work on Metro 3. It was, as Englert put it, "mostly an act of pride, because we had to have our own MIDI program—we had been happy with M but we had to go further and make a program including some algorithms that M did not offer." Metro 3 allowed a composer to compose up to eight independent voices, with controls for each voice, ranging from deterministic to random, for timbre, tempo, rhythm, loudness, and melody patterns. Englert used Metro 3 to compose *Sopra la Girolmeta* (1991).

•

By the mid-1980s, Francisco Kröpfl in Argentina was beginning to move away from fixed structures to processes based on transformations and interactions. His *Mutation II* (1985), for example, was about interactions. As he explains, "I wanted three different sound characters to confront each other as if they were characters in a play, and I imagined those sounds in their evolutions and confrontations."

In 1990, Kröpfl's ideas on transformation were recast into realtime software by Miguel Calzon as AREM (Algoritmos para la Reinterpretacion de Estructuras Musicales / Algorithms for the Reinterpretation of Musical Structures), written with MAX. AREM took an input such as what someone might play on a keyboard, analyzed it in terms of pitch and rhythmic characteristics to decide the probabilities with which one characteristic followed another, and then used those probabilities to cause transformations in the playback. In his *Incursions in the Arem* (1993), what Kröpfl plays on a keyboard is played back along with the transformations, giving the impression of a keyboard instrument with its own personality responding to its performer.

•

Bruno Spoerri's musical ideas were congruent with Intelligent Music's software. He said, "I was very happy when control software began to appear in 1987, like Intelligent Music's M and Jam Factory, that did something more than sequencers or score programs or note lists." Spoerri, a professional jazz saxophone player and composer based in Zürich, Switzerland, had been since the 1960s interested in improvisation with electronics. Like most improvisors, he welcomed serendipity. He tells a short story: "From the beginning, I was interested in using electronics in live, improvisational situations and I welcomed the accidents, so one of my best performances was in the days of analog synthesizers, in the 1970s, when I played on a hot afternoon in open air at the Montreux Jazz Festival and one of my synthesizers started to make strange sounds that it never made before—it was great!"

Spoerri began to use small computers in performance in the early 1980s. He remembers:

> I didn't see any way to do anything important with a computer. Until, that is, I heard Hans Deyssenroth in, I think, 1981. Hans was a member of the electronic progressive band Brainticket. He was working with a tiny KIM-1 computer and he wrote a program that controlled a Moog synthesizer. His program improvised. It sounded almost like Weather Report. Then computers began to interest me, so we got together and he did a program for me for a Commodore 64, a little computer. That program was a sort of echo and looping device, and I did some concerts with it.

Spoerri was interested in using a computer as a controller, not as a sound generator, and he wanted to learn more about it. He became one of the ringleaders of the Swiss Society for Computer Music because, as he said, "I found that it was impossible for someone to buy the necessary equipment out of private money, so I thought the only way to do something interesting was through an organization." In fact, the Swiss Society for Computer Music, conceived by Bruno Spoerri and Tonino Greco, was founded in 1982 at a table in Spoerri's garden near Zürich. Spoerri and Greco were soon joined by Gerald Bennett and Rainer Boesch as the core group. Their first public event, in February 1983, was a two-day conference at Radio Studio Zürich, with guests Max Mathews and Jean-Claude Risset and a concert by Brainticket.

The next step occurred in 1984, when Spoerri, Greco, Boesch, and Bennett founded the Swiss Center for Computer Music. (The founders represented all of the linguistic regions of Switzerland plus Bennett's native English—as Greco said, "We have a German Swiss, an Italian Swiss, a French Swiss, and an American Swiss.") Fortune had it that 1984 was the so-called "Year of Music" in Switzerland, and the Swiss government was particularly interested in funding musical projects. The newly formed center received a grant, basic equipment was purchased, including a DMX-1000 digital synthesizer, and activities began. In 1985, there was a course in programming the DMX-1000; in 1986, there were MIDI courses and an international workshop in music notation by computer; and in 1988, David Zicarelli did a workshop called "An Introduction to MIDI Programming." Meanwhile Bennett used the center to work in software synthesis, and Greco and Boesch developed a program called Musicologo for musical education. Further, Boesch and Daniel Weiss conceived and built a DSP board made to fit inside the Apple II. Boesch performed with it in concerts until the Apple II became obsolete.

Spoerri developed a personal and portable performance-oriented system and used it to program dynamic interactive processes. In *Controlled Risk* (1986), for example, he set up a MIDI feedback situation. He describes it:

> I used a pitch-to-MIDI converter from the saxophone and fed back the output of the synthesizer into the pitch-to-MIDI converter again. In a

way, it's a controlled use of mistakes. There's an inherent delay, about twenty milliseconds, enough to trigger a new note. Then there were mistakes in pitch detection, mostly at a fifth or octave. The result was that as soon as it didn't get a new note from the saxophone, it started spreading out the pitches it caused to be played and it even did some rhythmic things that I can't explain. And the result was that it reminded me of some early Chris McGregor and Brotherhood of Breath pieces, where they played almost in unison, then they spread out and came together again. The point was to use the mistakes of the machine as a sort of controlled randomness. I was never interested in letting the synthesizers do exactly what I wanted because I always used them as improvising partners, to augment my playing and give me further cues for what to play next.

Spoerri's next pieces were *Drum Song* (1986), for which he used Jam Factory, and *Rue du Cherche-MIDI* (1987), for which he used M. In both pieces, he played notes that were played back as transformed pitch and rhythm patterns while he continued to play, and he used the notes he played to control the way the software transformed what he played. He continues:

The important thing for me was to have a partner in the computer who threw balls at me, who gave me a reason to react in a certain way, but who would react in a logical way. I didn't know *exactly* what the software would do, but I knew *about* what it would do, and so the action of the program is half foreseeable and half not predictable. Which was great. The foreseeable part made me feel that it was part of my performance; the unpredictable part gave me cues for doing something.

Then Spoerri began to use MAX (a prerelease version), which in his words, "let me expand my ideas." In a performance of *A Digit for Dr. Diamond* (1989), his relationship with the computer went through different states. First, the computer reacted to certain pitches with simple accompanying notes, then it began to echo phrases and transpose them with a delay, then it played arpeggios where the intervals and the range of the arpeggios were changed according to the loudness with which he played, and then it became more active, composing its own notes. In his words:

The main idea of it is that leadership goes from me gradually over to the computer and I have to follow the computer towards the end of the piece, rather than it following me. At the end of the piece, it doesn't react to me at all. I just react to it. The benefit for me, in improvising especially in free jazz, is that the formal aspects of music very often get lost, and here I'm using the controlling force of the computer to bring me into a formal framework for my improvising.

•

In summary, during the 1970s and 1980s many composers and performers gained experience in creating and working with realtime interactive processes. By the mid-1990s, a substantial body of knowledge had been formed and the idea had become credible. And people began to say that there were two reasons to use electronics in making music. One was access to sound. The other was interaction.

• • •

Chapter Twelve

Where Are
We Going?

As Bruce Pennycook said, "The players that we see on a day to day basis out there making music are the players of traditional instruments—I'd like to have my pieces played live in the kind of venues that attract music lovers as those venues have for hundreds of years." Pennycook's concern, accordingly, is not only to extend the concert tradition but also to extend traditional instruments and to do it in a way that is practical. In his view, "We need to build instruments that are inexpensive, highly portable, simple to use, and that performers will enjoy using—I'm thinking also of automated mixing, in-hall acoustic feedback systems that do automatic adjustments, and small, self-powered high fidelity loudspeakers that can be put in the milieu of the performers so that from the audience's viewpoint the sound seems to come from the players."

Taking it yet a step further, particularly in his *Praescio* compositions, he has explored ways in which chamber music performers can trigger and control electronically generated accompaniments. In *Praescio-I* (1986), for example, a saxophone player presses a MIDI footpedal. In *Praescio-II Amnesia* (1988), for soprano, flute, violin, cello, and keyboard synthesizer, the keyboard player triggers sequences of notes and effects. In *Praescio-III The Desert Speaks* (1988), for harpsichord and electronics, the different registers of the harpsichord are used to trigger different accompaniment events in a precomposed list. *Praescio-V Frontline* (1990), for trumpet, saxophone, and computer-MIDI system, written for himself and Dexter Morrill for a European tour, uses special software called MIDI-LIVE which is controlled by switches installed on the trumpet and saxophone. As Pennycook describes it, "Numerous tightly coordinated events were triggered in rapid succession by the saxophone and trumpet to produce a rapid repartee of gestures." *Praescio-IV* (1990), completed shortly after *Praescio-V*, uses special keys on a clarinet to trigger electronic events. As he remarks, referring to *Praescio-IV*, "Players that have never encountered electronic music before are so excited about having truly responsive control over the computer, compared to playing with tape, that they can't stop talking about it."

•

In 1981, for the first performance of his *Sonic Waters*, Michel Redolfi delighted swimmers by launching underwater loudspeakers from the coast of California into the Pacific Ocean. Quickly concluding, however, that swimming pools were musically superior to the ocean, his subsequent performances have been in public pools, where audiences have happily floated and dived while listening to his underwater concerts. *Sonic Waters*, performed with a Synclavier, was soon followed by *Sonic Waters II* (1983–1989), performed with a Synclavier II. Other underwater pieces included *L'écume de la Nuit* (1984, Waves of the Night), composed for the Roman baths in Strasbourg, and *Crysallis* (1992), an underwater opera composed for the Olympic pool in Grenoble. And why? Why do concerts underwater? He answers: "It's a high-tech experience in a very sensual environment . . ."

But a swimming pool, as verily it is said, is not a concert hall. And Redolfi's swimming-pool compositions comprise but one example of departures from the traditional. Many composers of electronic music, at least in particular projects, have stepped aside from the concert tradition to create unusual types of presentations. Indeed, it seems as if electronic music in its many and various manifestations has lent itself extremely well to a wide variety of venues, including the concert hall but also including extravagant environments, art-and-technology, interactive installations, CD-ROM, and the World Wide Web.

There was the Philips Pavilion at the Brussels World's Fair in 1958, among the first of the extravagant environments, for which Iannis Xenakis designed the building. There was the Pepsi Pavilion at Expo '70 in Japan, perhaps the most ambitious of the extravagant environments, with artificial fog, a gigantic spherical mirror, robots, a lighting system designed by Tony Martin, lasers by Lowell Cross, and music by David Tudor, Gordon Mumma, and others. There were spectacles with sound and light, lasers, images, and fireworks created and produced by Christian Clozier in the mid-1980s, at the Piazza San Marco in Venice, at the Château de Chambord in the Loire Valley, at the Château de Versailles, at the Bourges Cathedral, and at many other locations throughout Europe. Clozier's spectacles were site specific. As Françoise Barrière, one of his partners, wrote: "Each show is carefully conceived and minutely thought out in order to celebrate the place or the monument in front of which it happens, making use of its architecture, its environment, its cultural aura . . ."

And there were Xenakis' *polytopes*, as he called them, multimedia spectacles of light and sound. There was the *Polytope de Montréal* (1967) at the French Pavilion at Montreal Expo, which included tapes of orchestral sounds and 1,200 strobe lights mounted on a structure of steel cables. There was the polytope at Persepolis in Iran (1971), with an eight-track tape of transformed instrumental sounds, with flashlights, fires, and projections. As Xenakis describes it, "They asked me to do a show with music on the mountain dominating Persepolis, in Iran—I did it with school children bearing electric torches, going to the top of the mountain and coming down, and with projectors making shapes on the mountain." There was the *Polytope de Cluny* (1972), with computer-controlled strobe lights, lasers, and tape. One entered the T-shaped hall of the Roman Baths at Cluny, at the intersection of the Boulevard Saint-Michel and the Boulevard Saint-Germain in Paris, sat against a wall, and watched and listened. There was the *Polytope of Mycenae* (1978), a spectacle of lights, movement, and music surrounding the Mycenae Acropolis in Greece. And there was the *Diatope* (1978), with 1,600 pinpoint lights, four lasers, 400

Iannis Xenakis' Diatope, as installed outside the Centre Pompidou in Paris in 1978. The public entered the tent and sat on a plexiglass floor, lit from below. Each show was about twenty minutes' duration and consisted of computer-controlled lasers, pinpoint lights, and sound. Photo by Joel Chadabe.

mirrors, diverse optical effects, and as music, *La Légende d'Eer* (1977), commissioned by and composed principally at the WDR studio in Cologne. The *Diatope*, exhibited first at the Centre Pompidou in Paris and then shown at other locales in Europe, was housed in a large, red, steel-supported tent, its shape reminiscent of the 1958 Philips Pavilion. One entered the tent and sat on a translucent plexiglass floor with soft colored lights below. Each show was forty-six minutes. Pinpoints of lights in varying patterns flashed through the space, lasers formed and reformed colored outlines of shapes above, and sounds came from all around. The music and lights were not synchronized. As Xenakis said, "The music doesn't have to be connected to the lights—we have ears *and* eyes."

•

Woody and Steina Vasulka, video artists and more, active through the 1980s and 1990s in all manner of combining musical technology with visuals and other technologies, had begun as early as 1970 to combine electronic music with video imagery. From their perspective, the electronic arts, including music, were about process, and the different electronic arts, including music and video, were simply different ways to display the same core process. In 1970 in New York, they bought a Buchla synthesizer through an ad in the *Village Voice*, and they collaborated with Rhys Chatham on a first attempt to control video with audio signals. In their words:

> Our basic interest was combining electronic music and video. In fact, from our point of view, there was no division between electronic music and electronic video. In New York, there was not much that we would call unassigned video, not many people that would think of video as a subject of its own investigation. Video was mostly considered a continuation of film, or had a political or social agenda, but our approach had no social agenda. We were curious about this new material, and the closest cousin was the latest products of electronic music and the synthesizers. So we immediately used audio synthesizers to generate patterns on the screen and we learned that it was the same material, differently displayed.

•

In *Well* (1969), Tony Martin used vibrating mercury and various transducers to sense the movements of people's hands and control sounds and images. In *Sunspots* (1981), Liz Phillips used theremin-type devices to detect the movement of people in a gallery space and control sound accordingly. In *Talkshow* (1988), Paul Lansky, in his words, "let speech become the activator of rhythmic and speech templates, with the sounds made by synthesizers." And Lansky adds: "The best time I had with it was when I set it up as an installation to improvise with its own output, so it became a kind of automaton—it would go on for five or ten minutes and then quiet down and someone would go in and

Tony Martin's Well (1969) as seen at the Howard Wise Gallery, New York City, in October 1969. Photo courtesy Tony Martin.

Liz Phillips' Sunspots I & II (1979–1981) as it appeared in 1981 at Soundings, an exhibition at the Neuberger Museum, State University of New York at Purchase. The screen on the left and the copper tubing on the right act as theremins, responding to the proximity of people and allowing spectators to influence the music produced by the synthesizer in the cabinet at the rear left. Photo by Joel Chadabe.

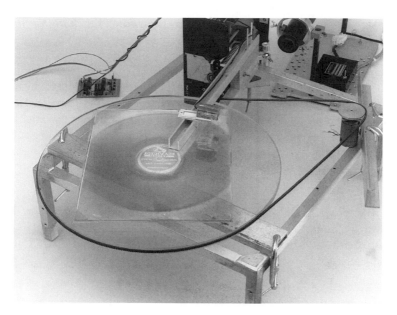

*Paul DeMarinis' Ich auch Berlin(er) (1993), an example
of electronic music as a gallery installation.
Photo by Patrick Sumner. Courtesy Paul DeMarinis.*

clap or shout and it would go again . . ." Paul DeMarinis describes his *Ich auch Berlin(er)* (1993), a gallery installation:

> A tribute to the Berlin(er) brothers, Emil, Irving, and John Fitzgerald. A gelatin dichromate hologram of a 78 rpm record of the 'Beer Barrel Polka' is rotated on a transparent turntable and played by a green laser. Once I realized that only light reflections were needed to make the recorded grooves audible, it became apparent that a hologram (the memory of light reflecting from a surface) would suffice to play music. Here, sans needle, sans groove, the band plays on.

Il Giardino di Babele (1990), an installation composed by Ron Kuivila for the Soccer World Cup in Florence, consisted of three elements: a *trompe l'oeil* blue moon on the top floor of the tower in the piazza Poggi; a garden in which the alarms and chimes of 500 watches started sounding at nightfall and continued in staggered fashion throughout the next hour; and a playing field in which people's movements affected sounds. In Kuivila's *Der Schnueffelstaat* (1991) at the Technorama in Winterthur, Switzerland, images in a video projection changed from "smart bomb" crosshairs to rectangular Swiss flags when a video sensing system detected motion in the room. For *Singing Shadows* (1994) at the New York Hall of Science, Kuivila programmed a video sensing system to scan shadows on a panel and control musical processes according to their changing shapes.

For *In Thin Air* (1995), David Behrman's idea was to re-create in a gallery installation the types of interactive performing situations that he'd worked with in his earlier pieces. As he said, "I wanted to give those experiences to any interested person, even someone who knows nothing about music . . ." So he assembled an input system of footpedals, buttons, and an array of light-beam sensors designed by James Lo and placed them around the installation so that members of the public would feel invited to use them. He explains:

> You explore. And you may be surprised, and that's part if it. It's not always a one-to-one relationship between a gesture and a musical result because the algorithm is in between you and the music. There's an interplay between knowing what will happen and being surprised.

•

Barton and Priscilla McLean have earned their living with interactive installations. They came into electronics through university work. They had worked with Iannis Xenakis at Indiana University, and Barton McLean subsequently directed studios at Indiana University at South Bend and at the University of Texas at Austin. But they came into their own after leaving the university environment and touring as The McLean Mix. Two threads developed through their work: nature and interactivity. Priscilla McLean's *Beneath the Horizon I* (1978) included a tape of whale sounds. And in a performance of *In Wilderness Is the Preservation of the World* (1985), which included projections and environmental and animal sounds, as she said, "The audience was performing with us . . ."

Interactivity was the generating idea in their collaborative *Rainforest*. For one thing, they had been exploring the idea of large mixtures of musical and visual, and human and environmental, elements. For *Rainforest Images* (1993), for example, the McLeans recorded sounds in the Peruvian Amazon, Australia, and other far-flung places; they recorded humans improvising with didjeridoos, voices, and other instruments at their concerts and installations; they recorded sounds in studios at the Canberra School of the Arts, University of Wyoming, and elsewhere; and they processed their sounds in collaboration with Panaiotis, using the Expanded Instrument System at the Oliveros Foundation studio in Kingston, New York. After four years of collecting material, they put it together in a forty-eight-minute organic mix of human, nature, and electronic sounds. It took a year, as Barton McLean said, "all without a marriage counsellor." He subsequently composed a videotape of *Rainforest Images* with images he had shot on a trip to the Peruvian Amazon and then mixed and edited with video artist Hasnul J. Saidon at iEAR Studios in Troy, New York.

For another thing, as Barton McLean said, "Over the last ten years or so, I've found that audiences are increasingly disinclined to want to sit still and listen to a full concert." The McLeans began to develop *Rainforest* through experiments in local venues at which they invited the public to improvise with equipment that they'd set up beforehand. Then they went to el Yunque, a national park in Puerto Rico. As Barton McLean recalls, "We were there at night walking from the top of the mountain down to the bottom and we heard various strata of sounds depending upon the altitude, and each stratum was totally different—as we went downward, we could hear them blending into one another as in a huge electronic composition."

And so *Rainforest* took shape and name. In an installation, a taped drone of recorded and synthesized sounds and continuous projections of rainforest images provide an atmosphere in which members of the public are invited to perform on electronic and acoustic instruments. Does it work? The McLeans answer:

Barton:	We've learned to adapt our presentation to the level of sophistication of the audience. We're as at home with an audience with no prior experience as with an audience that's technologically-oriented.
Priscilla:	We're going on the premise that our work will be satisfying to our host . . .
Barton:	What we do is not a part of ordinary experience, so there's usually some apprehension when we arrive. We try to allay their fears and assure them that the large commitment they've made to hire us is not going to be a disaster.
Priscilla:	At the Nature Sound Society at the Oakland Museum, the audience came up on stage en masse and performed for a half-hour.
Barton:	In Stamford, Connecticut, on New Year's Eve 1992, we had over 1,000 participants in the *Rainforest* installation—of all types, adults, children and in between. It was cold out and they came with their mittens on. And there were masses of people trying to get at the equipment to make sounds . . .
Priscilla:	In September 1990, at the Canberra Institute of the Arts, people were waiting at the door at 9 A.M., and the art students were playing the didjeridoo, slap sticks, singing, and improvising with the *Rainforest* sounds.

•

As personal computers and CD-ROMs became normal consumer items in the early 1990s, the idea of artistic interactivity at home became a common thought. Some people, of course, had thought of it much earlier. Whereas a compact disc might bring a concert hall into one's living room, Max Mathews had reasoned that an interactive approach would actually let someone conduct:

"The Radio Baton and Conductor Program," as he explained, "may create another way of experiencing music, where instead of passively sitting and listening to a compact disc, you could buy the score to a piece of music on a floppy disk and conduct your own interpretation of the music." And the initial goal of Intelligent Music, founded in 1983, had been to develop an interactive instrument for the home entertainment market. The following words are excerpted from an early Intelligent Music business plan:

> The definitive characteristic of Intelligent Music's interactive instrument is that it generates musical information by itself as it plays. It shares control of the music with a user, thus compensating for the user's lack of previously acquired skill. It allows anyone to participate in a sophisticated musical process through performing, conducting, improvising, composing, interacting with the instrument in any other way . . .

Interactivity at home means that an amateur, perhaps without talent or skill, can participate in a rewarding way in a musical process. Is it possible? Yes, because the aspect of musical performance which requires skill, namely playing the notes, can be eliminated from the performer's tasks. Is it good? Yes, because it allows people to participate in musical processes at a meaningful artistic level whether or not they have previously studied a musical instrument. Laurie Spiegel, in 1987, said it well:

> This is a very exciting time for music. With the advent of computers, many of music's past restrictions can begin to fall away, so that it becomes possible for more people to make more satisfying music, more enjoyably and easily, regardless of physical coordination or theoretical study, of keyboard skills or fluency with notation. This doesn't imply a dilution of musical quality. On the contrary, it frees us to go further and raises the base-level at which music making begins. It lets us focus more clearly on aesthetic content, on feeling and movement in sound, on the density or direction of experience, on sensuality, structure, and shape—so that we can concentrate better on what each of us loves in music that lies beyond the low level of how to make notes, at which music making far too often bogs down.

●

Morton Subotnick's *All My Hummingbirds Have Alibis* (1993), the first musical composition created specifically as a multimedia CD-ROM, allows a listener at home to select the ordering of sections and choose which visuals are seen—score, pictures, or words—as the music plays. It was published by The Voyager Company under the direction of Jane Wheeler. In her words, "We're interested in artists, authors and composers creating works for this medium, we're trying to do new things—we're more like a research group than a standard commercial venture . . ." She continues:

One of the things we ask ourselves when we undertake something is: "Does this project need to be done with interactive media?" One thing that was really important to Mort's work is that the music was based on the Max Ernst collage novels. What we're able to do is to combine the images that inspired the work and the notation and the ballet section where he turned the images themselves into a visual ballet. And this is not possible in any other medium. Composers have to compose more than the music element; they have to start working with visual artists and thinking of the visual. The right combination of visual imagery and music can have a tremendous impact. There are certain things that have been done on stage, and I think the same can be true of the computer, as a new chamber art medium. It's the intimacy of it, it's you and it, and the relationship is very close.

Peter Gabriel's *XPlora 1* allows a listener at home to use a mouse to position the faders of an on-screen mixer. Todd Rundgren's *No World Order* invites a listener at home to function something like the conductor of an orchestra, manipulating a variety of on-screen controls to affect various aspects (Rundgren calls them "flavors") of the music. The following is from his liner notes:

> Standard music CDs are like amusement park cars that run on tracks. *No World Order* removes the track; you can drive wherever you want in the park. You control the tempo, the mood, the mix, and the freedom with which musical events are selected. Speed up the tempo. Reverse the order. Change the mix. Overthrow conventional expectations and create something entirely new.

Is the level of interaction in these CD-ROMs interesting enough to warrant the trouble? Well, it's a beginning. But Subotnick offers a better answer: "If a piece does not need new vision and new experience or new expressive qualities, then you don't need a performer." And how, then, do you bring vision, experience, and expressive qualities to a performance without bringing the notes and sounds? By performing, as Subotnick explains, "such things as loudness, tempo, pacing between notes, crescendos, pedalling, the nuances—the musician is to the music what a conductor is to any orchestra." Max Mathews, in fact, had been thinking along the same lines. Referring to his Conductor Program, Mathews said:

> I wondered what useful function computers could serve in live performance. It seemed to me that there were many things that I did *not* want the computer to do—like to limit or interfere with or contribute to the expressive arts of the music—because those are the domain of the performer.
>
> But it also seemed to me that there were a number of aspects of music where the performer didn't need any freedom of choice. The sequence of

notes to be played, for example, was an area in which the computer could legitimately help a performer in making it easier to do things correctly. And this led to the concept of the *expressive sequencer*, where the predetermined parts of the music were in the computer memory as a sequence of notes or chords or events, but where the performer was controlling everything about the way those notes got played . . .

•

Gabriel, Rundgren, Subotnick, and Mathews view the listener at home as a performer. But Laurie Spiegel's idea was to turn the listener at home into a composer. She began to work with personal computers in the late 1970s following her work with GROOVE at Bell Labs. She tells it:

> In 1978, Jef Raskin, one of the original crew at Apple and also a fine musician, showed up at my loft with a prototype 48k Apple II as a present. He said, "I'm going to take a nap in your back room and by the time I wake up I want you to have written a program for it." And by the time he woke up, I had written a program . . .

In 1979, she worked as a codeveloper of the Apple II-based alphaSyntauri music system, which she used to compose *Nomads* (1981) and *A Harmonic Algorithm* (1981). In 1981, she worked with the McLeyvier, a hybrid system named after its designer David McLey, extending its operating system into what she called IMP (Interactive Music Processor). Although the McLeyvier never got to market, Spiegel used it for several compositions, among them *Three Modal Pieces: A Cosmos, A Legend, A Myth* (1983), *Harmonic Rhythms* (1983), and *Immersion* (1983). And she said: "I found most wonderful its linguistic interface and the fact that it was extremely realtime savvy in design—it could play without the slightest glitch in sound while loading files from disk, displaying and updating music notation on the screen, and expanding disk-based macro commands in its music language."

In 1985, she finished Music Mouse. Earlier, at Bell Labs in about 1973, she and Max Mathews had coined the term *intelligent musical instrument* to describe an instrument that first sensed its performer's intent by the type and context of the performer's actions and then extended the performer's controls to execute the music automatically. She adds, "Intelligent instruments let people play music on a compositional level."

Music Mouse is an intelligent musical instrument realized as software for Macintosh, Amiga, and Atari computers. How does it work? Vertical and horizontal keyboards are shown graphically on the computer's screen. A performer moves a mouse through an on-screen grid of vertical and horizontal lines that simultaneously intersect both keyboards, thereby aligning the mouse, at every moment, with a note on each keyboard, thereby causing two notes to play simultaneously. The software automatically generates additional musical material. The type of material, whether additional contrapuntal lines, for example, or melodic ornamentation or chordal harmony, is determined by which keys are pressed on the computer's alphanumeric keyboard. And the result is that the performer gets back far more than was played. Spiegel continues:

> The software interprets the player's actions and outputs music which can be thought of and experienced as a transformation of the player's physical movement. The actual music produced will vary with an action's context, history, and position in what can be thought of as a multidimensional musical space.

Spiegel used Music Mouse to compose *Cavis Muris* (1986) and most of her compact disc *Unseen Worlds* (1987-1990). She continues:

> In coding Music Mouse, I tried to minimize violations of musicality while allowing maximal variety of output. I used constraints, logical tests, filtration, transformation, a loosely enforced bias toward continuity in all dimensions, and very careful specification of non-user-settable constants for harmonic progression and modulation. The touchiest part of this task was in the area of transitions between scales, modes, or contrapuntal voicings when they are switched from the ASCII keyboard during performance. For me, the most interesting material tends to happen when

A screen shot of Laurie Spiegel's Music Mouse. A performer moves the mouse through the grid on the right, thereby selecting and playing simultaneously two notes pointed to by the "polyphonic cursor" along the vertical and horizontal keyboards. The software adds two notes to produce four-voice harmony, according to the various settings shown in the parameter table on the left.

Music Mouse – An Intelligent Instrument

Voices: 1 2 3 4	MIDI Chan: 1 2 3 4
Harmonic Mode:	Octatonic
Treatment:	Chord
Transposition:	-10
Interval of Transp:	5
Pattern:	4 = OFF
Mouse Movement:	Contrary
Pattern Movement:	Parallel
Articulation:	Half-Legato
Loudness:	100
Sound:	99
Velocity:	100
ModWheel:	0
BreathControl:	64
FootControl:	64
AfterTouch:	64
Portamento:	0
Displaying:	Output
Group = OFF	Tempo1 = 100
MIDI Output ON	Tempo2 600

336 Where Are We Going?

Music Mouse is played with only minimal mouse movement but with lots of use of the qwerty keyboard to change the compositional, orchestrational and other interpretive variables. Music Mouse is like a traditional instrument in that the same sequence of actions by the performer will always produce the same musical results and all sound is in direct response to player action. Nothing is random. The player is in control.

Warren Burt was also in control, with the help of Donald Buchla's Lightning, in a performance of his *Sound Effects Improvisation* at the Perth Institute of Contemporary Art in 1993. He explains:

I know the range of pitches that I want, but I actually don't care which one of those pitches is happening . . . A few small changes in range settings and I can generate a lot of music. If I were using a sequencer, I'd have to specify a lot of detail which in this particular piece is actually superfluous because really what I'm looking for is a statistical character to the music. I'm trying to generate controllable clouds of sound. So I feel relief at not having to specify the detail.

In summary, the software that animates Music Mouse and *Sound Effects Improvisation* automates the musical detail, allowing the performer to make broader gestures, to compose while performing, to pilot the music through time, as if using a fly-by-wire system to fly the music through a musical space. Iannis Xenakis' words come to mind: "With the aid of electronic computers the composer becomes a sort of pilot . . ."

But if the performer is composing, what has the composer done? In the two-stage process of design-then-do, the composer has designed the instrument and its sounds so that the performer can do the music. And as part of the design, the composer has defined the connections between the performer's controls and the musical variables. The composer has determined, in other words, what happens when the performer does this or that. The software-generated ornamentations in Music Mouse follow the performer's lead as if they were kindred airborne objects flying in formation. In *Sound Effects Improvisation*, sound objects realign and regroup in various designs and distributions as if the act of flying through the musical space caused turbulence.

•

The intelligent musical instrument may also be programmed to produce unpredictable elements to which the listener at home can react. Remember what George Lewis said: "as soon as the computer generates something independent, a performer can react to that and go with it." Remember how Bruno Spoerri put it: "The important thing for me was to have a partner in the computer who threw balls at me, who gave me a reason to react in a certain way . . ." Remember the whole history of interactive composing instruments.

New musical ideas generated in the software, perhaps as interpretations of what a performer has just played, perhaps as completely new information, provide cues for a performer's ongoing actions. The software does something to which the performer reacts, the performer does something to which the software reacts, and the music takes its form through that mutually influential and responsive interaction. In such a situation, the listener at home is an *interactive* composer, in other words, an improviser.

•

The traditional musical roles of performer, composer, and improviser can be realized in a wide variety of ways. Remember also that music can be a social activity, that people can come together to play chamber music, to improvise, to sing. It may be, for example, given likely improvements in Internet technology, that a listener at home in the near future will be able to play any one of these roles as a participant in a large group, contributing to a holistic composition while socializing with many other listeners at home around the world; and it may be that the materials of the composition will include images and text as well as music. Thinking of the World Wide Web, one might question whether interactive music will be separable from interactive multimedia.

In September 1995, Carla Scaletti introduced *Public Organ: An Interactive, Networked Sound Installation* simultaneously on the World Wide Web and at the International Computer Music Conference in Banff, Canada. She describes it:

> A sometimes-humorous-sometimes-serious commentary on the Internet, *Public Organ* invites participants to experience linking, lurking, looping and collective thinking through interaction with everyday objects: a television, a radio, a telephone, a spray can, a camera, and a book.

As composer, Scaletti defined the process by which participants interacted. Linking, lurking, and looping meant exchanging information, taking in information, and going through old information. She defined the performance devices ("everyday objects . . .") that participants used and she allowed participants to introduce their own material. As she said, "Web participants will be able to contribute graffiti and images of themselves that will be instantly incorporated into the installation." She described the music that the instrument played: "They will also be able to view images and hear sounds from the physical installation as well as see and talk to other installation participants." And she articulated the underlying concept—that while we act as individuals we participate in a total world—by quoting a passage from *The Lives of a Cell*, a collection of essays by biomedical researcher Lewis Thomas:

> The human brain is the most public organ on the face of the earth, open to everything, sending out messages to everything . . . We pass thoughts

around, from mind to mind, so compulsively and with such speed that the brains of mankind often appear, functionally, to be undergoing fusion.

●

There is no conclusion. The electronic musical instrument of the mid-1990s, like the electronic technology from which it is made, is still at a formative stage. There is no general understanding as to the best types of performance devices, or sound generators, or software. And nothing quite seems to work really well. As composer Terry Fryer put it, "It's like early automobiles—at the turn of the century you had to carry a mechanic to keep things going . . ."

Yet it will all eventually come together: interactive media, interactive composing, intelligent musical instruments, multimedia; listeners at home as performers, conductors, composers, improvisers, and participants; more ergonomic and sensitive performance devices; more expressive and powerful sound generators; more sophisticated, flexible, and creative software; and, of course, supersensitive extended-functionality improvements of traditional instruments for the concert hall.

And perhaps, as we better understand the human process of making music and as we become more aware of the nature of the relationships between people and the musical instruments they play, our understandings will lead us toward using technology more wisely in designing instruments that will be optimally beneficial to human creativity. As that happens, the electronic musical instrument, in its myriad manifestations, is likely to become the most ergonomic, sensitive, expressive, powerful, sophisticated, flexible, creative, socially beneficial, altogether rewarding instrument ever developed. And as we learn how to make it, we'll learn how to play it—and the other way around.

● ● ●

NOTES ON SOURCES
AND MATERIALS

Although much of the music mentioned in this book is available on compact disc, it is not easily found through normal stores. For access to materials, contact Electronic Music Foundation, a not-for-profit organization formed specifically to disseminate information on the history and current development of electronic music:

Electronic Music Foundation　　　　　(518) 434-4110 Voice
116 North Lake Avenue　　　　　　　　(518) 434-0308 Fax
Albany NY 12206　　　　　　　　　　EMF@emf.org
USA　　　　　　　　　　　　　　　　http://www.emf.org

In writing this book, I relied largely on my own experience in the field during the last thirty years as well as personal familiarity with most of the places and events described. I also conducted more than 150 interviews with composers, researchers, and entrepreneurs between the summer of 1993 and the spring of 1996, most of them in person, a few of them by telephone, fax, and e-mail. I did extensive followup to each interview, as appropriate, to verify factual information and correlate what had been said with information in articles, the annual reports of various organizations, concert programs, conference proceedings, and so on. The first few interviews were conducted by taping the conversations. It soon became clear, however, because of the time required to transcribe the tapes, that it would take a few decades rather than a few years to finish writing this book. Consequently, I changed my technique to taking dictation by typing directly into a computer while people were speaking. In some cases, when the person interviewed was speaking French or Italian, I did a simultaneous translation. I edited each interview to put it in the form of a concise and readable statement and then verified each edited statement by sending it to the person interviewed for approval or corrections.

In the following notes, listed by page numbers, the full name of the person interviewed is cited for the first time in each chapter that an interview is quoted. Only the last name is cited for all subsequent quotations from the same interview within the same chapter. Printed sources and general references are cited in their contexts. Recommendations for further reading, hopefully to be found in libraries when they are out of print, can be found at the beginning of the notes for each chapter. I have kept these recommendations to a simple minimum, consistent with the overview character of this book. For those who seek additional sources, extensive bibliographies can be found in many of the recommended books.

Preface

vii　"And now, in this the twentieth century": John Philip Sousa, "The Menace of Mechanical Music," reprinted in *Computer Music Journal*, 1993, 18:1, pp. 14–15.

-　"Put another nickel in": Lyrics to *Music Music Music!*, a popular song by Stephen Weiss and Bernie Baum, 1950.

viii　"We also need new instruments": Edgard Varèse, "The Electronic Medium," a lecture at Yale University, 1962. Reprinted in "The Liberation of Sound," in Elliott Schwartz and Barney Childs, eds., *Contemporary Composers on Contemporary Music* (New York: Holt, Rinehart and Winston, 1967), p. 207.

-　"Electronic music exists only on tape": Herbert Eimert, "What Is Electronic Music?" in *Die Reihe* Vol. 1 (Philadelphia: Theodore Presser, 1958), p. 2.

-　"I think that the electronic tape piece": Interview with Luciano Berio in Barry Shrader, *Introduction to Electro-Acoustic Music* (Englewood Cliffs, NJ: Prentice Hall, 1982), p. 183.

ix　"Conventional instruments produce various noises": Harry F. Olson, *Music, Physics and Engineering* (New York: Dover Publications, 1967), p. 415.

ix   "These effects": Quoted in David H. Paetkau, *The Growth of Instruments and Instrumental Music* (New York: Vantage Press, 1962), p. 342.

xi   "Composers who rival Cage": Alexander Fried, *San Francisco Examiner*, March 28, 1964.

-   "We ask ourselves": From a review of the Conference on Electronic and Concrète Music, broadcast on Radio Basel, Switzerland, in May 1955. Quoted in Otto Luening, "Origins," in Jon H. Appleton and Ronald C. Perera, eds., *The Development and Practice of Electronic Music* (Englewood Cliffs, NJ: Prentice Hall, 1975), p. 15.

-   "The actual musical input": John Rockwell, *The New York Times*, March 6, 1986.

One: The Early Instruments

For general information on early electronic instruments, see Hugh Davies' articles in Stanley Sadie, ed., *The New Grove Dictionary of Musical Instruments* (New York: Grove's Dictionaries, 1984). See also Thomas Rhea, *The Evolution of Electronic Musical Instruments in the United States* (PhD dissertation, George Peabody College, 1972); Richard Schmidt James, *Expansion of Sound Resources in France, 1913–1940, and Its Relationship to Electronic Music* (PhD dissertation, University of Michigan, 1981); and Albert Glinsky, *The Theremin and the Emergence of Electronic Music* (PhD dissertation, New York University, 1992). See Reynold Weidenaar, *Magic Music from the Telharmonium* (Metuchen, NJ: Scarecrow Press, 1995) for a superb account of the story of the Telharmonium. For a description of Hugh Le Caine's work, see Gayle Young, *The Sackbut Blues* (Ottawa: National Museum of Science and Technology, 1989).

1   "setting the clavier stool": Harry Partch, *Genesis of a Music* (New York: DaCapo Press, 1974), p. 384.

-   "Any musical innovation": Plato, *The Republic.*

2   "'Exactly,' said Lewis": E. T. A. Hoffmann, "Automata," in *The Best Tales of Hoffmann,* trans. Alexander Ewing (New York: Dover Publications, 1967), pp. 96-97.

-   *Ether*: See definition of "Inaudible Music" in Nicolas Slonimsky, *Music Since 1900* (New York: Charles Scribner's Sons, 1971), p. 1458.

-   "Dear Balilla Pratella, great Futurist composer": Quoted in *Futurismo* (New York: Abbeville Press, 1986), pp. 560–562.

6   "It did run perfectly in tune with itself": Reynold Weidenaar, *Magic Music from the Telharmonium* (Metuchen, NJ: Scarecrow Press, 1995), p. 186.

7   "I conceived of an instrument": Quoted in Robert Moog, "Out of Thin Air," *Keyboard Magazine*, February 1992.

8   "to carry out Lenin's dictum": Nicolas Slonimsky, in his article on the theremin, *Music Since 1900* (New York: Charles Scribner's Sons, 1971).

9   "they dropped it like a hot potato": From Robert Moog, "Controller Oddities," *Keyboard Magazine*, March 1993.

-   "none of the dancers who tried it": Quoted in Robert Moog, liner notes to *The Art of the Theremin*, Delos CD 1014.

10   "Ms. Rockmore actually uses fingering patterns": Ibid.

11   "In the Soviet Union at that time": Robert Moog, "Out of Thin Air," *Keyboard Magazine*, February 1992.

12   "attracts us like a message": Obukhov dossier at the Bibliothèque Nationale, Paris, quoted in Richard Schmidt James, *Expansion of Sound Resources in France, 1913–1940, and Its Relationship to Electronic Music* (PhD dissertation, University of Michigan, 1981), p. 38.

-   "Sala is convinced of the necessity": Lejaren Hiller, "Technical Report #4," University of Illinois Experimental Music Studio, June 1962.

13   "He was making the instruments one by one": Jean-Claude Eloy, personal communication.

-   "The keyboard facilitates rapid execution": Personal communication to David H. Paetkau, quoted in David H. Paetkau, *The Growth of Instruments and Instrumental Music* (New York: Vantage Press, 1962), p. 342.

15   "They were ecstatic reports": Milton Babbitt, personal communication.

-   "I didn't want to splice tape": Babbitt.

-   "the possibility of entirely new tone complexes": Harry F. Olson, *Music, Physics and Engineering* (New York: Dover Publications, 1967), p. 415.

-   "a 750-vacuum-tube affair": Richard Boulanger, "Interview with Roger Reynolds, Joji Yuasa, and Charles Wuorinen," *Computer Music Journal*, 1984, 8:4, p. 48.

16   "I talked to Harry Olson": Babbitt.

-   "Vladimir and I": Babbitt.

-   "Then came a great two years": Babbitt.

17   "I realized that there was a tremendous discrepancy": Babbitt.

18 "I wrote a trill": Babbitt.
-   "In the notation": Babbitt.
-   "In a nutshell": Babbitt.
-   "The notion": Babbitt.
-   "stole everything that was stealable": Babbitt.
-   "The composer of the future": Quoted in Reynold Weidenaar, op. cit. p. 215.
19 "Music is an art not yet grown up": From a statement by Percy Grainger on Free Music, December 6, 1938, stored in an exhibition case at the Grainger Museum, University of Melbourne, Australia. Reprinted in *Recorded Sound: Journal of the British Institute of Recorded Sound*, January-April 1972, p. 16.
-   "Grainger wanted a composer's machine": Burnett Cross, "Grainger Free Music Machine," *Recorded Sound: Journal of the British Institute of Recorded Sound*, January-April 1972, pp. 17–21.
20 "Kangaroo Pouch": Ibid.

Two: The Great Opening Up of Music to All Sounds

For general background to John Cage's early work, see Richard Kostelanetz, ed., *John Cage* (New York: Praeger, 1970). See also John Cage's writings: *Silence* (Middletown, CT: Wesleyan University Press, 1961); *A Year from Monday* (Middletown, CT: Wesleyan University Press, 1963); and *M* (Middletown, CT: Wesleyan University Press, 1973).

For the history of the phonograph, see Roland Gelatt, *The Fabulous Phonograph, 1877-1977* (New York: Macmillan, 1977). For further information on early magnetic recording, see Marvin Camras, *Magnetic Recording Handbook* (New York: Van Nostrand Reinhold, 1988).

Lowell Cross' "Electronic Music 1948-1953," in *Perspectives of New Music*, 1968, 7:1, pp. 32–65, presents an insightful overview of the first tape studios. See also Pierre Schaeffer, *A la Recherche d'une Musique Concrète* (Paris: Editions du Seuil, 1952) and *Traité des Objets Musicaux* (Paris: Editions du Seuil, 1966). For the history of the Cologne studio, see Marietta Morawska-Büngler, *Schwingende Elektronen: Eine Dokumentation über das Studio für Elektronische Musik des Westdeutschen Rundfunks in Köln, 1951–1986* (Cologne: P. J. Tonger, 1988). For further insight into the Cologne studio, see Karlheinz Stockhausen's articles in *Die Reihe* Volume I, V, and VI (Bryn Mawr, PA: Theodore Presser, 1959).

Varèse' lectures are collected in "The Liberation of Sound," in Elliott Schwartz and Barney Childs, eds., *Contemporary Composers on Contemporary Music* (New York: Holt, Rinehart and Winston, 1967). See also Chou Wen Chung, "A Varèse Chronology," in Ben Boretz and Edward Cone, eds., *Perspectives on American Composers* (New York: W.W. Norton, 1971), and Louise Varèse, *Varèse: A Looking-Glass Diary* (New York: W.W. Norton, 1972).

21 "Absolute, True, and Mathematical Time": Quoted in Max Born, *Einstein's Theory of Relativity* (New York: Dover Publications, 1962), p. 57.
22 *Lundi Rue Christine* was first published in *Soirées de Paris*, II:19, 1913. The French text is:
    Trois becs de gaz allumés
    La Patronne est poitrinaire
    Quand tu auras fini nous jouerons une partie de jacquet
    Un chef d'orchestre qui a mal à la gorge
    Quand tu viendras à Tunis je te ferai fumer du kief
    Ça a l'air de rimer
-   "We must throw wide the window": Claude Debussy, "Monsieur Croche the Dilettante Hater," in *Three Classics in the Aesthetics of Music* (New York: Dover Publications, 1962).
-   "Music was born free": Ferruccio Busoni, *A Sketch of a New Aesthetic in Music* (New York: G. Schirmer, 1911).
23 "Sir and Dear Friend": Quoted in William W. Austin, *Music in the Twentieth Century* (New York: W. W. Norton, 1966), p. 165.
-   "The score of *Parade*": Jean Cocteau, "Le Coq et l'Arlequin," in *Le Rappel à l'Ordre* (Paris: Librairie Stock, 1926), pp. 32, 58.
-   "Antheil has made a beginning": Ezra Pound, "George Antheil and the Theory of Harmony," written in 1927, quoted in Nicolas Slonimsky, *Music Since 1900*, 4th ed. (New York: Charles Scribner's Sons, 1971), p. 434.
24 "Now Mr. Mutt's fountain": Quoted in Anne d'Harnoncourt and Kynaston McShine, eds., *Marcel Duchamp* (New York: Museum of Modern Art, 1975), p. 289.
-   "a combination readymade": Ibid.
25 "Since other men": John Cage, *M* (Middletown, CT: Wesleyan University Press, 1973), p. 32.
-   "Structure in music": John Cage, "Forerunners of Modern Music," in *Silence* (Middletown, CT: Wesleyan University Press, 1961), p. 62.

25   "I felt the need": John Cage, liner notes to *The 25-Year Retrospective Concert of the Music of John Cage*, produced by George Avakian. The concert took place May 15, 1958 at Town Hall in New York. The quote was reprinted in "[On Earlier Pieces]" in Richard Kostelanetz, ed., *John Cage* (New York: Praeger Publishers, 1970), p. 127.
-    "the structure": John Cage, "Music as Process," in *Silence* (Middletown, CT: Wesleyan University Press, 1961), pp. 19–22.
26   "I believe that the use of noise": John Cage, "The Future of Music: Credo," in *Silence* (Middletown, CT: Wesleyan University Press, 1961), pp. 3-6.
-    "wherever we are": Ibid.
-    "Certainly the idea": Pierre Schaeffer, *A la Recherche d'une Musique Concrète* (Paris: Editions du Seuil, 1952), pp. 18-19.
-    "Here I am": Ibid.
-    "This determination": Ibid. p. 22.
27   "At that point": Pierre Henry, personal communication.
-    "I found my voice": Henry.
-    "A lot of the *Symphonie*": Henry.
28   "There being nowadays": Oberlin Smith, "Some Possible Forms of Phonograph," *The Electrical World*, September 8, 1888.
29   "risk of instantly decapitating anyone": Desmond Briscoe and Roy Curtis-Bramwell, *The BBC Radiophonic Workshop* (London: BBC, 1983), pp. 11-12.
-    "thrashed ungovernably about": Ibid.
30   "The center of the Magnetophone production": Quoted in Mark Mooney, Jr., "The History of Magnetic Recording," *Hi-Fi Tape Recording*. From a reprint of the article that does not identify the issue of the magazine in which it was originally printed.
-    "Bing Crosby started transcription broadcasting": Ibid.
32   "There was a riot": Henry.
-    "*Le Voile d'Orphée* existed within the larger *Orphée*": Henry.
33   "It was the *Symphonie*": Henry.
-    "It gave me a taste": Henry.
-    "I left because he wanted me to leave": Henry.
34   "It was a question of recording a door": Henry.
-    "The idea of musique concrète": Iannis Xenakis, personal communication.
-    "At that time": Xenakis.
-    "I was not paid": Xenakis.
-    "It's interesting for me": Xenakis.
35   "I did *Bohor*": Xenakis.
-    "Musique concrète wasn't at all a music of noises": François Bayle, personal communication.
36   "to follow the process suggested by Dr. Meyer-Eppler": Quoted in Otto Luening, "Origins," in Jon H. Appleton and Ronald C. Perera, eds., *The Development and Practice of Electronic Music* (Englewood Cliffs, NJ: Prentice Hall, 1975), p. 13. Luening received the information directly from Meyer-Eppler.
-    "*Musica su Due Dimensioni*": Ibid.
37   "I, in turn, assert": Pierre Boulez, "Eventually . . .," originally published in *Revue Musicale*, 1952. Reprinted in Pierre Boulez, *Notes of an Apprenticeship*, trans. Herbert Weinstock (New York: Alfred A. Knopf, 1968), p. 148. Weinstock's translation reads "the dodecaphonic language" instead of "serialism," but since the terms are equivalent in this context, I used "serialism" for consistency.
-    "Goethe's primeval plant": From a lecture by Anton Webern, February 19, 1932. Subsequently reprinted in Willi Reich, ed., *The Path to the New Music*, trans. Leo Black (Bryn Mawr, PA: Theodore Presser, 1963), p. 53.
-    "It is certain": Herbert Eimert, "What Is Electronic Music," in *Die Reihe,* Vol. I (Bryn Mawr, PA: Theodore Presser, 1959), pp. 6-9.
38   "a sine-wave is recorded": Karlheinz Stockhausen, "Two Lectures," in *Die Reihe,* Vol. V (Bryn Mawr, PA: Theodore Presser, 1961), p. 61.
-    "When I went to Cologne": Gottfried Michael Koenig, personal communication.
39   "Wherein lies the difference": Karlheinz Stockhausen, "Two Lectures," in *Die Reihe,* Vol. V (Bryn Mawr, PA: Theodore Presser, 1961), p. 59.
-    "The lines and words": Karlheinz Stockhausen, "Music and Speech," a lecture given at Darmstadt in 1959. Reprinted in *Die Reihe*, Vol. VI (Bryn Mawr, PA: Theodore Presser, 1961), pp. 57–58. For further discussion of the use of the text, see Karlheinz Stockhausen, "Actualia," *Die Reihe*, Vol. I, pp. 45–51.
-    "In the composition": Karlheinz Stockhausen, "Music and Speech," a lecture given at Darmstadt in 1959. Reprinted in *Die Reihe*, Vol. VI (Bryn Mawr, PA: Theodore Presser, 1961), pp. 57–58.

40   "In my *Gesang der Jünglinge*": Karlheinz Stockhausen, "Two Lectures," in *Die Reihe,* Vol. V (Bryn Mawr, PA: Theodore Presser, 1961), p. 68.

41   "from the Imperial Japanese Court": Karlheinz Stockhausen, liner notes to Deutsche Grammophon LP 137012.

42   "Today, only three years later": Ibid.

-   "National anthems": Karlheinz Stockhausen, liner notes to Deutsche Grammophon LP 139422.

43   "It was an experimental time in Tokyo": Joji Yuasa, personal communication.

-   "but there was of course no electronic studio": Toshi Ichiyanagi, personal communication.

-   "It was very lively": Ichiyanagi.

-   "I was more or less known": Yuasa.

-   "I tried to compose": Joji Yuasa, "The Shadow of Tape Music on Instrumental Music," in *Contemporary Music Review*, 1987, I:2, p. 65.

44   "Same name as Mayuzumi's piece": Yuasa.

-   "We wish him well": Quoted in Otto Luening, op. cit. p. 15.

-   "We transported our equipment": Ibid.

45   "The result": Ibid.

-   "We were met": Ibid.

-   "Did not seem to detract." Ibid.

-   "We wrote a report": Ibid.

-   "In 1955": Ibid.

46   "I assisted him": Mario Davidovsky, personal communication.

-   "Life at that time": Davidovsky.

47   "From 1960 to 1970": Otto Luening, op. cit. p. 21.

-   "My major goal": Davidovsky.

-   "The sound was very new for me": Luciano Berio, personal communication.

-   "A few weeks later": Berio.

48   "radio had come to be seen": Alvise Vidolin, "Avevamo nove oscillatori . . ." ("We had nine oscillators . . ."), a talk given at the Civica Scuola di Musica, Milan, November 16, 1989.

-   "the idea of a radiophonic art": Luciano Berio, "Prospettive nella Musica," *Elettronica*, 1956.

-   "Bruno and I immediately agreed": Berio.

-   "The idea of the studio": Berio.

49   "The musician may have a clear idea": Alfredo Lietti, "Gli Impianti Tecnici dello Studio di Fonologia Musicale di Radio Milano," *Elettronica*, 1956.

-   "What I emphasized": From "Interview with Luciano Berio," in Barry Shrader, *Introduction to Electro-Acoustic Music* (Englewood Cliffs, NJ: Prentice Hall, 1982), pp. 179-183.

50   "I attempted to establish": Luciano Berio, "Poesia e Musica—un' esperienza," *Incontri Musicali III*, 1958.

-   "At that time": Shrader, op. cit.

-   "to experiment": Henri Pousseur, liner notes to BVHAAST CD 9010.

51   "purely a radio-program work": Luciano Berio, liner notes to Turnabout LP 4046.

52   "We all knew about tape recorders": Tristram Cary, personal communication.

-   "Three of them replied": Cary.

-   "I was using recorded sound": Cary.

-   "It really put my studio": Cary.

53   "Meanwhile, at about this time": Cary.

-   "I decorated the whole place": Cary.

-   "It seemed perfectly obvious": Cary.

54   "It's pretty primitive": Cary.

-   "In those days": Cary.

-   "Compared to the early ones": Cary.

55   "It was John's idea": David Tudor, personal communication.

-   "I worked closely with John": Tudor.

-   "I lived in the Village": Earle Brown, personal communication.

56   "We simultaneously cut and spliced": Brown.

57   "Having finished *Williams Mix*": Brown.

-   "We had eight mono Magnacorders": Brown.

58   "I don't remember why it stopped": Brown.

-   "It was like hearing an echo": Quoted in Otto Luening, op. cit. p. 20.

-   "More clearly": John Cage, "Edgard Varèse," originally published in *Nutida Music* (Stockholm), Fall 1958. Reprinted in John Cage, *Silence* (Middletown, CT: Wesleyan University Press, 1961), p. 84.

-   "colors are not used": Wassily Kandinsky, *Concerning the Spiritual in Art* (New York: Wittenborn, 1972). Originally published in Germany in 1912.

58　"The role of color": Edgard Varèse, "New Instruments and New Music," a lecture at Mary Austin House, Santa Fe, 1936. Reprinted in a collection of Varèse' lectures called "The Liberation of Sound," in Elliott Schwartz and Barney Childs, eds., *Contemporary Composers on Contemporary Music* (New York: Holt, Rinehart and Winston, 1967), p. 196.

59　"nonelectronic synthesis": Milton Babbitt, "Edgard Varèse: A Few Observations of His Music," in Benjamin Boretz and Edward T. Cone, eds., *Perspectives on American Composers* (New York: W. W. Norton, 1971), p. 46.

-　　"I have always felt the need": Edgard Varèse, "The Electronic Medium," a lecture at Yale University, 1962. Reprinted in Schwartz and Childs, op. cit. p. 207.

-　　"Our musical alphabet": Quoted in *The New York Telegraph*, 1916. Reprinted in Chou Wen-Chung, "Open Rather than Bounded," in Boretz and Cone, p. 49.

-　　"The acoustical work": Quoted in Peter Manning, *Electronic & Computer Music* (Oxford: Clarendon Press, 1985), p. 9.

60　"I was a civil engineer": Xenakis.

-　　"I got to Le Corbusier through an acquaintance": Xenakis.

61　"I will make you a *poème électronique*": Le Corbusier, *Le Poème Electronique* (Paris: Editions de Minuit, 1958), p. 23.

-　　"They asked Le Corbusier to design something": Xenakis.

-　　"a spectacle": Edgard Varèse, "Spatial Music," a lecture at Sarah Lawrence College, 1959. Reprinted in Schwartz and Childs, op. cit. pp. 206–207.

-　　"There is an idea": Edgard Varèse, "Rhythm, Form and Content," a lecture at Princeton University, 1959. Reprinted in Schwartz and Childs, op. cit. p. 203.

Three: Expansion of the Tape Music Idea

63　"In exchange for time and space": Francisco Kröpfl, personal communication.

-　　"about ninety cubic meters": Kröpfl.

64　"quite critical of the military government": Kröpfl.

-　　"conceivable only by a Latin American": Kröpfl.

-　　"When I came in": Gustav Ciamaga, personal communication.

65　"Beckett's script was remarkable": Desmond Briscoe and Roy Curtis-Bramwell, *The BBC Radiophonic Workshop* (London: BBC, 1983), p. 18.

-　　"applied electronic music": Brian Hodgson, personal communication.

-　　"In those days": Hodgson.

66　"Delia took the manuscript": Hodgson.

-　　"No whooshes": Hodgson.

67　"reduced to a kind of characteristic inarticulate utterance": Bengt Emil Johnson, liner notes to *The Pioneers*, Phono Suecia PSCD 63.

-　　"to 'freeze' the words": Lars-Gunnar Bodin, liner notes to *The Pioneers*, Phono Suecia PSCD 63.

-　　"all the textual layers": Bodin.

-　　"I did everything": Sten Hanson, personal communication.

68　"The placement of loudspeakers": François Bayle, "A Propos de l'Acousmonium," in *Recherche Musicale au GRM* (Paris: La Revue Musicale, 1986), pp. 144–146.

-　　"The morpho-concept": François Bayle, personal communication.

69　"The proposition of *Synchronisms*": Mario Davidovsky, personal communication.

-　　"With a live instrumentalist": Davidovsky.

-　　"I went in": Jacob Druckman, personal communication.

-　　"I very quickly discovered": Druckman.

-　　"to exaggerate": Druckman.

-　　"Like looking in a mirror": Druckman.

-　　"Despite the rhythmic aspect": Davidovsky.

-　　"It was always possible": Jan Williams, personal communication.

70　"As usual, I wanted instruments involved": Earle Brown, personal communication.

-　　"They had a machine": Brown.

71　"Suffering from the 1960s tangle": Salvatore Martirano, personal communication.

-　　"In *Underworld*": Martirano.

-　　"I was against the war": Martirano.

-　　"It was played on a Magnavox": Martirano.

72　"a music that would happen by itself": Lukas Foss, personal communication.

-　　"The answer perhaps": Lukas Foss, "A Mini-History," program notes for a performance of *MAP* at the Brooklyn Academy of Music, March 2, 1979.

-　　"Another friend": Jean-Claude Eloy, personal communication.

-　　"Visiting him at his home in Cologne": Eloy.

73   "I used to meet her in Japan": Eloy.
74   "I tried to have this one project": John Cage, "On Roaratorio," his acceptance speech for the Karl Sczuka Prize for the best radio poetry composition of the year, given at the Donaueschigen Music Festival in 1979, printed in a booklet with Mode CD 28/29.
-    "My first idea": Ibid.
-    "I hope that someday": Ibid.
75   "Tapes *can* be used": John Cage, personal communication.
-    "I am sitting in a room": Alvin Lucier and Douglas Simon, *Chambers* (Middletown, CT: Wesleyan University Press, 1980), pp. 30–34.
-    "Record your voice on tape": Ibid.
76   "I didn't choose to use tape": Ibid.
-    "I was fascinated": Eliane Radigue, personal communication.
-    "When you make three tapes": Radigue.
-    "With a synthesizer": Radigue.
77   "The audience was bathed in sound": Radigue.
-    "I use tape because": Radigue.
-    "The voice belongs to": Steve Reich, liner notes to Elektra/Nonesuch CD 979 169-2.
78   "I wanted to bypass editing": From "Interview with Pauline Oliveros," in Barry Shrader, *Introduction to Electro-Acoustic Music* (Englewood Cliffs, NJ: Prentice Hall, 1982), pp. 184–187.
-    "about a total of seven months": Eloy.
-    "from abstract to concrète": Eloy.
-    "What are Japanese sounds?": Eloy.
-    "I had to go very far": Eloy.
-    "I transformed the sounds": Eloy.
79   "The focus": Maggi Payne, personal communication.
-    "I took a word": Payne.
-    "Oh, man": Payne.
-    "I have a great affinity": Payne.
-    "Control": Payne.
-    "I'm looking at the movement of people": Phill Niblock, personal communication.
-    "We went to a studio": Niblock.
80   "The sound": Annea Lockwood, personal communication.
-    "I view the whole world": Lockwood.

Four: Out of the Studios

For further information on Alvin Lucier's work, see Alvin Lucier, *Reflections* (Cologne, Germany: MusikTexte, 1995).

81   "to make electronic music live": John Cage, "[Cartridge Music]" in Richard Kostelanetz, ed., *John Cage* (New York: Praeger Publishers, 1970), p. 144.
-    "The title *Cartridge Music*": Ibid.
82   "Cage decided to find out": Merce Cunningham, "A Collaborative Process Between Music and Dance," in Peter Gena, Jonathan Brent, and Don Gillespie, eds., *A John Cage Reader* (New York: C. F. Peters Corporation, 1982), pp. 114–115.
-    "I did wonder about our feet stepping on the wires": Ibid.
-    "The general principle": Ibid.
83   "I undertook an experiment": Karlheinz Stockhausen, liner notes to CBS LP 32110044.
85   "Recently I worked four days": "Conversation," *Source Magazine*, July 1967, 1:2, p. 105.
-    "hither and yon": Pauline Oliveros, personal communication.
-    "really a loose association of individuals": Oliveros.
86   "I had a variable speed machine": Oliveros.
-    "I would record acoustic sounds": Oliveros.
-    "Certain areas on the sides of the tank": Concert program notes by Ramon Sender.
-    "One of us had found a tape": Morton Subotnick, personal communication.
87   "The house was going to be torn down": Subotnick.
-    "At that point": Subotnick.
88   "It was five or six feet tall": Subotnick.
-    "He would borrow pieces": Subotnick.
-    "It was an era of happenings": Ramon Sender, personal communication.
-    "We used the city environment": Sender.
-    "Everything got reviewed": Subotnick.
89   "I was back there saying goodbye": Sender.
-    "It was quite a show": Sender.

89   "That was a major event for us": Oliveros.
90   "I started burning out": Sender.
-    "In order for us to receive the money": Oliveros.
-    "I wanted the studio": Oliveros.
-    "if the Tape Center": Subotnick.
-    "It was a very amazing time": Oliveros.
-    "Before the Rockefeller Foundation grant": Subotnick.
91   "were often like those we played live": Gordon Mumma, personal communication.
-    "a type of envelope generator": Mumma.
-    "The performers were isolated": Mumma.
-    "Only Ashley and I were musicians": Mumma.
92   "Music has to be *about* something": Robert Ashley, "Groups," *Source Magazine*, January 1968, 2:1, p. 21.
-    "I think that over the last twenty years": Robert Ashley, personal communication.
93   "I projected hands at the piano": Tony Martin, personal communication.
94   "We didn't hear anything": Subotnick.
-    "All the wax in my ears melted": Pauline Oliveros, "Some Sound Observations," *Source Magazine*, January 1968, 2:1, p. 78.
-    "sinister nightclub vocalist": Robert Ashley, "Wolfman," *Source Magazine*, July 1968, 2:2, p. 5.
-    "The technical notion": Ashley.
-    "The performer no longer": Will Johnson, "First Festival of Live-Electronic Music 1967," *Source Magazine*, January 1968, 2:1, p. 51.
-    "A musical instrument": Mumma.
96   "The soloist seats himself comfortably": Gordon Mumma, "Alvin Lucier's *Music for Solo Performer 1965*," *Source Magazine*, July 1967, 1:2, p. 69.
97   "I had made the acquaintance": Alvin Lucier and Douglas Simon, *Chambers* (Middletown, CT: Wesleyan University Press, 1980), pp. 70-73.
-    "Most of the time": Alvin Lucier, personal communication.
-    "I use technology for acoustical testing": Lucier.
98   "I often draw a geometric form": Lucier.
-    "I've got to reduce the music language": Lucier.
-    "They just don't appeal to me": Lucier.
-    "It's a simple use of technology": Lucier.
-    "Flexibility, portability": David Tudor, personal communication.
-    "The microphones": Tudor.
99   "Get some friends together": Joel Chadabe, *Reports and Reflections*, unpublished manuscript.
100 "Electronic resources": Mumma.
-    "A few months later": Mumma.
101 "Duchamp came up": David Behrman, personal communication.
-    "It was Gordon": Behrman.
-    "Alvin Lucier had a concert": Ashley.
102 "The variety of those pieces": Mumma.
-    "We went everywhere": Lucier.
-    "Then Sonic Arts Union": Ashley.
103 "original results": Frederic Rzewski, "A Short History of MEV," January 1991, unpublished manuscript.
-    "Form for a music": Frederic Rzewski, "Plan for Spacecraft," *Source Magazine*, January 1968, 2:1, p. 67.
104 "MEV was just a bunch of friends": Frederic Rzewski and Richard Teitelbaum, personal communication.
105 "This was to be the first": Billy Klüver, "9 Evenings: Theatre and Engineering, A Description of the Artists' Use of Sound," 1980, unpublished manuscript.
-    "only those sounds": John Cage, program notes to 9 Evenings: Theatre and Engineering.
106 "So according to the pitches": Tudor.
-    "I had established discrete switching": Tudor.
-    "The silence was deafening": Tudor.
-    "And there's more": Tudor.
-    "There was a lot to take care of": Tudor.
-    "I was Klüver's boss": John Pierce, personal communication.

Five: Computer Music

For an introduction to the fundamentals of computer music and a detailed description of the operations of Music V, see Max V. Mathews, *The Technology of Computer Music* (Cambridge, MA: MIT Press, 1969). For a further description of the technology, see also Charles Dodge and Thomas A. Jerse, *Computer Music* (New York: Schirmer Books, 1985), and F. Richard Moore, *Elements of Computer Music* (Englewood Cliffs, NJ: Prentice Hall, 1990). The definitive source for the development of the technology is Curtis Roads, *The Computer Music Tutorial* (Cambridge, MA: MIT Press, 1996).

For anthologies of articles from *Computer Music Journal*, see Curtis Roads and John Strawn, eds., *Foundations of Computer Music* (Cambridge, MA: MIT Press, 1985) and Curtis Roads, ed., *The Music Machine* (Cambridge, MA: MIT Press, 1989).

108 "turned out to be": Max Mathews, personal communication.
- "It was immediately apparent": Mathews.
- "I was Executive Director": John Pierce, personal communication.
- "It was terrible": Mathews.
109 "To me, it sounded awful": John R. Pierce, *My Career as an Engineer* (Tokyo: University of Tokyo Press, 1988), p. 107.
- "It was the first": Mathews.
- "The program was also terrible": Mathews.
- "when things really came together": Mathews.
- "The implications are dizzying": Liner notes to Wergo CD 2033-2.
- "How can we introduce": Gerald Strang, "The Problem of Imperfection in Computer Music," in Heinz von Foerster and James W. Beauchamp, eds., *Music by Computers* (New York: John Wiley & Sons, 1969), pp. 133–139.
- "Dear computer": Patte Wood, "Recollections with John Robinson Pierce," *Computer Music Journal*, 1991, 15:4, pp. 17–28.
- "had built a number": Ibid.
- "allegedly to do psychoacoustics": Ibid.
110 "an exhausting, nerve-racking experience": James Tenney, "Computer Music Experiences: 1961–1964," *Electronic Music Reports #1* (Utrecht: Institute of Sonology, 1969).
- "One day I found myself *listening*": Ibid.
- "a curious history of renunciations": Ibid.
- "There are no theoretical limitations": Max Mathews, "The Digital Computer as a Musical Instrument," *Science*, November 1963.
111 "I decided I wanted to do music": Jean-Claude Risset, personal communication.
- "I was amazed when I got there": Risset.
- "Max had several ideas": Jean-Claude Risset, "Computer Music Experiments 1964-...," *Computer Music Journal*, 1985, 9:1, p. 11.
- "The palette of computer sound": Ibid.
- "I recorded trumpet samples": Ibid.
- "I came in at about 10 A.M.": Risset.
112 "We used to send the Music V program": F. Richard Moore, personal communication.
113 "People from Princeton": Moore.
- "We were continually driving": Barry Vercoe, personal communication.
- "At Princeton, way back in 1969": Jonathan Harvey, personal communication.
- "I drove": Ed M. Thieberger, "An Interview with Charles Dodge," *Computer Music Journal*, 1995, 19:1, pp. 11-24.
- "Operating under those conditions": Moore.
114 "Management tolerated music": Mathews.
- "Bell Laboratories was in those days": Pierce.
- "Walter Brattain stopped me in the hall": Pierce.
- "I got on the bandwagon": Wood, op. cit.
- "I would typically spend the day": Mathews.
115 "Max's article": John Chowning, personal communication.
- "there I was": Chowning.
- "The sounds we could make": Chowning.
116 "We'd have at least four hours": Larry Austin, personal communication.
- "I was trying to produce bell-like sounds": Chowning.
117 "It means that you get control": Jim Aiken, interview with John Chowning. Originally printed in *Keyboard Magazine*, September 1978. Reprinted in *Synthesizers and Computers* (Milwaukee, WI: Hal Leonard, 1985), pp. 10–14.
- "Pete had this design": Chowning.
- "It was an amazing machine": Chowning.

117   "to have some basis": Chowning.
118   "It was a scientific lab": Risset.
-     "Although I had just settled in Marseilles": Jean-Claude Risset, "Computer Music Experiments 1964-...," *Computer Music Journal*, 1985, 9:1, pp. 11–18.
-     "I felt personally engaged": Gerald Bennett, personal communication.
-     "In summer 1972": Chowning.
119   "I would go to Paris": Mathews.
-     "In the initial period": Risset.
120   "It's largely a question of exploration": Risset.
121   "I went back to work with Godfrey": Vercoe.
-     "During that time": Vercoe.
-     "By that time": Vercoe.
122   "Instead of having one big single mainframe": Vercoe.
-     "Now we had our own computer": Vercoe.
-     "essentially a viola concerto": Vercoe.
-     "I was having a problem": Vercoe.
-     "The question that interested me": Moore.
123   "At one time": Moore.
-     "It's like asking how much music": Moore.
-     "If you were there late at night": Moore.
124   "What Max and I agreed": Thieberger, op. cit.
-     "I asked him if he had any texts": Ibid.
-     "The first stage": Charles Dodge, personal communication.
-     "a different kettle of fish": Dodge.
125   "I surrounded Caruso's voice": Dodge.
-     "I got so interested": Dodge.
-     "One day in 1977": Bennett.
-     "That was a revelation": Xavier Rodet, personal communication.
-     "After a few years": Rodet.
-     "You just gave a few symbols": Rodet.
-     "What interested me in CHANT": Bennett.
126   "We were able to make any sound": Rodet.
-     "Because CHANT was a physical model": Rodet.
-     "We cannot go on": Rodet.
127   "Generality": Chowning.
-     "There was no limit": Moore.
-     "The process of thinking carefully about a problem": Chowning.
-     "I experimented with sounds moving in space": Chowning.
-     "the piece that I consider the best": Chowning.
-     "It was an exhilarating experience": Chowning.
-     "in composing sounds": Risset.
128   "I built the sounds component by component": Risset.
-     "I like the idea that a musical score": Risset.
-     "Sometimes by mistake": Risset.
-     "I like many natural sounds": Risset.
-     "John Grey, a researcher": Johannes Goebel, personal communication.
-     "over the next ten years": Goebel.
129   "I was interested": Goebel.
-     "From the digital domain I took ideas back": Goebel.
-     "We are questioning": Goebel.
-     "one can generate": Goebel.
-     "the perfect instrument": Goebel.
-     "Before the microscope": Harvey.
-     "It's a haunting sound": Harvey.
-     "was superhuman": Harvey.
-     "the boy is the vivos": Harvey.
130   "All my work": Harvey.
-     "Computer synthesis": Harvey.
-     "I simulated an Indian oboe": Harvey.
-     "I was in the marvelous position": Harvey.
-     "The timbral combinations": Harvey.
-     "to make new sonic discoveries": Denis Smalley, personal communication.

130 "My musical ideas come out of the sounds": Smalley.
131 "The first story has sounds": Annea Lockwood, personal communication.
-      "Over a period of years": Smalley.
132 "was based on the idea": François Bayle, personal communication.
-      "I made a demonstration of GRM techniques": Bayle.
-      "which worked out": Bayle.
-      "The idea was to make a form in the air": Bayle.
133 "The sound world is infinite": Curtis Roads, personal communication.
-      "You might ask a painter": Roads.
-      "I recently had a chance": Roads.
-      "I've done a lot of tape pieces": Paul Lansky, personal communication.
-      "The surface of the piece": Lansky.
134 "I like to project": Lansky.
-      "I sometimes use the computer as a camera": Lansky.
-      "The piece": Lansky.
-      "*Still Time* was conceived": Paul Lansky, liner notes to CRI CD 683.
135 "The human voice": Dexter Morrill, personal communication.
-      "I was simply bowled over": Morrill.
-      "I think Joe felt sorry for me": Morrill.
-      "my computer music career began": Morrill.
-      "John, Lee, and John Grey": Morrill.
-      "The Stanford group": Morrill.
-      "I carried the work very far": Morrill.
136 "It's great": Morrill.
-      "I met Stan Getz": Morrill.
-      "The slightly angry": Trevor Wishart, personal communication.
-      "You can now treat sound": Wishart.
-      "I'd figured out a methodology": Wishart.
-      "I wanted to create a myth": Wishart.
137 "a journey into an alternative world": Trevor Wishart, liner notes to *Red Bird*, October Music CD.
-      "the sinister Fly": Trevor Wishart, notes in the score to *Red Bird*.
-      "I was lucky enough": Trevor Wishart, liner notes to *Red Bird*, October Music CD.
-      "There were all those composers": Wishart.
-      "a daunting task": Richard Orton, "A Brief, Informal History of the CDP," in *Yearbook 1989* (York, United Kingdom: Composers' Desktop Project Ltd.).
138 "The computer science crowd": Ibid.
-      "We didn't have any capital": Wishart.
-      "We all began to see in the project": Orton, op. cit.
-      "out of a passion": Quoted in an e-mail message from Richard Orton, 1995.
-      "We gradually became aware": Tom Endrich, "The Organisation and Administration of the CDP," in *Yearbook 1989* (York, United Kingdom: Composers' Desktop Project Ltd.).
-      "We believe very strongly": Ibid.
-      "We have been very encouraged": Orton, op. cit.
139 "Now on Atari Falcon": Orton, op. cit.
-      "I like programming": Wishart.
-      "You can now do almost anything": Wishart.
-      "It turns out": Austin.
-      "It's Billy Klüver's idea": Pierce.

Six: Synthesizers

For a description of the workings of the early analog synthesizers, see Joel Chadabe, "The Voltage-Controlled Synthesizer," in Jon Appleton and Ronald Perera, eds., *The Development and Practice of Electronic Music* (Englewood Cliffs, NJ: Prentice Hall, 1975). For descriptions and the technical details of many specific synthesizers, see Mark Vail, *Vintage Synthesizers* (San Francisco: Miller Freeman, 1993). For a definitive overview of analog technology applied in music, including synthesizers, see Allen Strange, *Electronic Music: Systems, Techniques, and Controls* (Dubuque, IA: Wm. C. Brown, 1983).
140 "I found myself designing bigger and better theremins": Robert Moog, personal communication.
-      "a big, fat color picture": Moog.
-      "And along comes Herb Deutsch": Moog.
141 "We talked for about an hour": Herbert A. Deutsch, *Synthesis* (Sherman Oaks, CA: Alfred Publishing, 1985), pp. 19–20.

141 "He invited me to a concert": Moog.
-      "I spent about eight hours a day": Deutsch, op. cit.
-      "And then it was my turn": Moog.
142 "So there I was": Moog.
-      "It kept us busy": Moog.
-      "It was in our 1967 catalog": Moog.
143 "In 1967, I got a call from Paul Beaver": Moog.
-      "Chris Swanson started": Moog.
144 "It was in *The New York Times*": Moog.
-      "I made a recording": Larry Austin, personal communication.
-      "I started practicing on it": John Eaton, personal communication.
145 "I wanted the keyboard": Eaton.
-      "You hear the difference": Eaton.
-      "Over more than a ten year period": Eaton.
-      "It encouraged me": Eaton.
146 "I tried all kinds of different things": Eaton.
-      "a lot of telephone-type things": Morton Subotnick, personal communication.
-      "We put an SOS out": Subotnick.
-      "this glorious three-track Ampex": Donald Buchla, personal communication.
-      "It was a typical studio": Buchla.
-      "that this idea of cutting and splicing": Subotnick.
147 "The first thing I built there": Buchla.
-      "This is the wrong way": Subotnick.
-      "my first idea": Buchla.
-      "I regarded things that you touch": Buchla.
-      "But this was all on paper": Subotnick.
-      "I played with it": Bill Maginnis, personal communication.
-      "I called it the *Electric Music Box*": Buchla.
148 "They thought they wanted": Buchla.
-      "My method": Subotnick.
-      "When I got the commission": Subotnick.
149 "I was collaborating with Buchla": Subotnick.
-      "I couldn't stand cutting up tape": Peter Zinovieff, personal communication.
-      "I'd been messing about": Zinovieff.
150 "I began moonlighting": David Cockerell, personal communication.
-      "He was into the most complete sequencing": Tristram Cary, personal communication.
-      "We got in touch with DEC": Zinovieff.
-      "The computer couldn't really do anything": Zinovieff.
-      "So I wrote to a DEC instructor": Zinovieff.
-      "I began to take myself seriously": Zinovieff.
-      "planned London's first": Cary.
-      "Believe it or not": Cary.
-      "that we should make something to sell": Zinovieff.
-      "Don asked if David": Cary.
151 "Peter suggested": Cary.
-      "He wasn't much interested in tonal music": Cockerell.
-      "The BBC had decided to buy a Moog": Brian Hodgson, personal communication.
152 "It arrived with David Cockerell": Hodgson.
-      "was to raise money": Cary.
-      "It was quite big": Zinovieff.
-      "That's my gift": Zinovieff.
153 "He did *Glass Music*": Zinovieff.
-      "He wasn't interested in programming": Zinovieff.
-      "He put standard modules in it": Moog.
-      "We all worked on it": Moog.
-      "We had very little luck": Moog.
154 "By early 1970": Moog.
-      "Bill Waytena watched us slowly die": Moog.
-      "There was so little room": Tom Rhea, personal communication.
-      "When you can sell stuff": Rhea.
-      "I worked for six or seven different marketing regimes": Rhea.
155 "Salespeople can affect history": Rhea.

- "We began hearing things": Moog.
155 "The only sound I could ever find": quoted in Jim Aiken, "Plug It In, Crank It Up," *Keyboard Magazine*, January 1995, p. 33.
- "I thought we could sell 100": Moog.
156 "I learned what a synthesizer was all about": Tom Oberheim, personal communication.
- "All the synths at the time": Oberheim.
- "At first, it was a kind of curiosity" : Oberheim.
- "not liking it too much": Dave Smith, personal communication.
- "right up my alley": Dave Smith.
- "Keyboard Magazine": Dave Smith.
157 "I decided to take a chance": Dave Smith.
- "It barely worked": Dave Smith.
- "We had all kinds of problems": Dave Smith.
- "A typical musical evening": F. Richard Moore, personal communication.
- "The problems associated with Piper 1": Andrew James Gabura, *An Analog/Hybrid Instrument for Electronic Music Synthesis* (University of Toronto: PhD dissertation, 1973), p. 31.
158 "We were using computers": Gustav Ciamaga, personal communication.
- "would scan through the oscillators": Ciamaga.
- "What the 'hybrid computer' method": Andrew James Gabura, op. cit. p. 34.
- "GROOVE is a hybrid system": M. V. Mathews, F. R. Moore, and J. C. Risset, "Computers and Future Music," *Science*, January 25, 1974, 183: 4122, pp. 263-268.
- "components that I could lay my hands on": Max Mathews, personal communication.
- "We programmed the patcher": Moore.
159 "It provided a control": Moore.
- "In principle, GROOVE was the ultimate": Laurie Spiegel, personal communication.
- "Life in those days": Moore.
- "did a little work": Mathews.
- "were so complex": Emmanuel Ghent, personal communication.
160 "When Bob Moog saw it": Ghent.
- "Well, we had the same idea": Ghent.
- "Dick was writing": Ghent.
- "The computer was used": Ghent.
161 "By changing a number": Ghent.
162 "on developing my ideas": Spiegel.
"I was extremely excited": Spiegel.
- "It was incredibly liberating": Spiegel.
- "We were allowed to use the computers": Spiegel.
163 "They were all studies": Ghent.
- "It opened opportunities": Ghent.
- "a very large and quite elaborate hybrid system": Buchla.
- "an instrument": Buchla.
- "I find commercial synthesizers": Buchla.
164 "I often hear the comment": Buchla.
165 "old hat now": Cockerell.
- "We used it to control the 100 or 200 devices": Zinovieff.
- "My goal": Zinovieff.
- "It epitomized the way I wanted to work": Zinovieff.
- "People were invited to whistle": Zinovieff.
166 "We thought we might be able to sell this": Cockerell.
- "One of EMS' endeavors": Zinovieff.
- "I enjoyed those years": Cockerell.
- "It was almost an ultimatum": Lars-Gunnar Bodin, personal communication.
167 "it was very complicated": Bodin.
- "The software was poor": Bodin.
- "The Swedish Waterfall Company": Tamas Ungvary, personal communication.
168 "I realized": Ungvary.
- "It was some kind of drug": Ungvary.
- "I had to make *my* music": Ungvary.
- "There was no real computer music course": Ungvary.
- "I could not mix technical work": Ungvary.
- "When I was composing": Ungvary.
169 "When the evaluation report was finished": Bodin.

169   "For the next year": Bodin.
-      "I soon discovered": Stan Tempelaars, personal communication.
-      "Quite naturally": Gottfried Michael Koenig, personal communication.
-      "It was a rather small studio": Koenig.
170   "Why don't we speed it up": Koenig.
-      "It was a very general device": Koenig.
-      "Composers often use your equipment": Tempelaars.
-      "The group thought" : Tempelaars.
-      "a combination of Greek and Latin": Tempelaars.
-      "And eight years later": Tempelaars.
-      "In those days you had to punch in your data": Koenig.
-      "This was the rich time of the university": Tempelaars.
-      "After the first sounds": Tempelaars.
171   "The weakness of VOSIM": Tempelaars.
-      "We got the feeling": Koenig.
-      "this was pretty cool": William Buxton, personal communication.
-      "I'm a computer programmer": Buxton.
-      "Well, I guess you're going to": Buxton.
-      "Writing manuals and teaching": Buxton.
-      "I'd been corresponding with some people": Buxton.
172   "They asked": Buxton.
-      "It always struck me": Buxton.
-      "It turned out": Buxton.
-      "Every time it played a note": Buxton.
-      "The problem was": Buxton.
173   "I figured there were three activities": Buxton.
-      "Everything was graphical": Buxton.
-      "I had a strong group": Buxton.
174   "The question was": Jon Appleton, *21st-Century Musical Instruments: Hardware and Software*
       (New York: Brooklyn College ISAM Monograph Number 29, 1989), p. 22.
-      "made a number of suggestions": Ibid.
-      "I offered the opinion": Sydney Alonso, personal communication.
-      "We had a little homemade computer": Alonso.
-      "We were aware": Alonso.
-      "The idea was": Jon Appleton, personal communication.
-      "They were line numbered files": Appleton.
175   "Kemeny met with Norton Stevens": Alonso.
-      "The next week": Alonso.
-      "Part of the conditions": Alonso.
-      "In April 1977": Alonso.
-      "My input was": Appleton.
176   "Our first musical sale": Alonso.
-      "The flux of the waves": Michel Redolfi, personal communication.
-      "I was fascinated": Redolfi.
-      "A fellow by the name of": Alonso.
177   "I guess they asked me some questions": Appleton.
178   "The instrument had become so large": Appleton.
-      "It had a glutton's heaven": Spiegel.
-      "We had six weeks": Spiegel.
179   "When we got the thing out": Spiegel.
-      "The Palladium crew": Spiegel.
180   "I played guitar like a dilettante": Giuseppe Di Giugno, personal communication.
-      "I was impressed by this as a curiosity": Di Giugno.
-      "I talked with him after his lecture": Di Giugno.
-      "At that time, at Frascati": Di Giugno.
-      "got to know the contemporary electronic music scene": Di Giugno.
-      "I'd like to meet you": Di Giugno.
-      "We had had only nine oscillators": Luciano Berio, personal communication.
-      "He had stopped in Rome": Di Giugno.
181   "We can do this": Di Giugno.
-      "Synthesizers should be made for musicians": Di Giugno.
-      "There were many things that were impossible": Di Giugno.

181   "At that point, after some reflection": Di Giugno.
-   "I've never seen another machine": Marc Battier, personal communication.
182   "And so in 1983": Di Giugno.
-   "So I said to Boulez": Di Giugno.
-   "studied various architectures": Di Giugno.
-   "He said, 'For two years'": Di Giugno.
183   "it let me continue": Di Giugno.
-   "I used ideas": Miller Puckette, personal communication.
-   "The idea was to give the flutist": Philippe Manoury, personal communication.
-   "In spring 1987": Puckette.
184   "It had been hard and long": Manoury.
-   "In August 1988": Manoury.
-   "What was so good about the new MAX": Manoury.

Seven: The MIDI World

For further information on MIDI, see Gareth Loy, "Musicians Make a Standard: The MIDI Phenomenon," and Christopher Yavelow, "Music and Microprocessors: MIDI and the State of the Art," in Curtis Roads, ed., *The Music Machine* (Cambridge, MA: MIT Press, 1989). See also Craig Anderton, *MIDI for Musicians* (New York: Amsco Publications, 1986), and Jeff Rona, *MIDI: The Ins, Outs & Thrus* (Milwaukee, WI: Hal Leonard, 1987).

186   "Only the Mellotron": Advertisement in *Contemporary Keyboard*, September/October 1975.
-   "We sold the first one": Sydney Alonso, personal communication.
-   "A couple of austere businessmen-scientists": Alonso.
-   "They would show up at AES shows": Alonso.
-   "We were a corporation": Alonso.
187   "The General Development System": Back-cover ad, *Keyboard Magazine*, October 1983.
-   "We got a commission from Peter Baumann": Marco Alpert, personal communication.
-   "We figured": Alpert.
188   "We caused a bit of a stir": Alpert.
-   "sort of hugged it": Dave Rossum, "E-mu Emulator," in Mark Vail, ed., *Vintage Synthesizers* (San Francisco: GPI Books, 1993), p. 201.
-   "That was really the start of sampling": Alpert.
-   "kicked off the affordable drum machine market": Alpert.
-   "It was a phenomenon": Alpert.
-   "At Digital Keyboards": Back-cover ad, *Keyboard Magazine*, October 1983.
-   "I was writing a drum machine program": Roger Linn, personal communication.
189   "It was very crude and expensive": Tom Oberheim, personal communication.
-   "I wrote to EMS": Felix Visser, personal communication.
-   "After three days": Visser.
-   "Why did they do this": Visser.
-   "I worked myself into a state": Visser.
-   "Three months": Visser.
190   "And, of course, still no Syrinx": Visser.
-   "We were just beginning to start": Visser.
-   "We were happily selling our phaser": Visser.
-   "We didn't make a whole lot of money": Visser.
-   "I announced": Visser.
-   "about a zillion": Visser.
-   "It marked the beginning": Visser.
191   "In the early 1980s": Visser.
-   "My cousin Peter": Stephen Paine, personal communication.
-   "Peter was blown away": Paine.
-   "We were determined": Paine.
-   "We didn't always make corporately sensible decisions": Paine.
-   "You could buy": Paine.
192   "into the expensive stuff": Paine.
-   "the only handmade pianos": Paine.
-   "It was based on transputer technology": Paine
-   "the first high-tech professional outlet": Rene Rochat, personal communication.
-   "We were showing": Rochat.
193   "Spye was located outside of Rome": Rochat.

193 "I had such a lot of fun": Rochat.
- "Spye wasn't really financially viable": Rochat.
- "We couldn't find anything of interest": Visser.
194 "I liked classical music": Ikutaro Kakehashi, personal communication.
- "It's wasted energy": Kakehashi.
195 "The theory behind MIDI": Tom Oberheim, "Turmoil in MIDI-Land," a compilation of interviews by Dominic Milano for *Keyboard Magazine*, June 1984. Reprinted in *Synthesizers and Computers* (Milwaukee, WI: Hal Leonard, 1985), pp. 81–89.
- "I discussed the necessity of a standard": Kakehashi.
- "The very first contact": Dave Smith, "Turmoil in MIDI-Land," a compilation of interviews by Dominic Milano for *Keyboard Magazine*, June 1984. Reprinted in *Synthesizers and Computers* (Milwaukee, WI: Hal Leonard, 1985), pp. 81–89.
196 "We knew from the start": Smith, op. cit.
- "I think that MIDI has been brought on": Oberheim, op. cit.
- "The only thing I won't give in on": Carmine Bonanno, "Turmoil in MIDI-Land," a compilation of interviews by Dominic Milano for *Keyboard Magazine*, June 1984. Reprinted in *Synthesizers and Computers* (Milwaukee, WI: Hal Leonard, 1985), pp. 81–89.
197 "to exchange ideas": Kakehashi.
- "the price is even more remarkable:" Dominic Milano, "Keyboard Report," *Keyboard Magazine*, October 1983, p. 80.
- "At Sequential": Dave Smith, personal communication.
- "What turns me on is innovation": Linn.
- "Because we were underfinanced": Dave Smith.
198 "Synclavier bought keyboards from us": Dave Smith.
- "We knew we were taking a chance": Dave Smith.
- "Japanese companies": Dave Smith.
- "Well, then I wanted to make something": Linn.
199 "I raised my expenses": Linn.
- "combined a lot of MIDI implementation": Oberheim.
- "My involvement": Oberheim.
- "I bought a ticket": Visser.
200 "We wanted to achieve visibility": Visser.
- "When I was designing booths": Visser.
- "We thought": Alpert.
- "We showed it at the NAMM show": Alpert.
201 "I got this board working": Dave Oppenheim, personal communication.
- "I bought some Oberheim modules": Oppenheim.
- "I turned thirty": Oppenheim.
- "I hadn't known": Oppenheim.
202 "We shipped the first stuff": Oppenheim.
- "I called him up": Al Hospers, personal communication.
- "It was an eye-opener": Hospers.
- "There was no music software industry": Hospers.
- "Karl was fiddling around": Manfred Rürup, personal communication.
203 "The feedback was completely lousy": Rürup.
- "A company called Music Data": Rürup.
- "The funny thing": Rürup.
- "They all had Ataris": Rürup.
- "People often have good musical ideas": Rürup.
- "I was interested in tablas": Peter Gotcher, personal communication.
- "They loved the sounds": Gotcher.
204 "went on to sell 60,000 drum chips": Gotcher.
- "We saw the convergence": Gotcher.
- "Editing": Gotcher.
- "George Lewis": David Wessel, personal communication.
- "It quickly became clear": Wessel.
- "My concept": Wessel.
- "I started the MIDI LISP project": Wessel.
205 "LOGO was used quite a bit in France": Yann Orlarey, personal communication.
- "We had many discussions": Orlarey.
- "We wanted to do things with music": Pierre Lavoie, personal communication.

205 "It was a good idea": Lavoie.
206 "was so complete": Orlarey.
- "how using a computer": Jean-Baptiste Barrière, personal communication.
- "How to solve": Barrière.
- "It was an experiment": Barrière.
- "Our concern": Barrière.
207 "You might have considered it": Barrière.
- "It's an aid-to-composition system": Barrière.
- "It seemed clearly superior": David Zicarelli, personal communication.
208 "Miller solved the problem": Zicarelli.
- "My interest": Zicarelli.
- "I took a program": Zicarelli.
- "It was also necessary to modify the scheduler": Zicarelli.
- "Over the last five years": Zicarelli.
- "There's also a set of five objects": Zicarelli.
209 "MAX is simply the most exciting MIDI technology": Carter Scholz, "Opcode Max," *Keyboard Magazine*, April 1991.
- "accessible to a lot of people": Christopher Dobrian, personal communication.
- "There's a sharp conceptual division": Zicarelli.
- "My work includes editing and control software": Richard Zvonar, personal communication.
- "They were running Vision": Antony Widoff, personal communication.
210 "One of the other things I did": Widoff.
211 "They had to make sure": Widoff.
- "They're stadium shows": Widoff.
212 "Electronic music is all over the place": Robert Ashley, personal communication.

Eight: Inputs and Controls

213 "I was doing designs": Iannis Xenakis, personal communication.
- "How would you relate probabilities to shapes?": Xenakis.
214 "Anybody, even myself or you": Richard Dufallo, "Interview with Iannis Xenakis," in *Trackings* (New York: Oxford University Press, 1989), pp. 171-174.
- "Composing with a graphic score": Gerard Pape, personal communication.
- "I didn't find it a problem": Joji Yuasa, personal communication.
215 "I could imagine what would happen": Yuasa.
- "It was easy for me". Yuasa.
- "Sometimes the pages": Pape.
- "I tried to find an input structure": Vincent Lesbros, personal communication.
- "from wooden bells": Marc Battier, personal communication.
216 "from traditional keys and knobs": Max Mathews, "Foreword" to Curtis Roads and John Strawn, eds., *The Foundations of Computer Music* (Cambridge, MA: MIT Press, 1985).
- "I can imagine": Morton Subotnick, personal communication.
217 "One extreme": Neil Rolnick, personal communication.
- "I was the ghost": Subotnick.
- "We had twenty contact mikes": Subotnick.
- "I decided it was time": Subotnick.
- "I thought we could get a computer": Subotnick.
218 "able to listen to a flute performance": Barry Vercoe, personal communication.
- "For example, when the players": Subotnick.
- "I was imagining": Joan La Barbara, personal communication.
219 "to score the piece": Tod Machover, personal communication.
- "means taking more": Machover.
- "You need to get detailed information": Machover.
- "In *Begin Again Again* ...": Machover.
220 "It would be silly": Jim Aiken, an interview with John Chowning, originally printed in *Keyboard Magazine*, September 1978. Reprinted in *Synthesizers and Computers* (Milwaukee, WI: Hal Leonard, 1985), pp. 10-14.
- "I'd take a trip": John Eaton, personal communication.
- "I also wanted to make the instrument more sensitive": Eaton.
- "So Bob and I started talking": Eaton.
- "It was just so complicated": Robert Moog, personal communication.
221 "I went to CBS": Gregory Kramer, personal communication.

221   "I was looking for that link": Kramer.
222   "I could control the signal processing": Kramer.
-     "I was very excited about it": Eaton.
-     "Well, it's exciting": Dorothy Martirano, personal communication.
-     "because commercial equipment was so expensive": Martin Hurni, personal communication.
-     "The more I looked": Hurni.
-     "Bob Moog gave me the idea": Hurni.
223   "It was my entry point": Nicolas Collins, personal communication.
-     "to the uninitiated": Nicolas Collins, "Low Brass: The Evolution of Trombone-Propelled Electronics," *Leonardo Music Journal*, 1991, I:1, pp. 41–44.
224   "The process of making interactive art": Paul DeMarinis, personal communication.
225   "Got rid of the tuba": Gary Lee Nelson, personal communication.
-     "to feel the need": Nelson.
-     "It was pretty smooth": Nelson.
-     "What the audience saw": Nelson.
-     "I'd play a note": Nelson.
226   "It's a single block of maple": Chris Chafe, personal communication.
227   "I'd like to apply": Chafe.
-     "When he blows a note, he moves": Chafe.
-     "I want to get out of this": Chafe.
-     "I assumed that with a MIDI standard": Donald Buchla, personal communication.
228   "It has twenty-five keys": Bruno Spoerri, personal communication.
-     "It feels good": Spoerri.
-     "allows you to create instruments in space": Buchla.
-     "When the clubs flip": Buchla.
-     "It's not that I like technology": Michel Waisvisz, personal communication.
-     "I'm afraid it's true one has to suffer": Volker Krefeld, "The Hand in the Web: An Interview with Michel Waisvisz," *Computer Music Journal*, 1990, 14:2, pp. 28–33.
-     "Once one takes formal structure as a synonym": Ibid.
-     "There is a kind of physical excitement": Waisvisz.
-     "It really became my instrument": Waisvisz.
229   "I got a Power Glove": DeMarinis.
-     "I used the recorded text": DeMarinis.
-     "In my part of the piece": Laetitia Sonami, personal communication.
-     "There was a beauty of expression": Sonami.
230   "This is for me the ultimate instrument": Sonami.
-     "One has to think of overall systems": Max Mathews, personal communication.
-     "By that time there were a lot of pieces for tape": Mathews.
231   "The wires were always breaking": Mathews.
-     "I needed continuous information": Mathews.
232   "I'd spend pretty much every weekend there": Richard Boulanger, personal communication.
-     "Brook forbade me": Andrew Schloss, personal communication.
-     "I heard that they had some sort of Radio Drum": Schloss.
-     "I started to think of the Radio Drum": Schloss.
-     "combined the flexibility of the Music V approach": David Jaffe, personal communication.
233   "Andy had been working": Jaffe.
-     "I found it responded very quickly": Jaffe.
-     "The coupling of the piano": Jaffe.
-     "We need controllers": Schloss.
234   "like a generalization of a hand drum": Schloss.
-     "What's great for me": Schloss.
-     "I played solo cornet": Gordon Mumma, personal communication.
-     "I made a set of accelerometer belts": Mumma.
-     "I had been writing a lot of dance music": Mark Coniglio, personal communication.
235   "You have two hands": Rolnick.
-     "what waveform is produced": Moog.
-     "I really took it on": DeMarinis.
-     "We were the first generation": DeMarinis.
-     "It was like an untuned radio": DeMarinis.
236   "to design a series": Godfried-Willem Raes, "A Book of Moves," unpublished article, 1993.
-     "It was the first movement-driven system": Spoerri.
-     "They had the impression": Spoerri.

236 "There's always a performer": Spoerri.
- "with big movements": Spoerri.
237 "a kind of drum duo": Spoerri.
- "the smaller the movement": Spoerri.
- "It was a fairground installation": Warren Burt, personal communication.
238 "One guy said": Burt.
- "An outer ring of spaces": Burt.
- "I never found it magical": Burt.
- "I wanted to be fascinated": Burt.
- "as musicians we've spent years": Rolnick.
- "If you're dealing with a new paradigm": Rolnick.
- "What was lost": Peter Otto, personal communication.
239 "You just touched the technology": Waisvisz.
- "I thought, 'How could I'": Waisvisz.
- "I saw a spider web": Waisvisz.
- "I was never a dancer": Xavier Chabot, personal communication.
- "California was an enormous influence": Chabot.
- "In the context of Kiva": Chabot.
240 "I went to Japan": Chabot.
- "It's long-term research": Moog.

Nine: Making Sound

John R. Pierce, *The Science of Musical Sound* (New York: Freeman and Company, 1992) provides a general background on sound. For a focus on hearing, see Juan G. Roederer, *Introduction to the Physics and Psychophysics of Music* (London: Springer-Verlag, 1973). See also John R. Pierce and Edward E. David, Jr., *Man's World of Sound* (New York: Doubleday, 1958).
241 "MIDI?": Bruno Spoerri, personal communication.
- "Engineers are interested": Joel Ryan, personal communication.
- "I began to realize": Ryan.
242 "The rules of thumb of engineering": Ryan.
- "eliminates all the contingencies": Ryan.
- "Nature gave us vocal chords": Stan Tempelaars, personal communication.
- "We need an intelligent sound generator": Tempelaars.
- "to research the equilibrium": C. Cadoz, A. Luciani, and J. Florens, "Responsive Input Devices and Sound Synthesis by Simulation of Instrumental Mechanisms: The Cordis System," in Curtis Roads, ed., *The Music Machine* (Cambridge, MA: MIT Press, 1989), pp. 495–508.
243 "the possibility of creating": Ibid.
- "Speech is portable synthesis": Chris Mann, personal communication.
- "Before writing the piece": Trevor Wishart, personal communication.
- "I was always very interested": Joan La Barbara, personal communication.
- "I asked the musicians": La Barbara.
- "In work sessions": La Barbara.
- "I found that you could extend the voice": La Barbara.
244 "You become very familiar": La Barbara.
- "There are so many factors": La Barbara.
- "My vision of a very romantic plot": Ivan Tcherepnin, personal communication.
- "The whole box was a resonating chamber": Tcherepnin.
245 "I was trying to use the santur": Tcherepnin.
- "a seamless transition": Simon Emmerson, personal communication.
- "I was interested in extending the timbral world": Emmerson.
- "It was a different sort of live music": Emmerson.
246 "Maderna mentioned": Alcides Lanza, personal communication.
- "I was using a Putney synthesizer": Lanza.
- "My main intention": Alcides Lanza, program notes to a concert at Espace/Musique, Ottawa, January 16, 1994.
- "I always saw that I wanted an electric voice": Lanza.
- "I couldn't find an electronic piano": Robert Ashley, personal communication.
247 "Edge's guitar sound": Antony Widoff, personal communication.
- "The source signal": Widoff.
248 "Now, with electronics": Stephen Montague, personal communication.
- "Without the electronics": La Barbara.
249 "are actually double texts": La Barbara.

249   "I thought about": La Barbara.
-   "I use the computer": Kaija Saariaho, personal communication.
-   "environmental and singing": Saariaho.
-   "I processed the sounds": Saariaho.
-   "I was interested in the contrabass": Saariaho.
250   "built between the covers": Hugh Davies, personal communication.
-   "I began to amplify": Davies.
-   "I began to use small coiled springs": Davies.
-   "Typically for my microsonic world": Davies.
-   "many of my ideas": Davies.
-   "Korg had started a new engineering division": Dave Smith, personal communication.
-   "What makes this instrument so impressive": Greg Rule, "Keyboard Reports," *Keyboard Magazine*, March 1995.
252   "Most people that play": Julius Smith, personal communication.
-   "is understanding how to do": Julius Smith.
-   "Ultimately, we'll build a high-quality physical device": Julius Smith.
-   "There are no limits": Julius Smith.
253   "How do you create a sound": David Jaffe, personal communication.
-   "He got real excited": Jaffe.
-   "I liked the possibilities": Jaffe.
-   "would probably be the path of least resistance": Perry Cook, personal communication.
254   "as fun hacks": Cook.
-   "It was one of the first revealing things": Cook.
-   "What physical models do": Cook.
-   "Why tie yourself to the physical world?": David Wessel, personal communication.
-   "The point of physical systems": Jean-Claude Risset, personal communication.
255   "Trying to speak more directly": Wessel.
-   "So here I give you 200 inputs": Julius Smith.
-   "In fly-by-wire systems": F. Richard Moore, personal communication.
256   "An *adaptive* system": Wessel.
-   "We analyze sounds": Wessel.
-   "I'm very annoyed": Gottfried Michael Koenig, personal communication.
-   "not referring to a given acoustic model": Koenig.
-   "You could generate": Koenig.
-   "allows me to work": Herbert Brun, personal communication.
257   "All sound is an integration of grains": Iannis Xenakis, *Formalized Music* (Stuyvesant, NY: Pendragon Press, 1992), p. 43. First published as *Musiques Formelles* (Paris: Editions Richard-Masse, 1963).
-   "One of my goals": Barry Truax, personal communication.
-   "a landmark piece": Truax.
-   "I had the wonderful experience": Truax.
-   "on the flow of a river": Toru Iwatake, "An Interview with Barry Truax," *Computer Music Journal*, 1994, 18:3, pp. 17–24.
-   "You can repeat or magnify instants": Ibid.
258   "If you have a good orchestra": Julius Smith.
-   "In general, nobody programs synthesizers": Dave Smith.
-   "We've determined that what people have always wanted": Dave Smith.
-   "I need an entirely new medium": Edgard Varèse, "Music as an Art-Science," a lecture at the University of Southern California, 1939. Reprinted in a collection of Varèse' lectures collectively called "The Liberation of Sound," in Elliott Schwartz and Barney Childs, eds., *Contemporary Composers on Contemporary Music* (New York: Holt, Rinehart and Winston, 1967), p. 200.
-   "The easier a system is to use": Risset.
-   "I've never used any software": Truax.
-   "The most interesting music": Paul Lansky, personal communication.
-   "If we're composers": Ashley.
259   "With electronic sound, we're in a completely new era": Risset.
-   "I love factory sounds": Ashley.
-   "The only constraints": Larry Austin, personal communication.
-   "Csound started": Barry Vercoe, personal communication.
260   "I had previously used Moog": Richard Karpen, personal communication.
-   "as a toolkit": Lansky.
-   "The ideal": Dave Smith.

260   "It's what's going to happen": Dave Smith.
261   "The best tool at that time": Adrian Freed, personal communication.
-      "My intention": Freed.
262   "Some sampled sounds": Curtis Roads, personal communication.
-      "I did not conceive the sections": Roads.
-      "just decided to stay": James Dashow, personal communication.
263   "The important thing": Alvise Vidolin, personal communication.
-      "In 1990": Dashow.
-      "My software was more flexible": Dashow.
-      "Several of us got together": Miller Puckette, personal communication.
264   "It was everything I was looking for": Cort Lippe, personal communication.
-      "I invited everyone I knew": Guiseppe Di Giugno, personal communication.
-      "I left rubber": Sylviane Sapir, personal communication.
-      "I fell in love with Venice": Sapir.
-      "to go to Venice": Sapir.
265   "There's an enormous distance": Sapir.
-      "When the chip arrived": Sapir.
-      "We gave examples": Sapir.
-      "I wanted to have a hybridization": Luciano Berio, personal communication.
-      "The problem is to perform": Vidolin.
-      "Our work together in the 1980s": Vidolin.
-      "In the 1980s, Nono worked in live electronics": Vidolin.
-      "What was so much fun": Carla Scaletti, personal communication.
266   "I just showed up": Kurt Hebel, personal communication.
-      "They had microprocessors": Scaletti.
-      "CERL was a unique situation": Hebel.
-      "Nobody took the CERL group very seriously": Scaletti.
-      "It was difficult to get in": Scaletti.
-      "One night Kurt showed up": Scaletti.
267   "I was teaching": Scaletti.
-      "At that time": Scaletti.
-      "We bought the components": Scaletti.
-      "And that's when we redid the interface": Scaletti.
-      "The design took from June to August": Hebel.
-      "Kyma was born out of a kind of greediness": Scaletti

Ten: Automata

For a history of using computers to compose music, see Lejaren Hiller, "Music Composed with Computers—A Historical Survey," in Harry B. Lincoln, ed., *The Computer and Music* (Ithaca, NY: Cornell University Press, 1970). For the details of Hiller's first experiments, see Lejaren A. Hiller, Jr., and Leonard M. Isaacson, *Experimental Music* (New York: McGraw-Hill Book Company, Inc., 1959).
268   "Morning and Evening Amusements": Arthur W. J. G. Ord-Hume, *Barrel Organ* (New York: A.S. Barnes and Company, 1978), p. 75.
-      "Supposing, for instance": Quoted in Edmund A. Bowles, "Musicke's Handmaiden," in Harry B. Lincoln, ed., *The Computer and Music* (Ithaca, NY: Cornell University Press, 1970), pp. 3-20, with the footnote: R. Taylor, *Scientific Memoirs*, III, London, 1843, p. 694.
269   "The Talking Turk": E. T. A. Hoffmann, "Automata," in Alexander Ewing, trans., *The Best Tales of Hoffmann* (New York: Dover Publications, 1967), pp. 96-97.
-      "Vase containing the 89 notes": Marcel Duchamp, "The Bride Stripped Bare by Her Bachelors, Even. Musical Erratum, 1913." As reprinted in Anne D'Harnoncourt and Kynaston McShine, *Marcel Duchamp* (New York and Philadelphia: Museum of Modern Art and Philadelphia Museum of Art, 1973), p. 264.
-      "It is thus possible": John Cage, "Composition," in *Silence* (Middletown, CT: Wesleyan University Press, 1961), p. 59.
-      "What actually happened": John Cage, "Interview with Roger Reynolds," in Elliott Schwartz and Barney Childs, eds., *Contemporary Composers on Contemporary Music* (New York: Holt, Rinehart and Winston, 1967).
270   "Cage arrived in Albany": Joel Chadabe, *Reports and Reflections*, unpublished manuscript.
272   "One evening, he fixed a meal": Larry Austin, personal communication.
-      "Yes and no": Tamas Ungvary, personal communication.
-      "The geophysicists at Goddard": Ed M. Thieberger, "An Interview with Charles Dodge," *Computer Music Journal*, 1995, 19:1, pp. 11–24.

272   "The logic stuff": Michel Waisvisz, personal communication.
273   "They produce a hell of a lot of nonsense": Waisvisz.
-        "The last performance was in Spain": David Tudor, personal communication.
-        "the first substantial piece of music": Lejaren Hiller, liner notes to *Computer Music from the University of Illinois*, Heliodor LP 25053.
-        "I had been working": Ibid.
274   "Messages are themselves a form of pattern": Norbert Wiener, *The Human Use of Human Beings* (New York: Avon Books, 1973), p. 31.
-        "Jerry Hiller called me": Larry Austin, "An Interview with John Cage and Lejaren Hiller," *Computer Music Journal*, 1992, 16:4, pp. 15–29.
-        "The original idea": Ibid.
275   "I must admit": Ibid.
-        "The simplest": Ibid.
277   "Each tape, once it is started": Ibid.
-        "It's the first piece": Ibid.
-        "When you get right down to it": John Cage, "Foreword" to *A Year from Monday* (Middletown, CT: Wesleyan University Press, 1969).
-        "entertaining a suspicious character": Herbert Brun, personal communication.
-        "When I arrived": Brun.
-        "It was extremely intelligent": Brun.
278   "My desire was to prove": Brun.
-        "could recognize patterns": Brun.
-        "Due to the preoccupation": Brun.
-        "Instead of approaching again the aesthetic question": Herbert Brun, program notes for *For and By Herbert Brun*, a festival of lectures and concerts of Brun's music, May 5–8, 1988, at the University of Illinois at Urbana.
-        "A FORTRAN program": Ibid.
279   "It may be well to remind people": Brun.
-        "The laws of the calculus of probabilities": Iannis Xenakis, *Formalized Music* (Stuyvesant, NY: Pendragon Press, 1992), p. 8. First published as *Musiques Formelles* (Paris: Editions Richard-Masse, 1963).
-        "I was interested in automating what I had done before": Iannis Xenakis, personal communication.
-        "In most human relations": Iannis Xenakis, op. cit. p. 134.
280   "Freed from tedious calculations": Ibid. p. 144.
-        "I needed to make a program": Gottfried Michael Koenig, personal communication.
-        "I worked on it continuously": Koenig.
-        "Actually ...": Koenig.
-        "The model": G.M. Koenig, "PR1XM: Operating Manual" (Utrecht: Institute of Sonology, 1980).
281   "I took only the most basic elementary parameters": Koenig.
-        "PR-1 was meant to replace the very strict idea of a series": Koenig.
-        "I made *regularity* and *irregularity* as extremes": Koenig.
-        "In step 4": Koenig.
-        "You could have an irregular structure": Koenig.
-        "I opened up PR-1 more and more": Koenig.
282   "Although I was not trying to compose a piece of music": G.M. Koenig, liner notes to BVHAAST CD 9001/2.
-        "I started being interested in generative grammars": Otto Laske, personal communication.
283   "With hindsight": Laske.
-        "I walked in as a refugee": Barry Truax, personal communication.
-        "It wasn't that obvious": Truax.
-        "It was a wonderful opportunity": Truax.
-        "Laske was seeing music as an activity": Truax.
-        "The original printouts": Truax.
-        "There's a better way": Truax.
-        "A couple of months later": Truax.
-        "I could say, 'I want five sounds . . .'": Truax.
284   "a huge collection of sequencers": Gustav Ciamaga, personal communication.
285   "Through the late 1960s": Austin.
-        "I made music that was unpredictable": Austin.

Eleven: Interaction

- For a more complete explanation of interactive composing, see Joel Chadabe, "Interactive Composing: An Overview," in Curtis Roads, ed., *The Music Machine* (Cambridge, MA: MIT Press, 1989), pp. 143–148.
287 "It demanded a new performance technique": Jan Williams, personal communication.
288 "My father was a builder": Salvatore Martirano, personal communication.
289 "I always thought": Martirano.
- "Serialism was in the air": Martirano.
- "There's the presentation of an idea": Martirano.
- "I was talking with him": Martirano.
- "the interesting thing was": Martirano.
290 "A data base": Martirano.
291 "In performance": Salvatore Martirano, program notes to Horizons '84, a concert sponsored by the New York Philharmonic, June 5, 1984.
- "It was too complex to analyze": Martirano.
- "How can we know the dancer from the dance?": Yeats' "Among School Children" from *The Tower*.
292 "My software automatically composed": Joel Chadabe, *Reports and Reflections*, unpublished manuscript.
293 "The equipment was terribly primitive": Giuseppe Englert, personal communication.
- "We had four or five VCS-3s": Englert.
294 "time definition": Englert.
- "I bought a Synclavier": Englert.
- "the ideal tool for realtime performance": Englert.
- "I could invent even sounds": Englert.
- "When I wrote software for electronic music": Englert.
- "We can, then, describe composition as the realization of a network": Giuseppe G. Englert, "Automated Composition and Composed Automation," in Roads, op. cit., p. 132.
- "They are neither musical sequences": Giuseppe Englert, liner notes to *Juralpyroc*, Gallo LP 30-380.
- "Pretty soon I had the feeling": Englert.
295 "The perfect program": Englert.
- "I had seen an ad": Jim Horton and John Bischoff, personal communication.
296 "They used to have communist party meetings": Horton.
- "We went out on stage": Tim Perkis, personal communication
- "He just couldn't believe": Horton
- "We'd played for quite awhile": Bischoff.
- "It had just run its course": Perkis.
- "It just knocked me out": Chris Brown, personal communication.
297 "It took hours": Perkis.
- "The emphasis": Bischoff.
- "Pieces done by The Hub defined ways of interacting": Brown.
- "Very simple, minimal music": David Behrman, personal communication.
- "Occasionally, the Cunningham musicians": Behrman.
298 "I went to work at Mills": Behrman.
299 "I had a strong interest in the changing states": Behrman.
- "The relationship": Behrman.
- "It was the first time": George Lewis, personal communication.
- "The deciding moment": Lewis.
300 "It was a simple bass player": Lewis.
- "He had made pieces that were listening": Lewis.
- "In performance": George Lewis, "Improvisation with George Lewis," in Curtis Roads, ed., *Composers and the Computer* (Los Altos, CA: William Kaufmann, 1985), pp. 75–87.
- "When you're playing with someone else": Lewis.
301 "I felt that we needed": David Rosenboom, personal communication.
- "I was looking for": Rosenboom.
302 "It was very stimulating": Rosenboom.
- "Evoked responses are very tiny": Rosenboom.
- "The computer generates some starting musical structure": Rosenboom.
- "So to predict when to look": Rosenboom.
303 "I look for performers": Rosenboom.
- "First we designed the front panel": Rosenboom.
- "It seemed to me": Rosenboom.

303   "There was a strong sense": Larry Polansky, personal communication.
-      "We were also interested": Polansky.
-      "We started working on the idea": Rosenboom.
-      "No musical idea": Polansky.
304   "Often your software": Polansky.
-      "I don't distinguish between the idea and the piece": Polansky.
-      "Using ideas about musical perception": Rosenboom.
305   "There are hundreds of possible simple interacting processes": Polansky.
-      "The title": Larry Polansky, "Live Interactive Computer Music in HMSL, 1984-1992," *Computer Music Journal*, 1994, 18:2, pp. 59-77.
-      "I made musical discovery machines": Peter Beyls, personal communication.
-      "Oscar was designed": Peter Beyls, "Introducing Oscar," in *Proceedings of the International Computer Music Conference 1988* (San Francisco: International Computer Music Association, 1988).
306   "Oscar wanted to express its personality": Beyls.
-      "Oscar is approaching the complexity barrier": Beyls.
-      "I lived in the hills just outside Adelaide": Felix Hess, personal communication.
307   "Each machine had a microphone": Hess.
-      "The machines listened": Hess.
-      "that was a rough design": Hess.
308   "I'm interested in machines which communicate": Hess.
-      "I gave these machines stereo hearing": Hess.
-      "They're very silent": Hess.
-      "Playing with ensembles": Roger Dannenberg, personal communication.
-      "The sound was very crude": Dannenberg.
-      "It really did a good job": Dannenberg.
-      "The problem was what to do": Georges Bloch, personal communication.
309   "Our idea": Dannenberg.
-      "We put the first concert together": Dannenberg.
-      "Melodic material was analyzed": Bloch.
-      "I used to twirl knobs": Richard Teitelbaum, personal communication.
-      "working in the brain wave lab": Teitelbaum.
310   "It was the first extensive improvising": Teitelbaum.
-      "I used to play my synthesizer with my toes": Teitelbaum.
-      "Sometimes I tried to match and approximate": Teitelbaum.
311   "How is an electronic instrument different": Teitelbaum.
-      "I wanted to do something": Teitelbaum.
-      "I'd already been very much inspired": Teitelbaum.
-      "The computer functions": Richard Teitelbaum, "Digital Piano Music," unpublished manuscript, 1982.
-      "As my system is presently configured": Ibid.
312   "We did five days of soldering": Teitelbaum.
-      "I thought of a system that gets out of control": Teitelbaum.
-      "it really worked well": Martirano.
313   "It was a performance program": Martirano.
-      "There were fifteen orchestras": Martirano.
-      "Musicality emerges": William Walker, Kurt Hebel, Salvatore Martirano, and Carla Scaletti, "ImprovisationBuilder: Improvisation as Conversation," in *Proceedings of the International Computer Music Conference 1992* (San Francisco: International Computer Music Association, 1992), p. 192.
314   "The Listener was sensing": Robert Rowe, personal communication.
-      "Spaarney could hear what the computer was doing": Rowe.
-      "I was trying to make a model": Rowe.
-      "I programmed the Listener": Rowe.
-      "For example, you could tell the program": Rowe.
315   "I took the approach": Rowe.
-      "a working model of my ideas": Rowe.
-      "We wanted it to look at more than one player": Rowe.
316   "I was working with Tony Widoff": Joel Chadabe, *Reports and Reflections*, unpublished manuscript.
317   "Most computer tools are rendering tools": David Zicarelli, personal communication.
318   "M suggests a way of working": Antony Widoff, personal communication.

318 "The electronic sounds": Joel Chadabe, liner notes to *After Some Songs*, Deep Listening DLCD 001.
-    "The only resources I had available": Carl Stone, personal communication.
-    "I became interested in the continuous transformation": Stone.
319 "I could freeze a moment of sound": Stone.
-    "I would make urban recordings": Stone.
-    "Through practice": Stone.
-    "A day or two before Christmas": Stone.
-    "I considered M to be my instrument": Stone.
-    "At first, we used Intelligent Music's M": Englert.
320 "mostly an act of pride": Englert.
-    "I wanted three different sound characters": Francisco Kröpfl, personal communication.
-    "I was very happy": Bruno Spoerri, personal communication.
-    "From the beginning": Spoerri.
321 "I didn't see any way": Spoerri.
-    "I found that it was impossible": Spoerri.
-    "We have a German Swiss": Tonino Greco, personal communication.
-    "I used a pitch-to-MIDI converter": Spoerri.
322 "The important thing for me": Spoerri.
-    "let me expand my ideas": Spoerri.
-    "The main idea of it": Spoerri.

Twelve: Where Are We Going?

324 "The players that we see": Bruce Pennycook, personal communication.
-    "We need to build instruments that are inexpensive": Pennycook.
325 "Numerous tightly coordinated events": Bruce Pennycook, "Machine Songs II: The PRAESCIO Series—Composition-Driven Interactive Software," *Computer Music Journal*, 1991, 15:3, pp. 16–25.
-    "players that have never encountered": Pennycook.
-    "It's a hi-tech experience": Michel Redolfi, personal communication.
-    "Each show is carefully conceived": Françoise Barrière, personal communication.
326 "They asked me to do a show": Iannis Xenakis, personal communication.
327 "The music doesn't have to be connected to the lights": Xenakis.
-    "Our basic interest": Woody and Steina Vasulka, personal communication.
-    "let speech become the activator": Paul Lansky, personal communication.
-    "The best time I had with it": Lansky.
329 "A Tribute": Notes to "The Edison Effect," a show of Paul DeMarinis' work at the San Francisco Art Institute, 1993.
330 "I wanted to give those experiences": David Behrman, personal communication.
-    "You explore": Behrman.
-    "The audience was performing with us": Priscilla McLean, personal communication.
-    "all without a marriage counsellor": Barton McLean, personal communication.
331 "Over the last ten years or so": Barton McLean.
-    "We were there at night": Barton McLean.
-    "We've learned to adapt": Barton and Priscilla McLean.
332 "The Radio Baton and Conductor Program": Max Mathews, personal communication.
-    "The definitive characteristic": Joel Chadabe, Intelligent Music business plan, October 20, 1985.
-    "This is a very exciting time for music": Laurie Spiegel, "Introduction," *Operating Manual for Music Mouse* (1987).
-    "We're interested in artists": Jane Wheeler, personal communication.
333 "One of the things we ask ourselves": Wheeler.
-    "Standard music CDs": Todd Rundgren, liner notes to *No World Order*, Electronic Arts CD-ROM.
-    "If a piece does not need new vision": Morton Subotnick, personal communication.
-    "such things as loudness": Subotnick.
-    "I wondered what useful function computers could serve": Mathews.
334 "In 1978, Jef Raskin": Laurie Spiegel, personal communication.
-    "I found most wonderful": Spiegel.
-    "Intelligent instruments let people": Spiegel.
335 "The software interprets the player's actions": Spiegel.
-    "In coding Music Mouse": Spiegel.
336 "I know the range of pitches that I want": Warren Burt, personal communication.
337 "A sometimes-humorous-": Carla Scaletti, personal communication.
-    "Web participants": Scaletti.
338 "It's like early automobiles": Terry Fryer, personal communication.

INDEX